The Frontier in History

A SEVEN SPRINGS CENTER
PROJECT

The Frontier in History

North America and Southern Africa Compared

Edited by
HOWARD LAMAR AND
LEONARD THOMPSON

New Haven and London:
Yale University Press

Published with assistance from the foundation
established in memory of Rutherford Trowbridge.

Designed by James J. Johnson
and set in Linotron Trump type.
Printed in the United States of America by
The Murray Printing Co., Westford, Mass.

Library of Congress Cataloging in Publication Data
Main entry under title:

The Frontier in history.

Includes bibliographical references and index.
1. Frontier and pioneer life—West (U.S.)—Addresses, essays, lectures.   2. Frontier and pioneer
life—Africa, Southern—Addresses, essays, lectures.
3. West (U.S.) — History—Addresses, essays, lectures.   4. Africa, Southern—History—Addresses,
essays, lectures.   I. Lamar, Howard Roberts.
II. Thompson, Leonard Monteath.
F596.F88   978   81–3008
ISBN 0–300–02624–2   AACR2

Contents

List of Maps

Maps follow page 337

Foreword

Seven Springs Center's aim is to promote scholarship, creativity, and understanding concerning matters of intellectual, cultural, and public significance. Accordingly, the Center warmly welcomed the suggestion by Professors Howard Lamar and Leonard Thompson of Yale University that it sponsor a systematic comparison, under their guidance, of the frontier experience of peoples—indigenous and intrusive—in southern Africa and North America. This volume is the richly rewarding result of the scholarship they have inspired, selected, and assembled, and the Center is greatly indebted to them.

The project was supported in large part by a much appreciated grant made to Seven Springs by The Rockefeller Foundation. Allocations were also made from corporate contributions in support of the Center's programs.

Joseph N. Greene, Jr.

Mount Kisco, N.Y.
March 1980

Preface

This book is the outcome of professional cooperation over a number of years. We first conducted a joint graduate seminar on comparative frontier history at Yale University in the spring semester of 1971. Discovering that students of American and African history relished the challenge of being obliged to stretch beyond their regional specializations, we have repeated the seminar in alternate years. By the late 1970s, the subject having given rise to numerous vigorous cross-cultural debates and some excellent seminar papers, we decided to plan a book, to consist of a carefully structured series of essays by the most appropriate scholars. Following a conference at Seven Springs Center in April 1979, at which the essays were discussed, each author made substantial revisions in his first draft.

We introduce the book in the first chapter. Here, it remains for us gratefully to acknowledge the contributions of many people. We thank Joseph N. Greene, Jr., and his staff at Seven Springs Center, and the Rockefeller Foundation, for their generous support. We also thank the members of the Yale-Wesleyan Southern African Research Program, who submitted drafts of the first chapter to critical scrutiny, and the donors of that program—the National Endowment for the Humanities and the Ford Foundation. Not least, we pay a tribute to the authors of the various essays, who have given much time and thought to meeting our editorial requests, and to the following scholars who also took part in the discussions at Seven Springs and, in most cases, supplied written comments on essays: Charles Ambler, Robert Baum, Jeffrey Butler, William Cronon (a most efficient conference rapporteur), Leonard Doob, George Fredrickson, Stanley Greenberg, Leonard Guelke, Alastair Hennessy, Francis Jennings, John Juricek, Richard Ralston, Robert Shell, Deryck Schreuder, Jane Scott, and Jerome Steffen. Recently several of the above people have continued to provide substantial suggestions and

Leonard Guelke supervised the production of the four southern African maps. We have also benefitted from comments and criticisms by Colman Cooke, William Foltz, Robert Harms, and Dunbar Moodie.

Others, too, have made valuable contributions to this book. Marty Achilles, Pamela Baldwin, and Mary Whitney typed most of the manuscript; William Worger compiled the index; and Barbara Folsom, copyeditor, and Charles Grench, history editor, brought expert and sensitive professionalism to the production of the book by the Yale University Press.

Howard Lamar
Leonard Thompson

New Haven, Connecticut
May 1981

The Frontier in History

1

Introduction

1

LEONARD THOMPSON AND HOWARD LAMAR

Comparative Frontier History

The dominant tradition in historical scholarship is one that deals in single cases. The time, energy, and talents of the typical historian are fully engaged in the discovery, organization, and interpretation of data on the history of his own society or his own culture. This focus has created a tendency for mainstream historians to refrain from questioning some of the fundamental assumptions that are current in their own environments. Historians who specialize in the history of alien cultures have not made much impact on their own society, nor have their perspectives greatly influenced many of the most prominent historians who dominate the profession. Moreover, the parochialism of some of the most talented and widely read professionals percolates down to the popular mind in a simplified form, stripped of nuance and qualification. The cultural chauvinism that is a regular concomitant of human conflict is, wittingly or unwittingly, propagated by many historians.

This phenomenon is conspicuous in frontier historiography. In South Africa, the migrations of the *voortrekkers* from the Cape Colony to the interior in 1836 and the following years form the centerpiece of Afrikaans historiography; but despite all the attention that has been paid to their Great Trek, there has been little attempt to distinguish what was truly original about it by systematically comparing it with other mid-nineteenth-century landward migrations that were prompted by ideological as well as economic factors, such as the Mormon migration to Utah.[1]

1. For example, C. F. J. Muller, ed., *Five Hundred Years: A History of South Africa* (Pretoria and Cape Town, 1969); also idem, *Die Oorsprong van die Groot Trek* (Cape Town and Johannesburg, 1974). There are broader perspectives in W. K. Hancock, "Trek," *Economic History Review*, 2d ser. 10, n. 3 (1958):331–39, and E. A. Walker, *The Great Trek*, 5th ed. (London, 1965). P. J. van der Merwe has written the following distinguished works on the *trekboer*: *Die Noordwaartse beweging van die Boere voor die Groot Trek (1770–1842)* (The Hague, 1937), *Die*

In the United States, Frederick Jackson Turner, father of the famous frontier hypothesis that the frontier experience shaped both the American character and American institutions, has exerted an extraordinarily profound influence over his successors.[2] His ideas were formulated in a nationalist ethos permeated by social Darwinism and the rise of the United States to the status of a major world power during the 1890s. Ray Allen Billington, his principal interpreter, continued to claim that the American frontier experience was unique and that it is therefore incomparable,[3] leaving Americans to stand apart even from the history of western Europe, the region from which most American immigrants came. In fact, of course, everything is unique; but everything is also related to other things in systematic and comparable ways. One of the least persuasive claims of the frontier hypothesis is that American frontiersmen had faith in the equality of all men, an assertion which is contradicted by the fact that these same frontiersmen excluded Indians, Mexicans, and blacks from equal status.[4] Indeed, Turner and most of his successors have almost completely disregarded the fact that two societies were involved in the frontier process in North America: an indigenous Indian society as well as an intrusive European one.

From the perspective of this volume, the experience of the indigenous society is as significant as the experience of the intrusive one. In this respect we agree with Jack D. Forbes, who has defined a frontier as "an intergroup situation."[5] Furthermore, despite numerous and far-reaching variations, we consider that the frontier should be seen as a phenomenon with common

---

Trekboer in die geskiedenis van die Kaapkolonie (1657–1842) (Cape Town, 1938), and Trek: Studies oor die mobiliteit van die pioniersbevolking aan die Kaap (Cape Town, 1945).

2. Turner's paper was first published in The Annual Report of the American Historical Association for the Year 1893, pp. 199–207; it is also available in the Bobbs-Merrill Reprint Series in History, no. H-214. Among the most perceptive of the many appraisals of Turner's work are: Stanley Elkins and Eric McKittrick, "A Meaning for Turner's Frontier," Political Science Quarterly 59 (1954):321–53, 565–602, which, too, is available in the Bobbs-Merrill Reprint Series, no. H-64; Richard Hofstadter and Seymour Martin Lipset, eds., Turner and the Sociology of the Frontier (New York and London, 1968); Richard Hofstadter, The Progressive Historians (New York, 1969), pt. 2; David M. Potter, "Abundance and the Frontier Thesis," in People of Plenty (Chicago, 1958), pp. 142–65; and Jackson K. Putnam, "The Turner Thesis and the Westward Movement: A Reappraisal," Western Historical Quarterly 7 (1976):377–404. There are useful bibliographical essays in Hofstadter, The Progressive Historians, pp. 470–77, and Ray Allen Billington, Westward Expansion: A History of the American Frontier, 4th ed. (New York, 1974), pp. 666–71.

3. Ray Allen Billington, "Frontiers," in The Comparative Approach to American History, ed. C. Vann Woodward (New York, 1968), p. 76.

4. Ibid., p. 80. Billington, who has written copiously on Turner and the American westward movement, summarized his ideas in The American Frontier Thesis: Attack and Defense, American Historical Association Pamphlet no. 101, 1971 ed.

5. Jack D. Forbes, "Frontiers in American History and the Role of the Frontier Historian," Ethnohistory 16 (1968):207.

basic characteristics wherever and whenever it has existed in history. As Robin F. Wells has written, a frontier system is "a distinct socio-cultural type."[6] On the other hand, neither Forbes nor Wells is very helpful in setting limits to the frontier concept. In particular, Forbes sees a frontier situation as continuing to exist so long as there are ethnic differences between indigenous and immigrant communities, or between succcessive immigrant communities, long beyond the time when, in our perspective, the zone has ceased to be a frontier. While "an inter-group situation" is intrinsic to our definition of a frontier, it is only part of a full definition.

The comparative approach has been used by anthropologists ever since their discipline began to emerge in the nineteenth century. Today, committed though they have become to intensive field research, anthropologists still conceptualize their material in a universal framework. Sociologists and political scientists also use general models and take cognizance of institutions in Africa and Asia.[7]

Historians have been less committed to systematic comparative studies. The great French medievalist Marc Bloch used comparisons as a method of testing hypotheses, but the scope of his work was limited to western Europe, and predominantly to medieval western Europe.[8] At the global level, Arnold Toynbee regarded "civilizations" as the only intelligible fields of historical study, and his mammoth *Study of History* is structured as a comparative study of civilizations; but his work was uneven and he failed to provide a consistent meaning for his basic concept.[9] During the last three decades, however, some historians—including Bloch's successors in the Annales school—have been applying the comparative approach more rigorously than Toynbee and across a wider range of human experience than Bloch. Slavery is a notable example of an institution that has been receiving comparative treatment from historians.[10] Recently, some have extended their purview beyond the history of slavery in Western culture to include

6. Robin F. Wells, "Frontier Systems as a Sociocultural Type," *Papers in Anthropology* 14 (1973):6–15.

7. Shmuel N. Eisenstadt and Barrington Moore, Jr., are notable contemporary examples.

8. Marc Bloch, "Pour une historie comparée des sociétés européenes," *Revue de Synthèse Historique* 46 (1925):15–50; English translation without footnotes, "Toward a Comparative History of European Societies," in *Enterprise and Secular Change*, ed. Frederic C. Lane and Jelle C. Riemersma (Homewood, Ill., 1953), pp. 494–521; William H. Sewell, Jr., "Marc Bloch and the Logic of Comparative History," *History and Theory* 6 (1967):208–18.

9. Arnold J. Toynbee, *The Study of History*, 10 vols. (London: 1935–54). In the last four volumes of this work, Toynbee shifted from "civilizations" to "higher religions" as the intelligible fields of historical study.

10. Laura Foner and Eugene D. Genovese, eds., *Slavery in the New World: A Reader in Comparative History* (Englewood Cliffs, N.J., 1969); David Brion Davis, *The Problem of Slavery in Western Culture* and *The Problem of Slavery in the Age of Revolution, 1770–1823* (Ithaca, N.Y., and London, 1966, 1975).

precolonial African versions of slavery.[11] They have been preparing the way for scholars to formulate general hypotheses concerning the rise and decline of property in human beings, as well as the varied forms that the institution has assumed in different periods and different political cultures and economic systems. Adopting an even broader perspective, historians may eventually attempt general histories of labor systems and provide explanations for why different systems have prevailed in different times and places.

Comparative frontier historiography is much less mature than comparative slavery historiography. It has suffered from two main methodological weaknesses. First is a lack of clarity in defining the subject and a lack of rigor in identifying and classifying comparable entities within the subject. Such a judgment is not meant to denigrate the useful and careful testing of the Turner hypothesis on specific frontiers. Works by Paul F. Sharp, Fred Alexander, and H. C. Allen, and the provocative essays in Walker D. Wyman and Clifton B. Kroeber's well-known *The Frontier in Perspective* all test aspects of Turner's hypothesis on the Australian, Canadian, and other frontiers; and W. K. Hancock has written an imaginative essay applying Turner's ideas to southern Africa.[12] In 1977 David Harry Miller and Jerome O. Steffen edited a symposium entitled *The Frontier: Comparative Studies*, in which they permitted each author to attach his own meaning to the term *frontier*. The result is a series of scholarly essays on societies as disparate as the Roman Empire and modern Brazil, without any organizing principle or common factors of analysis.[13] We ourselves, when we conducted our first graduate seminar at Yale University on this topic in 1971, committed the same error.

Second, the historical discipline is such that most individuals are essen-

11. Frederick Cooper, *Plantation Slavery on the East Coast of Africa* (New Haven, Conn., 1977); Suzanne Meiers and Igor Kopytoff, eds., *Slavery in Africa: Historical and Anthropological Perspectives* (Madison, Wis., 1977). On comparative history in general, see the articles on "Comparative History in Theory and Practice" in the *American Historical Review*, vol. 85, no. 4 (October 1980); also George M. Fredrickson, "Comparative History," in *The Past Before Us: Contemporary Historical Writing in the United States*, ed. Michael Kammen (Ithaca, N.Y., 1980), pp. 457–73.

12. Paul F. Sharp, "Three Frontiers: Some Comparative Studies of Canadian, American, and Australian Settlement," *Pacific Historical Review*, vol. 24 (November 1955); Fred Alexander, *Moving Frontiers: An American Theme and Its Application to Australian History* (Melbourne, 1947); H. C. Allen, *Bush and Backwoods: A Comparison of the Frontier in Australia and the United States* (East Lansing, Mich., 1959); Walker D. Wyman and Clifton B. Kroeber, eds. *The Frontier in Perspective* (Madison, Wis., 1957); W. K. Hancock, *Survey of British Commonwealth Affairs*, 2 vols. in 3 (London, 1937–42), 2 (1):1–72.

13. David Harry Miller and Jerome O. Steffen, eds., *The Frontier: Comparative Studies* (Norman, Okla., 1977), p. 6. Most of the essays in this book are specific studies without any comparative features; but there are illuminating comparative passages in David Harry Miller and William W. Savage, Jr., "Ethnic Stereotypes and the Frontier: A Comparative Study of Roman and American Experience," pp. 109–37.

tially one-region specialists who have looked rather cursorily beyond the case they know to find matching attributes elsewhere, instead of attaining a higher level of abstraction and giving the different regions treated equal weight. Thus, American frontier historians tend to regard the American case as a model against which they have analyzed and evaluated other frontier histories. This was the conceptual basis Marvin W. Mikesell used in an important review article, "Comparative Studies in Frontier History," in 1960.[14]

Here, building on ideas advanced by Martin Legassick and by Hermann Giliomee, and by several of our students in unpublished essays, as well as on an article by Marc Bloch and more recent publications by Giovanni Sartori, William Sewell, and others, we and the other contributors are attempting to overcome these weaknesses by pooling our knowledge of two distinct regions, defining our concept of a frontier in universal terms, and explaining its application at different levels of analysis.[15]

We regard a frontier not as a boundary or line, but as a territory or zone of interpenetration between two previously distinct societies.[16] Usually, one of the societies is indigenous to the region, or at least has occupied it for many generations; the other is intrusive. The frontier "opens" in a given zone when the first representatives of the intrusive society arrive; it "closes" when a single political authority has established hegemony over the zone. When the frontier has closed in a given zone, the intruders may have exterminated the indigenous people (as in Tasmania); they may have expelled them (as in North America from east of the Mississippi); they may have subjected them and incorporated them into their own political and economic system (as in South Africa); the intruders may themselves have been incorporated by the indigenous people (as happened to the Portuguese in the Zambesi valley between the sixteenth and nineteenth centuries); or

14. Marvin W. Mikesell, "Comparative Studies in Frontier History," *Annals of the Association of American Geographers* 50 (March 1960): 62–74.

15. Martin Legassick, "The Griqua, the Sotho-Tswana, and the Missionaries, 1780–1840: The Politics of a Frontier Zone" (Ph.D. diss., University of California, Los Angeles, 1970), pp. 1–29, 634–68, and "The Frontier Tradition in South African Historiography," *The Societies of Southern Africa in the Nineteenth and Twentieth Centuries*, University of London, Institute of Commonwealth Studies 2 (1971): 1–33; Hermann Giliomee, "The Eastern Frontier, 1770–1812," in *The Shaping of South African Society 1652–1820*, ed. Richard Elphick and Hermann Giliomee (Cape Town and London, 1979) pp. 291–337; Giovanni Sartori, "Concept Misformation in Comparative Politics," *American Political Science Review* 44 (1970): 103–53; and the articles by Marc Bloch and William H. Sewell, Jr., listed in note 8 above. Alastair Hennessy, in *The Frontier in Latin American History* (Albuquerque, N. Mex., 1978), uses a conceptual framework compatible with ours.

16. The term *frontier* has had a checkered history. John T. Juricek, "American Usage of the word 'Frontier' from Colonial Times to Frederick Jackson Turner," *Proceedings of the American Philosophical Society* 10, no. 1 (February 1966): 10–34, and Fulmer Mood, "Notes on the History of the Word 'Frontier,'" *Agricultural History* 22 (April 1948): 78–83.

they may have reached a stalemate (as was the case with the eighteenth-century frontier of New Spain in the provinces of Texas and New Mexico).

Most cases are more complex than we have indicated so far. Two or more intrusive peoples may be competing with one another as well as with the indigenous inhabitants for control of the frontier zone (as with the French and English in the Mohawk and Hudson River valleys); or the indigenous populations may be so sharply divided among themselves that they persist in devoting more energy to their competition with one another than to resisting the intruders. In some cases it may not be possible to distinguish between indigenes and intruders: such frontier zones are areas where two societies meet and compete (as with the French and the Germans in the Rhineland, or the Germans and the Slavs in eastern Europe). However, there are three essential elements in any frontier situation as we conceive it: territory; two or more initially distinct peoples; and the process by which the relations among the peoples in the territory begin, develop, and eventually crystallize. We shall examine these three elements separately.

First, the geography of a given frontier zone provides the opportunities and sets the limits for human activity there. The geographical variables include temperature and precipitation; contours and catchment areas; soils, vegetation, minerals, and fauna; and the spatial relationship between the frontier zone and the territory from which the intruding people originate. The carrying capacity and attractiveness of land varies prodigiously, from near zero in the case of deserts to very high figures in the case of exceptionally well-favored areas; so that those who, following Turner, have attempted to define frontier zones in terms of population density are not providing a useful tool.[17] Even within the United States, which was Turner's concern, there were immense differences in the carrying capacities of different sections of the frontier. Furthermore, in the course of time discoveries and technological advances have dramatically altered a territory's attractiveness and carrying capacity, as when gold was discovered in California in 1848 and on the Witwatersrand in 1885, or when dry-farming techniques assisted in the intensive white settlement of the North American Great Plains.

Second, the qualities of the basic cultures of the interacting societies go some way toward explaining the nature of their interactions. Hunting, herding, mixed farming, and industrial societies all have different capabilities and different ranges of social structures, political organizations, and belief systems. Further, no society is monolithic. Within a single society, different

---

17. Throughout the period 1870 to 1914, "the U.S. Census considered a density of between two and six per square miles to indicate a 'frontier' condition." David J. Wishart, Andrew Warren, and Robert H. Stoddard, "An Attempted Definition of a Frontier Using a Wave Analogy," *The Rocky Mountain Social Science Journal* 6 (1969): 73–81.

groups have different interests: fathers and sons; men and women; towns-people and countrypeople; and regional, ethnic, and class rivals. Occupational differences, especially among intruders, are often highly significant. Hence, Frederick Jackson Turner and other historians have classified frontiers according to the occupations of the intruders: missionaries, traders, pastoralists, cultivators, speculators, administrators, soldiers, and so on.[18] Such analytic devices are fruitful, for the objectives, methods, and effects of the various categories differ quite profoundly, provided we recognize that in practice individuals often perform more than one occupational role, and that several types of intruders are usually present in a given frontier zone at the same time.

In many cases, rival segments within both the indigenous society and the intrusive one compete with each other in a frontier zone. Indeed, in every contact situation, even where relationships are predominantly violent, crosscutting ties quickly develop across the major cleavage. Thus intruders acquire allies among indigenous peoples. In virtually every confrontation between incoming whites and Indians in North America and whites and Africans in southern Africa, whites were able to form and manipulate such alliances. In Natal, for example, the army of the Zulu king Dingane was crushed in 1840 by regiments controlled by his half-brother Mpande, who had allied himself with Afrikaner *voortrekkers*. But this was not just a one-way process. In North America Indians benefitted temporarily from Anglo-French competition for control of the Hudson, Mohawk, and Saint Lawrence River valleys, and in southern Africa, Africans took advantage of Anglo-Afrikaner tensions, as in 1868, when Moshoeshoe persuaded the British to annex his kingdom of Lesotho rather than allowing it to be carved up by the Afrikaners of the Orange Free State.

The extent of the technological and organizational gap between the interacting societies is also significant. By the time of Christopher Columbus and Vasco da Gama, Europeans already possessed several advantages over American and African societies, and the gap increased dramatically during the industrial revolution, reaching its greatest extent in the 1880s and 1890s. Whites were then able to establish hegemony over the remaining frontier zones in North America and southern Africa at a low cost in lives and money, with the use of quick-firing machine guns and of logistics that were far superior to those of the native Amerindians and Africans.

A frontier process has a beginning and, at least potentially, an end. In the opening phase, except when it takes the form of a military expedition as it did in the Spanish conquest of Mexico and Peru, the members of the intrusive society are usually too few to be perceived as a threat to the established

---

18. This analytical approach has been used very effectively by W. K. Hancock, *Survey of British Commonwealth Affairs*.

indigenous order. Even so, the actions of the first intruders, who may not themselves be farmers, may quickly initiate profound systemic changes in the indigenous society. The material goods they introduce may cause intense competition to control or monopolize them among segments of the local population and may damage the interests of the local people who previously made and exchanged goods that served equivalent purposes. The power of the intruders and the ideas they purvey may shake the confidence of some of the indigenous people in the validity of their own belief systems and the respect for their own political and cultural leaders, including their intermediaries with supernatural forces.

Gradually, therefore, members of the indigenous society may become aware that the intrusion constitutes danger to their autonomy and identity. This process of erosion is often intensified by an increase in the number of intruders and by the arrival of new categories of intruders, especially of settlers—as when farmers followed missionaries and peripatetic traders into the interior of North America and southern Africa with the manifest intention of becoming permanent inhabitants of the region. In such cases there then ensues a more or less open conflict for use of the natural resources of the region—land and water supplies—and eventually for physical control over the entire territory and all its inhabitants. The termination of the process is most clearly indicated by political events—that is to say, when one group establishes political control over the other. Once that has been done, the frontier ceases to exist. This does not mean that the relations between the inhabitants then become static, but rather that a new structural situation has been created and that the ongoing historical process is no longer a frontier process. Subsequent relationships are relations of ethnicity and class within a single society, not frontier relationships between different societies.

One should not assume that the intrusive society necessarily emerges as the winner in the struggle for hegemony in a frontier zone. History is replete with abortive frontiers. In North America, for example, the white intruders were palpably the losers in Raleigh's "Lost Colony" in North Carolina. Moreover, distinguishing winners from losers depends upon one's time frame. One generation of people may more than hold their own in a frontier zone and the next generation may be overwhelmed.

There are great differences in the extent of the powers that are wielded by victorious regimes when frontiers close. Numbers are a key factor. In the nineteenth century, enough Europeans settled in Australia and New Zealand as well as North America to eliminate the possibility of a subsequent reversal of power. White settlement was not so conclusive anywhere in Africa. Reversals of power have already occurred in Algeria, Kenya, Malawi,

Zambia, Angola, Mozambique, and Zimbabwe, all of which contain former frontier zones that were closed under European control. At the present time, the white ascendancy is being challenged in Namibia and even in South Africa itself. In other cases, frontier zones have been contested for many generations, or even centuries, with frequent swings of control, as in the frontier between Egyptians and Nubians in the valley of the Nile.[19]

Within the genus frontier it is possible to distinguish various species and subspecies as one descends the ladder of abstraction. At the highest level, one might take cognizance of everything that is discoverable about frontier processes in the human experience, bearing in mind that all empires, many states, and numerous acephalous societies have generated frontier processes. There were frontier processes in precolonial America and Africa, as when Pueblo-dwelling agriculturalists and Apachean hunter-collectors confronted one another in present-day New Mexico and Arizona, and when Bantu-speaking farmers migrated into southern African territories previously inhabited only by Khoisan-speaking hunter-collectors and herders.[20] At an intermediate level, there are species that can be studied globally within a given time span, such as the frontiers created by the Roman Empire, or those created by the expansion of Europe and of commercial and industrial capitalism in the modern era. At a still lower level, there are regional subspecies of the great imperial frontiers. This perspective emphasizes the mobility of frontier zones—as in modern North America as a whole, where they moved in a generally westward direction until, by the end of the nineteenth century, the entire subcontinent and its surviving indigenous peoples had been incorporated into an economic and political system dominated by people of European origin. This is the classic perspective of American frontier historiography. Finally, at the local level, small areas can be studied in depth to reveal the great complexities that exist when two quite small communities confront one another, as Richard Metcalf has shown in seventeenth-century Connecticut and Richard Elphick has demonstrated in the Cape peninsula and its immediate hinterland in the second half of that century.[21]

In selecting a perspective, we have kept in mind the limits we have ascribed to the term *frontier.* Otherwise, we are in danger of resorting to what Giovanni Sartori calls *"conceptual stretching,* or conceptual straining, i.e.

19. William Y. Adams, *Nubia: Corridor to Africa* (Princeton, N.J., 1977).

20. Margaret Kinsman, "The Heartlands Frontier: A Comparative Study of Interaction between Agriculturalists and Hunter Collectors in the American Southwest and Southern Botswana" (seminar paper, Yale University, 1977).

21. P. Richard Metcalf, "Who Should Rule at Home? Native American Politics and Indian-White Relations," *Journal of American History* 61 (1974): 651–65; Richard Elphick, *Kraal and Castle: Khoikhoi and the Founding of White South Africa* (New Haven, Conn., 1977).

to vague, amorphous conceptualizations" that "lose connotative precision."[22] Historians often fall into this logical trap. Frederick Jackson Turner,
for example, argued that the American pioneers' confrontation with the wilderness was so overpowering that it reduced all of them to social and physical conditions of rough equality. In his view, these enforced egalitarian conditions fostered a sense of democracy that in turn accounts for the American
political system. The complex problems of cause and effect are ignored for a
dramatic and attractive, if very broad, conceptualization of the nature of the
United States. Similarly, Walter Prescott Webb's stimulating work, *The
Great Frontier,*[23] actually embraces the entire process of European expansion in the modern age, which is a legitimate and important field of study
but deprives the word *frontier* of substantial content.

This book compares two subspecies of the frontiers created by the expansion of Europe and of commercial and industrial capitalism in the modern age—those in North America and in southern Africa.

William Sewell has claimed that the term *comparative history* can
have three meanings. First, as with Marc Bloch, it may be a method of testing hypotheses. Second, it may mean a comparative perspective, which off-
sets the historian's tendency toward parochialism. Third, *comparative
history* may be applied to "studies which make systematic comparisons between two or more societies and present their results in a comparative
format."[24]

With respect to Sewell's first meaning, neither he nor Bloch would expect us to propose an overarching hypothesis that purports to identify all the
relevant variables, to distinguish independent from dependent ones, and to
organize them into a single, systematic model of the frontier throughout
history. We do not believe it is possible to create such a hypothesis; and even
if it were theoretically possible, the data are so incomplete and many of
them so ambiguous that it is not possible in practice. In any case, it would
be naive to essay such an overarching hypothesis on the basis of the two
cases studied in this volume. Nevertheless, our knowledge of the two cases
does enable us to propose several hypotheses about the frontiers created by
the expansion of Europe. For example, we discover that in both the cases we
have studied, Europeans did not establish hegemony over frontier zones
without exploiting the internal divisions among the indigenous societies;
and we also find that mass conversions of indigenous peoples to Chris-

22. Sartori, "Concept Misformation in Comparative Politics," pp. 1034, 1035.
23. Walter Prescott Webb, *The Great Frontier* (Boston, 1952); likewise D. W. Meinig, "A
Macrogeography of Western Imperialism: Some Morphologies of Moving Frontiers of Political
Control," in *Settlement and Encounter: Geographical Studies Presented to Sir Grenfell Price,*
eds. Fay Gale and Graham H. Lawton (Melbourne, 1969).
24. Sewell, "Marc Bloch and the Logic of Comparative History," p. 218.

tianity did not occur in the frontier epoch, but did take place in some cases after whites had established hegemony.

Regarding Sewell's second meaning, we believe that as historians in the unstable, interdependent, contemporary world, we have a peculiar responsibility to combat the parochial tendencies that have been produced by ultraspecialization in our profession. Hence our work has been imbued with the desire to rise above regionalism and operate in a comparative perspective. This method has prompted us to seek to enrich our understanding of one situation by our knowledge of another—that is to say, to raise questions about our individual regions that we might otherwise have ignored. For example, knowledge of the southern African frontier experience should provoke Americanists to explain why native Americans played such an insignificant role in the economic systems created by white immigrants, except, temporarily, in the fur trade; whereas knowledge of the devastating effects of disease on the native Americans should provoke southern Africanists to probe more deeply than hitherto into the population trends among indigenous Africans.

Third, much as we would have liked to structure this book as a series of systematic comparisons of two regional frontier processes, that has not been practicable, because not enough scholars possess sufficient control over the history of both regions to apply this method effectively. Instead, we present most of the material as a series of paired chapters by specialists, one a North Americanist, the other a southern Africanist, each pair dealing with a major facet of the frontier process. However, in the chapter that follows this one, we ourselves highlight the most conspicuous similarities and differences in the frontier processes in the two regions and try to account for them. We recognize that this is rough, preliminary work. But we hope it may prepare the way for others to embark upon more profound, more tightly structured, and more productive enterprises.

2

LEONARD
THOMPSON AND
HOWARD LAMAR

The North American and Southern African Frontiers

In this chapter we set the stage for the studies that follow by making some general comparisons between the contexts of the frontier processes created by white expansion in North America and southern Africa.[1] In North America we focus mainly on the region embodied in the continental United States excluding Alaska—an area of just over three million square miles with a present population of about 220 million people (1979), although several authors make excellent use of the French and English experience in Canada in their essays for this volume. By southern Africa, we mean the region now comprising the Republic of South Africa, Botswana, Lesotho, Swaziland, Namibia (formerly known as South West Africa), Zimbabwe (the former Rhodesia), and Mozambique south of the Zambesi River—an area of about 1.3 million square miles with about 45 million inhabitants (1980). This book deals mainly with the most durable and effective frontier processes in each region: that initiated by England and sustained by the independent United States itself in the North American case, and that initiated by the Netherlands and sustained by Great Britain and independent Afrikaner republics in southern Africa. However, references are also made to the Spanish, Dutch, and especially the French frontiers in North America and the Portuguese and German frontiers in southern Africa.

The North American and southern African frontiers had much in common. Both were products of the same general process: the expansion of Europe and of capitalism. Both had roughly the same chronology. Following

1. The chapters that follow examine the histories of the North American and southern African frontiers and provide ample documentation; George Miles reviews the historiography of each of these frontiers; and the Index is thorough. Consequently, to avoid repetition, the footnotes in this chapter refer to quotations, to specific works mentioned in the text of the chapter, and to a few statements that are not dealt with elsewhere.

the voyages of Columbus (1492–) and da Gama (1497–) and subsequent probings along the seaboards, Europeans established their first effective bridgeheads in both regions in the seventeenth century (Virginia, 1607; New England, 1620; the Cape Peninsula, 1652). Thereafter, frontier zones successively closed and came under white control and new zones opened up, as whites moved westward in North America and north and east in southern Africa.

There were, however, substantial differences in the extent of the European involvement in the two regions, and hence in their political and economic systems. During the age of discovery, indeed, most Europeans regarded North America as well as southern Africa as potential stepping-stones to Asia—hence the persistent search for a northwest passage by English and Dutch seamen; but whereas they soon recognized that North America had its own intrinsic attractions, the only substantial merit seaborne explorers saw in southern Africa, before diamonds were discovered in 1869, was the strategic location of the Cape peninsula.

North America was much more accessible than southern Africa. In the 1820s the voyage from England to New York in sailing ships averaged about five and a half weeks, compared with between nine weeks and three months for the voyage to Cape Town; by 1840, steamships were taking between one and two weeks to New York and about three weeks to the Cape. Also, the Atlantic coastline of North America contained numerous natural harbors that provided shelter for colonial settlements and bridgeheads for expansion inland, and it was pierced by numerous rivers, many of them navigable for 50 to 100 miles inland and several of them navigable deep into the continent. In stark contrast, there were scarcely any natural harbors on the southern African coastline—ships were frequently wrecked by storms in Table Bay—and not a single southern African river was penetrable from the sea by ocean-going ships. Moreover, in southern Africa a series of obstacles impeded movement inland from the Cape peninsula—the sandy Cape flats, the Cape mountain ranges, and then the arid Karroo—whereas there were no formidable barriers to the expansion of settlement into North America from the east coast to the Appalachians, through which there were easy mountain passes to the vast fertile areas beyond. Conditions comparable to those encountered in southern Africa existed only in the Great Plains, desert, and Rocky Mountain areas of the trans-Mississippi West.

These effects were intensified by the location and extent of natural resources in the two regions. In North America, the rainfall, the soil, and the pasture were suitable for crop production, or at least for stockfarming, virtually all the way from the Atlantic Ocean to the 100th meridian running through the Great Plains, beyond which the rainfall was less than twenty inches a year. But while true deserts existed in the Great Basin, Arizona, and southeastern California, the West Coast and hundreds of river valleys in and beyond the Rocky Mountains had a sufficient rainfall or water supply to promote agriculture. On the other hand, the western three-fifths of southern Africa has less than twenty inches of rain a year—much of it less than ten inches—and with preindustrial technology it permitted at most very extensive stockfarming. The only exceptions were a small area with a Mediterranean-type climate near the Cape peninsula and the adjacent south coast, and a strip along the Kunene River in the north of Namibia.

Consequently, there was a radical difference in the scale of European migration to the two regions. By 1700 there were about 200,000 Europeans in the English colonies in North America, but only about 1,200 in the Cape Colony; in 1800, over four million in the United States and only 20,000 in southern Africa; and in 1900, when the frontier era had ended in both regions, about 67 million in the United States and just over one million in southern Africa. Furthermore, North America's attractiveness and accessibility made it the scene for intense competition and major wars among rival European powers from the seventeenth century through the Napoleonic wars. No such rivals contested the Dutch East India Company's control of the Cape Colony before the French revolutionary and Napoleonic period, after which Britain's supremacy in most of southern Africa was not challenged by other European powers before the 1880s, when Germany annexed South West Africa and Portugal gave effect to her old claims in Mozambique.

Besides being the scene for international rivalries, a situation that involved claims to frontier lands not yet occupied, from an early stage colonists in the English North American colonies possessed considerable local autonomy. In the War of Independence they acquired full national status, when political responsibility for developing and controlling the most dynamic frontiers in North America passed from London to a limited federal government which was eventually located in Washington. In effect, control passed from highly centralized but distant overseers to local participants.

In South Africa, on the other hand, the Dutch authorities gave the colonists very little say in the formulation of official policy (though they did acquiesce in considerable de facto local autonomy in the frontier zones), and Great Britain did not begin to delegate political power to locally elected bodies until the 1850s. Even then, although Britain recognized the Boer republics as being nominally independent in 1852 and 1854, and the Cape Colony and Natal as having responsible self-government in 1871 and 1893 respectively, she wielded considerable power throughout most of southern Africa until after the end of the nineteenth century—especially over frontier zones where white colonies and republics contested control with African polities.

In North America, massive successive immigrations from various parts of continental Europe, notably Germany, Ireland, and Italy, as well as from Great Britain, and the incorporation into the United States of territories with French- and Spanish-speaking communities in the nineteenth century, made ethnicity an important factor in intrawhite relationships. Nevertheless, English cultural predominance, firmly implanted in the thirteen colonies at an early stage, was never seriously challenged south of Canada. The English language became the lingua franca and the sole official language of the United States. In southern Africa, on the other hand, the century and a half of Dutch rule left an enduring legacy. After the British conquest in 1806, there were two distinct, competitive white communities, and the advantage that the newer British community possessed from its connection with the powerful and wealthy imperial metropole was offset by the fact that the Afrikaners were always more numerous than the British in the region. The only comparable situation in the United States occurred in New Mexico after the American conquest in 1846. There, while Anglo-American authority was supreme, Spanish-American citizens greatly outnumbered the Anglo population and thus exercised considerable influence in local government and insisted on Spanish as a second official language in the territory.

Into both regions the European immigrants carried with them ethnocentric attitudes that were deep-seated in Western culture. Ignorant of the needs of local societies, they assumed that they were not depriving the inhabitants of anything if they occupied land that was not already built on, cultivated, or grazed by domestic animals. When they did knowingly deprive local societies of their resources, they assumed that they were justified in doing so on the ground that the native populations had not used them effectively, or that their customs and mores stamped them as savages or barbarians. By the nineteenth century many whites were concluding that Indians and Africans were genetically inferior—a conclusion that was reenforced when respected European scientists produced schemes classifying people in racial categories, with whites preeminent and Indians and Africans far below them. But as David Harry Miller and William W. Savage, Jr., have observed in a recent study, derogatory stereotypes of alien peoples as subhuman often accompany an expansionist ideology, and not only make atrocities possible, but indeed encourage them.[2] Thus the white communities in both our regions were able to suppress any moral scruples they may have had about pursuing their own interests at the expense of the native societies where they deemed it necessary. Moreover, in some cases they had

2. David Harry Miller and William W. Savage, Jr., "Ethnic Stereotypes and the Frontier: A Comparative Study of the Roman and American Experience," in *The Frontier: Comparative Studies*, ed. David Harry Miller and Jerome O. Steffen (Norman, Okla., 1977).

the added impetus of powerful ideological drives, as with the Puritans in New England.

On their part, Indians and Africans often treated their first white visitors as they were accustomed to treating all visitors—hospitably. In numerous places, including Virginia, they helped white settlers or castaways to survive by providing them with food. Such hospitality was not simply an act of naivete. Most of the indigenous societies in both North America and southern Africa could be characterized as inclusionist rather than exclusionist; that is to say, they readily assimilated strangers as well as making use of their ideas, their techniques, and their weaponry.

However, it was not long before it dawned upon the indigenes that they were up against a completely new type of person whose impact was more fundamentally devastating than anything they had previously experienced. Whites soon assumed control over areas of land that were regularly used by hunters and collectors, or seasonally by transhumant pastoralists, or periodically by slash-and-burn cultivators. Moreover, they assumed *exclusive* control of such areas, whereas Indian and African leaders could not transfer the ownership of land; they could merely grant people the right to make use of land subject to specified conditions. Whites also behaved arrogantly, showing that they ignored the spiritual forces which the natives believed ensured the fertility of the land and the continuity of life. Thus Indians and Africans came to regard white people as lacking in humanity.

The most numerous element in the pre–da Gaman population of southern Africa were mixed farmers, who owned cattle and sheep, grew sorghum and other crops, smelted metals and attached iron blades to the wooden shafts of their digging implements and spears, and spoke one of several quite closely related Bantu languages. Living in settlements ranging from single-family hamlets to towns with over ten thousand inhabitants, they were organized in chiefdoms that also varied greatly in size. A chief ruled in conjunction with kinsmen, councillors, and village headmen, but male commoners also participated in making important decisions that affected the entire polity. Chiefdoms sometimes split into two or more autonomous polities, especially when rival kinsmen contested the succession to a deceased chief. Young men often indulged in raiding cattle from neighboring settlements, but so long as the population was not large enough to cause shortages of land, game, and water supplies, serious warfare was probably infrequent—and so far as we know this remained the case until toward the end of the eighteenth century. Religous beliefs and rituals were typical of those in small-scale, isolated communities. In a chiefdom, the living, the dead, and those yet to be born were regarded as forming a social continuum, and in times of trouble people sacrificed animals to the shades of their ancestors or the ancestors of their chief, who could influence them for better or worse.

Bantu-speaking mixed farmers had begun to infiltrate into southern Africa from the north at the beginning of the Christian era, and thereafter they gradually became more numerous by further infiltration as well as by natural increase. By the seventeenth century they had established control over virtually all the land that was suitable for agriculture in the better-watered eastern two-fifths of the region. As they did so, they killed some of the earlier inhabitants, drove others into the mountains and western deserts, and absorbed others by marriage. However, they did not penetrate into the arid areas west of the twenty-inch rainfall line. There, descendants of the ancient inhabitants remained unchallenged until the advent of white intruders. San, who became known to whites as Bushmen, were hunters and gatherers like their ancestors; Khoikhoi, whom whites called Hottentots, had acquired sheep and cattle from Africans farther north and become transhumant pastoralists. Possessing relatively unstable economies and weak social and political institutions, the San and Khoikhoi were far less competent to cope with the problems created by the white intrusion than were the Bantu-speaking farmers.

We do not have enough information to do more than speculate about the numbers of the pre–da Gaman inhabitants of southern Africa. There may have been about two hundred thousand San and Khoikhoi hunters and herders and between two and four million Bantu-speaking farmers.[3]

People whom whites were to name Indians have lived in North America for a very much longer time than Bantu-speaking farmers have lived in southern Africa. The first immigrants entered Alaska across the Bering Strait land-bridge from Asia during the late Pleistocene period at least 19,000 and perhaps as many as 40,000 years ago. Significant immigration probably ceased about 10,000 years ago, so that a truly isolated and distinctive set of Amerindian societies emerged. For reasons we do not understand, there were migratory drifts of peoples from one area of North America to another for many hundreds of years, but by the time of Columbus, people had occupied every habitable part of the continental United States for many centuries. Scholars have estimated that the number of Indians living north of Mexico was between two and a half and ten million; perhaps five million is as good a guess as can be made from the evidence available. Because many small groups had lived in discrete areas for many years, Indians were much

3. We know of no systematic attempt to estimate the number of Bantu-speakers. Richard Elphick estimates that there were "no more than 100,000 Khoikhoi in the southwestern Cape," in *Kraal and Castle: Khoikhoi and the Founding of White South Africa* (New Haven, Conn., 1977), p. 23.

more differentiated than the Bantu-speaking inhabitants of southern Africa; they had had so much more time to adapt to the different environments in which they lived. Over two hundred different languages were spoken in North America; scholars have grouped them into more than fifty quite distinct language families and half a dozen basic language stocks. They practiced a vast variety of subsistence activities, with numerous different forms of hunting and collecting and agriculture. However, they had no iron tools, and pastoralism, which was common in much of the Old World, was completely absent in the Americas; there were no sheep, no cattle, and no equivalent domesticated animals such as the horse or the pig. Mobility in North America was due to the search for game and farmland, not pasturage.

Eleanor Leacock has divided the region that is now the continental United States into seven areas, each characterized by a distinctive indigenous economy.[4]

1. Perhaps the most elaborate societies could be found in the Southeast where the culture of agricultural people had reached a peak shortly before the European discovery. The fertile lands of the Southeast not only provided maize and vegetables, but the woods teemed with game. An early white observer called it one vast deerpark. The Indians of the region were village dwellers and had elaborate ceremonial centers and rituals that reflected influences from the distant Valley of Mexico.

2. In the Northeast there was a series of woodland cultures stretching from Virginia to Canada and consisting of small groups or sometimes loose confederations of polities, where agriculture and also hunting and fishing were the mainstays of life. Along the shores south of the Saint Lawrence, the population, which depended on seasonal seafood, was fairly dense.

3. The mid-central and eastern plains areas were an extension of the eastern agricultural area, but there were local variations in the food supply. In the Great Lakes region the population depended on wild rice for food— along with hunting and fishing—and used the birchbark canoe for travel. On the eastern plains a combination of buffalo hunting and farming was practiced.

4. In the Southwest, where dramatic prehistoric climatic changes had produced a semiarid, even desert, environment, earlier hunting and gathering societies had evolved into a series of town-dwelling—or Pueblo—Indians living in multistoried adobe or stone communal houses. The Pueblo peoples were the most efficient agriculturalists north of Mexico. Some groups practiced flood-plain agriculture, while others in present-day Arizona developed canals to supply water for crops. As in the Southeast, the Pueblo peoples had experienced a mysterious material and cultural decline

4. Eleanor Burke Leacock, "Introduction," in *North American Indians in Historical Perspective*, ed. Eleanor Burke Leacock and Nancy Oestrich Lurie (New York, 1971), pp. 9–10.

before white contact, a decline due in part to a sustained period of drought and disease, and also—around the time of Columbus—to an invasion by nomadic Athabascan hunter-raiders who had moved down from the north. Here in the sixteenth and seventeenth centuries a true frontier zone existed between two Indian cultures.

5. The Great Basin was the home of desert cultures where widely scattered bands, scarcely larger than an extended family, depended on the gathering of seeds and wild vegetables and occasional hunting.

6. In California yet another kind of hunting-and-gathering economy could be found. Here the beneficent environment provided acorns, seeds, game, and seafood plentiful enough to maintain a dense population and a relatively stable mini-village life. However, a seemingly simple lifestyle hid an elaborate sense of territoriality and an intense religiosity.

7. In the Pacific Northwest plentiful sources from the sea and the forest sustained a wood and hunting culture that enabled inhabitants to lead a richer life in material terms than any other nonagricultural group in North America. Based on salmon fishing and whaling, hunting and wood products, the economy supported a caste society whose members ranged from wealthy aristocratic leaders inordinately proud of their ancestry, to slaves. The culture was distinguished by a flourishing array of art forms with wood as the medium, as well as an elaborate set of social and religious rituals.

The social and political systems of the peoples of North America were as varied as their economic systems. As in southern Africa, most polities were quite small in size; but in North America, except in parts of the Southeast which were influenced by the large-scale and highly stratified societies of Mexico, leadership roles were more widely diffused than was general in southern Africa: for example, military and civil authority among the southeastern Creeks was often vested in different men. In some cases, such as in Iroquois polities, women played a larger role in decision making than in other societies, and in the semiarid areas, Indian "tribes" separated into smaller bands for survival at various times of the year but united to conduct a summer hunt. Some tribes approximated a system of hereditary chiefdoms; in others, the leader might simply be the best warrior or the best provider.

Still, in many respects the peoples of North America and southern Africa had common qualities—qualities that have been widespread among preindustrial, preliterate societies throughout the world. The scale of effective organization, whether economic or political, was generally small. Though most people believed that there was a single Supreme Being who reigned over all the world, their sacred objects, their cosmologies, and the deities that directly affected their lives were highly localized. People were conscious of being embedded in their natural environments; they respected nature and tried to live in harmony with it. Since there were constraints on the hoarding of wealth, the rights of users of property took precedence over the nominal rights of owners, so that gross differences in economic levels were rare. Social stratifications, also, were limited. Though clientage systems were common, outright property in human beings did not exist in southern Africa. Where slavery did occur in North America, it tended to be a less severe and more flexible institution than in modern Western slave systems. While captured adult males might be killed by the victors, women and children were often absorbed into the households and eventually accepted into the society of the conquerors.

In both regions, powers of leaders were balanced by the rights of subjects; ordinary people took part in political discussions, and an effective decision was one that embodied the consensus of the community. As in other cultures, leaders differed greatly in power and in behavior; whites were not justified in creating a stereotype of a tyrannical and capricious chief. Society emphasized communal rather than individual goals, and antisocial conduct was curbed by informal controls such as peer-group ostracism as well as by ritual proceedings that had the effect of law. People identified with different groups in different contexts: a family, a lineage, a clan, a residential community, a political community, or a cultural community; but each of these groups could incorporate new members or expel old ones, and none of them completely dominated the rest. Tribes did not exist in the sense in which whites would use the term—as static, bounded ethnic populations.[5] Despite the absence of polities comparable with European nation-states, people were politically active and cleavages within polities and among polities were the stuff of political life. However, in the age of Columbus and da Gama, the population levels in neither region had reached the stage of acute competition for resources such as land and water; consequently, so far as we know, warfare was limited by recognized rules and there was no tradition of indiscriminate violence.

There were also significant differences between the two regions before they experienced the impact of white intrusion. Several have already been mentioned. One difference proved to be a major determinant of the outcome of the frontier processes in the two regions. Having been an isolated population for some ten thousand years, despite the variety of their adaptations to

5. Morton H. Fried, *The Notion of Tribe* (Menlo Park, Calif., 1975), is a general criticism of the concept. Robert F. Berkhofer, Jr., "The Political Context of a New Indian History," *Pacific Historical Review* 40 (August 1971):357–82, and William T. Hagan, *The Indian in American History*, American Historical Association Pamphlet no. 240 (1971 ed.), specifically reject the application of the term *tribe* to the Indian peoples of North America. The editors and authors of *The Oxford History of South Africa*, ed. Monica Wilson and Leonard Thompson, 2 vols. (Oxford, 1969–71), and *African History*, Philip Curtin et al. (Boston, 1978), avoid applying the term to the peoples of southern Africa.

local environments the Indians of the Americas were genetically a unique and remarkably uniform population. In their long period of virtually complete isolation from the rest of mankind, they had benefitted from the absence of epidemic diseases such as smallpox and measles; but this also meant that they were particularly vulnerable to such diseases when they were brought to the New World. Genetically, the peoples of southern Africa were far less isolated and consequently far less vulnerable. They formed the southwestern fringe of a population continuum extending through Africa, Asia, and Europe. Among them, the Bantu-speaking mixed farmers were somewhat less isolated, and therefore probably somewhat less vulnerable, than the Khoikhoi herders and the San hunter-collectors.

In southern Africa the frontiers advanced in four phases. First, between 1652 and about 1700, whites consolidated a bridgehead on Table Bay and also acquired control of the arable land within thirty or forty miles distance. Second, during the eighteenth and early nineteenth centuries many whites became *trekboers*—extensive stockfarmers—and occupied land in the arid interior, eastward toward the Fish River and northward toward the Orange. A third stage began in 1835, when organized groups of stockfarmers migrated into the better-watered eastern two-fifths of the region, where by 1870 they had occupied much of the fertile land. Later this movement became known as the Great Trek, the participants, *voortrekkers*. Finally, in the last thirty years of the century, whites gained control not only of the remaining territory up to the Limpopo River, but also of Namibia (South West Africa), Zimbabwe (Rhodesia), and Mozambique.

During the first two phases, despite their meager resources, whites were able to gain control of vast areas because the indigenous Khoisan hunting and herding peoples were too few, too weak, and too divided among themselves to prevent it. In the later phases, white advances into the areas previously controlled by Bantu-speaking farming peoples were facilitated by the catastrophic intra-African disturbances known as the *Mfecane*—wars sparked off between 1816 and 1828 by the rise of Shaka's military Zulu state that disrupted and demoralized most of the African chiefdoms throughout the region, left desirable areas on the highveld grasslands and in Natal denuded of their inhabitants and thus open to settlement, and provided whites with ready-made allies, such as the Mfengu and other refugees from Shaka. The culmination of white expansion in the region was accelerated by the growth of the world's largest diamond- and gold-mining industries which, from 1869 onward, brought an infusion of European technicians and capital and a railroad system deep into the interior.

In North America the frontier phases were more numerous and more complex than those in southern Africa. Yet, paradoxically, they were simpler in the initial stages, for unlike the native African population, who were identified as three distinct cultural and economic groups, the Indian populations along the Atlantic coast were relatively homogeneous. There was no hunter-fisher-gatherer group, pure and simple, on the Atlantic coast, although some came close to that in Nova Scotia, Newfoundland, and along the Saint Lawrence. There were no pastoralists, for Indians possessed neither cattle nor horses. There were no pure agricultural groups on the Atlantic coast, although some Indian polities were devoted to the cultivation of maize.

Actually, the first frontier settlement at Jamestown was preceded by a debilitating wave of European diseases which considerably weakened the Atlantic coast populations. Even so, whites had a difficult time expanding inland until 1676, when Indians were defeated in two local wars: King Philip's in New England and Bacon's Rebellion in Virginia.

The second phase began with expansion up the coastal river valleys westward where, in contrast to southern Africa, the land sometimes proved richer than that on the coast. By 1760 white settlement and control had reached the Appalachians; but here again the achievement was marked by the French and Indian War (1754–63), which was part of a larger European imperial conflict—the Seven Years' War between Britain and France. In this and in the American War for Independence (1776–83), Indians chose to ally themselves with one side or the other or to remain neutral.

The third phase, 1763–1815, was marked, first, by the American Revolution which resulted in the creation of the United States, and second, by Indian resistance throughout the 1790s to whites expanding into the area between the Appalachians and the Mississippi River. That expansion into Kentucky, Tennessee, and Ohio has often been portrayed as the quintessential pioneering experience in American history, where small groups of whites had to battle both the forces of the wilderness and hostile Indians in order to survive. But it is useful to remember that despite the American Revolution, the cis-Mississippi West remained an international frontier. After 1783 the British, now entrenched in Canada, developed diplomatic relations with the Indians in the Ohio country and in Florida. The Spanish in Louisiana continued to seek anti-American alliances with Indian tribes living in present-day Alabama and Mississippi.

Despite the fact that the United States secured full political rights to the Old Northwest in the Jay Treaty of 1795, it did not establish actual political hegemony over the cis-Mississippi West until the close of the War of 1812 with Great Britain. Thereafter the United States had full control over the Old Northwest and the Old Southwest, and acquired Florida in 1819.

The fourth phase—a series of westward thrusts across the entire continent—actually began when Napoleon Bonaparte acquired the Louisiana

Territory from the Spaniards in 1800 and sold it to the United States in 1803. The purchase of the Louisiana Territory not only gave the Americans a foothold in the trans-Mississippi West, it gave them a claim to Oregon and a portion of the Pacific coast. The acquisition of Louisiana triggered a burst of expansionist diplomacy that ended with the close of the Mexican War in 1848. In this short forty-five-year period, the United States annexed Texas, Oregon, California, and the Spanish Southwest.

It was also in this period that the United States, now clearly in possession of vast lands beyond the borders of white settlement, initiated a policy of relocating all major Indian tribes from east of the Mississippi to reservations west of that river. That removal in turn set up pressures on indigenous Indian groups who lived in the area or had moved onto the Great Plains once they had acquired horses. The pressure of the newly arrived eastern groups on the western ones led to conflicts along a vast front from Texas to the Dakotas. In the case of the powerful Sioux bands, it led to their own aggressive expansionist policy, which displaced or upset other Plains groups. The coming of Anglo-American authority also disrupted long-standing trade, tribute, and warfare patterns that existed between the Mexican settlers of Texas and New Mexico and the Apache, Comanche, Navaho, and Pueblo Indians, as well as the relations between the indigenous groups themselves. The new American presence in California after 1848 was disastrous for local Indians, who were pushed off the land or killed by miners. Similarly, the American presence in the Pacific Northwest created tensions and led to Indian wars and frontier raids. By 1850 no Indians west of the Mississippi could fail to be aware that although they were still free, whites now affected nearly every aspect of their lives.

Meanwhile, groups of American "voortrekkers" occupied distant Oregon and settled eastern Texas and the arid lands of the Great Basin. They had also begun to penetrate, by land and sea, pastoral Mexican California. Superficially, the parallels to white occupation of the Orange Free State or the Transvaal are tantalizing, for in each of these regions the local Anglo-American population seized the lands of both Indians and Spanish-Mexicans and practiced a doctrine of "popular sovereignty" by establishing independent provinces or republics for a time. With the exception of the Mormons in Utah, however, these American trekkers were the cutting edge of an aggressive American nationalism rather than a retreat from imperial or metropolitan authority.

The fifth frontier phase began when settlers, having leap-frogged the Great Plains and desert areas in search of rich lands and good climate in California, discovered gold in that province in 1848. The California gold discoveries set in motion a population rush and triggered a mineral frontier that expanded constantly until 1878 and led to the occupation of most of the remaining areas of the American West. Agricultural penetration of the Great Plains and other regions of the West overlapped with the mining frontier and lasted until 1890. Even thirty years of Indian resistance on the Great Plains and in the Southwest between 1860 and 1890 did not stop this occupation. Historians, in fact, now call American expansion in the latter half of the nineteenth century one of the most successful examples of conquest by flood population in world history, a process which, aided by simultaneous revolutions in transportation, mining, and agricultural technology, did not force whites to accommodate to the presence of the native population anywhere.[6]

Americans celebrate this fifth and closing phase of their frontier period with expressions of ethnocentric nationalism and praise of the pioneering efforts of the individual frontiersman. These are the very characteristics we associate with the Great Trek in southern Africa. But it is worth noting that the American occupation had the sympathy of the federal government and benefitted from the presence of federal troops, a national land system, and the absence of political separatism. Put another way, Washington, D.C. was not an imperial government so far as the American pioneer was concerned, but an ally, however crotchety, rule-ridden, and paradoxically ineffective that government could be at times.

As has been suggested above, white advance in North America was punctuated by frequent small wars; on the other hand, it was not facilitated by warfare among the indigenous peoples themselves on a scale comparable to the African Mfecane; nor did mineral discoveries have such profound immediate effects there as did the diamond and gold discoveries in southern Africa. Moreover, the native response to the mineral boom was different in the United States in that Indians were scarcely ever viewed as a possible labor force in the areas of either mining or farming.

The principal reason for these differences, as has been mentioned earlier, was disease. Whereas in southern Africa the Bantu-speaking farmers were not very much more seriously affected than were the white intruders themselves by such diseases as smallpox, that virus was catastrophic for American Indians when brought in by the whites. Introduced into northeastern America via the Spanish invaders of the Caribbean islands, Mexico, and Florida and via European fishermen along the Newfoundland Banks and the Saint Lawrence estuary, smallpox devastated Indian communities along the eastern seaboard before the English colonists arrived. The disease frontier continued to advance ahead of the human frontiers throughout the con-

6. Malcolm J. Rohrbough, *The Trans-Appalachian Frontier: Peoples, Societies and Institutions, 1775–1850* (New York, 1978), p. 407.

tinental United States. Southwestern tribes were hard hit by smallpox in the 1780s; the Plains Indians were decimated by smallpox epidemics beginning in 1837. The extent of these disasters can never be quantified with any precision, but some scholars estimate that the Indian population of North America declined to one twenty-fifth of its pre-Columbian size.[7] Whatever the figures may have been, European-borne disease exacted a gigantic toll from the Indian peoples and thereby made a vital contribution to the establishment of white hegemony throughout the Americas.

Decimated by disease, war, a flood tide of white immigration, and a shrinking land base and food supply, it is not surprising that Indians numbered only one quarter of one million in North America—one-third of 1 percent of the total population—when the frontiers closed at the end of the nineteenth century. In contrast, Bantu-speaking Africans numbered about six million, or nearly 80 percent of the total population of southern Africa. In sum, North America was a region of large-scale white immigration and natural increase and of catastrophic indigenous population collapse, while in southern Africa far fewer white immigrants settled and the stronger element in the pre–da Gaman population maintained an overwhelming numerical superiority.

There were other substantial differences between the historical processes in the two regions. Except at the very beginning and the very end of the frontier era, the southern African frontiers were far more peripheral to the market economy than those of North America. Despite the facts that for the first century and a half white settlement in southern Africa took place under the auspices of a commercial company, and that the Cape peninsula and the neighboring arable lands performed a minor but useful role in the capitalist system, during the eighteenth century the white pastoralists who dispersed beyond the arable belt loosened their links with it. Transportation was exclusively by horse and by ox wagon on tracks that were subject to seasonal inundations. The pastoralists did obtain a few imported goods— firearms and ammunition and perhaps a few groceries and some clothing— in exchange for farm produce and for sheep and cattle they sold on the hoof to itinerant traders from Cape Town, but there was no market for the bulk of their flocks and herds and there were no real towns in the colony except Cape Town. It was not until diamond and gold mining began toward the end of the nineteenth century that the means existed for full-blooded capitalist practices to flourish in southern Africa. As A. G. Hopkins has said in an-

7. Wilbur R. Jacobs, "The Tip of an Iceberg: Pre-Columbian Indian Demography and Some Implications for Revisionism," *William and Mary Quarterly* 31, no. 3 (January 1974): 125.

other context, "It was not the will to achieve that was lacking, but the means of achieving which were limited."[8]

In North America every factor—the environment, the land, the indigenous people, and the organization and impulse of the initial British settlers—conspired to make the frontier an integral part of the European system of merchant capitalism. North America from the Atlantic coast to the Mississippi was a vast woodland teeming with fur-bearing animals, and the shallow coastal waters were full of fish. The forests themselves provided timber for ships and masts, and the southern pineries of the Carolinas supplied pitch and resin. Within twenty years after settlement, commercial production of tobacco in Virginia enabled the settlers to enjoy a remarkable period of prosperity and thus to reproduce, among the planter gentry at least, British rural lifestyles in the New World. Meanwhile, New Englanders developed trade relations with Europe, Africa, and the Caribbean islands, carrying goods in the holds of their own ships. Furs, foodstuffs, timber, and rum flowed from the ports of the northern and central British colonies, while tobacco, rice, indigo, pitch, and a huge deerskin trade stemmed from the ports south of Philadelphia.

In addition to the organized commercial network of agricultural producers, merchants, and carriers, one of the keys to this early success was the Indians themselves. While they were not a source of labor, they were producers of furs and skins as well as buyers of white goods. By 1650, English frontier traders had pushed their pack animals, loaded with trade goods, to the Appalachians, and by 1700 all the way to the Ohio and Mississippi valleys. So great was the incentive to trade, that in New York colony the Iroquois nation fought cognate tribes to gain control of the fur trade in their area. The North American frontier was thus not only capitalist in spirit; the white entrepreneur who first exploited it developed a frontier trade network that stretched hundreds, even thousands, of miles beyond the actual frontier of white settlement. A vast, usable system of waterways and portages facilitated this penetration.

This system brought native populations into a relationship that intensified the traditional hunting aspects of the Indian economy without bringing about an overt dependence on the whites or a close daily exchange of goods and services as existed in the clientage system in southern Africa. Thus the Indian was at the same time much better off, in the sense that he could profit from a sale of furs, and yet worse off, in the sense that, not only did he come to depend on the trade for a livelihood, but he had come to view white goods as necessary for his existence. Trade relations continued as a major initial determinant of Indian-white acculturation clear across the

8. A. G. Hopkins, *An Economic History of West Africa* (London, 1973), pp. 293–94.

continent. Although white commercial hunters must bear a major responsibility for killing off the buffalo, in the second half of the nineteenth century the Plains Indians also helped bring about their own destruction by killing off their own major food source, the buffalo, for robes which they sold to whites in return for ammunition, trade goods, sugar, and coffee. The demise of the buffalo was speeded after 1870 by white market hunters who also killed buffalo for robes. Only then did a vast trading system that had flourished at various times in various parts of the continental United States over a three hundred-year period come to an end. Without any remaining territorial or economic base, the Indians were forced onto reservations where the government instituted a dole system for food and clothing.

To discuss either capitalism or the frontier without discussing the role of the land itself would be to distort both the American experience and its meaning. Frederick Jackson Turner felt that the American frontier was synonymous with the availability of free land. Certainly the trekboers also held the attitude that land existed for the taking on various frontiers of southern Africa. Today, when wealth is conceived of in many forms, it is difficult to realize how much a land theory of wealth dominated preindustrial society in North America and southern Africa.

If the frontier meant "free land," European social, legal, agrarian, and capitalistic concepts and assumptions gave it a whole universe of added connotations. Each of these spawned entrepreneurial expectations that had enormous consequences for the native population. Land in frontier Virginia, for example, was used not only to raise tobacco but to pay for the passage of immigrants. Colonists sought land to create English-style estates. During the nineteenth century, whites in southern Africa, as earlier in North America, purchased and held vacant lands in the expectation that increased immigration would double their value; land located at a distance was purchased so that it could be sold on the market like futures in grain, gold, or any other commodity. Further, whites in both regions conceived of land as being like clothing in the sense that, if it wore out, one could discard it and move on to more fertile areas. A search for new lands meant population movement, and that meant a change in the relation of the seat of government to population. Such movements by whites also invited contests with Indians or Africans and with fellow white competitors for clear title.

Land was also a substitute for money in that both the British government, and later the American government, paid citizens for military duty with land warrants, and by a series of national land acts offered virtually free lands to promote settlement throughout the nineteenth century. In the later nineteenth century, the Afrikaner government did much the same in the Transvaal. Both of these actions encouraged and perpetuated the speculative concept and the disruption of indigenous polities.

What is perhaps the most important aspect of land on a frontier, however, is what is least measurable: the implications of ownership. To own no land was to have no status. In America, to own a hundred acres was to be a subsistence or yeoman farmer with perhaps the right to vote; to own a thousand acres was to aspire to be a gentleman and an office holder; to own ten thousand acres, although the owner may not have had a farthing in his pocket, was to be a lord. On the southern African frontier, it became customary for a trekboer to have effective ownership of six thousand acres, and the custom was maintained among the voortrekkers. Free land, therefore, not only inspired aggressive expansion into indigenous areas for social and psychological reasons, it perpetuated hierarchical concepts of society and fostered forced labor systems on the so-called free frontiers of both North America and southern Africa. It is ironic indeed that "free land" has been seen as the primary causal agent in the development of "democracy."

If capitalism, whether mercantile or landed-agrarian, played two different roles in the two regions, so did religion. Contrary to what is often asserted by white South African historians, the Europeans who settled in the Cape Colony in the seventeenth and eighteenth centuries did not form a Puritan community.[9] Most of them were Dutchmen or Germans who took their discharge at the Cape rather than in Europe, having been recruited in the Netherlands into the service of the Dutch East India Company, where pay was low, conditions of work were severe, and the death rate was appallingly high, especially on the long sea voyages. Scarcely any such people were particularly religious. There were exceptions, notably the one hundred and fifty French Huguenots who settled in the colony in 1688–89, but they were not numerous enough to determine the colonial mores. One consequence of this was that in the nineteenth century the established white population came increasingly to regard British and continental European missionaries as aliens and to resent their pleas for humane dealings with the indigenous peoples.

Nevertheless, British and continental European missionaries were a major factor in southern African frontier history throughout the nineteenth century. They were often the first white people to settle inside African chiefdoms. Chiefs found them useful as informants about white culture and scribes for the conduct of written diplomacy with white authorities, and in some cases treated them as royal councillors. Missionaries made scarcely any converts so long as a chiefdom was autonomous, but once the frontier had encompassed the chiefdom and closed around it, Africans began to flock to the mission churches, anxious to harness the sources of white power by

9. This hypothesis occurs in an extreme form in W. A. de Klerk, *The Puritans in Africa: A Story of Afrikanerdom* (London, 1975).

adopting white remedies once they were confronted with phenomena that their ancestors had never encountered during their lifetimes. By the end of the nineteenth century, for example, about a quarter of the African population of the Cape Colony regarded themselves as Christians. Complex processes of cultural synthesis continued thereafter. By the middle of the twentieth century, more than half the African inhabitants of the region professed Christianity, many of them as members of independent churches under African control. Thus the closing of the southern African frontiers—that is to say, the establishment of white political and economic hegemony—did not mark the conclusion of a cultural process. Rather, it created a material framework within which Africans were obliged to make more radical adaptations than in the past.

In North America, at the very beginning both the English government and the English settlers declared that it was their duty to convert the "savage" and to civilize him. They either blissfully or deliberately ignored the fact that Catholic missionaries working for Spain had already settled in Mexico and Central and South America and established outposts in Florida and the Carolinas. By the seventeenth century such missionaries had penetrated New Mexico and by the eighteenth, Texas and California. Nor did they care to admit the influence of French Catholic missionaries on the Indians in Canada and the Mississippi Valley. The British represented a second and variant wave of European Christianity to reach some North American Indians. Nevertheless, Puritan missionaries—such as John Eliot—tried to create "praying towns" of Christian Indians in Massachusetts modeled on the white Puritan towns. Such a totalitarian approach to conversion was doomed to failure. Even so, during the seventeenth and eighteenth centuries missionaries worked among Indians and by the nineteenth had produced both converts and some unexpected results.

First, their efforts often fragmented rather than united a "tribe" or group, so that while some Indians still adhered to old beliefs, others accepted Christianity and white culture, while still others sought a compromise. Ironically, the acculturated Indians were not accepted in white society, and in times of war Christian Indians were attacked along with the rest. Second, Christianization played a major role—with its millenarian doctrine of the Second Coming—in fostering Indian revitalization movements among the Iroquois, the Cherokee, the Sioux, and other Plains tribes between 1800 and 1900. Whites simply had not expected the Indians to make an imaginative adaptation of Christian ideas either as an "additive" to their own religion—to use Richard Elphick's apt term—or as a weapon against acculturation to white ways. In southern Africa, too, the missionaries created divisions in local societies, and even the most westernized Africans were denied social and political equality with the whites. Christianity may also have influenced one of the most catastrophic millenarian episodes of all time when, in 1856–57, many Xhosa killed their cattle and destroyed their crops in the belief that such a demonstration of faith in their ancestors' demands, as revealed in a vision, would cause the whites to disappear.

At the same time that English and later American missionaries were busy at their task, Catholic missionaries in the northern borderlands of New Spain were attempting to convert New Mexican Indians in the seventeenth century, and Texas, southwestern, and California Indians in the eighteenth. Here the process operated under very different assumptions and conditions. The Indian neophytes, for example, always outnumbered the Spaniards, so that compromise and mutual accommodation were necessary attributes of conversion. In the course of time, native religion in the Southwest was modified but not suppressed. In the eyes of the Spanish crown, conversion also had a very practical purpose: it would create both a loyal borderland citizenry and a needed labor force for the missions and the ranches. In California, converted Indians usually became herdsmen for cattle. There, as nowhere else in the continental United States, did something similar to the South African clientage system exist for a time.

Even so, the Spanish system was destined not to last. Despite the earlier Jesuit efforts to convert Indians in the Southwest, and the later efforts by the Franciscans there and in California, after 1821 the newly independent Mexican government began to dismantle the mission system in its northern provinces. The Anglo-American conquest of California and the Southwest in 1846 sounded the final death knell of the system. Beginning in 1869, a new American policy of *total* assimilation—the so-called Peace Policy—assigned Protestant missionaries as agents to Indian reservations in the West where they were expected to Christianize their charges and to teach them agriculture. Another aim of the policy was to break the power of the traditional chiefs so that the assimilation process could be accelerated. In essence, the original Puritan concept of total assimilation was revived under the more secular auspices of the national government. Seldom in history has an indigenous society been so subjected to a simultaneous attack on its religion, culture, economy, and political institutions as in the American West between 1867 and 1890. This policy of cultural genocide led many Indians to lose hope and commit suicide. Others joined such revitalization movements as the Ghost Dance or the Native American Church, or resorted to military resistance. In the end all resistance proved fruitless and by 1890 the last "frontier" war—the Battle of Wounded Knee between Indians and whites—had taken place. (It should be noted that the powerful urge of the white majority to force the Indian minority to conform was not based entirely, or even principally, on racial as distinct from cultural prejudice. Throughout the nineteenth century Americans harassed the Latter-Day

Saints, or Mormons, because of their belief in polygamy, and exhibited an intense hostility to Catholic immigrants.)

A vital difference between the North American experience and the experience of southern Africa can be found in the use of indigenous people for labor. From the very beginning the colonizers of southern Africa were not self-sufficient: they used the labor services of both imported slaves and indigenous peoples. In the seventeenth and eighteenth centuries, slaves were brought in by sea from tropical Africa, Madagascar, and southeast Asia to work for the Dutch East India Company and for the townsmen and grain and wine farmers of the southwestern Cape Colony. During the same period, as the local hunting and herding societies collapsed, those survivors who did not retreat beyond the advancing settlers became their clients, working as herdsmen and domestic servants in return for squatting rights. In the nineteenth century, Bantu-speaking Africans performed these roles in the eastern part of the region, and after minerals were discovered it was they who did most of the manual labor in the construction of railroads and in the mines.

Again the contrast was startling when compared to the North American experience. Although some of the first white settlers attempted to enslave Indian laborers, they soon turned instead to a dependence on European emigrant labor and black slaves from Africa. The beneficence of the American environment, the self-sufficiency of many of the white communities, and the decline in the Indian population meant that, as settlements developed, the Indian came to have no practical economic function in the white world, a view that helps to explain why Indians were constantly removed from the paths of white advance.

Yet another difference may be found in the history of native land ownership in the two regions. In southern Africa, whereas scarcely any land was left in the possession of the Khoisan hunting and herding peoples (with a few exceptions in Botswana and Namibia), the Bantu-speaking farming people retained effective occupation of considerable tracts of land as the frontiers closed around them. They held all the land in Lesotho (Basutoland), nearly half of Swaziland and Zimbabwe (Rhodesia), most of the arable land in eastern Botswana and northern Namibia, much of Mozambique, and, in scattered fragments, about one-third of the eastern two-fifths of the present Republic of South Africa (including the Transkei and other former reserves that are now so-called independent states). This outcome was the result of piecemeal decisions that white governments adopted mainly because the Africans were too numerous and too powerful to be completely expropriated. In time, however, whites came to realize that it was safer to accept the permanent existence of African reservations than to attempt to disperse the entire African population throughout the region as a simple, landless proletariat. Whites also found that reservations provided an advantageous basis for their labor needs. Although the reservations were large enough to provide most Africans with an economic cushion, they were not so large as to make it possible for African communities to feed and clothe themselves and pay the taxes that were demanded of them without releasing a high proportion of their manpower as migrant labor. Hence, as the frontiers closed toward the end of the nineteenth century, production for the market in the areas occupied by whites was becoming based on a reservation system combined with a system of industrial segregation, with high wages and secure employment for whites and low wages, minimal social services, and intermittent, migrant employment for Africans.

In the United States, white attitudes toward land—described earlier—produced a removal and reservation system that performed a very different role. At first a reservation was seen as a specific area in which Indians could live more or less as they pleased. However, by the nineteenth century reservations were reduced in size, and agents and army units were sent there to oversee every aspect of Indian life. In 1887 the government instituted a new policy of assimilation through "severalty"—that is, giving Indians individual homesteads of 160 acres or less so that they could become self-sufficient farmers. The remaining reservation lands were thrown open to the whites. The practical result of this misguided reform was that of the 130 million acres still owned by the Indians, 90 million were thrown open to public sale. In short, the Indians had not only lost a continent, they were physically confined to tiny reservations whose resources were not sufficient to sustain life. Not until the Second World War did substantial numbers of Indians escape the reservations to join the armed forces or to find jobs in war industries. So great did the exodus become, that in 1970 nearly 40 percent of those Americans we call Indian lived in cities.

By the end of the nineteenth century there were substantial differences in the modes and degrees of white control in the two regions. Although white governments had proclaimed supremacy over the entire southern African region, actual white power was still very limited in many areas. It was most effective where two conditions existed: the presence of a strong settler community and the collaboration, or at least the acquiescence, of significant segments of the African population. These conditions were fulfilled to a considerable extent in the self-governing British colonies and the Boer republics. Over 90 percent of the white population of the region lived there, and the traditional cleavages among the Africans were compounded by newer divisions between the majority who were still looking to their own traditions for inspiration and a growing minority who looked outside their own traditions in seeking ways of coming to terms with the intrusive forces. The modernizers differed among themselves as to how that should be done, but nearly all who were well-equipped to cope with the whites had been educated in mission schools and were inclined to pursue cautious, nonviolent, reformist policies. Only after another generation had passed would significant numbers of black South Africans turn to revolutionary actions. In Basutoland and Bechuanaland Protectorate, the British were content to keep the peace with minimal outlays of money and personnel by supporting the traditional chiefly hierarchies and allowing them to do most of the work of administration. In Rhodesia, German South West Africa, and Portuguese Mozambique, on the other hand, the colonial regimes did not succeed in creating strong links with the African population and were still depending very largely on main force.

It would be difficult to exaggerate how much more complete the white takeover of North America was when compared to the African experience. By 1890, disease, war, the reservation system, and the destruction of the internal Indian leadership system, combined with Christianization and assimilation, had reduced the Indian population to less than 250,000 persons. They were, indeed, wards of the nation without political rights or the power of the vote, and without any land base or labor role in the new white industrial society.

Finally, as the frontiers closed toward the end of the nineteenth century, there were great contrasts between the terms under which the surviving members of the indigenous societies had been subjected to white control in the two regions. In southern Africa, the indigenous peoples had become an integral part of an increasingly capitalist economy, in which the categories of class and race had merged to form one of the most rigidly stratified systems in the modern world. In a typically trenchant sentence, Lord Milner, the last great British proconsul in the region, expressed his hopes for the future soon after war broke out between Great Britain and the Boer republics in 1899: "The *ultimate* end is a self-governing white Community, supported by *well-treated* and *justly* governed black labour from Cape Town to Zambesi."[10] The foundations for such a fulfillment had been laid during the frontier era. Reservations that were substantial but nevertheless insufficient for an increasing African population constituted a uniquely effective solution to the labor problem. White governments could manipulate the quantity of African labor by balancing incentives such as taxation against restrictions such as pass laws; and they could keep African wages down by placing the main burden of African support on the reservations. In addition, the black elite, their education provided by Christian missions, bestowed legitimacy

10. Sir Alfred Milner to Sir Percy Fitzpatrick, 28 November 1899, in *The Milner Papers (South Africa) 1897–1905*, ed. Cecil Headlam, 2 vols. (London, 1931–33), 2: 35.

on the system by pursuing the chimera of equality in the British imperial order, as embodied in the forms but not the practice of the Cape colonial franchise laws.

In the United States, on the other hand, a curious and indeed cruel, dilemma existed for the Indians. They were told to relinquish their culture; and beginning in the 1870s, as one product of the Peace Policy, white-run boarding schools were established to wean Indian children from the traditional language and ways of their parents. But those youths who learned to read and write, or decided to farm or develop a craft skill, were not accepted either socially or as a part of the labor force. However, although there were gross inequalities, stratification in American society was not nearly so rigid as in southern Africa; there were powerful egalitarian traditions and forces that were eventually to benefit Indians as well as more powerful minorities, but that process was not to bear fruit until the second half of the twentieth century when Indians moved to the city. There a pan-Indian movement eventually developed, led by Indians who were at home both in their own and in white culture. Backed by a government that had finally become respectful of Indian culture in the 1930s, and sympathetic to Indian property claims in the 1960s, Indians launched a new struggle to obtain opportunities, funds, and lands long denied them.

The following chapters written by eight authors examine the processes that cumulatively produced these divergent outcomes. They shift the focus from the broad perspectives of this chapter to specific facets of the history of individual frontier zones in particular periods. While there is no reason to anticipate the conclusions of those analytical narratives here, the fact of juxtaposing an essay by a North American expert and one by a southern African expert on a common topic has produced insights beyond the comparative approach that neither the editors nor the other authors expected. Some of these deserve special comment here.

In his chapter on the American frontier process, for example, Robert Berkhofer has called attention to the fact that while the long-range process of opening and closing frontiers has a ring of inevitability about it, the comparative approach suggests that outcomes are by no means predictable. Indians in the preindustrial era were few but seldom enslaved (although whites sometimes sent captive Indians to Caribbean islands as slaves); blacks in America were numerous, but until the Civil War the vast majority remained unfree. The indigenous peoples of southern Africa, though vastly outnumbering the whites, were enfeoffed by a symbiotic clientage system in a pastoral society that was more subsistence than capitalist. And yet when an industrial and capitalist society came to southern Africa after the discoveries of diamonds and gold in 1869 and thereafter, both poor whites and poor Africans failed to benefit economically and became, instead, the urban poor.

Thus Berkhofer not only questions the assumptions of progressive historians about frontier history, he poses the most fundamental questions about the nature of capitalism, the interactions of peoples, economies, and cultures, and the tantalizing factor of persistence. He also raises questions about when a frontier really closes and how, if traditional polities change over time, stereotypical definitions of "peoples" and "sides" develop. Taken together, these questions suggest that there was indeed a frontier period with distinctive qualities, but that each regional frontier had its own qualities. To study process during the frontier period rather than slavery, labor systems, government, or other traditional approaches to the history of a region or a country, is to confront the dynamics of history itself.

Herman Giliomee's chapter on process on the southern African frontier analyzes the way in which frontiers open and close by focusing on three topics: land and subsistence farming, caste and class relations, and the political order in the Eastern Cape, the Orange Free State, and the Transvaal. At once one is struck by what "peoples," land, process, and "sides" meant in southern Africa; for unlike American historians who speak only of Indians, southern Africans speak of San, Khoikhoi, and Bantu-speaking farmers, and identify the Griquas as well. Unlike the case on the North American frontier, these groups more or less lived with one another and were constantly interacting with one another as well as with the whites. Thus, in analyzing the southern African frontier a different definition of people and "sides" from that of the American frontier must be found. Futhermore, land, though abundant in southern Africa, was for the most part ranch land or near-subsistence farmland; and though there was a potential surplus of labor, there was no market. The internal variations on the three frontiers treated by Giliomee compared with those on the North American frontier assist us in gaining a better perspective on what was distinctive and what was common in the frontier process.

Internationally, perhaps no aspect of frontier history has received more attention than the way in which white populations established hegemony over indigenous populations and their lands. This has variously been called European overseas expansion, imperialism, pioneering, or nation-building. Clyde Milner and Christopher Saunders, in their chapters on political processes on the two frontiers, bring a new perspective to this familiar subject: first, by exploring the nature of the local indigenous polities; second, by tracing the interface between them and local white polities in the open phase of the frontier; and finally, by assessing the impact of mass settlement, technology, and the metropole in bringing about the closing of the frontier. Both scholars agree with Berkhofer that the so-called inevitable outcome of this interaction was far from inevitable. Milner finds, for example, that although Indians were so culturally diverse that they could never achieve political unity beyond a local level, their disunity was often matched by a white disunity—local and international—so great that the Indians did not have to face the fundamental question of survival until the 1760s, almost 180 years after first contact.

Using a very different approach, Saunders describes the theme of disunity on the southern African frontier as an intricate web of power struggles based on conflicts between black and black, white and white, and black and white. He concludes that there were long periods of rough equilibrium (open phase) between the indigenous and white populations up until the 1870s. Both he and Milner also make the crucial point that power during the open frontier period was conceived of in terms of allegiance rather than political territory or racism. It took the united national power of the United States to defeat the Indians and the backup of British military force to close the frontiers of southern Africa.

By concentrating on political processes rather than systems, they demonstrate again the wisdom of discussing "sides" and "peoples" rather than national or ethnic groups. In that connection, it is worth noting that both scholars independently concluded that up until the closing of the frontiers, Indian-Indian and Khoikhoi-Khoikhoi relations took precedence over Indian-white or African-white relations, and that whites on both frontiers sought native alliances in order to survive. Moreover, both also suggest that neither Indians nor Africans ever basically restructured their polities to meet the white threat. Read in conjunction, the two chapters offer remarkable new insights into the actual workings of local political processes that lasted hundreds of years on some frontiers.

Any serious comparative study of frontier interaction must give full attention to the social and economic orders of both indigenous and intrusive societies and the factors that altered each between the opening and closing dates. In his discerning chapter on the social and economic frontiers of North America, Ramsay Cook points out that Europeans came to trade and exploit the products of the wilderness as well as to settle. In turn, the Indians were anxious to trade and had access to furs as a valuable medium of exchange. But that basic wish was vitally compromised by the impact of disease, the ease with which goods penetrated the interior, and the fact that the native network of hunters and middlemen who, while using European technology and goods to their immediate advantage, were competing with one another so fiercely that in the ensuing wars, population displacements, and economic struggles they destroyed the one economy that might have given them a rough equality with the whites. Here again the complex theme of disunity, and of peoples and sides, surfaces in economic form. Here, too, is a vivid case study of the way merchant capitalism could seize and shape a native economy. No sooner had the Indians become dependent on the whites than the latter moved from the fur trade to agricultural settlement.

Robert Ross's chapter on the social and economic processes on the southern African frontier makes the important point that both the indigenous population and the Boer population were land seekers, and thus both were engaged in "pioneering," so to speak. Each encountered the other outside areas of regularly constituted authority. Thus, while both Ross and Cook note that the economic interface between peoples was essentially private rather than public, they provide a different perspective on the theme of individualism that Turner identified as a frontier trait.

They also discuss Turner's familiar theme of frontier mobility, but with an ironic twist of meaning. Advancing pioneers in North America, at least during the national period after 1780, advanced by their own will—but they had the blessing of the government. White mobility on the southern African frontier was also a private act, but it was often a flight from government. Nonetheless, the hiving off of young persons in southern Africa from their well-landed parent families in order to search for estates of their own bears a remarkable resemblance to the American process and suggests that generational attitudes in a frontier situation need further study.

Again both authors find that the end of the frontier in both regions sometimes meant a decline in economic security and/or status for both frontier indigenes and frontier whites in southern Africa, and for both Indians and white agricultural pioneers in the Great Plains region of the United States. Whether it took the form of a mining economy in southern Africa, with its need for a vast pool of cheap labor, or the workings of the international grain market in the United States where the farmer, having pushed Indians off the land, used industrial farming techniques so successfully that he soon suffered from overproduction and depressed prices, the results were both grim. In both instances the rise of industrial capitalism was a major factor affecting the well-being of these frontier groups.

The last two chapters of this volume describe religious and cultural processes on the two frontiers. James Axtell and Richard Elphick agree that Christianity was, in Elphick's words, a "revolutionary" challenge that deserves comparison with revolutionary ideology; or, as Axtell expresses it, "conversion was tantamount to a complete transformation of cultural identity." Here we encounter a substantially different kind of frontier, one in which the white "side" was not prepared to compromise, whereas in other areas of contact Indians and whites and Africans and whites not only understood one another but maneuvered in recognizable ways to achieve their own economic, social, and political ends. At the same time, whites could not agree on the role of religion in changing the status of the African or the Indian. Once converted, were they to remain second-class citizens or become equals? Again Axtell's and Elphick's chapters remind us of the theme of disunity that other authors have identified with the frontier condition.

And finally, perhaps as much as any of the authors, Axtell and Elphick demonstrate the limited meaning of the "closed" frontier by suggesting just how rarely the missionaries ever succeeded at total conversion, and just how frequently cultural frontiers persisted beyond the time of the establishment of political hegemony by one side. Their analysis of cultural and religious interaction greatly assists our efforts to define more precisely the very nature of opening and closing frontiers.

2

Phases and Processes

3

ROBERT F.
BERKHOFER, JR.

The North American Frontier as Process and Context

The word *process*, like the word *frontier*, has an ambiguous meaning. In American English, in fact, the term *frontier* depends for its most important historical meaning and imaginative connotation upon the several meanings of *process*. *Process* can mean any set of changes that in aggregate lead to some end. It can also mean a single sequence in a set or series of recurring sequences. The word therefore may also designate the cumulative effects of such a series of recurring sequences. The word *frontier* in American understanding denotes both a series of recurring sequences of white settlement as the English and the Americans advanced into the interior of what is now the United States, and the overall results of those sequences for comprehending the impact of the frontier upon American life and history in general.

White settlement upon the American frontier was seen as a series of repetitive sequences as early as the era of the American Revolution by such men as Crevecoeur and Benjamin Rush, but this approach to Anglo-American expansion only became the foundation of American historical scholarship with the writings of Frederick Jackson Turner. He combined the sequential and the aggregative meanings of *process* so well in his frontier interpretation of the American past, that westward expansion seemed to explain as well as describe all the virtues which nineteenth-century Americans prided themselves on possessing in contrast to other peoples. Through recurring process he delineated the advancing frontier zone, and the cumulative sequences in turn produced the frontier as an analytical concept for him. Thus Turner fused space and time in his interpretation, by stressing sequence in any one area over time and also the resulting effects of all these sequences for all of the territory ever considered frontier at any one time. The power of the frontier as an interpretive concept in American history therefore rested, in reality, upon Turner's poetic fusion of the several meanings of *process* into a single overall continuum for the American experience.[1]

Today such an approach to American history in general and to the frontier in particular is questioned on at least two counts. First, the sequence of the stages of white settlement postulated that people actually moved westward in accordance with nineteenth-century social-evolutionary theory. Today not only do we deny that American expansion recapitulated the stages of human cultural evolution, but also we no longer believe in the idea of progress that is presumed by such an interpretation of human history.[2] Second, Turner's interpretation of the frontier solely in terms of sequences of white settlement is condemned as too ethnocentric, if not racist, in its neglect of nonwhite peoples, especially the First Americans, as settlers. Because Turner believed in the superiority of white progress and social evolution, he either excluded Indians and other races entirely from the stage of American history, or relegated them to minor roles in the grand drama of settling the continent. His conception of the frontier is criticized today for resting upon too narrow a definition of who produced and participated in the frontier process(-es).[3]

Leonard Thompson and Howard Lamar seek to remedy the ethnocentrism of the older definition of the frontier by defining it as a territory or zone in which two or more "distinct peoples" interact and the "process by which the relations among peoples in a territory begin, develop, and eventually crystallize." Though solving the problem of ethnocentrism by including nonwhite as well as white peoples as part of the frontier experience, this new definition still leaves two major problems: the ambiguity of the words *process* and *peoples*.

How should we understand the word *process* under this new definition if we deny the older notion of sequence based upon social evolution? If *process* merely means the sum of changes occurring during white-Indian inter-

---

1. John Juricek, "American Usage of the word 'Frontier' from Colonial Times to Frederick Jackson Turner," *Proceedings of the American Philosophical Society* 110 (February 1966): 10–34, discusses the changing meaning of the term *frontier*. Henry Nash Smith, *Virgin Land, The American West as Symbol and Myth* (Cambridge, Mass., 1950), treats the imagery that culminated in Turner's view of American history.

2. Robert F. Berkhofer, Jr., "Space, Time, Culture and the New Frontier," *Agricultural History* 38 (January 1964): 21–30, and William Coleman, "Science and Symbol in the Turner Frontier Hypothesis," *American Historical Review* 72 (October 1966): 22–49, stress the presuppositions of Turner, especially his social evolutionary biases. David A. Nichols, "Civilization over Savage: Frederick Jackson Turner and the Indian," *South Dakota History* 3 (Fall 1972): 383–405, points out the implications of such thinking for Turner's image of the Indian.

3. Jack D. Forbes has long argued for a concept of the American frontier as a place of Indian-white interaction; see his "The Indian in the West: A Challenge for Historians," *Arizona and the West* 1 (Autumn 1959): 206–15; "Frontiers in American History," *Journal of the West* 1 (July 1962): 63–73; and "Frontiers in American History and the Role of the Frontier Historian," *Ethnohistory* 16 (Spring 1968): 203–35.

action, then we can continue to speak of the overall process of frontier inter-action. If, however, *process* also denotes a series of recurring sequences, then scholars seem less sure of its applicability to white-Indian history. In spite of the general impression that frontier interaction between Indian and white peoples manifested much repetition across tribes and white nations, across space and time, scholarship in the field has not advanced greatly beyond the case study of the individual tribe. While we desperately need more such studies of specific tribes, we also need the larger perspective af-forded by comparison across tribes. Lacking the existence of such scholar-ship, this essay can only suggest the nature of process(-es) involved in Indian-white interaction on the frontier.[4]

Clear as the notion of a "distinct people" seems at first impression, this term also poses problems of definition for the study of frontier interaction. While the idea of a people appears evident enough in any given place at a specific time, what does the term mean when considering the frontier as a whole throughout time? Who constitutes a people (and why) was an impor-tant outcome of the frontier as process. Those peoples called Indians by Eu-ropeans were divided into hundreds of tribes and thousands of societies. Even who was a member of a tribe at any one time and what a tribe was, changed greatly over time. Only the ultimate result of frontier interaction would seem to justify the conception of these peoples as Indians. Not only were whites divided by nationality, but even within nationalities whites dif-fered in occupation, class, and religion. For example, should English and American settlers be considered one or two peoples during the history of frontier expansion? Should fur traders and farmers be analyzed as occupa-tional groupings regardless of nationality during frontier interaction with In-dian tribes? Thus, who was a distinct people on the frontier depended upon the results of frontier interaction itself, especially when considering the pro-cess in aggregate. Might does not determine right in frontier history, but it did determine the semantics of frontier history and the ultimate phraseol-ogy of what came to be thought of as "sides." Perhaps this determination of who was considered a people was the most important outcome of frontier interaction from the viewpoint of the Seven Springs symposium.[5]

4. A good example of comparative scholarship is Edward H. Spicer, *Cycles of Conquest: The Impact of Spain, Mexico, and the United States on the Indians of the Southwest, 1533–1960* (Tucson, Ariz., 1962). James A. Clifton, *The Prairie People: Continuity and Change in Potawatomi Indian Culture, 1665–1965* (Lawrence, Kans., 1977); Deward E. Walker, Jr., *Conflict and Schism in Nez Perce Acculturation: A Study of Religion and Politics* (Pullman, Wash., 1968); and Thomas S. Abler, "Factional Dispute and Party Conflict in the Political Sys-tem of the Seneca Nation (1845–95): An Ethnohistorical Analysis" (Ph.D. diss., University of Toronto, 1969), offer models for the type of individual tribal histories we need to understand process and context in frontier interaction.

5. The problem of defining a tribe is covered below. Charles M. Hudson, *The Catawba Nation* (Athens, Ga., 1970), explores the varied meanings given a tribal name over time.

From these few comments about process and peoples, one can see that even the briefest investigation of frontier interaction must look at the creation of both senses of process and the creation of the various peoples as they came to be defined by frontier interaction itself. To see the connection between peoples and processes, one should consider at the very least the following topics:

1. the process of interaction or the long-term trends and consequences of the meeting of peoples considered as the aggregate of changes, because these outcomes determined not only who was considered a people but also the very notion of what happened in a significant manner on the many frontiers;

2. the framework or structure of interaction that made for these long-term consequences for both peoples and process;

3. the processes of interaction, or the degree to which we can find sequential recurrence, or the second meaning of *process*, and the nature of the context of such processes for each tribe;

4. the context of these contexts that made for the final consequences of the frontier interaction and its implication for understanding the frontier as concept and image. The ultimate context of frontier as process would seem to be the overall history of the frontier.

THE PROCESS OF INTERACTION: LONG-TERM CONSEQUENCES AND AGGREGATE CHANGES

If we measure process by the overall outcome of the interaction between whites and Indians as distinct peoples, then the general consequences for the original inhabitants of what is now the United States were much the same for tribe after tribe, regardless of when and where they occurred or how much the tribes differed among themselves. Such variations as duration of the frontier phase, changes in white and Indian societies, economies, and governments, the diversity of tribal cultures, and shifting international and intertribal alliances, all seemed to make little difference in the end for the white taking of Indian lands or the incorporation of Indians into a white nation—often in the face of tribal resistance. While this statement seems true in general for Spanish and French relations with Indian peoples in the Americas, this discussion will concentrate on English and American relations with Indian peoples, with only a few examples being drawn from Spanish and French experiences for comparison. Likewise, I shall concentrate on the continental United States today, using Canada and Mexico as illustrative comparisons now and then.

Major Trends in Indian-White Relations

The most evident general result of the frontier process was white acquisition of the lands of the native inhabitants and often displacement of tribespeoples from locales native to them (at least at the time of first contact with
whites). The English colonial system accomplished the transfer of land title
and occupancy from Indian to white hands both in legal theory and in practice through the land disposal system, the court system, and even the general economy and cultural values. What the English colonial system created,
the new United States adopted without basic change as its own Indian policy, its own land-disposal system, and its general cultural values. As this
land was absorbed into the English and American settlement process, Indians native to these lands, or at least occupying them at the time of contact,
were confined to smaller tracts, removed or encouraged to migrate, or dispersed in some other way. Long before the removal policy became official
under Andrew Jackson and the Congress in 1830, or before the classic reservation was developed to contain the Plains tribes, the process of forced or
voluntary migration and the reduction of Indian territory to small enclaves
was practiced in the English colonies.[6]

The success of this white acquisition of territory may be seen in the
proportion of the contiguous forty-eight states still in trust for Indian tribes
and individuals to the amount alienated to white owners and government
holdings. By the end of allotment in the 1930s, only about 2 percent of the
lands of the forty-eight states remained in trust for Indians, and the very fact
that these lands were held in trust for Indian people by the federal and state
governments suggests who held the title to them in theory as well as in
fact.[7]

Accompanying the transfer of land title in law and in actual ownership
was the transfer of sovereignty over those lands in theory and in fact. From
the very beginning of English settlement, that nation, like most other European nations, claimed sovereignty over the lands of America and their inhabitants. Since the actual transfer of sovereignty depended upon the balance of power between white and Indian societies on any given frontier,
assertion of white sovereignty had to be supported by armed conquest or by
peaceful settlement and actual jurisdiction.[8]

6. Wilcomb E. Washburn, *Red Man's Land/White Man's Law: A Study of the Past and
Present Status of the American Indian* (New York, 1971), is a good introduction to the history
of white policies toward Indians and their implications for native territories and legal status.

7. Computed from table 1 in Theodore W. Taylor, *The States and Their Indian Citizens*
(Washington, D.C., 1972), pp. 176–77.

8. The best guide to the complicated subject of English land title and sovereignty is John
T. Juricek, "English Claims in North America to 1660: A Study in Legal and Constitutional

As the balance of power shifted from an Indian tribe to the white "side" on a frontier, so did the relationship between native and white political and legal jurisdictions and agencies. If in this process a tribal people retained its customary political institutions or some modification of them, those institutions bore a changed relationship to English and American governments from that which obtained during an earlier phase of contact. That altered relationship limited what Indian political institutions could do effectively within their own jurisdiction, and certainly what they could achieve vis-à-vis other tribes and whites in general. In other words, the principal turning point would seem to be the loss of political autonomy by the natives and the gaining of authority over a tribe's members by white political agencies, whether colonial, state, or federal.[9]

Just as significant as the previous trends, and perhaps both cause and result of them, was the changing relationship between native and white populations in a frontier area over time. While warfare between white and Indian peoples certainly contributed to demographic decline in some tribes, all tribes were profoundly affected by native susceptibility to Old World diseases. Whether or not one accepts all of the upward revisions of aboriginal population figures, the decimation of Indian peoples in the area now designated the United States (as elsewhere in the Americas) by the later nineteenth century was enormous. Scholars agree that the total Indian population in the United States reached a nadir of approximately a quarter of a million in the second half of the 1800s. This figure, depending upon the estimator, represents a decline of 60 to 98 percent of the total tribal populations in that area before white contact. Some tribes almost entirely disappeared as a result of disease and conquest.[10] Such severe demographic decline had profound implications for tribal leadership succession and the nature of governance, economic subsistence and patterns of survival, and even for conversion to alien religions and customs. Whereas near the end of the nineteenth century a quarter of a million Indians survived on and off the

History" (Ph.D. diss., University of Chicago, 1970). Compare Francis Jennings, *The Invasion of America: Indians, Colonialism, and the Cant of Conquest* (Chapel Hill, N.C., 1975), chap. 7.

9. Edward P. Dozier, "Forced and Permissive Acculturation," *American Indian* 7 (Spring 1955):38–45; Evon Z. Vogt, "The Acculturation of American Indians," *Annals of the American Academy of Political and Social Science* 311 (May 1957):137–46; and Edward H. Spicer, ed., *Perspectives in American Indian Culture Change* (Chicago, 1961), chap. 8, all stress the importance of the balance of power between Indian and white societies in understanding the history of their interaction.

10. Good starting places for the changing estimates of native population are: Henry Dobyns, *Native American Historical Demography: A Critical Bibliography*, The Newberry Library Center for the History of the American Indian Bibliographical Series (Bloomington, Ind., 1976); Wilbur R. Jacobs, "The Tip of the Iceberg: Pre-Columbian Indian Demography and Some Implications for Revisionism," *William and Mary Quarterly* 31 (January 1974):123–32; Jennings, *Invasion of America*, pp. 16–31.

reservations, the white population reached fifty-five million persons not counting blacks or Asians—or five times the most generous estimates of precontact tribal populations.[11]

Perhaps the most significant result of the frontier as overall process was the concept of whites and Indians as "sides." During the prolonged competition between whites and Indian peoples for land and cultural hegemony, the frontier became identified as a combat zone in white minds (and probably Indian also), and the various tribal peoples continued to be considered "Indian" by white policymakers and settlers' alike. Similarly, English and Americans in aggregate became a single oppressive entity in Indian relations. Of course, both Indians and whites recognized ethnic and national differences, religious and political differences, occupational and class differences in their dealings with each other, especially over time in any one area; but the eventual outcome was that each group became a "people" in addition to the individuals constituting the "sides." Thus, although western expansion made the United States the nation it was (and is), it also generated a process whereby policy leaders and intellectuals of that time, and historians since, came to see the Indians as being on one side and the whites on the other.[12]

Major Consequences for Indian Lives

Major changes took place in tribal ways of life as a result of white-Indian interaction on the frontier, but historians and anthropologists find it difficult to specify the exact nature of all these changes. Clearest are the economic and political transformation of Indian lives during this interaction. Far less clear are what might be called cultural changes. Although Indians no longer live as they once did (neither do whites for that matter), it is difficult to say with precision, when examining personality, values, and general world views, just what did change. Some changes are evident, but the persistence of certain basic attitudes and values defy scholarly consensus. Moreover, we should not assume that all changes were forced or that Indian cultures would have remained static without white invasion and stimulus.

Although it is difficult to generalize about economic relationships between Indian and white peoples, most tribes were denied sufficient resources after "conquest" to maintain their traditional life-styles yet at the same time were not really integrated into the white economic system on a

11. White population computed from *Historical Statistics of the United States, Colonial Times to 1970* (Washington, D.C., 1975), ser. A91–104, p. 14.

12. The white invention of the "Indian" and the perpetuation of that concept comprise the theme of Robert F. Berkhofer, Jr., *The White Man's Indian: Images of the American Indian from Columbus to the Present* (New York, 1978).

sustaining basis. Whether or not one looks at John Eliot's praying towns or at the classic reservation in the last half of the nineteenth century as internal colonies, one is impressed less with the economic subordination of Indians tribe by tribe than with the exclusion of Indians from the basic English and American economic systems except peripherally (excluding the special cases of the fur and hide trades). After the frontier closed, some tribespeoples engaged in menial labor, craft production, grazing, and farming. Whether Indians were integrated into the lower classes in rural areas or were isolated on enclaved lands, their usual place in the larger American economy was one of poverty and exclusion except at the lowest and most tenuous levels.[13]

As the balance of power shifted from a given tribespeople to the white "side" on a frontier, not only did the relationship between native and white political authority and agencies alter, but so in many instances did the nature of native political institutions. If individual Indians left their enclaved lands, they became directly subject to white governments. If they stayed on enclaved lands in communal aggregations, they were still subjected to the jurisdiction of white governments in theory and, as far as such jurisdiction could be enforced, in fact. Thus, the extent to which traditional tribal governmental procedures and agencies were recognized was a matter of white inability to suppress such practices and institutions and to Indian persistence. Factions arose (some would say continued to endure) over strategies of coping with white intrusion and influence, if not coercion, for change in traditional Indian life-styles and institutions. In meeting such challenges, response frequently took the form of changes in Indian political practices. Over time, these institutional changes often produced tribal governments that were partially modeled on white ways of governance. New kinds of jurisdiction, decision making, and scope and authority of tribal government therefore developed, and in the end the size of the tribe often changed along with the nature of its government. The consolidation of tribal-wide governments following a white American model and the adoption of constitutions by the Southern "Civilized Tribes" in the first half of the nineteenth century are probably the best examples of radical transforma-

---

13. Whether Indian enclaves can be considered as internal colonies depends upon the definition. See, among other references on internal colonialism: John Walton, "Internal Colonialism: Problems of Definition and Measurement," in *Latin American Research*, vol. 5; Wayne A. Cornelius and Felicity M. Trueblood, eds., *Urbanization and Inequality: The Political Economy of Urban and Rural Development in Latin America* (Beverly Hills, Calif., 1975), pp. 29–50; Michael Hechter, *Internal Colonialism: The Celtic Fringe in British National Development, 1536–1966* (London, 1975); Joseph G. Jorgenson, *The Sun Dance Religion: Power for the Powerless* (Chicago, 1972), pp. 89–93; and George P. Castille, "Federal Indian Policy and the Sustained Enclave: An Anthropological Perspective," *Human Organization* 33 (Fall 1974): 219–28.

tion along these lines, but other tribes experimented with similar develop-ments in reaction to white pressures.[14]

Tribal members experienced changes in their life-styles and perhaps in their values as a result of contact and continued interaction with whites. Some changes were voluntary; some were the involuntary results of white policy enforced by army and annuity. Because it is difficult to measure cul-tural change with any degree of precision, scholars are divided over (a) what changed as the consequence of white pressure and what persisted in spite of the pressure for change, and (b) how changed or continuous native values and life-styles would have been under more autonomous circumstances. Re-gardless of these problems, all agree that many changes did take place in native habits and life-styles over time. Less clear are fundamental altera-tions in values. Although Indians do not live as they once did, many Indians have not joined the mainstream of American culture even today—particu-larly if they still call themselves Indian. This tendency to cultural per-sistence as well as change poses a fundamental problem in analyzing the frontier period of white-Indian interaction. The problem can be seen in the retention of native languages as well as in the adoption of English, and in the survival of native religions alongside adopted Christian religions and syn-cretic or new nativistic ones.[15]

Major Trends for English and American Life

The long-term consequences of frontier interaction for white life seem ei-ther painfully clear or terribly obscure. The main results, of course, were white possession of Indian lands and resources to be exploited according to English and American methods, territory to be settled and governed and lived on in the English and American modes, and the opportunity for auton-omous social and cultural development with little or no hindrance from In-dian power and influence. More obscure are the ways in which the presence of Indian peoples affected English and American imagination, beliefs, or val-

14. Robert F. Berkhofer, Jr., "Native Americans," in John Higham, ed., *Ethnic Leadership in America* (Baltimore, 1978), pp. 119–49, treats these changes in general. For specific tribal histories particularly addressed to these changes, see Clifton, *The Prairie People*, and Walker, *Conflict and Schism in Nez Perce Acculturation*. Lester Hargrett, *A Bibliography of the Con-stitutions and Laws of the American Indians* (Cambridge, Mass., 1947), lists law codes for a few other tribes besides the Southern ones.

15. Perhaps one could construct a chart of assimilation to gauge the result of frontier inter-action for cultural and social change over time. Following Milton Gordon, *Assimilation in American Life: The Role of Race, Religion, and National Origins* (New York, 1964), one could look at marital amalgamation, social structural assimilation, transacculturation, and complete ethnic identification in order to determine the nature and degree of change in a tribe. Whether these categories are precise enough or whether analysts would agree upon their measurement is another problem. An ambitious effort is Spicer's *Cycles of Conquest*.

ues. Although a large literature explores the many Indian contributions to Anglo-American life, the authors usually list the many concrete and specific items adopted by whites, such as drugs, foods, clothing, modes of transportation, and words, or they assert tenuous, even doubtful, influences on American character, values, or institutions. As a result, it is easier to see the material contributions made to white life by the first Americans than it is to understand the more complicated influences that might have affected Anglo-American ways of perceiving and understanding the world or the nature of white institutions. A major contribution of Indians to Anglo-American life was the very idea of *the* Indian. One result of actual contact and interaction was therefore the Indian of imagination and ideology that figured so prominently in captivity narratives, political speeches, dime novels, and motion pictures.[16]

From the viewpoint of this discussion, the most powerful influence was the changed meaning given to the concept of the frontier by the presence of Indian peoples between white settlements and the outer boundaries of what England and the United States claimed as part of their sovereign territory in North America. This presence created an anomaly between municipal area and international boundary that became the new meaning of frontier for Americans. In the end, the settlement of this area by whites produced so many conflicts that the frontier in Anglo-American experience was perceived more as a zone of conflict than one of cooperation. Such conflict fostered the notion of "sides" and ultimately the idea of "peoples" in interaction. To understand why the frontier became a zone of competition rather than of cooperation in the Anglo-American experience and why such sides developed, we must turn to the persisting framework of frontier interaction.

THE FRAMEWORK OF INTERACTION ON THE FRONTIER

The remarkable similarity of results over time for so many tribal societies vis-à-vis English and American societies suggests a continuity in the framework, or what we might call the structure, of frontier interaction. This framework depends less upon the place or time of contact than upon the respective natures of the two "sides" interacting. The repeated long-term

16. Virgil Vogel, "The American Indian Impact on History and Culture," in Vogel, comp., *This Country Was Ours: A Documentary History of the American Indian* (New York, 1972), pp. 433–51, provides an extensive bibliography on the subject of his title. Felix S. Cohen, "Americanizing the White Man," *American Scholar* 21 (Spring 1952): 177–91, and Edwin F. Walker, "League of the Iroquois—The Inspiration for the United States of America," *Masterkey* 22 (July 1948): 135–37, offer some of the more tenuous and unhistorical contributions of Indian impact upon American character and institutions.

consequences of frontier interaction for so many Indian peoples came from the basic continuity of white values, goals, policies, and practices over three centuries. The recurring patterns of white-Indian interaction stemmed from the general similarity of tribal sociopolitical organization across the vast area that is the United States today. Therefore, it is the combination of white goals and Indian tribal sociopolitical organization which explains how individual contacts between Indian and white societies became an overall process.

Continuity of White Goals

Two major goals dominated white policies toward Indian peoples: (1) the expropriation of native resources and the acquisition of their lands; and (2) the transformation or elimination of native cultures in favor of approved white models. As true of French and Spanish as of English and American policies, these aims shaped all the many supposed policy changes implemented over the centuries before the closing of the Anglo-American frontier. Extermination or genocide was not an official policy explicitly espoused by any white government, but military operations against Indian peoples were usually justified in the name of achieving the two major goals of expropriation or assimilation. The remarkable persistence of these basic goals stemmed from the continuing commitment of most English and American leaders and their fellow countrymen to capitalism in its several forms and from their feeling of ethnic superiority to the tribal cultures they encountered.[17]

From the economic point of view the frontier was part of the larger English and American economies. Capitalist values and institutions dominated the white side of the framework of frontier interaction no less in the earlier period of the European system of commerce than during the period of nineteenth-century industrialism.[18] So the fundamental question for understanding white-Indian interaction on the frontier becomes: what were the resources available in the area that is now the United States and how could they be exploited according to the techniques and markets of the time? A basic answer already prevailed in the colonial period of Anglo-American his-

17. The argument in this and the next section relies heavily on my *The White Man's Indian*, part 4. Since an extensive bibliography accompanies my discussion of white goals and policy in that book, I shall provide only minimal references in this section and the next.

18. I say this in spite of such arguments as those advanced by James A. Henretta, "Families and Farms: *Mentalité* in Pre-Industrial America," *William and Mary Quarterly* 35 (January 1978):3–32, but see Immanuel Wallerstein, *The Modern World-System: Capitalist Agriculture and the Origins of the European World-Economy in the Sixteenth Century* (New York, 1974), who attempts a larger perspective on European settlement based upon a single world system of labor founded on capitalist expansion.

tory as well as in the nineteenth century, in regard to such resources as minerals, furs, and arable lands.

Precious metals were instantly usable in both European and American economies. From the viewpoint of the French and English of the colonial period, the Spanish obtained the best mines (and bodies to work them), for gold and silver fit the bullionist proclivities of the mercantilist outlook. Whenever gold and silver were discovered on the nineteenth-century United States frontier, the rush of whites intruding upon Indian lands soon expropriated these valuable resources for their own profit. But even lead and other base metals often produced the all too familiar intrusion of whites and the eventual dispossession of Indians. At times whites even contested salt licks!

Of all the white-Indian economic nexuses, the fur and hide trades appeared closest to being symbiotic. Although the trades transformed native hunting practices, patterns of economic subsistence, and even sectors of tribal cultures, still white commercial desires and institutions and Indian values and habits were far more compatible here than in mining or agriculture. The only problem with this symbiotic relationship was its temporary duration given the nature of the resources upon which it was based. Thus, for example, the beaver trade crossed the continent in less than two centuries, as white marketing practices and Indian desire for white trade goods quickly exterminated the slow-to-reproduce animal.[19]

Whether subsistence or commercial agriculture, farming as practiced by the English and Americans was totally incompatible with native economies. Even for tribal economies based in whole or part upon horticulture, the white demand for exclusive rights to the lands that produced the crops as well as to the produce of that land meant that no compromise could exist between native and white tenure. Since the basic frontier economy of the English and Americans developed in most areas into some form of agriculture based upon private property, the inevitable result for native title and occupancy was competition and subsequent loss, both because of white values and coercion and because of the nature of native sociopolitical organization. Perhaps if the tribes inhabiting the area that became the United States had been more like the Aztec and Peruvian societies, they would have survived as peons on the lands of their forefathers. The looser sociopolitical organizational forms of the Indians in the United States, however, hindered their easy mass enslavement or peonage.

In order to satisfy white aims, the Indians had to be dispossessed of the resource the whites wanted most to exploit to attain capitalist ends. There-

19. Harold Hickerson, "Fur Trade Colonialism and the North American Indians," *Journal of Ethnic Studies* 1 (Summer 1973): 15–44, argues that the fur trade seemed symbiotic only in relation to other white methods of commercial nexus and exploitation, for even it greatly changed native societies.

fore both English and Americans sought substitute labor in African slaves and indentured white servants rather than undertake the difficult task of enslaving Indians after conquest. Furthermore, they acquired native lands through removal or concentration of the Indians rather than attempting to incorporate them into a system of bondage or wage labor, because of the difficulties they presumed they would encounter in making workers of such individualistic (or obdurate) peoples.[20]

The industrialization of the United States in the nineteenth century speeded up these processes of economic accommodation and dispossession by providing faster transportation for settlers to the interior, by offering a larger market for frontier resources and production through that transportation system, and by inventing and proliferating new technology for the more rapid and more complete exploitation of frontier resources. Industrialism did not change the metropolitan-frontier economic relationship, nor did it change the fundamental premises of capitalism and private property. Rather, the transformation in the economic system and the technology that goes under the name of industrialism changed, not so much what was wanted from the frontier, but how fast it could be obtained. Thus the brief era of the canal and the railroad witnessed the expropriation of more Indian lands than did the previous two and a quarter centuries of English and American expansion.

Equally persistent as capitalist values in determining white policies and practices toward Indian peoples were the centuries-long attitudes of white cultural superiority to native societies. Not only was the view of the Noble Savage a minority opinion usually espoused for ideological purposes and to make polemical points, but even those who held this view seldom doubted that white society was generally superior to the Indian societies. The basis of such an argument was usually the same ethnocentric judgment of deficiency that underlay the image of the savage or degraded Indian. Whether the image of Indian deficiency and the ethnocentric evaluation of native cultures should be considered an independent variable or merely the epiphenomenon of white economic and military imperialism against Indian societies does not lessen the importance of this image in shaping either official policy or the efforts of religious groups to transform "Indians" into model citizens, religionists, farmers, and scholars. The efforts to tranform Indians through Christianity and "civilization" extended from the chartered

---

20. Enslavement of Indians did occur, but English colonists did not depend on such labor to any great extent. Still standard on this topic is Almond W. Lauber, *Indian Slavery in Colonial Times within the Present Limits of the United States* (New York, 1913); but see also William R. Snell, "Indian Slavery in Colonial South Carolina, 1671–1795" (Ph.D. diss., University of Alabama, 1972), and Lynn R. Bailey, *Indian Slave Trade in the Southwest: A Study of Slave-Taking and the Traffic of Indian Captives* (Los Angeles, 1966).

ends of the earliest English colonies to the assimilationist goals of United States Indian policy and private philanthropy at the end of the nineteenth century (and later).

The gap between ultimate goal and effective accomplishment of this transformation, so often pointed out in Anglo-American efforts to convert the Indians to Christ, farms, and schools, depended as much upon the nature of the Indian societies encountered by the English and Americans as it did upon the motivation of these two nationalities, as can be seen by comparing the French and Spanish "success" in these endeavors when dealing with the same levels of tribal sociopolitical organization. The basic premises of Hispanization and Francization were the same as those behind Anglicanization and Americanization: the need to convert Indians to the "proper" white ways of thinking and acting in those respective nations. Thus, civilization, as it was called then, and Christianity were inextricably linked in the cultural theory and practice of the times by all white political and religious leaders, regardless of nationality.

CONTINUITY OF OFFICIAL AND PHILANTHROPIC PRACTICES

English and American economic and cultural imperialism found its concrete expression in the continuity of official policy and so-called philanthropic practices over three centuries. Beneath the various programs advocated and implemented by sundry government officials, missionaries, and reformers lay similar basic approaches to Native Americans as "Indians." The English imperial and colonial governments, like later American federal and state governments, sought in the end the cession of tribal lands and the transformation of Indian lives. Public officials, opinion-makers, missionaries, and reformers, whether in the period of royal and colonial control, the era of early republicanism and later democratic politics, or the decades of post–Civil War partisanship, all agreed, despite ostensible conflict at times, upon the fundamental nature of the land system, of sovereignty, and of the ideal Indian. The actual execution of land transfer, political jurisdiction, and assimilative policies might have fallen short of the ideals explicitly espoused by some officials or religious leaders, but the need to gain Indian lands, to bring tribes under white jurisdiction, and to convert Indians to Christianity and "civilization" was never really questioned throughout the centuries of frontier interaction—even by those in seeming opposition to official policies or actual practices.

The whole United States land disposal system that divided the American landscape into the rectangular survey with fee-simple ownership was no more than the heritage of the approach originated by colonists and crown for the acquisition of Indian lands. Colonial governments in the seventeenth century claimed exclusive right to the position of intermediary in the transfer of land from Indian hands to private white ownership. Thus arose the practice of governmental insistence on the sole preemptive right to purchase Indian lands, the actual purchase of such lands by official government representatives through a treaty of cession, and the subsequent disposal by the government of land so obtained to individual white owners. This process became the regularized and official procedure for white acquisition of native lands, although it was often violated in spirit and in practice by white greed for Indian resources. Later, imperial control of Indian relations and subsequent federal policy adopted this general procedure with only slight modifications.[21]

White sovereignty and political jursidiction over tribal societies, like land transfer, originated in the colonial period and was adopted by the succeeding American governments. What sovereignty the crown claimed over native lands and peoples was gained in actual colonial control through seeming Indian acquiescence to such white symbols as flags and crosses, through military conquest, through white settlement, or by cession. Subsequently, what the crown had asserted was adopted as the foundation for federal extension of sovereignty over native territories and inhabitants. Actual white sovereignty brought a change of governance for a subordinated tribe. After conquest or subordination, its members became subject in some degree to white governments in addition to their own. The relationship between white and native governments and sovereignty was thus one of the balance of power between two groups in any one area. The so-called "Indian Country" was considered an anomaly under white governmental forms and sovereignty. It was never meant to be permanent, and it was never considered as a candidate for separate statehood.[22]

21. The colonial foundations of the American land transfer system from Indians are discussed in Marshall Harris, *Origins of the Land Tenure System in the United States* (Ames, Iowa, 1953), chap. 11, and Jennings, *Invasion of America*, chaps. 7–8. The abuses of the system are suggested in the title of Georgiana C. Nammack, *Fraud, Politics, and the Dispossession of the Indians: The Iroquois Land Frontier in the Colonial Period* (Norman, Okla., 1969).

22. Felix S. Cohen, *Handbook of Federal Indian Law* (Washington, D.C., 1941), pp. 5–8, examines briefly the changing meaning of "Indian Country." That some proposed to make part of the Indian Country into federal territories in the nineteenth century may be seen in: Annie H. Abel, "Proposals for an Indian State, 1778–1878," *Annual Report of the American Historical Association for the Year 1907* (Washington, D.C., 1908), 1 : 87–104; Ronald M. Satz, *American Indian Policy in the Jacksonian Era* (Lincoln, Neb., 1975), chaps. 5, 8. On sovereignty and jurisdiction in general, see: Juricek, "English Claims in North America to 1860"; Washburn, *Red Man's Land/White Man's Law*; and Cohen, *Handbook of Federal Indian Law*.

The official goal for native political institutions was shaped by white desire ultimately to assimilate Indians into the colonies and later into the United States as individuals. Under this ideal, no separate Indian political institutions ought to remain in existence. The white intention was always to bring an Indian people under an Anglo-American model of hierarchical government composed of native officials in the case of those tribes that were in transition toward assimilation, or later, as individuals, under the regular white governments when they had reached a more advanced degree of acculturation. Citizenship on the white model was to be substituted for kinship relations and tribal communalism on the Indian model. Those Indian political institutions that continued to exist after subordination therefore were tolerated or suffered to exist more through Anglo-American inability to exert total control than from any ideal of political pluralism. Treatment of tribal governments as "independent nations" through treaty and alliance was permitted only before greater actual white sovereignty could be achieved. If tribes on enclaved lands retained forms of tribal governance, these political institutions were suppressed, were not recognized as legal, or were considered an anomaly to be superceded by Anglo-American laws and political customs.

Official policy and private philanthropy were geared to the eventual acculturation of Indians to white ways and assimilation into the white society in some manner. Consolidation of tribespeoples upon enclaved lands, whether the praying towns of John Eliot or the classic reservations on the Great Plains, was justified for the "reduction" of Indians to "civilization" as well as for the economic gain of whites who moved to the lands vacated in the process of enclavization. While English and American governments funded few acculturative agents directly, they fostered such activity by declaring that Indian souls and bodies were available to such workers for the transformation of tribal life-styles and values. Missionaries, like traders, were therefore permitted to live in Indian Country. During most of the three centuries of Anglo-American frontier interaction, missionaries and their supporters were the primary proponents of the complete conversion of all Indians to Christianity—preferably Protestantism—and to civilization—definitely Anglo-American.[23]

23. The continuity of missionary goals and methods may be followed in: Francis Jennings, "Goals and Functions of Puritan Missions to the Indians," *Ethnohistory* 18 (September 1971):197–212, and his *Invasion of America*, chaps. 4, 14; R. Pierce Beaver, "American Missionary Motivation before the Revolution," *Church History* 30 (June 1962):216–26, and "Methods in American Missions to the Indians in the Seventeenth and Eighteenth Centuries: Calvinist Models for Protestant Foreign Missions," *Journal of Presbyterian History* 47 (June 1969):124–48; Robert F. Berkhofer, Jr., *Salvation and the Savage: An Analysis of Protestant Missions and American Indian Response, 1787–1862* (Lexington, Ky., 1965); Howard L. Harrod, *Mission among the Blackfeet* (Norman, Okla., 1971).

English and American governments used armed force to secure the "proper" outcome whenever the competition for lands, resources, sovereignty, or souls provoked tribal reprisals. Military force was disclaimed as the best official policy by almost all white governments through the centuries, but militia and army did support economic dispossession, legal jurisdiction, and cultural transformation often enough to include such coercion among the continuities on the white side of the framework of frontier interaction.[24]

The persistence of tribal societies and cultures in spite of all the white efforts to change Indian lives raises basic questions about the success and failure of Anglo-American policy in terms of its own ends. If the ultimate goal of white policy was social and cultural assimilation, then the persistence of tribal communities and cultures, changed as they may have been through interaction and enclavization, suggests failure. The failure to achieve the goals of assimilation must be ascribed to white racial barriers as well as to native resistance and tribal desire to retain traditional values and communal ways of doing things. White racial attitudes probably denied adequate financing to assimilative agencies that would enable them to make an all-out effort, just as they often barred acculturated Indians from citizenship and a place in American society. On the other hand, if Nancy Lurie is correct in her guess that there are about ten million Americans of Indian descent living today, then greater assimilation took place than a present-day survey of reservations and urban ghettoes would indicate.[25]

That Anglo-American policy did not totally eliminate Indians and Indianness (albeit a changed Indianness) reflects the peculiar humanity of that policy. Total extermination would have eliminated what was so often described in the past (and still far too often in the present) as the "Indian problem," but as Henry Knox, the first secretary of war, observed, such a policy was neither humane nor consistent with American ideals. On the other hand, the acquisition of Indian lands was so successful that tribes were denied the resources to maintain an economically viable life on their enclaves, and so the "Indian problem" was perpetuated. Thus the success of Anglo-American Indian policy in achieving economic benefits for whites simultaneously ensured its failure on economic grounds for Indians. And its

24. Historians, like politicians of previous centuries, debate the role of the white military in Indian relations. Leo E. Oliva, "The Army and the Indian," *Military Affairs* 38 (October 1974): 117–19, provides a brief introduction and bibliography on the topic, mainly with reference to the later nineteenth century. Francis P. Prucha, *The Sword of the Republic: The United States Army on the Frontier, 1783–1846* (New York, 1969); Robert M. Utley, *Frontiersmen in Blue: The United States Army and the Indian, 1848–1865* (New York, 1967); and *Frontier Regulars: The United States Army and the Indian, 1866–1891* (New York, 1973), integrate Indian warfare into United States military history.

25. Nancy Lurie, "The Enduring Indian," *Natural History* 75 (November 1966): 10.

failure to be harsher either in exterminating or assimilating the Indians also ensured its failure to transform Indian lives completely.

Tribe versus Nation-State: Implications of Indian Sociopolitical Organization

If Anglo-American goals and policies ensured inevitable conflict over Indian lands and souls, then what determined what or who was a "side" or a "people" in the contest? How, in other words, did the parties in competition know who were "we" and who were "they"? How Indians and whites bounded their social environments divided out-group from in-group relationships for their various societies. Not only were the two peoples ultimately incompatible in economics and culture, but their political bases differed as well. While all societies are permeable or hazy at their boundaries and shifting in total membership to some extent—never more so than on frontiers—I think that the terms *tribe* and *nation-state* characterize fundamentally different social and political self-understandings and relationships that lie at the core of Indian and white societies. These terms not only distinguish different internal relationships but also differing modes of bounding a society and conducting relations across societies. Moreover, the enduring tribalism of social and political relationships in Indian societies points to a consistency in the Indian "side" of the framework of frontier interaction from precontact to postconquest and beyond.[26]

Concepts of the nation-state and the tribe have both garnered a huge scholarly literature, so flexible and various have been their definitions. One can make too much of the differences between the two kinds of social and political organization, for often real societies seem to fuse in practice what scholars separate in concept and criteria. Neither tribes nor nations need coincide with cultural or linguistic groupings or other convenient social boundaries. On the other hand, one can make too little of the differences between the two forms as polity, for the terms are meant to designate fundamentally distinct ways of considering power and allocating authority when applied to frontier Indian and white interaction and, in the end, who and how many constitute the immediate and outer limits of the in-group so-

26. To ask how the competing groups conceived of themselves is not to adopt the racist thinking common to nineteenth-century Americans. Rather, the question is: who was a "race" and why were they perceived that way at the time?

Some scholars would abandon the use of the term *tribe* entirely because of the conceptual difficulties raised by its use. The reason I retain one sense of that term in discussing the differences between white and Indian political systems is the subject of this section. I have not distinguished among band, tribe, and chiefdom forms of organization, but rather have employed *tribe* for all of them as well as for an ethnic in-group. Whether I use *tribe* to mean the ethnic in-group or the political system of such a group will be clear from context.

ciety. Although individuals interacted in actual situations, their presumed membership in nation-state or tribe influenced how their behavior was perceived by the people at the core of their societies; and it was those people who shaped or determined the "sides" to the contest and therefore the ultimate meaning of tribalism and nationalism as it applied to frontier interaction.[27]

Scholars today have tried to clarify the concept of tribe as applied to American Indian societies by distinguishing the vaguer cultural and linguistic areas sometimes designated as tribes on modern maps from the narrower network of social and political relationships that existed within such areas. Even the ethnic in-group that thought of itself as a "people" and maintained peace within its social network did not have an all-embracing political system. Rather, political decisionmaking and sanctions took place within the several or many communities, villages, or bands that composed the ethnic in-group that whites and Indians thought of, or came to know, as a tribe. Often whites did not know, or even want to know, what were the actual political communities as opposed to the larger ethnic community they designated a tribe, when it came to land cessions, making war, and other activities of interaction. Regardless of how well whites understood these relationships—and some seemed well aware of these differences—it is the relationship between the actual political communities within a tribe and the larger ethnic in-group that is of greatest relevance for our understanding of what constituted a "side" for Indians in the framework of frontier interaction. In the end, who or what was an Indian side in the competition over lands and souls resulted from this dual meaning of *tribe*. Those peoples called Indian by the whites divided themselves separately by ethnic in-group and by political community, and these dual but not overlapping self-definitions, in turn, determined the size of territory involved, the number of people in that territory, and even the nature of the mobilization of resources and population for military conflict.

Of course, past white conceptions of nation-state social and political organization influenced how English and Americans approached Indian societies and what they considered their bounds. In fact, such nationalism partly accounts for the ethnocentric tendency to call Indian societies "nations" and to mistake the internal power relationships prevailing within Indian societies. Such ethnocentrism ranged from seeking powerful chiefs,

27. Good introductions to the conceptual problems in treating the tribe as an analytical unit are: June Helm, ed., *Essays on the Problem of Tribe*, Proceedings of the Annual Spring Meeting of the American Ethnological Society (Seattle, Wash., 1968); and Morton H. Fried, *The Notion of Tribe* (Menlo Park, Calif., 1975). I think Fried is too sweeping in his denunciation of *tribe* as concept, given the ethnographic evidence available, just as Marshall Sahlins, *Tribesmen* (Englewood Cliffs, N.J., 1968), presents too pat a neoevolutionary case for the concept.

earlier called "kings," to negotiate according to a modified form of international relations to arbitrarily aggregating Indian villages, bands, or communities into a "tribe" or a "nation" for the purposes of a diplomatic treaty or a land deal. French, English, and American officials tried to force some clan leader into being an overall chief of the Potawatomi for two and a half centuries, but the public role of such an *okama* was restricted by native custom and public opinion to speaking on behalf of clan interests. To have such a leader speak in the name of the tribe through delegated authority was possible, at best, if all the tribal communities and clans agreed. If disagreement prevailed, then no one individual could speak for all and no authority could or would be delegated to anyone from the tribe or even from a community. For this tribe, a "chief" in white terms was always a white invention.[28]

This confusion has persisted into modern scholarship and therefore it is still difficult to separate the social networks underlying political decision making from the larger ethnic in-group or confederation called the tribe.[29] Whether the Creeks, for instance, knew themselves as an ethnic in-group before white contact is uncertain. The possibly forty thousand Creeks spoke more than one language and were divided into a dozen to fifty towns (scholars' estimates differ widely) so autonomous that one authority speaks of them as tribes, which he defines as "a specifically named group of affinally interconnected kin units . . . governed by a supreme authority embodying the popular will (. . . [a] chief and other town officials), who own and defend a territory and possess a common language."[30] The largest village may have held two thousand people. The towns did not always preserve peace among themselves. Since in almost all tribes the political body was far smaller than what became known as the tribe, we find hundreds of tribes in the area that is now the United States but thousands of political communities. In practice, many of the tribal groupings known to us today may have resulted from white contact and pressure. The extreme example are those Creeks

28. Clifton, *Prairie People*, passim, but especially pp. 119–21. This author provides an ethnohistory that is particularly sensitive to the relationships among the nature of leadership, the size of tribal communities, and the intertribal and international context of that tribe's history.

29. The continuing controversy over the nature of Aztec government is a good example of the differing presuppositions held by white investigators about native American power and role relationships in governance. The century-old debate may be followed in Benjamin Keen, *The Aztec Image in Western Thought* (New Brunswick, N.J., 1971), chaps.12–15. That Atlantic coast political systems still pose problems of interpretation for historians and anthropologists may be seen in the commentary on governments in *Handbook of North American Indians*, vol. 15: *Northeast*, ed. Bruce G. Trigger (Washington, D.C., 1978). Compare the remarks of Charles Hudson, *The Southeastern Indians* (Knoxville, Tenn., 1976), pp. 202–39.

30. William C. Sturtevant, "Creek into Seminole," in Eleanor Burke Leacock and Nancy Oesterich Lurie, eds., *North American Indians in Historical Perspective* (New York, 1971), pp. 95–96.

who became known as Seminoles; but the Delawares, for instance, are a postcontact grouping of previously separate peoples.[31] The anthropologist Morton H. Fried goes so far as to assert that all tribes as ethnic groupings are the result of native peoples' responses to the military and territorial expansion of states. Tribes, in other words, are secondary organizations derived solely from contact between stateless and state peoples.[32]

The difference between Indian and white societies was not so much in unity or disunity but in how their respective internal political relationships were structured. The essence of that difference lay in the distinctive modes of social control embraced by stateless as opposed to state organization of peoples. People in states play up the role and power of leaders because of the state's hierarchical organization. Indians, on the other hand, thwarted the power of their leaders through many social devices. Indian societies, even those that seemed stratified to white eyes, curbed their leaders' quest for power through gossip and redistribution schemes, as well as through restriction of specific authority.

Whites had great difficulty understanding the seeming lack of power and the nature of social control in stateless Indian societies. As a result whites accused Indian tribes of both individualism and collectivism, of monarchy and anarchy. While some of these characterizations may have applied to different tribes, the contrasting descriptions are more attributable to the varying ways in which Indians and whites looked at power, its allocation, and methods of collective decision making and sanctioning. Indians and whites differed on the whole in regard to the nature and dispersion of power throughout a society, the degree of formalization of decision making, the specialization of political and other roles, and the degree of centralization of power and authority in a society.

On the spectrum of political processes and roles, Indian societies tended more to egalitarianism and white societies toward hierarchical relationships. Indian leaders, even so-called kings and paramount chiefs, ruled more through influence and ability than by monopoly of power and force. Thus, most native societies possessed positions of differing status but did not rank these statuses so as to produce social classes. Tribal social organization and political relationships were rooted in local or fictive kinship, while white societies increasingly depended on citizenship and ever-broadening territorial allegiance. The separation of functions into specific political, religious, economic, and other roles had proceeded much further in white than in Indian societies. Indian political coordination and leaders' au-

31. On the Delaware, see Ives Goddard, "Delaware," in *Handbook of North American Indians,* vol. 15: *Northeast,* p. 213.
32. Fried, *Notion of Tribe,* especially pp. 88–105.

thority rested on kinship influence in a local area, whereas white hierarchical relationships stretched across a territory regardless of family connections. Coordination and control rested upon distinctly different kinds of social and political organization in Indian societies than in white societies, no matter how frontier white settlements may have appeared to deny this generalization. Values and attitudes about leadership, governance, and power also differed fundamentally among stateless Indian societies and white states. These varying ideals and practices justify the basic distinction made between the terms *tribe* and *nation-state*.[33]

Thus, the ethnic in-grouping called a tribe varied fundamentally from the in-grouping called English or American. For even though the English and the Americans were divided by class, religion, state, or colony—or even frontier versus "the East"—when they looked to their own numbers or to see who their allies were in any given instance, they usually found a more inclusive in-group than the Indians who were labeled a tribe by the whites. When we add the concepts of power and size of the actual political communities to this equation of ethnicity, we see why population figures made less difference than the forms of political and social organization for the mobilization of military might and resources. Neither Indians nor whites united against each other as sides, but in the actual dividing of social boundaries, the English and the American societies, almost from the beginning of contact in a given area, possessed larger forces and connections to others of their kind elsewhere than did any one Indian society. Divided first by tribe and then by community, Indians seldom organized intertribal alliances and often failed to rally as a united tribal polity. Traditional tribal enemies remained enemies even in the face of hostile white invasion. Communities and bands rarely united politically or militarily as tribes against whites or other Indian societies.

This form of tribalism made for both the easy and the hard conquest of Indian peoples in the end. English and American advances had to proceed tribe by tribe, often tribal subdivision by tribal subdivision. In contrast, no Aztec or Inca empire awaited such relatively easy takeover of a large territory with a statelike political system. Even in this instance, the Spanish could count on the tribes only recently incorporated into the Aztec empire to fight on their side against their Aztec overlords. Diplomatic alliances

---

33. It is difficult to obtain an overall view of Indan tribal government and political systems, but see Harold E. Driver, *Indians of North America*, 2d ed. (Chicago, 1969), chap. 17. Compare the older Robert H. Lowie, "Some Aspects of Political Organization among the American Aborigines," in *Comparative Political Systems: Studies in the Politics of Pre-Industrial Societies*, ed. Ronald Cohen and John Middleton (Garden City, N.Y., 1967), pp. 63–88. John P. Reid, *A Law of Blood: The Primitive Law of the Cherokee Nation* (New York, 1970), provides a good overall detailed description of a tribal political system.

among Indian tribes were short-lived and relatively ineffective, in spite of the fame of such Indian leaders as Pontiac and Tecumseh. Such alliances had to face the localism and diffusion of power customary in native tribal outlook and practice.

White and aboriginal Indian warfare fundamentally differed in aim and execution before white contact because of the difference between tribal values and practices and those of nation-state political leadership and army. Indian tribes often had long-standing traditional enemies, but they did not make long-term plans for their conquest or ally forces across tribes for years. Rarely did more than a few warriors of a tribe engage in warfare with a few members of another tribe. Retaliation for insult or murder, and personal prestige and plunder were the causes of war rather than any desire for the incorporation of another whole society or its territory into a tribal domain. Such an approach to warfare did not mean that Indian warriors were not a challenging adversary to white hegemony. Even though native patterns of warfare changed as a result of white contact, the heritage of this difference for tribal competition and warfare with the English and Americans generally worked to the disadvantage of native peoples in the end. In many cases, what tribal values and practice encouraged, the demographic decimation of native peoples by white diseases only ensured.[34]

The similarity of Indian societies in regard to political power and social organization, in contrast to English and American society, had implications for the achievement by the English and the Americans of their goals, especially when contrasted with Spanish and French colonization. Spanish exploitation, whether economic, religious, or political, worked best in those areas of Latin America where dense, more statelike populations lived. Spanish conversion and exploitation therefore succeeded among the Aztec and Inca peoples, among whom Spanish overlordship in essence replaced a previous state mechanism of native exploitation. Both the French and the English, as well as the Spanish elsewhere, faced the same problems of exploitation and conversion among tribal peoples less hierarchically organized. I am sure that the English would have chosen to utilize the Indian peoples they encountered in the same way as the Spanish had in the "high civilizations" of the highlands of Latin America, but the statelessness of the tribes they encountered made such physical and spiritual exploitation far more diffi-

---

34. Discussions of the nature of warfare in stateless societies get as bogged down in conceptual clarification as the term *tribe*. See Keith F. Otterbein, "The Anthropology of War," in *Handbook of Social and Cultural Anthropology*, ed. John J. Honigman (Chicago, 1973), chap. 21, who provides a bibiliography on American Indian warfare up to date of publication. Driver, *Indians of North America*, chap. 18, tries to distinguish among feuds, raids, and warfare among tribal Americans before white contact.

cult. The problem for the French was ameliorated, at least in New France, by the lack of colonial French agriculture and the presence of the fur trade, which made the exploitation of Indians more compatible with native lifestyles and economy. In Louisiana, however, the French competed in the same ways and used the same forceful methods as the English had.[35]

Anglo-American interaction for three centuries is a history of conflict and competition because of the nature of the English exploitation of resources and the nature of stateless tribal organization. If the tribal peoples could not be used along with their resources as they employed them, then the English and Americans cleared away these peoples for their own supposedly "higher uses," in accordance with white values and their images of Indians. That the resulting conflict sooner or later worked to the disadvantage of the Indian peoples also depended upon the nature of the sociopolitical organization among those tribes. Though the differences between Indian societies and white societies were not so evident during the initial period of contact in any one zone, the differences between a stateless and a state group of people ultimately showed up in the mobilization of resources and persons for competition and conflict, in the respective sizes of the two "sides"—even what is considered a "side"—and the ability to gain allies or neutrality from other nations or tribes.

As I have said, the division of Indian peoples into stateless tribes meant that English and American "conquest" of what is now the United States had to proceed slowly, tribe by tribe, or even tribal community by tribal community. Moreover, once the tribe was dominated and enclaved, the nature of tribal political institutions continued to perplex and frustrate white officials and administrators. Some of this perplexity was deliberately fostered by tribal leaders. The continuation or development of factions prevented any one white acculturative policy from being implemented easily, if at all. Tribal political institutions, even if modified, often perpetuated Indian persistence as ethnic identity, and often as communal experience, for at least part of a tribe in defiance of white policies to the contrary. In this sense, the traditional distrust of the power of leaders that was natural to tribal political organization functioned for some Indian individuals to preserve tribal communities, their ways and values, and their self-identity in the face of white searches for powerful chiefs to effect change. At the same time as the resulting factionalism divided any given tribal community into different but shifting coalitions that favored and opposed various policies of coping with its options under white domination, it also hindered any united response to English and American sovereignty.

---

35. The French in Louisiana are particularly instructive on this point: Patricia Dillon Woods, *French-Indian Relations on the Southern Frontier, 1699–1762* (Ann Arbor, Mich., 1980).

PROCESSES OF INTERACTION: SEQUENCE AND CONTEXT IN TRIBAL HISTORY

Given the nature of the two "sides" in the framework of interaction and the continuity of the structure of contact, it seems possible that recurring events, even sequences, could be discovered in the process of interaction that would warrant the second meaning of *process* as a cumulation or pattern of repeated sequences. Tribal histories and the chronicles of white-Indian relations certainly reveal many similar events across tribes and time. Among the more obvious are treaties and land sales, miscegenation, factionalism, ethnic and diplomatic confederacies, religious revitalization movements, formation of reservations, warfare, and other social and cultural changes among interacting tribespeoples and whites. The important question then becomes: can these repetitive events and short-term sequences be ordered into longer sequences? The structural continuity of white values, goals, and practices and the similarity of tribal societies vis-à-vis white politicosocial organization hint at the possibility of an overall history of tribal-Anglo-American interaction based upon general sequences. Efforts to construct such sequences usually include a period of initial contact which offers friendly welcome to the white invaders and mutual cultural exchange; then a period of competition, conflict, and conquest; followed by a time of adjustment and accommodation by the tribes to their altered situation, which often includes removal or reduction.[36] Students of American Indian-white relations have found no one sequence to be applicable to all tribes at all times.[37]

What such efforts suggest at this stage in scholarship is a rough sequence of contexts in which various sets of events might recur, rather than a

36. For example, see Gary B. Nash, "The Image of the Indian in the Southern Colonial Mind," *William and Mary Quarterly* 29 (April 1972): 197–230; and Spicer, *Cycles of Conquest,* p. 16. Compare Brewton Berry, *Race and Ethnic Relations,* 4th ed. (Boston, 1978), pp. 149–56, for general efforts at cycles and sequences in race relations.

37. Basically, the whole aim of the many acculturation studies that became so important in the profession of anthropology, from Ralph Linton, ed., *Acculturation in Seven Indian Tribes* (New York, 1949), to Edward H. Spicer, ed., *Perspectives in American Indian Culture Change* (Chicago, 1961), was to construct just such sequences of interaction given the two sides in contact. The authors of the second volume concluded that no such overall sequence could be discovered which was applicable to all of the diverse tribes and different circumstances of contact. While it is still unclear whether or not various sets of sequences or cycles could be constructed, a recent text, Leacock and Lurie, eds., *North American Indians in Historical Perspective,* uses basic contexts as its supposed organizational framework.

On religious change and context, compare: Anthony F. C. Wallace, "New Religious Beliefs among the Delaware Indians, 1600–1900," *Southwestern Journal of Anthropology* 12 (Spring 1956): 201–16; Fred W. Vogel, "The American Indian in Transition: Reformation and Accommodation," *American Anthropologist* 58 (April 1956): 249–63.

uniform sequence of events and processes for all tribes. The contexts can be arranged into some sort of sequence based on the degree of interaction achieved for any one tribe. At the heart of the approach lies the relative power of the two sides in any one place and time and the nature of the economies and polities. This sequence of contexts suggests the role of the frontier in our analysis in spite of the variations of tribal society, place, and time. For any one tribe the sequence of contexts differed in overall duration as well as in the length of each phase. When the sequence started, the exact nature of the sequence, and its final outcome, also varied from tribe to tribe. Moreover, for some tribes, subsequences of contexts repeated themselves before the whole sequence was over. Anglo-American interaction with tribes in the southwestern United States, for example, often repeated contexts experienced under Spanish expansion centuries earlier.[38] In spite of these variations, however, the rough sequence of contexts suggests the dynamics of frontier interaction from contact to the closing of the frontier for any given tribe. While no specific sequence of whites invaded a tribe's territory, as was postulated by Turnerian interpretation, the differential size and impact of white settlement over time is basic to the scheme.[39]

The initial tribal context ends in the precontact period. Precontact, of course, is a catchall term for a very long period of time before a specific tribespeople and a white society encountered each other. It was a period of dynamic change from a tribe's origins to the era just before white contact. During these centuries, the original inhabitants of what was to become the United States migrated, developed their distinctive cultures and societies, underwent cultural change through invention and diffusion, and engaged in intertribal trade, warfare, and other relationships. While some tribal groupings as designated by modern observers may have formed in this period, many other Indian peoples still existed as ethnic communities smaller than what is currently referred to as the "tribe."

Scholars differ on the merits of dividing early white contact into indirect and direct contact. Indirect contact between a tribal group and white societies occurred without the direct meeting of representatives of the two peoples. Disease germs, trade goods, stories, images of each other, and other things were exchanged between the two "sides" through intermediaries.

38. For the repetition of some contexts in the history of southwestern tribes, see Spicer, *Cycles of Conquest*, and Spicer, "Yaqui," and Edward P. Dozier, "Rio Grande Pueblos," in Spicer, ed., *Perspectives in American Indian Culture Change*. The best book on the contexts of change within a tribe is Clifton, *The Prairie People*.

39. Malcolm J. Rohrbaugh, *The Trans-Appalachian Frontier: People, Societies, and Institutions, 1775–1850* (New York, 1978), finds no specific stages of occupational advance into cis-Mississippi America, although he implicitly notes the differential effects of population growth in the development of the frontier. The following scheme is a slight modification of the one I used in my article, "Native Americans" in Higham, ed., *Ethnic Leadership in America*.

Many plains tribes had obtained horses from other tribes before they had encountered any actual whites. I mention this phase to make two points: tribes changed habits and were affected by white influences before face-to-face contact with whites; this phase therefore began frontier interaction despite the lack of direct contact between the two sides. Any changes in tribal economy, culture, or political institutions were presumably the results of voluntary choice, for the tribe had control over its own destiny with the exception of the effects of disease or of war with and dispossession from other tribes caused by white trade and pressures. The white push from the east for beaver grounds and land sales, for example, created shock waves among tribal societies to the west long before a white first visited the homes of some of the tribes so affected.

Early direct contact as a context is distinguished from the preceding indirect context by actual encounters between a tribe and whites in an area and from the succeeding context by the small scale of the interaction. Not all of white pressure, let alone all white social agencies, was brought to bear upon the contact situation at this point. Traders, missionaries, emissaries, and "renegade" whites visited or settled in the tribe. Thus white pressures for change could be contained more or less within the traditional community framework and through traditional methods of social control. In other words, although cultural and perhaps social changes occurred, they were integrated into the larger traditional way of thought and life. Voluntary more than involuntary culture adaptation occurred during this phase for the individual communities of a tribal society still possessed sufficient autonomy and parity of power to control the amount and nature of white influence. The only fundamental changes in the traditional way of life occurred in economics and in the degree of intertribal warfare induced by changes in other tribes. Those individuals who adopted divisive white ways (for instance, religion) were sanctioned into conformity, or they formed new communities, a traditional way of handling deviation within the tribe. Treaties were more likely to deal with alliance, peace, or the cession of other Indian peoples' lands and were signed by some "chiefs" of some communities. The fur and hide trades probably operated in this context. Occasionally ethnic groups changed, or tried to change, their political organization to embrace more of the tribal ethnic group. Some Cherokee town leaders in the eighteenth century, for example, attempted to form a tribal-wide political community; but such efforts twice proved abortive.[40]

Increased and more intensive interaction characterizes another tribal context. Although it may be difficult to separate this phase exactly from the

40. These Cherokee efforts to organize a tribal-wide government are treated briefly in Frederick O. Gearing, *Priests and Warriors: Social Structures for Cherokee Politics in the 18th Century*, American Anthropological Association Memoir no. 93 (1962).

preceding one in terms of the amount of white pressure for change and the scale of intensity of interaction, its end point is clear: the creation of an enclaved territory or total dispersion. This phase is marked by serious competition for Indian minds and souls as well as lands. White agents for religions and for economic exploitation increased within tribal territory as white settlers crowded around the tribal boundaries (and often over them). Many more missionaries, greater pressure for land sales, intrusion by farmers, miners, or speculators presented tribal leaders and their peoples with stark options for change of beliefs, customs, and residence. Such competition frequently led to armed conflict. When external demands for change or concentration were great, then so too were factional demands for change from within. Politically, the various communities within the tribe may have attempted some consolidation of the tribe or part of it through the leadership of a faction. Demands for cession and increased white jurisdiction over tribal affairs came from government representatives and from white settlers. Competition and armed conflict usually ended with the relocation of the tribe upon a reservation or with the total dispersion of a people.

In the next context, tribal loss of autonomy came as whites consolidated their control over the larger context. This phase was usually marked by the enforced concentration of a tribal society on a reservation or other form of enclave. In the political side of this phase, the balance of power switched to white governments. Factionalism usually increased but did not become institutionalized as an accepted part of tribal political practices. A white-recognized tribal government, or one composed of acculturated Indians, was not the one usually accepted as legitimate by the traditional members of a tribe. As a result, such a government became just another faction opposed by the traditionalists. The economy of the tribe consisted of what whites allowed, what resources could be exploited, and what tribal members wished to do within that framework. Pressures for acculturation became more intense as white governments allowed or encouraged private religious groups to proselytize for plowing and the *ABCs*, as well as for religion. In fact, as a tribe's members became increasingly aware of religious conflict among the whites, one or more tribal factions utilized different white religions for their own ends.

The Seneca went through these latter contexts at the time of the American Revolution and during the early years of the republic. Many Seneca communities had been forced to move from traditional lands to seek the protection of British forts during the war. After the Revolution, some Seneca communities looked to American goods and allegiance while others remained within the British orbit. After the British soldiers removed from the forts on American soil in 1796, large land sales by those Seneca communities still resident in the United States, reduction to reservations, the entry of Quaker and Presbyterian missionaries to different groups of communities, the messianic visions of Handsome Lake in one group of those communities, and increased factionalism building upon old pre-Revolutionary divisions, all came within a few years. For the first half of the nineteenth century, the number of chiefs rapidly increased as various Protestant denominations gained converts or other leaders used them in factional fights, pressures for more land sales and removal mounted, and various "progressive" factions claimed tribal-wide governmental authority while traditional leaders formed counterorganizations. The adoption of a constitution and government along white American lines during the Seneca revolution of 1848 did not put an end to tribal factions nor ensure domestic stability through orderly succession of party leaders. Traditional Seneca distrust of powerful leaders, combined with the failure of traditional social controls, promoted enduring factionalism. How the Seneca lived in the three-quarters of a century between the Revolution and 1848 was repeated in broad outline in many other tribal histories.[41]

Tribal responses to increasing white pressures and change of autonomy were many: religious revitalization movements (Handsome Lake, Ghost Dance, and so on), last-ditch stands, passive resistance through factional splits, and antagonistic acculturation as time went on. Both Indian assimilation and Indian persistence were ways of coping with the loss of autonomy and the "powerlessness" of the classic enclave. Soon after the reduction of a tribe to an enclave, we can say that the frontier phase of white-Indian relations had ended, for the Indian society had been superseded mainly or entirely by white society on former tribal lands. (The term *frontier* might still apply to a white society at this point.)

Thus the postreservation, or modern, era provides the final context. For those tribes reduced to enclaves centuries ago, and subsequently subjected to total loss of lands or dispersion into the general white population, the appropriate phase after the preceding one should be called "postreservation." For those tribes which were concentrated last in the nineteenth century and which still possess relatively large reservations compared to most Indian tribes, this phase can be called "modern." The attributes of this context need not concern us too much; for regardless of whether it is postreservation or modern, it is clearly beyond the stage of frontier interaction. That some of its features may help us to judge the ultimate outcome of the process of frontier interaction or that the basic white goals of land cession, ex-

---

41. Parts of this story may be found in Anthony F. C. Wallace, *The Death and Rebirth of the Seneca* (New York, 1970); Robert F. Berkhofer, Jr., "Faith and Factionalism among the Senecas: Theory and Ethnohistory," *Ethnohistory* 12 (1965):99–112; Thomas S. Abler, "Factional Dispute and Party Conflict in the Political System of the Seneca Nation (1845–1895): An Ethnohistorical Analysis," (Ph.D. diss., University of Toronto, 1969).

ploitation of resources, and acculturation still operate in this period does not alter its postfrontier quality. This phase includes continuing Indian persistence as communities or enclaves or as individuals who see themselves as tribal Indians. Depending upon the time and recent federal policy, tribal government becomes an agency of the progressive faction and Bureau of Indian Affairs encouragement. Tribal economic relations are peripheral to the larger American economy and usually result in poverty for most reservation Indians.

While no one generalized tribal history emerges from this rough sequence of contexts, we can see how the Indian and the Anglo-American sides were created over and over again as one after another tribe passed through the various phases. The alteration in what was a tribe, who was a member of it, and the nature of political relations in the tribal in-group changed from context to context, but the continuity of Indianness due to communal desire and factional support, reinforced by Anglo-American racial prejudice against total assimilation, maintained the idea of tribal societies as a "side" to be subordinated as "Indians" against a "side" of triumphant, dominant English and Americans.

THE HISTORY OF THE ANGLO-AMERICAN FRONTIER AS OVERALL CONTEXT

In United States history it is difficult to talk about the history of white-Indian relations without recourse to the concept of the frontier. Conversely, it is equally difficult to think about the American frontier without some idea of tribal peoples, their settlements, and their succession by white settlements in most of what is the United States today. That tribal and frontier histories are so fused resulted from the overall process of the interaction between what came to be seen as two "sides." The results in aggregate of that process arose from the nature of the two sides which determined the framework or the context of the relationships, but the timing of that interaction stems from the overall history of Anglo-American invasion and expansion in North America. The history of Anglo-American settlement, in other words, provides the general context for the rough sequence of tribal contexts. Both the length of the frontier as aggregate process and the timing of individual tribal histories during the period from first contact to final subordination and enclavization lead us to a general view of the opening and closing of the frontier in American history.[42]

42. Ray A. Billington, *Westward Expansion: A History of the American Frontier*, 4th ed. (New York, 1974), is a standard account of white settlement of the area that is now the United States.

Two main factors dominate this general history and determine the timing and context of the rough sequence of tribal contexts: the diplomatic situation of England and America on the North American continent and the technology available for transportation and for exploitation of resources. If technology determined the speed of expansion, the diplomatic situation accelerated or hindered that speed. The frontier as physical geography in this view is less significant in the timing of Anglo-American expansion and native dispossession and subordination than diplomatic hegemony and technological innovation.

If one were to look at the history of all the tribal peoples as an artificial whole, then the timing for Indian autonomy would mirror in reverse that of Anglo-American expansion. Originally, only a few tribes had been subordinated by the English (or French or Spanish) during the first two centuries of European invasion. The English colonists and the later Americans were often disunited, and their internal divisions were exploited by shrewd native political leaders for economic and military advantage in the same manner as the international rivalries that separated white nations from each other. With the undisputed hegemony of the United States over its territory, the last and most famous Indian-white battles broke out on the Plains. At the same time, the railroad and the integrated national market economy of the United States only increased the ability of the army and the settlers to occupy this territory. No tribe could achieve its autonomy by appeal to international or internal rivals, as was done in earlier times. The last Indian battles also brought the usual attempts to transform these Indians, but the federal government and its missionary allies had greater wealth and resources of personnel at their command. The United States controlled the larger context in which a tribe must operate. Such ultimate control, however, left factional leaders free to operate and achieve ends they thought vital to the continuation of the tribe as a community. The ideal of federal policy in the latter part of the nineteenth century was to render Indians passive objects in their white-directed destiny, but in reality that policy never achieved such control over Indian lives.[43]

The passing of the frontier as a process for individual tribes meant the passing of it as overall process as well. Although the general history of Anglo-American frontiers determined the timing of the frontier phase of tribal contexts, the nature of the contexts and the histories of specific tribes suggest the limits of the traditional idea of the frontier as a place or time in interpreting American-Indian history. The frontier phase of Indian-white relations revolves around the nature of polities, power, and population inter-

---

43. Edward H. Spicer, *A Short History of the Indians of the United States* (New York, 1969), part 1, offers a chronology which he believes more appropriate to an aggregate tribal history than the one traditionally based upon white policy and Anglo-American expansion.

acting during a transition from tribal to white occupation of a given area of land. The conception of the frontier as overall process merely fuses as it aggregates the results of these many interactions between a tribe and Anglo-American society.

CONCLUSION

The persistence of the basic structure of frontier interaction between Indian and white peoples led to the persistence of Anglo-American perceptions of that process as well. Both the ideas of the Indian and of the frontier retained a fundamental nub of meaning amid changing specific contexts and definitions.

In the paradigm of race relations that ascribes attributes to the "they" as opposed to the "we," the white image of the Indian remained basically the same throughout the centuries of frontier interaction. Indians were considered to be deficient in economic, religious, political, familial, and cultural practices when compared to white values and institutions—unless a white alienated from his own society wished to hold up Indian goodness as a counterexample to white badness. In this sense, the native inhabitants of the United States became a single alien "other" whom whites used to measure their own progress and goodness. As the "Indian" became the alien other, then Americans became the bearers of just those superior virtues and institutions so needed by Indians in white eyes (although some white social classes were considered by their fellow countrymen as no better than "savages" themselves). Ethnocentrism, if not racism as well, reigned in the cultural distinction made by whites between Indians and whites and often in their legal definition of an Indian. Such imagery promoted the idea of sides in frontier interaction but did not necessarily create those sides. Only the continuing process of interaction created the sides as sides.

Such interaction also shaped the white idea of the frontier. The white view of nature was one of mastery in general, and so the frontier as physical environment represented what white society could and therefore should make of it. Certainly, the image of the deficient Indian combined with white economic desires fostered an image of an "empty" frontier, ready for white acquisition in spite of native inhabitants. The very definition of the frontier became the areas where Indians lived but also that were soon to be or were already in the early stages of white settlement. Where the Indians lived was "unsettled" in the proper sense and ripe for supersession and "proper" exploitation. Thus, during the centuries of active competition for resources and minds, the frontier was seen by whites as a zone of Indian-white conflict. In fact, the idea of the frontier where two societies or "sides" meet stems from this history of competition and conflict.

Turner's interpretation of American history merely reinforced or summarized a perennial white view of the frontier and Indians. The ultimate outcome of frontier interaction and process was the disappearance of the Indian from American history. The "winner's" struggle was featured only as long as competition kept the "losers" in white imaginations and policy. With the disappearance of the "Indian" as an active threat to ongoing white settlement, the "Indian" was relegated to the periphery of American concerns and was lost in the history books (until recently). Indian activism and white concern in recent times prompt a rethinking of this white-sided definition of the frontier. Such a redefinition poses new problems that are difficult to resolve satisfactorily without some resort to ideas of outcomes, process, and context. In that sense, it is difficult to exorcise completely the ghost of Frederick Jackson Turner from the idea of the frontier, for the teleology of the process created the idea of peoples, just as the nature of the peoples shaped the frontier process and its ultimate outcome.

4

HERMANN
GILIOMEE

Processes in Development of the Southern African Frontier

INTRODUCTION

This chapter discusses the main frontiers opened up by the Afrikaner[1] settlers in southern Africa. These frontiers were zones where processes of colonization occurred in a situation marked by a weak political authority and
quite often by conflicting claims to the land of two or more distinct societies existing there. The Afrikaner frontier is best understood by contrasting it with the American West of the nineteenth century, on the one
hand, and, on the other, the gradual westward expansion of the Xhosa people between the Mbashe and Sunday rivers on the south coast of southern
Africa in earlier centuries.

The American West in the nineteenth century was predominantly the
scene of capitalistic expansion. Initial white settlement was quickly followed by commercial and capitalist development and the growth of new
communities backed by the federal government and connected with the
heartland through the transportation revolution of America. With the help
of these resources, the indigenous peoples of America were quickly expelled
or exterminated. In contrast, the indigenous Xhosa people of southern Africa extended a particular social order and mode of subsistence production
in a process of inclusive expansion. A self-sufficient agricultural and pas-

I would like to thank Leonard Thompson, Howard Lamar, and other participants of the frontier
conference in the Seven Springs Center for illuminating discussions; Shula Marks and Stanley
Trapido for the opportunity to present a previous draft of this paper to their seminars in London
and Oxford, respectively; and André du Toit, Richard Elphick, Stanley Greenberg, and Leonard
Guelke for pertinent criticism and ideas. I owe a special debt of gratitude to Leonard Guelke and
his work on the historical geography of the frontier.

1. The term *Afrikaner* is used somewhat anachronistically since the frontiersmen did
not consistently and self-consciously refer to themselves as Afrikaners. But it is more convenient to use this term than something like Dutch/Afrikaner settlers.

toral people whose land was controlled by the community rather than by the individual, the Xhosa gradually established mastery over new territory and incorporated previously independent Khoikhoi herders into their society. During the initial stages of absorption the Khoikhoi were relegated to a subservient role, but biological mixing occurred freely and the Khoikhoi did not develop into a separate caste; rather, their descendants became Xhosa.[2]

The Afrikaner frontier fits in somewhere between the American West and Xhosa expansion. It was a mixed capitalist and subsistence frontier but with the subsistence element heavily predominant. The Afrikaners introduced the concept of private property, especially in the sense of individually owned land, and the idea of the family existing separately as a patriarchal unit while at the same time regarding itself as part of a distinct European cultural group and kinship network. In southern Africa the initial occupation by near-subsistence farmers was only very gradually followed by commercial development—in some cases after fifty years or more. Few in numbers and not backed by a strong central government, the near-subsistence farmers lacked the resources to sweep away before them the developed and organized Bantu-speaking indigenous peoples; indeed, extensive subsistence farming practiced by a small white settler population dictated the incorporation of large numbers of black workers into their society. These Africans formed a client and later a laboring caste; their descendants did not become Afrikaners.

The American, Xhosa, and Afrikaner variants of frontier expansion are by themselves enough reason to make any generalizations about the nature of political institutions or class relations on the frontier questionable, if not invalid. The focus should much rather be on different frontier processes which accompanied different types of settlement and colonization. Even if the focus were limited to the Afrikaner frontier experience, generalizations would be difficult to make. For it is clear that within the ambit of European expansion in southern Africa different frontier societies were produced which had to contend with different political and economic environments. A distinction can be made here among three classic types of white frontiersmen.

First, there was the transcolonial frontiersman who existed, as it were, beyond the frontier. Here one thinks of the small number of English traders who established a trading post at Port Natal in 1824[3] and of Coenraad de

<hr />

2. Gerrit Harinck, "Interaction between Xhosa and Khoi: Emphasis on the Period 1620–1750," in *African Societies in Southern Africa*, ed. Leonard Thompson (London, 1969), pp. 145–69; J. B. Peires, "A History of the Xhosa, c. 1700–1835" (M.A. diss., Rhodes University, 1976), pp. 81–84, 105–06.

3. Charles C. Ballard, "The Natal Frontier Experience: A Case Study of Cultural and Po-

Buys,[4] an Afrikaner who became the patriarch of a distinct mixed group, the Buys Bastaards. Living on their own among Bantu-speaking peoples far beyond the colonial border, these white men married black wives, adopted indigenous customs, and built up followings like African chiefs. A loss of European identity occurred, as these whites lacked the numbers and institutions to withstand the pressures of a vigorous indigenous culture.

Second, there was pioneer Afrikaner frontier society living on the frontier that was opening up. There a community of Afrikaners coexisted in a frontier zone with other ethnic groups competing for the land and its resources. There was usually a rough balance of power between the groups, and for a considerable period no group succeeded in establishing undisputed control over the area. There was such a phase during the first three or four decades of intensive contact between Afrikaners and Xhosa on the so-called Cape Eastern Frontier of the late eighteenth century.[5]

Third, there was settled frontier society living on what can be called the closing frontier. Here the consolidation of settlement had advanced much further, but both the pioneer and the settled societies should be considered as frontier societies in the sense that they were involved in processes of settlement and colonization in a context marked by a relative lack of power. From the Afrikaner point of view, settlement embraced notions of occupation of the land and control over all its resources; colonization involved not only the conquest of land but also the incorporation of the indigenous peoples; while lack of power usually had two dimensions—ineffective control by the white government over its own frontier offshoot (periphery) and the inability of any of the communities to establish its hegemony in the frontier zone. For Africans, as Martin Legassick has pointed out, the frontier meant something quite different: it was the first stage of a process in which their political power was eroded as they were absorbed into plural communities, and in which their material and social bases were transformed through their integration into a market economy linked with the industrializing and capitalist economy of Europe.[6]

This chapter is concerned with the most significant processes related

litical Change" (paper presented to the Association for Sociology in Southern Africa, Maseru, June 26–28, 1979).

4. R. G. Wagner, "Coenraad de Buys in Transorangia," in *The Societies of Southern Africa in the 19th and 20th Centuries* (University of London Institute of Commonwealth Studies), 4:1–8.

5. I have discussed this in detail in my "The Eastern Frontier, 1770–1812," in *The Shaping of South African Society, 1652–1820,"* ed. Richard Elphick and Hermann Giliomee (Cape Town, 1979), pp. 291–337.

6. Martin Legassick, "The Griqua, The Sotho-Tswana and The Missionaries, 1780–1840. The Politics of a Frontier Zone" (Ph.D. diss., University of California, Los Angeles, 1969), pp. 2–3. See also his chapter "The Northern Frontier to 1820: The Emergence of the Griqua People," in Elphick and Giliomee, *The Shaping of South African Society*, pp. 243–90.

to the opening of the frontier, and, more importantly, with the closing of the frontier—the transition of a pioneering frontier to a settled frontier. On the pioneering frontier, with its seemingly abundant land, the Afrikaners could start farming without much capital. Because it was far away from settled white society, they could take political and military action with the minimum of interference from their government. This situation gradually changed as the frontier began to close. The closing of the frontier cannot be reduced to a series of dates or a set of processes that come in any given chronological order. It is more accurate to think of a multiple closing—or a series of closings based on different aspects of the frontier. These comprise (1) economic closure, manifested in growing land and scarcity of resources, a shift from subsistence to commercial farming, and increasing control of the means of production by a specific class; (2) growing social stratification as discrete "races" or ethnic groups merged into a plural society with a given set of caste or class relationships; and (3) political closure, in the imposition of a single source of authority. Although not always interconnected, there was some link between the various "closures," as will be demonstrated below.

My generalizations about the frontier processes draw mostly from my research on the Cape Eastern frontier during the period 1770 to 1812. In the prevalence of near-subsistence farming and the absence of a strong political authority, the frontier which opened up there between 1770 and 1800 was in many ways similar to the Transorangia frontier pioneered by the Bastaards from 1800 to 1830, and the Afrikaner frontier in Transorangia and Transvaal from 1830 to 1870. From about 1800, the Cape Eastern frontier began to close after a much stronger central government had assumed control and land became scarce. These conditions were also found in the Free State (Transorangia) and Transvaal after the conquest of the African chiefdoms in the second half of the nineteenth century.

THE OPENING OF THE FRONTIER: PIONEERING AFRIKANER SOCIETY

Land and Near-Subsistence Farming

The opening of the Afrikaner frontier had to do, above all, with the initial occupation of land in order to start near-subsistence farming in a most extensive way and with the first phases of incorporation of laborers from indigenous societies, either through inducements or local controls.

The crucial feature of the pioneering stage of the frontier was abundance of land, near-subsistence farming, and the absence of regional markets. For whites, land was abundant during the first one hundred and thirty years of the settlement because the Khoikhoi could be easily dispossessed. In fact, dispossession occurred almost from the beginning of European settlement. For Khoikhoi, the loss of land was not sudden or dramatic. In the Cape Peninsula and its vicinity the Europeans practiced extensive agriculture and the transhumant, pastoralist Khoikhoi could exist on good land between European farms. Gradually, however, the Khoikhoi were squeezed out, and by the end of the seventeenth century those who wished to retain their independence had to retreat to the interior, beyond the first range of folded mountains.

In 1717, when the granting of freehold land ceased, there were just over 400 farms comprising an area of 75 square miles in a total area of 2,500 square miles.[7] Yet the Europeans considered the colony fully settled and began to speak of a land crisis. But a safety valve opened when the government started to issue grazing licenses to stockfarmers and lifted the ban on Europeans and other freemen bartering cattle with Khoikhoi. Out of these licenses evolved the loan-farm system, which allowed a stockfarmer the use of a minimum of six thousand acres of land for a small annual fee of 24 rixdollars, which was equal to the value of two cows. The *opstal* (fixed improvements) of a loan farm, though not the land, could be purchased. The average price of a loan-farm opstal during the mid-eighteenth century ranged from 300 to 500 guilders, compared to 6,000 to 10,000 guilders for an arable farm. Whereas the average cost of a working arable farm before 1770 was 15,000 guilders (including the price of the land), a stockfarmer needed only about 1,000 guilders to get started.[8] For Europeans without any capital the pioneering frontier offered the opportunity of becoming *bywoners*. These were tenant farmers who looked after their patrons' stock on a system of shares, which was often a first step toward an independent farming career.

On this frontier a peculiar life-style evolved after the beginning of the eighteenth century which, in some remote regions, lasted until the 1940s. There came into existence a special class of colonists, called *trekboers*, who practiced an economy in which hunting was intimately connected with transhumant stockfarming. In a country where game abounded, the pioneer could penetrate the interior with the assurance that he could always find food. Through hunting he also often obtained almost his only cash income

7. Leonard Guelke, "The White Settlers, 1652–1780," in Elphick and Giliomee, *The Shaping of South African Society*, p. 49.

8. Ibid., pp. 57, 64. For a fuller discussion, see Leonard Guelke, "The Early European Settlement of South Africa" (Ph.D. diss., University of Toronto, 1974). In Afrikaans there are the classic studies of P. J. van der Merwe, *Die Trekboer in die Geskiedenis van die Kaapkolonie, 1657–1842* (Cape Town, 1938) and *Trek* (Cape Town, 1945). More controversial is S. D. Neumark, *Economic Influences on the South African Frontier* (Stanford, Calif., 1957).

from the sale of ivory and ostrich feathers, whips, sjamboks, hides, and horns. These trekboers regularly trekked during the dry season to other pastures. Often accompanied by their families, they lived temporarily in wagons and tents, or in simple huts of reed or rush mats.[9]

In conditions of land abundance, European pastoral farmers could set themselves up on the frontier with little capital, practicing near-subsistence farming on a most extensive scale and drawing on the indigenous peoples for labor. The opening of new frontiers was propelled by a complex of political, economic, and social factors. Politically, expansion offered a refuge from the controls of the government and the wealthy farmers in the Cape Peninsula and vicinity. Socially, it was an escape from a catastrophic loss of status: with slaves providing the manual and skilled labor in the western regions of the colony, the European who entered service lost not only his independence but also his standing as a member of the dominant class. There was also an economic incentive. Expansion of near-subsistence farming was, as Leonard Guelke has shown,[10] not profitable from a commercial point of view. However, apart from all the political and social advantages, the pioneer farmer who directly exploited the existing resources and abandoned them when they were exhausted could support himself with much less effort than the commercial farmer who had to increase yields through manuring and weeding. As long as the frontier was still open, it was more economical for the frontiersmen to expand production by enlarging the size of their grazing lands than by using the already occupied area more intensively.

As a result of all these considerations, the Afrikaners outside Cape Town considered independent farming as the only suitable career for a freeman. As an administrator remarked, "One sends no children away from home—prejudice prevents one's children from serving another. They intermarry and then they must have a farm."[11] Until the late nineteenth century, whites nourished the expectation that cheap land would be acquired on the open frontier. In 1812 the first circuit court which visited the frontier reported that "all the young people of which many of the houses are full, have no other prospect than the breeding of cattle . . . all look forward to becoming graziers, and no person forms for himself any other plan of livelihood."[12]

The northward expansion of the trekboers in the nineteenth century

9. J. F. W. Grosskopf, *Rural Impoverishment and Rural Exodus*, in Report of the Carnegie Commission, *The Poor White Problem in South Africa*, 5 vols. (Stellenbosch, 1932), 1:35–36; van der Merwe, *Trek*, pp. 43–61, 99–106.

10. For an elaboration of this argument, see Leonard Guelke, "European Expansion and the Meaning of Frontier Settlement" (paper presented to an international conference for historical geographers, Los Angeles, 1979), pp. 4–5.

11. Cited by van der Merwe, *Die Trekboer*, p. 185.

12. Report of the Commission of Circuit, 28 February 1812, in *Records of the Cape Colony*, ed. G. M. Theal, 36 vols. (London, 1897–1905), 8:298–99.

and the Great Trek, which started in 1834, created a vast new pioneering frontier. In the Voortrekker States of Natal, the Orange Free State, and the Transvaal, the Cape system of land tenure was retained. The recognized method of initial settlement was the occupation of land not yet taken up by other whites. The new occupant would subsequently register his farm with the authorities; his title was subject to the payment of an annual quitrent. In the South African Republic (Transvaal) the quitrent was ten shillings for a farm up to about eight thousand acres, which was the average size, and a further two shillings and six pence for every additional hundred morgen. Under this system some colonists soon appropriated vast tracts of land. However, there were also considerable numbers of trekboers, especially in the Transvaal, who chose not to take up land, although the first settlers in the Natal and Transvaal were entitled to two farms as their "burgher right."

Landholders welcomed men who could assist them in defense, increase their income on a share-cropping basis, and provide some company on the isolated farms. As one such trekboer later explained: "There were many men, owners of good farms, who were only too glad if you came and stayed with them. You might very well be wealthier than the owner, and—'you were equally boss.'" [13] These men did not even consider themselves by-woners since their position was clearly not associated with social or economic inferiority as long as land was plentiful.

Caste and Class Relationships

On the pioneering frontier a plural society began to develop with its own caste and class relationships. Here farmers had to find labor in a situation where there were no market incentives or government labor compulsion. This meant that they were dependent on their own resources to attract laborers and induce them to stay in their service. However, this was especially difficult because the low man/land ratio enabled the indigenous societies to coexist independently with the pioneer settlers in the frontier zone. In the absence of any institutional resources, the pioneer farmers were generally unable to command large-scale unfree labor. However, at the same time the very absence of institutional controls enabled them to exercise a great degree of local control over their few clients and servants.

The rapid expansion of the trekboers in the eighteenth century extended a slender European superstructure over a vast area. On their unenclosed farms the trekboers needed dependable labor to herd their large flocks of sheep and cattle. They could not always acquire this by mere coercion as the opportunities for flight or theft were too great. Often a patron-

13. Grosskopf, *Rural Impoverishment and Rural Exodus*, p. 38.

client relationship evolved in which there was some quid pro quo between the contribution of the master in dealing justly with his clients and protecting them, and that of the client in the services he rendered. Trekboers would entrust a portion of their stock to a Khoikhoi clan, or clansmen would work for a year or two on a farm before returning to their people.[14] As a way of inducing indigenous peoples to serve them, frontiersmen could offer security in a country where beasts of prey roamed freely, and where San ("Bushman") "raiders" threatened the small herding communities. In the clientship tradition of Khoikhoi society it was common for a poor and insecure man to seek the protection of a patron to enable him to build up his livestock. A Khoikhoi client entering a colonist's service retained his livestock, and this was supplemented by payments in kind which he received for tending his master's cattle and accompanying him (or going in his place) on commandos against Xhosa and San. Three decades after trekboers had begun to settle in the frontier region of Camdeboo (Graaff-Reinet district), Khoikhoi still possessed considerable numbers of livestock. An *opgaaf* (census taken for tax purposes) of 1798 lists between 1,300 and 1,400 Khoikhoi in the district, owning 140 horses, 7,571 cattle and 30,557 sheep. One of these clients later told an official that until the turn of the century he and his clansmen living with the trekboers had nothing to complain of—"until that time the Hottentots were boors (farmers) and kept on their masters' land large flocks of their own."[15]

In such cases the transition from an independent herder to the client of a trekboer was not traumatic. The client retained his stock and maintained the bonds with his clan or kinsmen, preferably settling with them on the same farm. The latter arrangement evidently occurred on a large scale, for one of the major problems of the trekboers was the uneven distribution of labor. This happened because Khoikhoi refused to separate from their kinsmen who had settled with them on a farm. Thus the pioneering frontier, rather than being a place where new social and cultural institutions originated, was one where the disparate groups were often successful in maintaining conditions and institutions similar to those existing before contact.[16]

Ultimately it was, of course, the prevailing balance of power which determined whether on a particular frontier the Africans could retain a large

14. Guelke, "The Early European Settlement," p. 313.

15. Giliomee, "The Eastern Frontier," in Elphick and Giliomee, *The Shaping of South African Society*, p. 300. The statement by the Khoikhoi client is in D. Moodie, "Deposition of Platje Swartland, C. 1836," *Afschriften*, vol. 11.

16. See also the analysis of Khoikhoi cultural change in the Southwestern Cape by Richard Elphick in his *Kraal and Castle: Khoikhoi and the Founding of White South Africa* (New Haven, Conn., 1977), pp. 179–81.

measure of independence or whether whites could impose the forms of involuntary labor known in the settled parts. Because this power balance differed so sharply from one frontier to another, there existed a whole spectrum of labor relationships, ranging from those which almost involved a form of parity in status to others which rested purely on local coercion. There is evidence of the former especially in the northern Transvaal, where Afrikaners began to settle in the 1840s. Here the sparseness of the pioneer population and their inability to subjugate the stronger African chiefdoms strengthened the bargaining power of African labor. Consequently, the frontiersmen had to provide considerable incentives to Africans in order to acquire their services. In their hunting and raiding activities the Soutpansberg frontiersmen employed Africans in what can be called partnership relations. *Swart skuts* (black marksmen) were entrusted with guns by white patrons to engage in elephant hunting. H. W. Struben, who arrived in Soutpansberg in 1857, gave the following description: "Each hunter, according to his recognised value, was given a certain number of carriers to take his truck in, and the ivory out, and the hunters got a percentage on the ivory delivered. Some of these men were good elephant shots and made lots of money."[17]

By the 1860s so many Africans had acquired guns that they formed a distinct stratum of the hunting community of Soutpansberg. The problem facing the whites was to ensure the loyalty of these swart skuts at the head of hunting teams, something which could have been secured if the system was allowed to evolve into some permanent form of clientship, with rewards roughly commensurate with the services rendered. Conflicting interests within the white community, based on the competition for labor, prevented the formation of such stable relations. The desertion of black marksmen who kept their masters' guns indicated that the rewards of hunt labor were insufficient. Eventually they transferred their allegiance to Venda chiefs who launched a series of raids on the white settlement. Having lost their monopoly of guns, the Europeans by the late 1860s were forced to abandon the entire Soutpansberg district in the northern Transvaal.

However, the Soutpansberg experience was unusual. When Afrikaners had settled an area more fully, it was easier to dictate terms to laborers, maintain control, and track down those who absconded. But the increase of the number of employers also brought in its wake a greater element of competition and the risk of desertion to other masters. One of the perennial problems of the white frontiersmen was the shortage of labor amidst appar-

17. H. W. Struben, *Recollections of Adventures* (Cape Town, 1920), p. 86. This section on Soutpansberg is based on an illuminating study by R. Wagner, "Soutpansberg: The Dynamics of a Hunting Frontier, 1848–1867," to be published in *Economy and Society in Pre-Industrial South Africa*, ed. A. Atmore and S. Marks (London, 1980).

ently abundant supply. With labor evenly distributed among farms, employers constantly tried to entice servants from other farms. By the end of the eighteenth century, when the Eastern Frontier was fully settled, the Graaff-Reinet local authorities issued the first pass regulations to control Khoikhoi labor. They were directed specifically toward countering the practice of farmers enticing servants away from other farms.[18] However, because the district authorities did not have the means to enforce these controls, the master's dominance over his servants depended mainly on the extent to which he could offset the laborer's economic mobility with his own power.

The *inboek* system (indentureship) evolved out of the need to acquire a more stable labor force. Indentured labor was quite distinct from client labor and much nearer to mere coercion on the spectrum of labor relationships. It sprang from the incorporation of conquered Khoikhoi people into a society used to slave labor. Since children of a Khoikhoi mother and a slave father were technically free, frontiersmen in 1721 petitioned the government that such children be indentured for a number of years. The government did not respond to this request, but in 1775, when labor shortages became critical in the southwestern Cape, it allowed the indenturing of such children in Stellenbosch district until their twenty-fifth year. By the end of the eighteenth century, the informal indenturing of all Khoikhoi children (including those who did not have slave fathers) was widespread.

The indenture system can be regarded as a quasi-institutional form of labor. In analogy to slavery, the government legitimized the indenturing of legally free indigenous children. However, the masters' enforcement of their legal claims on indentured laborers depended on their own resources. Because they were so personally involved in the indenturing of children, frontiersmen tried to give the system a cloak of frontier paternalism. The rationalization in which this paternalism was rooted was that binding native children (and indirectly their families as well) to a period of service was justified because their destitute condition required the care and protection of a master; in exchange for this trouble and expense they could be assumed to have incurred the duty of protracted service.

Frontier paternalism was soon extended from child to adult labor, with the master arguing that they could make claims on their adult dependents in return for accepting responsibilities toward them. Their claim, "he is mine," in fact meant, "he is my responsibility, he is attached to me, he works for me." In turn, there was among laborers a paradoxical mixture of, on the one hand, resentment toward an oppressor who had taken away their land and exploited their labor, and, on the other, admiration for their mas-

18. Hermann Giliomee, *Die Kaap tydens die Eerste Britse Bewind, 1795–1803* (Cape Town, 1975), pp. 258–59.

ter's superior wealth and power. The words, "he is *my baas*" could indicate as much an identification with the master as a subservient relationship.[19]

However, especially where adults were involved, this subservient relationship ultimately rested on coercion. When the Afrikaners were faced with the Xhosa and Zulu peoples, who were much more resilient than the Khoikhoi, they acknowledged that paternalist inducements were not enough: force was needed to acquire labor. As a frontiersman in Natal expressed it: "There are no other means to rule the Kafirs but by fear; and Kafirs will not work for the white men unless they know that they will be punished when they refuse."[20]

The pioneering frontier was thus the scene of local coercion in contrast to the institutional coercion of the closing frontier, where the state and the market played a growing part in providing labor. Commandos on the pioneering frontier were raised in the first instance to retrieve stolen cattle, but soon the procurement of child labor became an important additional activity. Sometimes paternalist assumptions were involved. On the Eastern Frontier, where commandos were raised to exterminate the San, frontiersmen brought back San children and indentured them on the grounds that their parents had been killed and that this would prevent them from starving.[21] In other cases the paternalistic assumptions were absent. In Natal, where the Voortrekkers settled in the late 1830s, the slightly more than three hundred burgers who participated in the so-called Cattle Commando received permission beforehand to capture four native children each.[22] On the open frontier of the Transvaal, the Voortrekkers also resorted to indentureship not only of orphans but also of children captured on raids by commandos, or bartered by chiefs or their parents in periods of bad harvests and starvation. In parts of the Transvaal, a trade in indentured children was common practice.[23]

19. For a selection of documents which illustrate attitudes toward labor, see André du Toit and Hermann Giliomee, eds., *Afrikaner Political Thought, 1780–1854* (forthcoming), chap. 2. The relationship which existed until very recently between the "farm Bushmen" of the Ghanzi district of Botswana and the Afrikaner farmers is strongly reminiscent of that which existed on the pioneering frontier. For an analysis, see Margo Russel, "Slaves or Workers? Relations between Bushmen, Tswana and Boers in the Kalahari," *Journal of Southern African Studies* 2, no. 3 (1976): 178–97; Mathias G. Guenther, "Bushmen Hunters as Farm Labourers," *Canadian Journal of African Studies* 11, no. 2 (1977): 195–203.

20. Cited by B. J. Liebenberg, *Andries Pretorius in Natal* (Pretoria and Cape Town, 1977), p. 117.

21. This is a controversial issue in South African historiography. See the argument of P. J. van der Merwe, *Die Noordwaartse Beweging van die Boere voor die Groot Trek, 1770–1842* (The Hague, 1937), pp. 168–75.

22. Liebenberg, *Andries Pretorius in Natal*, pp. 117–20.

23. For indentureship, see W. Kistner, "The Anti-Slavery Agitation against the Transvaal Republic, 1852–1868," *Archives Year Book for South African History* (1952), 2:226–43; J. A. I. Agar-Hamilton, *The Native Policy of the Voortrekkers: An Essay in the History of the Interior*

In some cases there was also coerced adult labor, particularly in areas where the Voortrekkers had established control over small and broken chiefdoms which were only gradually beginning to recover from the ravages of the *Difaqane*. A particular form of adult forced labor in these conditions was tribute labor extracted from smaller kraals, which for short periods were compelled to provide additional hands for agriculture.

But because the power resources of the pioneering farmers were weak, purely coercive relations were unstable and often the means defeated the ends. Fear and intimidation as the basis of labor compliance meant both a pervasive insecurity for workers confronted by their masters' power and, conversely, frequent desertions. Labor relations without any bond of interest or loyalty gave rise, in the words of a frontier landdrost, to "the faithlessness of such Hottentots towards those whom they regard not as their masters but as their executioners, and whom they serve only through hunger or fear."[24] Thus a vicious circle arose in which the very consequences of forced labor required further coercive measures.

Frontiersmen unable to assert themselves sometimes looked to the government for help. By the end of the eighteenth century, a field-cornet, on behalf of some remote Stellenbosch farmers, proposed to the governor a solution which was unusual but reflected a common frustration:

> It is my humble request to your Honour to enact an ordinance prohibiting the Hottentots who are presently in this district from maintaining their kraals, and expelling them from there. . . . Thus I request that the Hottentots who have entered service should be put in leg-irons for a time when they steal or desert so that this nation can be tamed a little, as they are extremely devious. Once their conduct has improved sufficiently, the leg-irons might be removed.[25]

However, in a colony where there was just a small market for agricultural produce, largely because near-subsistence farming dominated the economy, the central government was little concerned to provide the frontier farmers with a docile and regulated work force. Because of the same lack of market opportunities, the frontiersmen did not make a concerted effort to find long-term solutions to their labor problems. It was only when commercial opportunities became available on the closing frontier that they sought to harness the labor of Africans more effectively.

---

of South Africa, 1836–1858 (Cape Town, 1928), pp. 164–95; Stanley Trapido, "Aspects in the Transition from Slavery to Serfdom: The South African Republic, 1842–1902," *Societies of Southern Africa* 6 (1976): 24–31.

24. This document will be published in du Toit and Giliomee, *Afrikaner Political Thought.*

25. This document, too, will be published in ibid.

The social stratification of the pioneering frontier was weakly developed. Khoikhoi and San, and to a lesser extent those Bantu-speaking Africans over whom control had also been established, were compressed into
an undifferentiated servile caste that was regarded as belonging to an inferior order of people. However, blacks who had not yet been subordinated
were considered more as alien than inferior. Predominant in the Afrikaner
frontiersmen's perception was cultural chauvinism rather than an immutable belief in their biological superiority. The Voortrekkers most commonly
regarded Bantu-speakers as cunning or cruel "savages" and "heathens."[26]
They strongly objected to mixing, but this was because they feared above all
that social equality would have dangerous political and economic consequences. This sentiment was well expressed by the Lydenburg authorities
in 1860, when they rejected the stand of missionaries that all Christians are
equals. They declared that "to expound the doctrine that confirmed Christian natives are of equal status with white men . . . will only have the result
that converts, and those who are not converts, will become yet more arrogant, haughty and untamable [ontembaar] than previously."[27]

But even all white men were not equals in the full sense of the word. At
the pinnacle of white society was a dominant class of landholders which
was fairly successful in ensuring that their progeny acquired similar status.
They tended to look down upon the landless poor in white society. However, they preferred to take on landless whites as bywoners rather than Bastaards or blacks; at the same time these poorer whites tended to identify
vigorously with the dominant Europeans and to secure their protection.[28] It
was only when land became exhausted that class strains became prominent
in white society.

The Political Order

The political order on the pioneering frontier was characterized by the lack
of a single controlling authority. The expansion of near-subsistence farmers
over a vast area ruled by a commercial company only interested in the Cape
as a halfway station for its ships had profound implications for the political
order. In order to maximize profits, the Company kept its complement at

26. See especially J. P. F. Moolman, "Die Boer se Siening van en Houding teenoor die Ban-
toe in Transvaal tot 1880" (M.A. diss., University of Pretoria, 1975), pp. 30–51, 70–89, 122.

27. Cited in J. D. Huyser, "Die Naturelle-politiek van die Suid-Afrikaanse Republiek" (D.
Litt. diss., University of Pretoria, 1936), p. 235.

28. For a fuller exposition, see Hermann Giliomee and Richard Elphick, "The Structure of
European Domination at the Cape, 1652–1820," in idem, eds., The Shaping of South African
Society, pp. 359–86. The class nature of white society at the Cape in the eighteenth century
and the practice of self-recruitment by the dominant class of landholders still await serious
research.

the Cape as small as possible. In the 1790s, the last years of company rule, there was a garrison of only a thousand men stationed at Cape Town at the tip of the colony. Any attempt by the government to improve political control was frustrated by the dispersed state of the population, which made tax collection a difficult task. Consequently, the government was unable to provide services and afford protection to the pioneering frontier, and the pioneers had to rely on themselves for political and military action.[29] This in turn produced a great measure of individualism and some frontier anarchy. Thus the lack of government control was directly related to extensive subsistence farming and low (white) population densities.

The establishment in 1786 of the Graaff-Reinet district, an area as large as Portugal today, only nominally increased the government's control over the frontier. The landdrost of Graaff-Reinet was assisted by only four or five *ordonnantie ruiters* (mounted police). He had to rely on colonists called *veldwachtmeesters* (later field-cornets) to ensure compliance with the laws in their respective divisions. But the field-cornets were dependent on their fellow colonists and normally chose to uphold the latter's interests. In a situation where colonists had free access to guns and considered it their right to fire on raiders, the landdrost could not remotely claim to monopolize the use of force. The first landdrosts of Graaff-Reinet despaired of instilling into the colonists a respect for their office and the laws. In 1786, Landdrost Woeke remarked that unless he was aided by fifty or sixty soldiers, "the rot will continue . . . and if not suppressed will increase to such an extent that everyone will act arbitrarily and do everything at his own sweet will."[30] In fact, the only lever the government had was its monopoly of the ammunition supply. This it used to quell rebellions and forestall frontier wars, but effective control over the Afrikaners on the Eastern Frontier was not established until 1800 when the British government, which had taken over the Cape Colony in 1795, stationed a contingent of troops there.

The lack of government control was compounded by the fragmented nature of both African and Afrikaner societies. An African chief identified primarily with his own small community. In matters of trade and external relations, he frequently regarded the interests of his chiefdom as being in conflict with those of other chiefdoms in the region. Like the Indians on the New England frontier, the Khoikhoi or Bantu-speaking peoples lacked a community of interests or a feeling of racial or national unity.[31]

There was also disunity in Afrikaner society, but not of the same sort.

29. This is well argued in Guelke, "European Expansion" (n. 10 above).

30. Giliomee, "The Eastern Frontier," in Elphick and Giliomee, *The Shaping of South African Society*, p. 298.

31. Alden T. Vaughan, *New England Frontier: Puritans and Indians, 1620–1675* (Boston, 1965), p. 62.

Although there is a danger of overemphasizing it, Afrikaners had a sense of belonging to a distinct group comprised of individuals with a common racial and cultural background and a similar legal status as freemen. This was both cause and effect of a high rate of endogamy, a sense that physical appearance was a badge of group membership, and an identification with European (Christian) civilization.[32] The disunity that did exist was the result of the disintegrative effect which the expansion of subsistence farming had on frontier society. Afrikaners on the frontier had little to bind them together politically except the commandos assembled to capture land, to seize cattle or retrieve those which were stolen, and occasionally to acquire child labor. The south African frontier certainly did not produce the same loyalty to a national government which Turner argued the American frontier did. In the eighteenth century, frontier colonists' requests for the extension of the colonial borders had limited objectives: they wanted a school and a church so they might remain part of the European cultural and kinship network; they desired to be incorporated into the landholding system of the colony in order to legitimize their occupation of the land; and they needed the government's sanction and its supplies of ammunition for commandos against indigenous enemies. They certainly did not intend to invoke a strong government which might protect their laborers or prevent them from acting against their enemies as they wished.

Government weakness meant that the Afrikaner landholders on the frontier sought to establish some local control in order to secure their property and pursue their political goals. Occasionally they collaborated with Africans, sometimes against other Africans but on occasion against whites, since there was some uncertainty of status on the pioneering frontier. As Martin Legassick has phrased it, "White frontiersmen expected all their dependents (save their families) to be non-white; they did not expect all non-whites to be their servants."[33]

To achieve their objective of expelling some "rebel" Xhosa chiefdoms from the Zuurveld, on the colonial side of the boundary, colonists on the Eastern Frontier formed an alliance with the Xhosa paramount chief. This alliance fought together in 1793 but then fell apart, allowing the Zuurveld Xhosa to launch a counterattack. When frontiersmen rebelled in 1795, 1799, and 1801 because the government would not allow further attempts to expel the Zuurveld Xhosa, both sides attempted to enlist nonwhite allies. The rebels tried to bring in the Xhosa, while Landdrost Maynier planned to use Khoikhoi troops against the rebels. In 1803, when Janssens, the first

32. This argument is expanded in Giliomee and Elphick, "The Structure of European Domination," in their *The Shaping of South African Society*, pp. 359–86.
33. Martin Legassick, "The Frontier Tradition in South African Historiography," *Societies of Southern Africa* 2 (1971): 19.

governor to visit the Eastern Frontier, arrived in Graaff-Reinet, he told the colonists frankly that if disorder in the district did not cease, "he would have to adopt such measures as would exterminate those who were the cause of the turbulence, even if it were possible only with the assistance of Kafirs and Hottentots."[34]

The leaders of the various parties of emigrants—Bastaards, trekboers and Voortrekkers—which left the Colony in the late eighteenth and early nineteenth centuries also sought to form alliances to strengthen their weak political bases. They often did so by intervening successfully in African succession disputes, as when the Voortrekkers supported Mpande against the Zulu chief, Dingane. But Africans could also play this game. On the hunting frontier of Soutpansberg in northern Transvaal, Africans intervened effectively in disputes between white factions. Africans as much as whites had a clear perception of how cleavages within the other society could be turned to their own advantage.[35]

The Afrikaners' involvement in African politics could not occur without putting some strain on the cohesion of their own society. That whites would always stick together was not a foregone conclusion. Ever since the end of the eighteenth century, large Afrikaner landholders in settled areas dreaded the rise of an armed and rebellious class of poor freemen of mixed racial origin who might threaten their predominance. In the 1780s some leading western Cape farmers expressed concern about frontier miscegenation and warned of the rise "of a completely degenerate nation who might become just as dangerous for the colony as the Bushmen-Hottentots are."[36] Soon afterwards Coenraad de Buys, having established a liaison with the mother of the Xhosa paramount, invaded the colony at the head of some Xhosa intending to expel the British troops from the frontier zone and set himself up as ruler. And the Slachtersnek episode of 1815 was in a sense a rebellion of poor, landless whites who threatened to form a cross-racial alliance against the propertied class. The rebels sought Xhosa help to challenge British control and threatened that those frontiersmen who refused to join the rebellion would be killed and their families and property given over to Xhosa.[37]

Even Voortrekker leaders sought the help of blacks against whites. There is evidence that Hendrik Potgieter, leader of the northern Voortrek-

34. D. G. van Reenen, *Die Joernaal van Dirk Gysbert van Reenen*, ed. W. Blommaert and J. A. Wiid (Cape Town, 1937), p. 209.

35. Wagner, "Soutpansberg." For another case study, see Philip Bonner, "Factions and Fissions: Transvaal/Swazi Politics in the Mid-Nineteenth Century" (paper for the Biennial Conference of the South African Historical Society, Cape Town, 1977).

36. Coenraad Beyers, *Die Kaapse Patriotte* (Pretoria, 1967), p. 326.

37. Hermann Giliomee, "The Burgher Rebellions on the Eastern Frontier, 1795–1815," in Elphick and Giliomee, *The Shaping of South African Society*, pp. 348–54.

kers, enlisted the help of Sekwati of the Pedi against his Voortrekker adversaries. Andries Pretorius considered Moshoeshoe as a potential ally in his struggle against the British in Transorangia, and his son Marthinus sought the help of the Basotho leader in his attempt to secure Transvaal control over the Afrikaners in the Free State.[38]

In peripheral frontier zones there is evidence of strategies that went further than temporary cross-racial alliances and tried to incorporate Africans in other than a merely laboring capacity. Hendrik Potgieter was poised ambivalently between a policy of establishing an exclusive white society and one aimed at setting himself up as an African chief, absorbing non-Europeans as subjects and allies in a larger political community. After his death the Soutpansberg settlement, which he founded, emphasized the latter trend. R. G. Wagner observes that it began as a tight Voortrekker society; however, as its hunting activities expanded, it incorporated other hunter-traders such as Albasini, a Portuguese trader, to develop its trading links with the outside world. It also incorporated African allies, such as the personal followings of the Buyses and Albasini, who helped to ensure its military domination over Venda villages from which tribute was exacted. Lastly it incorporated the *swart skuts*, Africans to whom it gave guns to expand its hunting and commercial activities.[39]

However, there was a distinct difference between the Afrikaner and Portuguese frontiersmen in southern Africa. Unlike the Afrikaners, who with a few exceptions remained tied to their culture and kinship network, the *prazeros* of Mozambique largely abandoned their European affiliations, became absorbed through intermarriage into the indigenous population, and shifted their loyalties to them.[40] Among both Portuguese and Afrikaner frontiersmen there was a constant interplay between the cultural traditions, material conditions, and political goals which shaped actions and attitudes with respect to land, labor, and the social order. But what ultimately separated them, especially when they lived in isolation in a peripheral area such as Angola, was a different worldview or ethos. Among the Portuguese, with their Catholic roots, there was a much fuller acceptance of Africans and mulattos as part of the family, as marriage partners, and as church members, and a general condonation of the rise of a mixed society.[41] Among the Af-

38. Leonard Thompson, *Survival in Two Worlds: Moshoeshoe of Lesotho, 1786–1870* (Oxford, 1975), pp. 142–44, 236–37.

39. Wagner, "Soutpansberg." See also Legassick, "The Frontier Tradition," pp. 18–19.

40. Allen Isaacman and Barbara Isaacman, "The Prazeros as Transfrontiersmen: A Study in Society and Cultural Change," *The International Journal of African Historical Studies* 8, no. 1 (1975): 1–39.

41. For a discussion of such an Afrikaner society, see W. G. Clarence-Smith, "The Thirstland Trekkers in Angola," *Societies of Southern Africa* 6 (1976): 42–51. See also Alistair Hennessy, *The Frontier in Latin American History* (London, 1978), pp. 19–25, 43–45.

rikaners, the Calvinist church adapted to the existing cleavages between white and black and formed no bridge between them. Afrikaner frontiersmen used black or brown sexual partners when expedient; however, persons with a black ancestry were stigmatized and mulattos were denied the prospect of advancing toward the status of whites. As the number of whites increased in a particular zone, the dominant families imposed the hegemonic values of a separate society.

To sum up the pioneering frontier: The first freeburghers on the seventeenth-century frontier inherited and transferred to their descendants the value of private landownership. The opening of the frontier encouraged them and their descendants to abandon the intensive methods of Dutch agriculture in favor of extensive ones. Seventeenth-century Netherlands agriculture was based on free labor; but because slavery was common in the Dutch colonies and because the sons of near-subsistence farmers preferred to have their own farm, slaves were imported to solve the labor shortage at the Cape. The trekboers of the eighteenth century brought to the interior the cultural tradition of slavery and were gradually able to transform free indigenous peoples into unfree laborers. Nineteenth-century white frontiersmen sought to implement these two principles—individual instead of communal holding of land, unfree instead of free labor—in the societies they were to found. To merge with African societies would put these, and also their goal to establish a separate society, at issue. At times the Boer state in the Transvaal was too weak to establish a political order on such principles. But once military and political supremacy was achieved, they became the core values of their society.

THE CLOSING FRONTIER: THE DEVELOPMENT OF A SETTLED SOCIETY

Land, Markets, and Towns

A distinct feature of the closing frontier is the change from abundant land resources and near-subsistence farming to a shortage of land leading to more intensive exploitation of the land resources and the gradual rise of commercial farming. In the place of long trips to a distant market and *smousen* (itinerant traders), came regional markets and towns. This in turn affected caste and class relations and the political order.

To Europeans with little capital at their disposal, the pioneer frontier of southern Africa seemed to offer almost the same abundant opportunities to make an independent living as the initial settlements in North America. It was only when the frontier began to close that the differences between the two settlements became starkly clear. With the exception of areas like the Piedmont and the Appalachian Mountains, commercial development quickly followed initial settlement on the North American frontier. On the southern Africa frontier, farming largely outside the market continued for much longer. Compared to the abundant resources of North America, resources in southern Africa were limited. Until the 1860s, land and game were virtually the only natural resources known to the colonists, and these fairly soon were exhausted. Also, compared to the settlement in America, capital was scarce. After the primary stage of land exploitation little was available to finance the improvement of pasture. There was no rapid secondary phase of settlement based on the exploitation of resources such as coal and minerals, with which North America had been blessed, to invigorate the frontier economy.[42] As a result, markets, towns, communications, and an industrial economy were slow to develop. And southern Africa never received the steady flow of European immigrants which North America did. Early in the eighteenth century the Dutch East India Company decided against assisted immigration of European artisans, agricultural laborers, and farmers who would work their own lands. Instead, slaves were imported, which meant that the arable part of the colony did not develop a large internal market. For long periods the pastoral farmers with their near-subsistence economy were dependent on Cape Town, the only town, for guns and ammunition, sugar, coffee, and cloth, but for the rest they had only tenuous links with the market. Their laborers were rarely paid in cash and remained largely outside the market system. Before the second half of the nineteenth century there were no African peasant communities which sold their surplus to towns. African societies lived in isolation conducting only a trickle of trade with the colonial markets.[43]

After the pioneer stage of settlement on the southern African frontier, there was no economic abundance, no people of plenty with a uniquely democratic vision as in North America. There was a lack of capital, a decrease of the money supply, growing cleavages between rich and poor, and a weakly developed institutional structure which struggled to provide a sense of national cohesion or to promote economic growth through administrative efficiency and political stability.

When land and game became exhausted, farmers who wished to retain their independence and wealth had either to find land elsewhere or to make the transition from their near-subsistence operations to a more intensive exploitation of resources, developing into commercial farming and a spe-

---

42. David M. Potter, *People of Plenty: Economic Abundance and the American Character* (Chicago, 1954).

43. Monica Wilson, "The Growth of Peasant Communities," in *Oxford History of South Africa*, ed. Monica Wilson and Leonard Thompson, 2 vols. (Oxford, 1969–71), 2:49–72.

cialized exchange economy. Because the conditions for sustained economic growth were lacking, capital investment in more intensive land use did not pay off immediately. Thus the closing of the frontier was a time fraught with insecurity for the Afrikaners as they tried to adapt to new economic imperatives.

In southern African history there were three occasions when this process impinged in a traumatic way on whites, who perceived it as nothing less than a survival crisis. These were: (1) the closing of the frontier of agricultural settlement in the southwestern Cape at the end of the seventeenth century; (2) the closing of the pastoral frontier in the eastern Cape from the end of the eighteenth century to the period of renewed trekboer expansion in the 1820s and the Great Trek; and (3) the closing of the Transvaal and Free State frontier toward the end of the nineteenth century. This discussion of the closing of the frontier will focus on these cases.

Two decades after the founding of the Cape settlement it was clear to the colonists that intensive agriculture had failed, and from then on the expansion of the settlement was based on extensive agriculture. By the end of the seventeenth century the colony was facing an economic crisis. With a small market that was easily glutted, overproduction was chronic. The poor roads and the low prices for agricultural products made it impossible for those on the fringes of the area of arable farming to compete with commercial farmers near Cape Town.

For more than a century the position was to remain the same: it was estimated that a wheat farmer who had to make a return journey of more than three days to Cape Town was unable to market his produce at a profit.[44] Not only the distances and quality of the roads but also the nature of the Cape market worked against the frontier farmer. Because there was no large domestic market, the farmers had to rely on passing ships to sell their surplus produce. Since such visits were irregular, profits were made either by those who could sell first or by those who could hoard their produce to sell at the most favorable prices.

During the first 150 years of white settlement loans were exceedingly difficult to obtain. It was very hard to find the capital for farming near Cape Town or for hoarding produce. The closing of the frontier of agricultural settlement at the end of the seventeenth century saw poor farmers sinking into debt as they failed to receive an adequate return on their capital. A young man without much capital could still set himself up as a stockfarmer on the fringes of the settlement, but droughts, epidemics, and "Bushmen" raiders could easily wipe out his stock. Land was ever more difficult to find. There was none available within the limits of the colony as defined by the govern-

44. W. S. van Ryneveld, "Beschouwing," *Het Nederduitsch Zuid-Afrikaansch Tydschrift* 8, no. 4 (1831):293.

ment, which in the 1690s strictly forbade settlement beyond the borders or even journeys into the interior.

The government's decision in 1703 to grant grazing permits beyond the colony's limits made possible the expansion of pastoral farmers into the interior. By the 1770s the Eastern Frontier zone extended as far as the Fish River, nearly 600 miles from Cape Town; but it, in turn, was confronted with serious economic problems. First, it was too far from the market, which at any rate was not very big, to allow the commercialization of the pastoral economy. An observer who visited Graaff-Reinet district at the end of the eighteenth century commented as follows:

> The distance is a serious inconvenience to the farmer. . . . If he can contrive to get together a waggon load or two of butter or soap, to carry with him to Cape Town once a year, or once in two years, in exchange for clothing, brandy, coffee, a little tea and sugar, and a few other luxuries, which his own district has not yet produced, he is perfectly satisfied. The consideration of profit is out of the question. A man who goes to Cape Town with a single waggon from the Sneuwberg must consume, at least, sixty days out and home.[45]

Second, the increase of population in a newly settled area led to a steady decline in the wealth of near-subsistence farmers as the available resources diminished. The number of pastoral farmers increased almost twelvefold between 1721 and 1780.[46] Nevertheless, unlike the American frontier, this increase was not large enough to support the development of a specialized exchange economy.[47] Nor could it provide the tax base for the improvement of transport facilities. The dispersion of the population made it even more difficult for the inefficient company administration to raise money to improve the transportation system. The large and virtually self-sufficient farms also precluded the growth of towns, which might have attracted people and encouraged them to start careers outside farming.

Thus, while frontier expansion was an escape hatch for a European lower class with diminishing opportunities, in the long run it only trans-

45. John Barrow, *Travels into the Interior of Southern Africa*, 2 vols. (London, 1806), 2:331.

46. Guelke, "The Early European Settlement," p. 260.

47. See the exchange between William Norton and Leonard Guelke on subsistence and commercial farming, in *Annals of the Association of American Geographers* 67, no. 3 (September 1977):463–67. Norton points out that a fundamental difference between the North American and the southern African experiences is the willingness of southern African settlers to locate on farms at distances from markets not compatible with commercial development. Guelke explains that in doing this the southern African settlers were not acting in a "noneconomic" way. The frontier offered people without much capital a reasonable subsistence, generally outside the exchange economy, combined with a measure of independence which many found preferable to wage labor.

planted the poverty of the seaboard to the outskirts of the settlement. The deterioration of resources combined with the increase of population was well summed up in 1776 by a visitor to the Eastern Frontier:

> In the Camdebo (Graaff-Reinet) there are about 30 farms of which about 25 are inhabited. If they will not begin to conserve artificially the grazing for their cattle, it is to be feared that the luxuriance of the grass that has already started to deteriorate markedly, though settlement in the area only began 7 or 8 years ago, will not last long, and this veld will become wholly deteriorated just like that which is nearer the Cape. This has already gone so far that one Jacobus Botha has had to move to the Great Fish River because he had no pasture for his cattle here; and A. van den Berg spoke of wanting to trek elsewhere because he could not maintain himself on his own farm.[48]

After 1780 the Eastern Frontier began to close rapidly, with further expansion blocked by the Xhosa in the east and temporarily by the San in the north. During the 1770s it was still possible for a young man with little or no capital to acquire land and start raising cattle. But by 1798 only 26 percent of the adult men listed in the opgaaf of the frontier district of Graaff-Reinet owned farms. By 1812 this had shrunk to 18 percent.[49] Large extended families stayed on a farm, leading to heavy overstocking of the land. In 1809 Colonel Collins found people almost everywhere in the Colony devoid of farms, some living with relatives, others wandering from place to place.[50]

As land became scarce, the strategies open to frontier farmers were few and unattractive. First, some tried "forcing in," that is, finding land between existing loan farms, but that did not help much. Cattle farming needed waterholes and all the good ones had been occupied at an early stage. Second, some hoped to mobilize support for driving back the Xhosa and San, and thus to continue expansion. However, white frontier society lacked the military resources to launch a successful expedition. In the frontier wars of 1793 and 1799–1802, it suffered heavy livestock losses and was forced to abandon a large area of the frontier district of Graaff-Reinet. Third, colonists could attempt to increase the carrying capacity of the land. The Colebrook-Bigge Commission of Enquiry which visited the colony from 1823 to 1826 expressed the hope that the increase of the population "will at last compel

48. (Cape Archives), Acc. 447, pp. 21–24.
49. Giliomee, "The Eastern Frontier," in Elphick and Giliomee, *The Shaping of South African Society*, p. 317; van der Merwe, *Trek*, pp. 54–55.
50. D. Moodie, *The Record; Or a Series of Official Papers Relative to the Condition and Treatment of the Native Tribes of South Africa*, 5 vols. (Cape Town, 1838–1842), 5:23–26 (Report of Colonel Collins, 1809).

them to contract the ranges of their cattle and to provide for them by raising artificial food."[51] But in the 1820s this transition was still too difficult to make for all but a few. The water supply was scarce and technical equipment, such as windmills, primitive. The distance from the market and the absence of easily marketable commodities did not justify a more intensive application of capital and labor.

Of the three alternatives, the Afrikaner frontiersmen strongly preferred the second—expansion of the area of subsistence farming in the eighteenth-century mold. However, this was resisted by the much stronger British government, which realized that such expansion would only lead to the duplication in other areas of the same cardinal problems of frontier settlement. As early as 1797, an official argued:

> As long as one may infringe upon the countries of the Cafirs, Bosjes-man, etc. to take their lands and to live upon the breeding of cattle, so long no person will be anxious about the state of his children, so long no sufficient number of hands will be obtained in the country itself to carry on the tillage, so long the inhabitants will never enter into the service of each other; and finally so long the importation of slaves will be necessary for the sake of the culture of grain. While on the other hand, one will never scruple to settle himself throughout the whole country of Africa among all the nations, and by so doing become like those wild nations.[52]

Andries Stockenstrom, landdrost of Graaff-Reinet and arguably the greatest authority on the Eastern Frontier, clearly realized the implications in the 1820s, when trekboers in large numbers began to expand beyond the limits of the colony in search of better grazing:

> Every stretch of migration throws the mass of our borders back in point of improvement, as long as it is not forced by a redundant population, or scarcity of food, which is far from being the case. . . . It is a curious fact that the complaints of the diminution of stock are accompanied by as loud a one that there is no market whatever for the little which remains, so that however impalatable I know the theory to be to my country men, I think it would not be unfortunate for the colony if the present distress of graziers were to throw numbers out of that line of life into more active ones, which we cannot expect to take place as long as a hope of the extension of the boundary exists.[53]

51. *Records of the Cape Colony*, 23 : 196 (Report of the Commissioners of Enquiry, 30 September 1825).

52. (Gubbins Collection, University of Witwatersrand), Replies to questions on the importation of slaves by W. S. van Ryneveld, 29 November 1797.

53. (Cape Archives), GR 6/15 Stockenstrom–Plasket, 1 December 1825.

From this perspective, the Great Trek was a dramatic escape, not only from the political controls which the British government imposed on frontier society, but also from all the difficult social and economic adjustments which the closing of the frontier required. It would remove both the threat of disastrous frontier wars and the calamitous loss of status entailed by entering someone else's service. It transplanted to the deep interior the pioneering frontier of the mid-eighteenth century, with its near-subsistence farming, undiversified economy, and lack of political controls.

In fact, just at the time of the Great Trek the frontier economy was slowly pulling out of its depression and there was an acceleration in the transition from subsistence to commercial farming. This was the long-term result of the increase of the colonial European population from 25,000 in 1800 to 237,000 in 1865. Together with the British drive (unlike that of the Company) to promote economic development and tighten up the collection of taxes, the population increase stimulated the development of roads, markets, and towns in the colony.

The economic history of the frontier town of Graaff-Reinet, established in 1786, provides a case study of the gradual transition toward the postfrontier stage of settlement and trade. In 1811 an official report noted the beginnings of trade in the town where twenty-five tradesmen had recently settled.[54] Townsmen were making a living from the produce of their vineyards and orchards situated near the Sunday River. The arrival of the more commercially oriented 1820 British settlers, the presence of the military establishment on the Eastern Frontier, and the development of a new harbor at Port Elizabeth promoted the growth of a regional market. By the 1830s the farmers of the district were bartering their produce for manufactured goods at Graaff-Reinet and had stopped obtaining supplies in Cape Town or from the *smousen.*[55]

It was wool that finally heralded the beginning of commercial farming. In the 1830s Graaff-Reinet was still producing very little wool and had hardly made a beginning with the breeding of merinos as a substitute for the thick-tailed Cape sheep. Gradually a switch toward cash-oriented farming took place as the prejudices and doubts of the conservative farmers were being broken down by the success which the newly arrived British settlers were achieving with wool.[56] Loans were becoming more readily available from Cape Town and even England. This led to greater activity in the building of dams and to experiments with new plows and reaping machines. The

54. *Records of the Cape Colony,* 8:299 (Report of the Commission of Circuit, 28 February 1812).

55. A. Steedman, *Wanderings and Adventures in the Interior of Southern Africa,* 2 vols. (London, 1835), 1:124.

56. H. B. Thom, *Die Geskiedenis van die Skaapboerdery in Suid-Afrika* (Amsterdam, 1936), pp. 272–330.

wool production of the district increased from 150,000 lbs. in the mid-1840s to 1,282,168 lbs. in 1855. By then Port Elizabeth was exporting nearly four times as much wool as Cape Town. In some areas land values multiplied by more than six times between 1843 and 1857. There was increasing agitation for improvement in the quality of the roads, but without much success. However, in 1879 the opening of a rail link between Graaff-Reinet and Port Elizabeth helped to assure the Graaff-Reinet market of a share of the wool and meat production in the area north of the Cape Colony.[57]

By the 1850s the transition of Graaff-Reinet from "frontier to midlands" was complete. In 1800 it was a cauldron of frontier conflict; by the mid-1850s the frontier had passed by. In some senses the frontier had closed much earlier: no more free land was available after the 1780s and the government had established full political control over the Afrikaner frontiersmen by the first decade of the nineteenth century. However, in other senses frontier closure only progressed gradually over the next four decades. There was the slow development of commercial farming and a regional market, and of control over the "Hottentot vagrants" and Xhosa "raiders." But by 1850 Graaff-Reinet was politically and economically settled. The expansion of the colony, the increase of the European population, and the establishment of new districts to the north and the east protected the Midlands region from frontier turmoil: It was now a leading producer of wool, a place where Mosenthal Brothers bought or bartered wool and "all description of produce" and extended credit to farmers through the financing of local storekeepers.[58]

The Graaff-Reinet case also applies in some respects to the frontier development in the area north of the Orange, where Afrikaners began to settle in the 1830s. There was a short mini-boom in wool, especially after the British established control over Transorangia in 1848.[59] For the Griquas (previously named Bastaards), the boom in wool spelled the end of their independent existence in the Transorangia area as they were edged out by trekboer and Voortrekker immigrants.[60] However, the British withdrawal from the Highveld in the 1850s ended the mini-boom and also decreased the degree to which the Free State economy was integrated with that of the Cape Colony. Despite the trade boost provided by the discovery of diamonds and gold, the

57. For a full and perceptive analysis of Graaff-Reinet, see Kenneth Wyndham Smith, "From Frontier to Midlands: A History of the Graaff-Reinet District, 1786–1910" (D. Phil. diss., Rhodes University, 1974), pp. 115–17 (published as Occasional Paper no. 20, Rhodes University Institute of Social and Economic Research, 1976).

58. Smith, "From Frontier to Midlands," p. 125.

59. D. Hobart Houghton, "Economic Development, 1865–1965," in Oxford History of South Africa, 2:4.

60. Robert Ross, Adam Kok's Griquas: A Study in the Development of Stratification in South Africa (Cambridge, Eng., 1976).

Free State only gradually made the change toward agricultural specialization and commercialization in the second half of the nineteenth century.

In terms of open conflict over disputed land, the Free State ceased to be a frontier region in 1868 when Britain assumed control over Basutoland. There were no large African reserves within its borders. Neither was there a large disparity in numbers between white and black: the 1890 census put the white population at 77,000 and the Africans at 128,000. However, lacking real commercial development and an effective government machinery, the Free State was still partly in the frontier stage until the late 1880s. Economic isolation resulted in largely subsistence farming; settlers waited for an improved transportation system and an increase in the population density before they would embark on farm improvements. Until 1870 there were no public highways to speak of, and the first bridge over the Orange River was only built in 1879. The population density gradually increased from 2.65 persons per square mile in the 1850s to 4.23 per square mile in 1890, with the highest densities in the east where there was a large concentration of Africans. Some wool was exported but wheat had to be imported from Basutoland and the Cape Colony. Agriculture consisted mostly of subsistence farming; and barter, with *smousen* playing a prominent role, comprised the bulk of trade.[61]

Eventually it was the Witwatersrand market, the railways, and the revenue from customs which ended precapitalist near-subsistence farming in the Free State. The Transvaal mines spurred agricultural development in the Northern Free State where land values increased sharply. Transport riding became an attractive alternative career for whites. In 1889 the Free State for the first time received revenue from customs. This enabled the government to strengthen its control over its subjects and to launch economic development projects. When the Free State entered the South African War in 1899, commercial farming was rapidly replacing subsistence farming. Farmers no longer relied primarily on barter to procure necessary items such as guns, building materials, and clothing, but aimed to sell a growing part of their production for cash in the market while still depending on unfree labor or sharecropping in their farming operations. But it would still take several decades before sufficient capital and coercive apparatus appeared to constitute the full transition to capitalist farming, involving maximization of profits, wage labor, and treatment of agricultural production as a business enterprise.

Throughout the second half of the nineteenth century, the Free State and Transvaal governments tried to attract white immigrants to promote

61. G. J. Lamprecht, "Die Ekonomiese Ontwikkeling van die Vrystaat van 1870 tot 1899" (D. Phil. diss., University of Stellenbosch, 1954).

economic growth and expand their tax base. But both governments had at early stages squandered their only real asset, land, through their liberal grants. In the Free State this land policy did not have the same disruptive effect on settlement as in the Transvaal. In 1874 the Bloemfontein *Friend* stated: "The country is filling up rapidly—in some of the older districts there being scarcely an unoccupied farm to be had."[62] By the end of the century, land was much better distributed among Afrikaners there than in the Transvaal. To be sure, there were large absentee landlord estates at the one end of the spectrum and, at the other, numerous small farms, the result of subdivision among heirs according to the Roman Dutch law of inheritance. But there was never the overcrowding of land, the acute poverty and the by-woner (tenant farmer) problem which Afrikaner society in Transvaal began to experience from the 1870s. Instead, a viable white middle class had developed in the Free State rural areas by the end of the nineteenth century, which enabled twentieth-century Afrikaner nationalism to draw its initial leader and support from this region.

If there is some resemblance between the Free State and the American frontier, particularly as far as the formative impact of the frontier on democracy and nationalism is concerned, the Transvaal represents a different case. In its political development it lies somewhere between the individualist democracy of the United States and the paternalist authoritarianism of Latin America. Its settlement pattern is reminiscent of the Latin American frontier where, as Alistair Hennessy has written, the "filling in" process did not occur because big landowners controlled the distribution of land. On both the Transvaal and the Latin American frontiers the white population was too sparse and the commercial links too weak to encourage the development of regional economies.[63]

Afrikaner occupation of the Transvaal was a slow and haphazard process. In the 1850s there were mainly two small strips of settlement—in the west from Potchefstroom to Rustenburg and the east from Utrecht to Soutpansberg. Large areas, including the Highveld proper, were unoccupied by whites. Settlement in the north had to be abandoned in the 1860s. Even as late as 1886 there was a ratio of less than one white per square mile in the Transvaal. The overwhelming majority of the roughly 60,000 Afrikaners of the Transvaal, an area of about 71,600 square miles, was concentrated in the southern half of the republic.[64] The filling-in process did not occur. By the

62. Cited in ibid., p. 33.

63. Hennessy, *The Frontier in Latin American History*, p. 48.

64. For detailed discussions, see F. J. Potgieter, "Die Vestiging van die Blanke in Transvaal (1837–1886) met spesiale verwysing na die verhouding tussen die mens en die omgewing," *Archives Year Book for South African History* (1958), 2:1–208; A. N. Pelzer, *Geskiedenis van die Suid-Afrikaanse Republiek, I: Wordingsjare* (Cape Town, 1950); R. Cornwell, "Land and Politics in the Transvaal in the 1880s," *Societies of Southern Africa* 4 (1974):29–40.

end of the century, half of the land to which whites laid claim in the Transvaal was unoccupied, being in the hands of absentee landlords or land companies.[65] In 1871 the government had temporarily stopped issuing land in an attempt to counter excessive land speculation, which left large areas of the country unoccupied, and to restore the credit of the state.[66] But by that time the chance of systematic colonization had been lost and the detrimental effects of the existing pattern of settlement were closing in on Afrikaner society.

The way in which the Transvaal had been occupied by whites made it very difficult to incorporate the region into the economic heartland of South Africa. The ports were too far away and the land was not suitable for the production of wool. A class of large landholders remained wealthy, but most farmers faced a crisis as the resources for extensive subsistence farming became exhausted. In most of the area, trade was reduced to a minimum and consisted mostly of barter. In the absence of exports the specie was soon exhausted and pioneer society became heavily dependent on merchant capital. In 1886, when gold was discovered, the Transvaal still was not self-sufficient in agriculture. D. M. Goodfellow, an economic historian, wrote some fifty years later:

> It became a commonplace, and a true commonplace, that the Transvaal scarcely responded to all the demand for foodstuffs created by the new industry. . . . The country had existed too long without markets and without commerce to be able to respond instantly to the great market which appeared with such suddenness in its midst.[67]

The great difficulty which the Afrikaners experienced in becoming cash-crop producers in the nineteenth century must partly be ascribed to their heritage of near-subsistence farming. Certainly factors such as the absence of a well-regulated labor force and the instability of agricultural prices weighed heavily, but the slow reaction of the Transvaal farmers to the new market can only be fully understood by taking into account the long-standing tendency among the average and the small farmer to produce only as much as was needed to purchase the necessary commodities.[68]

By the turn of the century there was no more cheap land available and game was all but wiped out. In terms of the availability of these easily ex-

65. Francis Wilson, "Farming, 1866–1966," in *Oxford History of South Africa*, 2:123.
66. Cornwell, "Land and Politics," p. 30.
67. D. M. Goodfellow, *A Modern Economic History of South Africa* (London, 1931), pp. 132–33.
68. For an unconvincing attempt to explain this phenomenon by portraying the Afrikaners as prisoners of their culture, see Randall G. Stokes, "Afrikaner Calvinism and Economic Action: The Weberian Thesis in South Africa," *American Journal of Sociology* 81, no. 1 (1975):62–81.

ploitable resources the frontier had closed. A new resource in the form of gold became available in the 1880s; however, most Afrikaners on the Witwatersrand sold mineral options cheaply. Some Afrikaners seized the opportunity of transport riding to the new towns. But the farming community as a whole was crushed in the 1890s by the rinderpest, which wiped out a large proportion of the cattle,[69] and the devastation of the South African War (1899–1902). Although the problem had existed long before, the term "poor white" was first used in 1890.[70] The "poor white problem" was soon to become a specter of white politicians, as the Afrikaner poor flocked to the cities in their last trek. As the seaboard in the eighteenth century exported its poor to the frontier, the frontier exodus of the early twentieth century exchanged rural poverty for urban indigence and squalor. During the second and third quarter of the century a maze of segregation and apartheid laws would be passed to protect the poor whites whom the frontier had pushed out.

Caste and Class Relations

Relationships between white and black on the pioneering frontier were shaped by the abundance of land, the lack of market incentives, and local rather than government recruitment and control of labor. On the closing frontier these relationships were mainly affected by declining land resources, a growing state role in the regulation of labor, and the demands of commercial farming. These variables influenced the treatment of laborers, but equally important was the extent to which the indigenous Bantu-speaking African society, as distinct from the Khoisan peoples, survived the impact of European colonization, withstanding not only their arms but also European diseases and alcohol as means of conquest.

For the Khoikhoi the southwestern Cape from the 1670s changed unmistakably to a rapidly closing frontier. The area became fully occupied by Europeans and slave labor was readily available. Khoikhoi who stayed in the area sank rapidly to a position where their status was not much higher than that of slaves. Indeed, by the turn of the century there were settlers who spoke of them in the same breath as slaves.[71] As Khoikhoi became poorer and unable to find alternative means of subsistence, farmers cut back on their meat and other provisions and their small livestock holdings became depleted.

69. C. van Onselen, "Reactions to Rinderpest in Southern Africa, 1896–97," *Journal of African History* 13, no. 2 (1972): 437–88.

70. A. N. Pelzer, "Die Arm-Blanke' Verskynsel in die Suid-Afrikaanse Republiek tussen die jare 1882 en 1899" (M.A. diss., University of Pretoria, 1937), p. 118.

71. Elphick, *Kraal and Castle*, pp. 179–81.

By the end of the eighteenth century, Khoikhoi had been squeezed out by whites and the expanding Xhosa from the few remaining unoccupied spaces on the Eastern Frontier. Without land they had lost the option to refuse their labor and exist outside someone's service. Local coercion had become increasingly effective. Once a Khoikhoi had become an apprentice or a debtor to a farmer, it was difficult to leave. Colonel Collins, an observer sympathetic to the colonists, reported in 1809:

> A Hottentot can now seldom get away at the expiration of his term. If he should happen not to be in debt to his master . . . he is not allowed to take his children, or he is detained under some frivolous pretence, such as that of cattle having died through his neglect, and he is not permitted to satisfy any demands of this nature otherwise than by personal service.[72]

After Britain occupied the Cape in 1806, the government tried to substitute contractual arrangements for the arbitrary power of the masters. But the coming of the British also linked the Cape more strongly with the channels of world trade, and the new government, much more than the Company, sought to provide the producers with a docile and regulated work force to supply an expanding market. Therefore it sanctioned some of the labor-repressive practices such as the indenture system. Within two decades the government reversed its position. The growing humanitarian movement in Britain and local pressure by reformers such as Dr. Philip and Andries Stockenström made it impossible to condone any longer the ill-treatment of indigenous peoples and involuntary servitude. A recent class interpretation suggests that the Cape government was also prompted by its conviction that large supplies of unfree labor were tied down on Afrikaner farms while the newly arrived British settlers were suffering acute labor shortages.[73] Ordinance 50 of 1828, which lifted the restrictions on Khoikhoi mobility, aimed at countering labor repression and increasing the flow of labor.

After 1828 there was for a short period a sharp increase of what frontier farmers termed "vagrancy." But because Khoikhoi had no land of their own and could seldom find alternative employment in towns, they were unable to improve their position materially. Andries Stockenström, a reformist frontier official, observed in 1836 that Khoikhoi were subjected to the same treatment as slaves, except that they could not be sold and were not bound to their master except by contract. Far removed from the magistrate, Stockenström went on, they were in a state of moral debasement and physical

72. Moodie, *The Record* (Report of Colonel Collins, 1809), 5:22.
73. See the argument of Suzie Newton-King in her chapter, "The Labour Market of the Cape Colony, 1806–1828," to be published in Atmore and Marks, *Economy and Society in Preindustrial South Africa.*

misery, because a farmer valued his slave more than his Hottentot servant who could not be sold.[74]

The farmers, on the other hand, received increasing institutional support for the control of labor. The Masters and Servant Ordinance passed in 1841, three years after the slaves in the Cape had been released, to a large extent erased the legal distinction which had formerly been maintained between slaves and Khoisan. Through this ordinance, the government put all laborers, who were almost all nonwhite, in a position of legal subordination to the master. In 1856, two years after the Cape Colony received representative government, the government even further tightened up on the control that masters could exercise over their labor. For African farm labor this law remained in force for more than a century.[75]

The steady deterioration of the status of Khoikhoi laborers was closely linked with the decline of Khoikhoi society during the first century and a half of European colonization. After the frontier began to close, Khoikhoi culture disintegrated; Khoikhoi and their descendants, the "Coloureds," became a laboring caste without the psychological support that a tribal affiliation and a culture of their own could provide. Disease and alcohol completely debilitated many.

In contrast, European diseases and alcohol made little impact on the Bantu-speaking societies. They recovered quickly from military defeat, with the temporary exception of the Xhosa who, during the first half of the nineteenth century, suffered several severe defeats at the hands of the British army and then dealt themselves a crushing blow with the cattle-killing of 1856–57. Further north, however, Africans soon recovered from the devastation of the *Difaqane*—the wars accompanying the rise of Shaka's Zulu kingdom. The population increased rapidly and the Zulu and Pedi states were focal points of power until they were conquered by the British toward the end of the 1870s. African culture remained an integral part of the lives of the majority of farm laborers. Compared to the Khoikhoi, African society entered the twentieth century strong in numbers and in spirit, not because of the benevolence of the whites, but because the Boer states were too weak to smash it militarily and because other means to conquest also proved ineffective.

On the closing frontier of the Orange Free State there was virtually no land that was not occupied by whites. What first worked in favor of Africans

74. *Imperial Bluebook no. 50 (1836)*, Aborigines Committee Report, question 2310. For a discussion of the significance of Ordinance 50, see Leslie Clement Duly, "A Revisit with the Cape's Hottentot Ordinance of 1828," in *Studies in Economics and Economic History*, ed. Marcelle Kooy (London, 1972), pp. 26–56.

75. Colin Bundy, "The Abolition of the Masters and Servants Act," in *South Africa: Sociological Analyses*, ed. A. Paul Hare et al. (Cape Town, 1979), pp. 373–79.

was a real shortage of labor, for according to the census of 1890, there were only some 70,000 African men to 40,000 white men in the republic. (Whites held the view that at least five African men were needed to work an average farm.) Second, while the market was still small and unstable, some large farmers considered African tenants paying rent in kind a more attractive proposition than investing capital in agricultural production. Third, the Free State government only gradually developed the means to coerce African labor. It issued pass laws to restrict the mobility of Africans, it levied taxes to force them to work, it legalized the apprenticeship of children, and after 1872 it passed several laws which aimed at limiting the number of heads of families on a farm to five. But despite all such efforts the government was unable to ensure a sufficient supply of labor to all farms. It did not have an efficient police force to execute its decrees. Especially in the north, wealthy whites with many Africans on their farms were powerful enough to resist the regulations limiting numbers, as repeated discussions in the Volksraad and complaints from frustrated small farmers show. The government also realized that if its African population was harassed too much, many would leave and settle in neighboring territories such as Basutoland and Natal. In 1893 *The Friend*, a Free State newspaper, succinctly summarized the situation:

> The native is as much at liberty to sell his labour at the best terms he can make as the farmer is to dispose of his crops. If the master is too exacting, the native leaves him and goes to one who is an easier man to get on with. If the laws are too oppressive, the native leaves the country altogether.[76]

"Squatting" emerged on the closing frontier as a working compromise to reconcile the needs of Africans and white farmers. For an African, a squatter farm provided a refuge from unfavorable working conditions, a place where he could pasture his cattle and reap his own harvest, and live together with his family and friends. By the end of the century, with the gold mines and railways offering wages four times higher than farm labor, farmers often had no option but to offer acceptable conditions to Africans. In particular, farmers responding to the Witwatersrand market by switching from subsistence to commercial farming needed a large supply of seasonal labor as well as a class of workers who would work the land they could not exploit themselves.[77] Two systems then evolved: farming-on-the-half, where Africans handed over half the crop to the farmer in return for the right to culti-

76. Cited by H. J. van Aswegen, "Die Verhouding tussen Blank en Nie-Blank in die Oranje-Vrystaat, 1854–1902" (D. Phil. diss., University of the Orange Free State, 1968), p. 634.

77. The labor "question" in the Orange Free State is discussed at length by van Aswegen, ibid., pp. 467–643.

vate, graze stock, and live on the land; and "Kaffir farming" in which absentee landlords let their land to rent-paying Africans.[78]

On the pioneering frontier, conflict between whites and Africans was over land and cattle. On the closing frontier of the Free State, the issues were labor and the response of a new class of Africans to the markets that were opening up. The smaller white farmers deeply resented the competition for the market which came from African peasants. In the 1890s a group of farmers from the eastern Free State demanded that the Volksraad prohibit "the large-scale grain-growing" of African peasants, since it was "impossible for white grain-farmers to compete against Coloureds."[79] Cooperation between European landholders and African peasants was also undermining white solidarity. Because the poor whites and bywoners were not prepared to do the same work as Africans and therefore set too many demands, white landholders increasingly considered replacing them with African peasants.[80]

It was in the Transvaal that the closing of the frontier produced the greatest transformation in social relations. In the Cape Colony the labor legislation of the 1840s and 1850s made all rural laborers legally subordinate to their masters. The Cape interior was ruled by a largely solidified white caste, with color the main sign of subordination. The Transvaal of the late nineteenth century, however, began to move toward a society which, compared with the rest of South Africa, was characterized more by a class and less by a caste relationship, with Africans enjoying greater mobility. To be sure, there were areas of the Transvaal where landholders could exercise sufficient local control to keep large numbers of black unfree laborers in a rigid, castelike condition of immobility and inferiority. By the end of the century, their numbers were swollen by the indenturing of newly defeated peoples. However, in this period too a new class of Africans was emerging between white landholders and African laborers, while in white society increasing class conflict was developing between the landholders and bywoners. To a large extent these developments were the result of the weakness of the central government and of white society at large in the Transvaal, in a period marked by the discovery of gold and the rise of commercial agriculture. The political autonomy of the Transvaal republic was considerably eroded during the last two decades of the nineteenth century. For fear of British intervention the Transvaal government did not feel free to pass legislation that would force Africans to work. In terms of the London

78. Colin Bundy, "The Emergence and Decline of a South African Peasantry," *African Affairs* 71, no. 285 (1972):369–88. For a full statement, see idem, *The Rise and Fall of the South African Peasantry* (London, 1979).

79. Van Aswegen, "Die Verhouding tussen Blank en Nie-Blank," p. 640; see also pp. 576, 581.

80. See the fascinating discussion on "The Labour Question" by R. J. F. in *The Friend* (Bloemfontein), 2 and 5 April 1895.

Convention of 1884, it was also obliged to demarcate reserves where the large African chiefdoms could live, taking into account the existing claims of these chiefdoms.[81] Besides the reservations, living space was also provided to Africans by the vast tracts of land held by absentee landlords or companies and by mission stations. Africans were also free to leave the territory and settle beyond its borders. And after the discovery of gold, a vast new field of alternative employment was open to them. According to an estimate of the South African Republic, there were 131,539 male Africans under its jurisdiction in 1895; of these, approximately 70,000 were working in the mines.[82]

In such conditions the coercive relationships between the master and the unfree indentured or tributary laborers were gradually transformed into what Stanley Trapido calls a "variety of unstable landlord-tenant linkages."[83] They were unstable because Africans had acquired a considerable degree of mobility and bargaining power. African tenants paying a cash or a labor rent for living on a farm, preferred to attach themselves to prosperous farmers owning fertile land where they could sow and pasture their cattle. They were often able to demand favorable terms in sharecropping arrangements. One farmer, for instance, had to accommodate forty families and provide pasture for their 400 cattle, but could only draw on the labor of three young Africans for the full year and an additional twenty for two months per year.[84] A mission journal wrote that "the Natives are not bound to the soil. . . . The Boers are obliged in self-defence to treat their people leniently."[85] Africans living together in the reserves or on large farms secured a considerable measure of psychological and cultural autonomy.

At the same time, economic differentiation and class strains began to appear in white society. As we have seen, half of the land to which whites laid claim in the Transvaal was unoccupied by the end of the century, being in the hands of large absentee landlords. Lands that were occupied were often heavily subdivided among as many as forty whites to a single farm. In some cases, subdivision of a farm led to the impoverishment of more than a hundred whites within three or four generations—the start of the so-called poor white problem. In the distribution of land the key role was played by the field-cornets. They inspected claims to the land before it was given out

81. For the constraining influence of the fear of British intervention, see Barend Johannes Krüger, *Diskussies en Wetgewing rondom die landelike arbeidsvraagstuk in die Suid-Afrikaanse Republiek met besondere verwysing na die Plakkerswette, 1885–1899*, Communications of the University of South Africa, C62 (Pretoria, 1966).

82. Ibid., p. 47.

83. Stanley Trapido, "Landlord and Tenant in a Colonial Economy: The Transvaal 1880–1910," *Journal of Southern African Studies* 5, no. 1 (1978): 26–58. This is a major reinterpretation of class relationships in the Transvaal.

84. Krüger, *Diskussies en Wetgewing*, pp. 12, 45, 56–57.

85. Cited by Trapido, "Landlord and Tenant," p. 28.

as farms and also auctioned land for which taxes had not been paid. Having prior access to information about land on the market, they often acquired substantial tracts and could attract large numbers of tenants. Toward the end of the century they constituted a class of notables that was well represented in the Volksraad.[86]

The obverse of the large number of Africans living on the farms of the wealthy was the labor shortage experienced by the small farmer. Obviously Africans would have to work harder on these farms; moreover, there was no status attached to working for a poor man. "It is known throughout the world that the poor rarely want to serve the poor,"[87] was a field-cornet's comment on the constant complaints of labor shortage. The Transvaal government responded by passing legislation limiting the number of African families on a farm to five. These laws had some restrictive effect on African mobility but did not prevent the wealthy from having as much labor as they required; neither did they supply the poor with the workers they wanted. Toward the end of the Transvaal republic, the government was both unwilling and unable to use effective measures to compel Africans to work or to redistribute African labor, and the small farmers were complaining vociferously that they were forced to work themselves and to "use their children as Kaffirs in order to hold their own" (staande te kunnen blijven).[88] With little land and hardly any labor at its disposal, the poorer section of white society was unable to survive economically in the rural areas. In 1899 the young Jan Smuts who, significantly, came from the caste society of the rural southwestern Cape, warned that if laws were not passed to protect the white farmer, their sons would have to become laborers, and the real (eigenlijke) nation of the republic would become a laboring class.[89]

The inequality of land and labor resources as the frontier closed transformed the previously fairly egalitarian Afrikaner society. It was a phenomenon that repeated itself. When the southwestern Cape frontier closed in the seventeenth century, poor whites were forced to enter the service of wealthy farmers. There was a minimum of social intercourse between landholders and white laborers. Significantly, white knechten (overseers) addressed their employers as "baas,"[90] which was to become the classic term denoting racial and class superiority. However, on the open frontier of the

86. Stanley Trapido, "The South African Republic: Class Formation and the State, 1850–1900," Societies of Southern Africa 3 (1973): 58.

87. Krüger, Diskussies en Wetgewing, p. 30.

88. Ibid., p. 10. See also B. J. Krüger, "Diskussies en Wetgewing rondom die Landelike Arbeidsvraagstuk in die Suid-Afrikaanse Republiek . . ." (M.A. diss., University of South Africa, 1965), p. 202.

89. Krüger, "Diskussies en Wetgewing" (diss.), p. 209.

90. G. C. de Wet, "Die Vrybevolking in die Kaapse Nedersetting 1657–1707," (D. Phil. diss., University of Stellenbosch, 1978), pp. 213–15.

eighteenth and nineteenth centuries, wealth was fairly evenly distributed among whites, with a tendency to become still more evenly distributed in the largely subsistence economy.[91] "That there is still no real class division among the true inhabitants of this colony [the whites] provides proof of the slight progress made in the welfare of the colony,"[92] Van Ryneveld observed in 1805.

White egalitarianism came under pressure toward the end of the nineteenth century when there was no more free land in southern Africa and farmers had to use their land more intensively. In 1879 a special commissioner on the northern frontier of the Cape Colony wrote: "it is the poorer class of farmers who, pressed out by their richer neighbours, move on in search of *vrygrond*."[93] Their time of crisis came at the end of the nineteenth century when there was no more *vrygrond* (free land) and farmers were rationalizing their farming operations to meet market demands. Also weakening their position was the fact that, whereas on the pioneering frontier the landholder needed his tenant farmers to join him (or go in his place) on commando, supervise his laborers, and provide company in his social isolation, on the frontier that had closed, the government could provide protection while government controls and the market compelled the Africans to work.

Although a sense of "white solidarity" remained, it was constantly being eroded, especially in the Transvaal, by landholders who exploited their tenant farmers, paying them even lower wages than nonwhite laborers, or pushed them out to the cities because they preferred black peasants, who were generally regarded as better laborers and producers.

Unable to exist as independent producers and unwilling to work as manual laborers, bywoners had little status. A Dutch visitor to the Transvaal remarked in 1890 that a man living on the farm of someone else, "does not count for much and is not held in esteem."[94] Early in the twentieth century the following definition of the bywoner was current: "everyone on a farm who is white but not a *baas*."[95] Black laborers on the farm no longer addressed and treated the bywoner as a *baas*. There was a growing social distinction between the farmer and the landless white. R. W. Wilcocks, a member of the Carnegie Commission of the 1930s on the poor-white problem, expressed a sentiment that was strongly felt during the preceding four decades: "[The farmer] often finds it difficult to strike a happy mean be-

91. For a full discussion, see Guelke, "The European Settlement of South Africa," pp. 335–36.

92. W. S. van Ryneveld, "Beschouwing," p. 124.

93. Van der Merwe, *Trek*, p. 60.

94. H. Blink, *De Zuid-Afrikaansche Republiek en hare bewoners* (Amsterdam, 1890), p. 98.

95. Grosskopf, *Plattelandsverarming en Plaasverlating*, in Report of the Carnegie Commission, *The Poor White Problem in South Africa*, 5 vols. (Stellenbosch, 1932), 1:121.

tween treating his European hand as a European, and so in a sense as still his equal, and at the same time as his subordinate."[96] To Wilcocks, the increasing economic equality between the large lower stratum of white society and the black population spelled the danger of the poor whites losing caste and becoming "the social equals of the great mass of non-Europeans."[97]

How far the class cleavages within Transvaal and Free State white society had developed became starkly clear when more than a fifth of the Afrikaners in the field were fighting at the side of the British by the end of the South African War. Of the roughly 5,000 "joiners," the vast majority had been bywoners. In some sense this treason was a rebellion against class exploitation. A recent study cites evidence of serious prewar bywoner discontent. In the 1880s and 1890s they had to go on commando against Africans without any recompense, to defend the property of landholders while their own families were destitute. The joiners of the Boer War clearly hoped that the British would offer them a better dispensation.[98]

In the end the Transvaal did not become a class society like Brazil. But its caste society might have been transformed had there not been such a short period between the 1880s, when the land resources became exhausted, and the birth of a new order dominated by the rapid industrialization of South Africa and politically by the South African constitution of 1909 which enfranchised all white men, thereby entrenching not only white supremacy but also white egalitarianism. Without this new order, the frontier that had made white egalitarianism possible might also have been instrumental in reordering society on the basis of class rather than race. Certainly the dominant class of landholders in Transvaal would have found it much more difficult than the southern planters to ensure that lower-class whites retain a sense of racial caste and solidarity.

The Political Order

Two overlapping trends characterized the political order of the closing frontier. First, there was the decline of regional strife and the establishment of control by the center over the periphery with its anarchic tendencies. Second, the central government with a modern bureaucracy took over the local administration in which the field-cornets had played a pivotal role. As we have seen, the British imperial government established a considerable mea-

---

96. R. W. Wilcocks, The Poor White (Report of the Carnegie Commission), 2:60.
97. Ibid., p. 63.
98. A. M. Grundlingh, Die "Hendsoppers" en "Joiners": Die rasionaal en verskynsel van verraad (Pretoria, 1979), pp. 232–36; Thomas Pakenham, The Boer War (Johannesburg, 1979), pp. 566–68.

sure of control over the Cape frontier during the first half of the nineteenth century. In the Free State and Transvaal this occurred only toward the end of the nineteenth and the beginning of the twentieth century, when a coalition of the imperial power and Afrikaner landholders finally closed the frontier.

On the pioneering frontier the authority vacuum produced endemic conflict which the frontiersmen attempted to resolve locally through the commando system. The decentralized nature of the commando system, in which regional commandants coordinated the activities of field-cornets under their command, made prompt action possible in the frontier zone but also bred regionalism and anarchy. When trekboer expansion was halted in the late eighteenth century, the government appointed two commandants, one for the northern frontier, where the "Bushmen" had forced the evacuation of several frontier divisions, and the other for the eastern divisions, which were intent on pushing the Xhosa over the Fish River. During the rebellions of the 1790s, Afrikaner society in Graaff-Reinet district split along these regional lines. The northern frontier divisions wished to concentrate the district's military efforts on the strife against the "Bushmen." The southeastern divisions ignored calls to enlist for commandos against the "Bushmen" and demanded an attack on the Xhosa. The rebellions of the 1790s were in fact nothing but a thinly disguised takeover of the district authority by the southeastern division, and they failed primarily because the northern frontiersmen first remained neutral and then opposed the rebellions.

Such conflicting regional loyalties often undermined the effectiveness of commandos. One of the chief reasons why the frontier colonists were unable to maintain themselves against the Xhosa in the period 1793 to 1811 was the continual bickering among military leaders and the general disunity which characterized the commando. The expulsion of the Xhosa from colonial territory in 1811–12 was due not so much to the presence of British troops, who only brought up the rear, but to British military officers who led the attacking force consisting of burgher militia and Khoikhoi. British intervention ended regional strife and radically changed the nature of the commandos on the Eastern Frontier. In the days of the pioneering frontier, commandos were often raised without the direct involvement, and sometimes even without the sanction, of the authorities. After the British had taken over, commandos were still called up, but they served essentially as auxiliary forces subservient to the British military and acted under much more effective government control. The constraints under which commandos then had to operate added to the sense of grievance and frustration that gave rise to the Great Trek. In 1836 Walter Currie recorded the comment of a frontier farmer on the turmoil in his division: "He thought they were worse off than fifty years ago; in those old times when they were robbed they redressed themselves, but now their hands are tied while the Kaffirs were loose."[99] These words caught the essence of the transition from the pioneering frontier to a situation where the conduct of frontier warfare had shifted from the periphery to the center, largely because the government was determined to control what John Galbraith has called the "turbulent frontier."[100]

In the Transvaal, regionalism based on personal loyalties to the respective commandant-generals had long thwarted attempts to establish central control. From 1845 onward there were continuous clashes between various groups of burghers, and several regional "republics" were created in the 1850s by discontented factions before all the burghers in the region were brought together under one flag and one constitution.[101] It was only in the 1870s that the Transvaalers started to coalesce under a stronger executive presidency, which developed under Burgers and Kruger, and that power began to shift from the localities to the center.

The gradual end of regional strife and anarchy was linked to another trend: the replacement of a "government of men" exercising arbitrary power, by a "government of laws" executed by a modern bureaucracy and a civilian police force. What law and order existed on the pioneering frontier in the Cape, Free State, and Transvaal had to be maintained by local agents acting according to their own lights and means. Police action in each division was the task of the field-cornets, who not only called up men for commandos but also acted as constables to arrest suspects, register labor contracts, resolve disputes between masters and servants, and investigate unnatural deaths. But while the field-cornets exercised some restraining influence, the landlords on their farms largely supplied their own interpretation of the law.

Gradually the pioneers' conception of the government and the law changed as the central government began to make its views felt. The change often came as a shock, as it did for a pioneer charged with murder after he had shot an African on his farm.

> I have a letter from my field cornet . . . in which he instructed us to 'put out of the way' any such creatures who do not want to surrender themselves. From our worthy commandant we have the same, also in writing. Indeed, this has been the law of the frontier since time immemorial. And now, for obeying the law and doing as has been done many

99. Quoted in C. F. J. Muller, *Die Oorsprong van die Groot Trek* (Cape Town, 1974), p. 193.

100. John S. Galbraith, "The 'Turbulent Frontier' as a Factor in British Expansion," *Comparative Studies in Society and History* 2 (1959–60): 150–68.

101. F. A. van Jaarsveld, *Die Eenheidstrewe van die Republikeinse Afrikaners, 1836–1864* (Johannesburg, 1951); J. A. du Plessis, "Die Ontstaan en Ontwikkeling van die amp van die Staatspresident in die Zuid-Afrikaansche Republiek, 1858–1902," *Archives Year Book* (1955), 1:1–271.

times to my knowledge and as every frontier resident does in such cases, we face the accusation of murder. This is intolerable.[102]

After the second British occupation of the Cape in 1806, the government of the Cape Colony wished to establish a modern polity with efficient military and administrative machinery. For a considerable period, however, the lack of financial resources prevented the attainment of this objective. The government hoped to take an important step toward this goal in 1828 when it replaced the courts of landdrosts and heemraden with resident magistrates. In terms of Ordinance 50, which granted the Khoikhoi legal equality, the power to register labor contracts was given to two new officials, the justice of the peace and clerk of the peace, of whom there was one for each district. The contracting of all servants was thus transferred to the district's capital. For a considerable period this system failed to have significant impact. A justice of the peace of Beaufort West district remarked in 1845 that most of the farms were 70 to 100 miles from the district headquarters, which made it too difficult to obtain redress: "Parties either submit to the evils . . . or in cases of petty thefts, ill conduct of servants, etc., they take the law into their own hands, and inflict such punishment as they think fit."[103]

In another respect, however, Ordinance 50 signaled an important phase in the closing of the frontier. Before 1828 field-cornets played a major role in the system of labor-coercion through enforcing the pass laws and stopping "vagrancy." After 1828 Khoikhoi were no longer required to carry passes and vagrancy was no longer a crime. The resident magistrates and justices of the peace then supervised much more closely the way in which the field-cornets exercised their police duties, and the main responsibility for patrolling the border and tracking down stolen cattle rested on the troops based at the military posts.

From the point of view of the colonists there was a major breakdown of law and order in the decade after 1828, with a sharp increase of "vagrancy" and also of cattle thefts by Khoikhoi and, on a larger scale, by Xhosa who had lost large tracts of land since 1811. The vagrants were men who were looking for better employment or refused to work for colonists in view of the extremely low wages. Instead they squatted on farms and lived from cattle they stole.[104] In an important sense the Great Trek sprang from the fact that the frontier had not yet completely closed in the far eastern part of the colony. It was no longer a pioneering frontier where the frontiersmen could impose their will through vigilante action. But the alternative forms of con-

102. [Free State Archives], GS 292, pp. 16–18.
103. Cited by Duly, "A Revisit with the Cape's Hottentot Ordinance of 1828," p. 38.
104. J. S. Marais, *The Cape Coloured People, 1652–1937,* 2d ed. (Johannesburg, 1957), p. 183; Muller, *Die Oorsprung van die Groot Trek,* p. 187.

trol of a modern industrial and capitalist society—the imperative of work or starve which forces people into productive activity, and an efficient police force compelling the lower classes to comply with the prevailing notions of law and order—were still virtually nonexistent. Commenting on the desirability of a vagrancy act, in 1829 the judges of the Supreme Court pointed out that the police force and prison discipline were insufficient to combat crimes arising from vagrancy.[105]

The weakness of the frontier administrative apparatus can be illustrated by a look at the one existing in the Albany district, from which many of the Voortrekkers came. Some 4,800 square miles in extent, the district in 1834 contained 4,202 whites, 5,949 free colored persons, and 156 slaves. At the district capital there were a resident magistrate, a clerk of the peace, and eight constables; there were also six field-cornets in the district.[106] Neither the military stationed at Grahamstown nor the field-cornets were able to act effectively against cattle raids and petty thefts. It was only in 1855 that a modern police force was established in the eastern part of the colony. This was the Frontier Armed and Mounted Police, which had an original strength of 17 officers and 500 other ranks.[107]

In the Voortrekker republics there was, by the end of the century, not nearly the same amount of government control as in the Cape Colony, which could draw on the expertise and resources of Britain. In the Free State the increased revenue flowing from the discovery of diamonds made possible some expansion of the bureaucracy. In 1889 there were 19 districts in this comparatively small territory. However, the state remained unable to enforce its laws with respect to "vagrancy" and the maximum number of African families on farms. Often the landdrosts and field-cornets were farmers who opposed these laws or feared resistance if they tried to enforce them. By the 1890s the *Rijdende Dienstmacht*, a mounted police force consisting of some 90 men who patrolled the districts, ensured a somewhat greater measure of government control and compliance with the laws.

In the Transvaal the field-cornets and commandants, who were all locally elected, were until the 1870s the chief sources of authority in the districts. It was mainly they who commandeered and distributed African labor; it is probable that much of the taxes Africans paid ended up as their property.[108] At first the state's machinery for raising taxes from its own citizens was hopelessly inadequate. However, administrative efficiency gradually increased. From the 1870s the landdrost, the only appointed official, be-

105. J. C. Visagie, "Die Katriviernedersetting, 1829–1839" (D. Litt. et Phil. diss., University of South Africa, 1978), p. 120.

106. *The South African Directory and Almanac for the Year 1834*, p. 204.

107. G. Tylden, *The Armed Forces of South Africa* (Johannesburg, 1954), p. 58.

108. Trapido, "Aspects in the Transition from Slavery to Serfdom," p. 26.

gan to replace the field-cornet as the government's agent in the rural areas. After 1886, although the executive machinery improved considerably as a result of the increased revenue from the gold mines, there was never any effective police force in the interior, and the commando remained the main instrument for police as well as military action in the Transvaal.[109] On the Witwatersrand the administrative apparatus was unable to meet the demands of a growing industrial economy.

It was a coalition between Afrikaner commercial farmers and British capitalist interests which finally completed the closure of the southern Africa frontier. This sprang from the strongly increased demand for cheap and abundant indigenous labor as the region rapidly began to industrialize after the discovery of the Witwatersrand gold fields.[110] Between 1886 and 1899, when war broke out, there was sharp competition for labor between the commercial farmers and the mining capitalists. Great tensions developed when it became clear to the mining capitalists that the Transvaal state, representing largely the interests of the commercial farmers, lacked the means to ensure a sufficient supply of labor to the mines or even interfered with its flow to the towns.[111] Some historians have recently rooted the origins of the South African War in the British desire to rationalize the control of the labor force and remove other obstacles to industrialization. After the war an uneasy alliance between "gold and maize" took shape. Although African peasants contributed a substantial part of the locally grown crops in the Transvaal, British imperial interests then chose to rely on the dominant class of Afrikaner society, not only for agricultural production but also to control the Africans in the rural areas and the white and black urban proletariat. State subsidies and credits enabled this class of large landholders to accumulate even more land and increase their profits at the expense of poor white and black peasant farmers.[112]

With the frontier finally closed, the decade after the war witnessed an assault on Africans who had succeeded in avoiding white demands for cheap labor. In the late nineteenth century it was the small white farmers who objected to African squatting; now it was the great landholders supplying a large but unstable market who insisted that the competition from African peasants be eliminated.[113] Land passed from the hands of absentee specula-

109. For an extensive treatment, see G. N. van den Bergh, "Die Polisiediens in die Zuid-Afrikaansche Republiek" (D. Phil. diss., Potchefstroom University, 1971).

110. A. Atmore and S. Marks, "The Imperial Factor in South Africa in the Nineteenth Century: Towards a Reassessment," *Journal of Imperial and Commonwealth History* 5, no. 3 (1974): 125–26.

111. Van den Berg, "Die Polisiediens in die ZAR," pp. 459–62.

112. Trapido, "Landlord and Tenant," pp. 52–58.

113. Ibid., p. 55; Tim Keegan, "Peasants, Capitalists and Farm Labour: Class Formation in the Orange River Colony, 1902–1910," *Societies of Southern Africa*, 9: 18–26.

tors and "Kaffir-farmers" to commercial farmers who demanded labor service instead of rent from African tenants and curtailed the number of cattle they were allowed to hold. The Land Act of 1913, which prohibited African land purchase, rent-squatting, and sharecropping, reflected the new dominance of the commercial farmer. For the African peasant farmer it had become "a fool's errand to find a new home for his stock and family."[114] Severely restricted in their rights of movement, African tenants were transformed into wage or serf laborers. Also in the first two decades of the twentieth century, the "Great Flight to the Cities"[115] of the Afrikaner rural poor began.

CONCLUSION

The southern Africa frontier differed in three major ways from the moving American frontier. What North America had, and southern Africa lacked, was the ferment of a frontier moving along with the ferment of industrial development from an early stage of settlement. Until the 1870s there was in southern Africa no major industrial and capitalist revolution occurring simultaneously with frontier settlement, each shaping and controlling the other. Nor before the 1870s was there the transportation revolution of America to link the frontier with the sources of technological and governmental change. On the frontier of the Cape Colony, and in the Free State and Transvaal, the initial settlement of near-subsistence farmers was only gradually followed by the development of commercial farming and the rise of markets and towns. The frontier in a particular area lasted much longer in southern Africa than in North America before it finally closed.

Second, unlike the North American frontier, which entailed the conquest of the land through the expulsion of the indigenous peoples, white expansion in southern Africa involved the colonization of the indigenous population as well as the land. On the Eastern Frontier of the Cape Colony, which opened in 1770, not all the land was expropriated, and Xhosa society did not disintegrate. In the Transvaal, where there was a resurgence of the African chiefdoms in the second half of the nineteenth century, the land was won but many of the people were not entirely vanquished. In fact, peasant farming, an essential feature of this frontier, is situated in the context of an "uncompleted colonization." The competitors for land on the frontier would meet again in the cities to compete for work and living opportunities.

Politically, "the frontier" conveys different meanings. Europeans think

114. S. T. Plaatje, *Native Life in South Africa*, 2d ed. (London, n.d.), p. 66.
115. *Die Groot Vlug* is the title of a pamphlet published in 1916 by D. F. Malan, the Afrikaner nationalist leader.

of a frontier as a borderline between countries or a line between antagonistic nations where the struggle for survival was the most intense. For American historians it means the moving line of settlements between established, organized society and the wilderness or desert beyond,[116] an area where opportunity beckoned and men lived as equals. To an Afrikaner, and perhaps also an African, the term "frontier" had both these meanings.[117] The pioneering frontier was a place where poor men could settle and escape subordination, where they could live as equals within their own community, relatively free from threats to their political and economic survival. But as the frontier began to close, the lower classes experienced impoverishment, subordination, and proletarianization—the heritage of the vast majority of Africans and at least a quarter of the Afrikaners by 1930. Thus the closing of the frontier in all its economic, social, and political dimensions had much more profound implications for twentieth-century southern Africa than it ever had for North America.

116. Louis B. Wright, *Life on the American Frontier* (New York, 1971), p. 13.

117. Significantly, in the Afrikaans language there is only the word *grens*, meaning border. To translate the American sense of the word *frontier*, one would probably have to use terms such as *grensgebied* or *pionierswêreld*.

3

Politics and the Frontier

5

CLYDE A. MILNER II   **Indulgent Friends and Important Allies: Political Process on the Cis-Mississippi Frontier and Its Aftermath**

One society's frontier may be another's front yard. For the American frontier north of Mexico and east of the Mississippi River, the political process in macro-context underscores this truism. During the colonial period, the expanding European powers in the cis-Mississippi area, France and England (and to a minor extent Spain), created a series of frontiers on the periphery of their empires, but on the ancestral homelands—the front yard—of America's natives. After the establishment of the United States, this imperial expansion continued across the Mississippi River. By the time the U.S. obtained its present national boundaries, the Spanish, Russian, and British empires, as well as numerous native groups, had lost all political claims within the trans-Mississippi West. Yet, the end result of white American domination can be too readily assumed in a simplistic ex post facto analysis. The various frontier zones often opened when intrusive whites came onto lands traditionally under the control of native polities. Although in general these European-American intruders chose to ignore or eradicate the American Indians' claim to the land which they inhabited, the situation on each frontier reveals a story of complex adjustment to resolve the issue of political control.

Many times, as the balance of power shifted on the frontier, the peoples of the two cultures needed one another's aid—sometimes as indulgent friends to a weaker party, sometimes as important allies to an equal power. Despite this search for allies and friends, disunity much more than unity characterized the political process on these frontiers, whether or not cultural lines were crossed. For example, the American Indians of the cis-Mississippi organized various styles of confederacies, but these larger polities often lacked cohesion and could create enmity. Similarly, the intrusive whites proved they could fight among themselves on both the local and in-

123

ternational levels of political organization. Only in the mid-nineteenth century, when the federal government of the United States dominated Indian policy, did the political disunity of the intruders largely disappear. For the Indians with their remarkable cultural diversity, such political disunity never disappeared.

Of course, cultural diversity and political disunity characterized native North America even before the arrival of Europeans. Such variation did not mean, however, that Indians lacked basic forms of political organization. American Indians had well-established polities with systems of leadership, traditions of war and revenge, and a history of forming alliances for trade, or to force tribute, or to conduct war. Many polities had clear distinctions between civil and military leaders, and councils as much as leaders could determine policy. In some cases, such as among the Iroquois, women played a major role in decision making. The scale of political organization varied from simple family groups, to small clusters of villages, to complex confederacies, to apparently autocratic states.

The latter example rarely appeared. In general, native leaders ruled more by consensus than by coercion. They gained their status as much by individual ability as by family or clan inheritance, and they retained their influence by public persuasion and personal example. Europeans regularly attributed more power to native leaders than they possessed. They were misidentified as "kings," "emperors," or "head chiefs," and were thought to control entire polities. This misconception served the purposes of the Europeans, who could readily recognize one leader and hold him responsible for all the actions of his people. Because of this, village councils or collections of civil and war chiefs could be ignored.

Yet over time, the impact of the white intruders created political changes within Indian societies. In some cases the power of Indian leaders grew because of the white insistence that these "chiefs" exerted more influence than they traditionally had. In other cases, these white-supported chiefs became a cause of internal divisions and greater disunity.[1]

On the international level in the two centuries that mark the colonial period before the American Revolution, the European powers also exhibited great disunity. These imperial rivalries, however, do not explain the long, failure-ridden process of attempted European settlement along the Atlantic coast, because at first the imperial powers of Spain, England, and France lacked an effective large-scale commitment to colonization. If gold or other wealth had been discovered, then the rapid military expansion of the Spanish Empire, which had occurred in the Caribbean and from Mexico southward, might have been duplicated by the French and English, if not by the

1. Wilcomb E. Washburn, *The Indian in America* (New York, 1975), pp. 42–51.

Spanish themselves. But exploratory expeditions, primarily by the Spanish, and coastal trade, a secondary vocation of some European fishermen, had not uncovered an easy source of wealth in this northern area of North America. With time, however, the underassessment of the economic potential of trade with the Indians changed. Nonetheless, during the period of first efforts at settlement, from 1521 to 1608, the early European colonists had little support from their home nations. These settlers, then, were left on their own to confront the native peoples in the area where they landed. In most cases, these natives already knew something of the Europeans because of trade connections, earlier expeditions, or knowledge passed on from Indian neighbors. In such a situation the indigenous residents held the upper hand. The political question on this earliest frontier, therefore, centered on European survival.

The "survival frontier" may be said to have begun in 1521 when Ponce de León, a would-be Spanish conquistador who had helped subdue the natives of Puerto Rico, failed to establish a colony on the west coast of Florida. The Indians quickly attacked the two hundred Spanish settlers, who suffered enough losses and injuries to convince them to return to Cuba. Native hostility also doomed Jacques Cartier's attempt in 1541 to establish a French settlement in the Saint Lawrence River valley. In Cartier's case, the local Iroquoian villagers had come to distrust the French leader, because during two earlier exploratory expeditions he had kidnapped important members of their community and taken them back to France. The first effort of the English in the 1580s on Roanoke Island also failed. Whether this "Lost Colony" perished from starvation, disease, and Indian attacks or simply chose to be absorbed by native neighbors remains an intriguing historical mystery.[2]

The aggressive response of a few Indians to European intrusion did not seem to disturb the imperial nations of Europe. Indians had not yet become a factor in the political plans of European nation states. Yet the presence of a European settlement in what another nation claimed as its New World domain could bring swift action. The Spanish established Saint Augustine in 1565 primarily to launch an attack on a settlement of French Huguenots on Florida's Saint Johns River.[3] After this bloody business, Saint Augustine remained a small isolated outpost of the Spanish Empire designed to protect the "inland passage" of gold-laden galleons on their way to Europe. Nonetheless, Saint Augustine represented the only permanent European settlement in the cis-Mississippi region during the 1500s. If Cape Town was a re-

2. David B. Quinn, *North America from Earliest Discovery to First Settlements: The Norse Voyages to 1612* (New York, 1977), pp. 143, 322–43; W. J. Eccles, *The Canadian Frontier: 1534–1760* (1969; reprint, Albuquerque, N. Mex., 1974), pp. 13–17.

3. Quinn, *North America*, pp. 240–321.

freshment station, Saint Augustine was a protection station, but each was an appendage and not an essential element in an overseas imperial system.

At Jamestown in 1607 and at Quebec in 1608, the English and French finally established their own permanent settlements in North America, not as way stations but as footholds for trade and exploitation. For different reasons, the survival of each colony depended more on the indulgence of local natives than on the imperialist plans of European nations.

MICRO-CONTEXT: SURVIVAL AND SEPARATION ON THE VIRGINIA FRONTIER

The approximately one hundred settlers at Jamestown established their coastal village in the midst of a somewhat centralized, quasi-feudal monarchy, a form of government which anthropologists consider "anomalous by American Indian standards."[4] Powhatan, the powerful leader of this local native empire, had inherited matrilineally only six of the thirty Algonkian-speaking communities that made up his domain. The expansion of his rule may be attributed to his personal charisma, political genius, and military success. Men of the Powhatan Empire were hunters, fishermen, and soldiers. Agriculture was women's work. War played a central role in both politics and culture. Women of the Algonkian communities could demand that war be waged for revenge, but the men might also wage war to control greater territory and extract tribute by conquest. In fact, the *weroances*, or chiefs, of each community along with their families were supported primarily from tribute. These weroances inherited their position matrilineally, but they surrounded themselves with counselors, or *cockarouses*, who were chosen from among leading families for their personal talents. To what extent the Powhatan Empire mirrored the local pattern of chiefs and counselors is unclear, as are the historic reasons for the empire's expansion on the eve of English settlement.[5]

What is clear is that Powhatan did not create the Powhatan "Confederacy," which may be attributed instead to Thomas Jefferson's democratic imagination. Powhatan ruled over a conquest state, which required of subject peoples homage, tribute, and occasionally relocation. Indeed, Powhatan's interest in consolidating his control over the Virginia coastal region, along with the challenge he faced from independent, inland polities, may well have led him to see the arrival of the English aliens as an op-

4. Christian F. Feest, "Powhatan: A Study in Political Organization," *Wiener Völkerkundliche Mitteilungen* 8 (1966):69.
5. Ibid., pp. 70–71, 75, 77–79; and Helen C. Rountree, "Change Came Slowly: The Case of the Powhatan Indians of Virginia," *Journal of Ethnic Studies* 3 (Fall 1975):1, 6–8.

portunity to establish a military/trade alliance. At first, this relationship seemed one-sided, because in the autumn of 1607 Powhatan supplied the food which saved the colonists from starvation. He also allowed his teenage daughter, Pocahontas, to become a kind of ambassador to the Jamestown colony by sending her to live there. The English responded in symbolic terms when the royal council of the Virginia Company instructed Captain Christopher Newport to undertake the coronation of Powhatan, complete with copper crown, red woolen robe, and English bedstead. Supposedly this event would make Powhatan a subject-king to James I of England. The Algonkian leader accepted these odd gifts in late 1608, but appears to have been oblivious to any English claims of sovereignty.[6]

In effective political terms such English claims were ludicrous. From 1607 to 1610, the settlement barely managed to survive until Captain John Smith reorganized most of the life of the colony, especially work details, along military lines. In part, Smith wanted to stop colonists from continuing to run off and live with the Indians. This new discipline stopped the runaways but did not grow more food, so Smith launched an aggressive policy of burning Indian fields and villages to extort food supplies. Powhatan soon cut off trade with Jamestown and forbade his emissary, Pocahontas, to visit the English settlement. He seemed determined to let the English colony starve to death without provoking a major war. This policy nearly succeeded. In the winter of 1609–10, the colonists were reduced to eating their own dead. By June, the remaining sixty survivors prepared to return to England. Only the arrival of 150 well-armed recruits prevented Jamestown's extinction. What followed for the next two years was the attempted military occupation of a region between the James and York rivers, primarily for the expropriation of the native corn crop. From 1610 to 1612 the English destroyed two Indian villages and displaced three small communities.

Powhatan also mounted attacks against the English, but the renewed strength of the colony may have convinced him that peace would be a wiser policy. Trade with the English in metal goods, especially tools, knives, and firearms, had increased Powhatan's own military power, for his empire appears to have expanded westward as he fought with the English on his eastern flank. To keep the English contained as a peaceful and important trade partner would be clever strategy for an expanding conquest state. In fact, the Powhatan Indians had given up many of their stone, wood, or bone weapons and tools for the metal European equivalents. They relied on the English for repair and replacement of these goods as well as for their supply of blue glass

---

6. Nancy Oestreich Lurie, "Indian Cultural Adjustment to European Civilization," in *Seventeenth-Century America: Essays in Colonial History*, ed. James M. Smith (Chapel Hill, N.C., 1959), pp. 39–44; Gary B. Nash, *Red, White, and Black: The Peoples of Early America* (Englewood Cliffs, N.J., 1974), pp. 55–57.

beads, which they considered analogous to their own shell-disc money. Possibly for these economic and political reasons, Powhatan agreed in 1614 to a resumption of peaceful relations. He underscored this policy when he permitted Pocahontas to marry the English widower, John Rolfe, that same year.[7]

Ironically, Rolfe became the indirect cause of the collapse of this peace. His experiments with West Indian tobacco created the cash crop which permitted Jamestown to succeed as an economic enterprise. This development secured a strong economic connection between England and Virginia which produced not only trade but immigration. The influx of new English settlers also created a demand for more land for tobacco cultivation. Furthermore, to encourage greater immigration, the Virginia Company ended the quasi-military organization which had characterized the colony since the days of John Smith. Virginia became a society dominated by tobacco planters, who greatly expanded the land base of the colony and brought on a nasty war.

Since 1607 the Powhatan Indians had not perceived the English as a threat to their domination of the area. They responded to the Jamestown settlement with generous friendship, attempted alliances, and sage peacemaking. Yet when the growth of the Virginia colony shifted the regional balance of power, the Powhatan Indians responded differently. In 1622, Opechancanough, the successor to the now deceased Powhatan, launched a well-organized, unified attack aimed toward driving the English from Virginia. Three hundred and forty-seven individuals, nearly one-third of the white population, died in this war, but the colony was not destroyed. In response, the English began a ruthless series of reprisals which devastated entire villages and increased the scale of slaughter. Conveniently, this uncompromising war brought more lands into the tobacco economy. In addition, a distinctly negative image of the Indian became evident in English accounts of the Virginia natives. They were depicted as vicious, lying savages who could be displaced without moral compunction. Indeed, when a peace treaty was negotiated in 1629, the colonial council rejected it and explained that a state of "perpetual enmity" would be of more benefit to the colony.[8]

Jamestown had passed beyond the issue of survival. Growth of population and increase of land holdings had become the dominant concerns. Pressed by such continuous expansion, the Powhatan Indians now faced their own crisis of survival. By 1644, whites outnumbered the Powhatan Indians, who for several decades had been reduced by warfare and the devastations of European diseases. Still, in that year the aged Opechancanough led a

7. Edmund S. Morgan, *American Slavery, American Freedom: The Ordeal of Colonial Virginia* (New York, 1975), pp. 73–79; Nash, *Red, White, and Black*, pp. 57–59; Lurie, "Indian Cultural Adjustment," pp. 47–48; and Rountree, "Change Came Slowly," pp. 1–2.

8. Morgan, *American Slavery, American Freedom*, pp. 90–101; Lurie, "Indian Cultural Adjustment," pp. 49–50; quotation from Nash, *Red, White, and Black*, p. 63.

final uprising. The English suffered more casualties than they had in 1622, but with 6,000 settlers now in the colony, the loss of approximately 500 lives did not have the same impact. No red or white allies seemed to have joined the Powhatan cause. Earlier efforts at conquest by the Powhatan Empire may explain why other Indian groups remained uninvolved. Perhaps for this reason, Opechancanough attempted to enlist the aid of the English colony of Maryland; but nothing happened. The Powhatan Indians stood alone and felt the full force of the Virginians' retaliation.

By 1646 the English colony was able to impose a formal peace, which established a line between red and white territory, extracted a yearly tribute in beaver skins, gave the colonial governor power of approval in the selection of Indian rulers, and required military assistance if the colony were attacked by other Indians. The Powhatan Indians had moved rapidly from a position of political equality to one of subservience, in which whites helped determine the formal native leaders. The days of the Powhatan Empire had ended. In addition, some historians believe that the treaty of 1646 marks the beginning of developments which would enforce cultural separation and eventually lead to the reservation system.[9] More significantly, the treaty of 1646 demonstrated that the tobacco economy of the southern Anglo-American colonies would not utilize Indian labor. Or, put in another light, the conflicts from 1607 to 1646 between the Powhatan Indians and the English settlers showed that the balance of political power might shift, but also that many Indians could resist absorption into white society.

Instead of Indian captives or African slaves, the labor force which *first* cultivated Virginia's tobacco consisted of white indentured servants from England itself. By the 1650s the frightening mortality which had plagued English settlers since 1607 had subsided, and many of these indentured laborers had begun to live out their terms of servitude and became freed men. They represented a new, unstable class of impoverished Englishmen who in their own way had also been victimized by the tobacco economy, as had the Powhatan Indians. Historian Edmund S. Morgan noted that by the 1660s,

> The new freedmen were multiplying in numbers every year, and, unable to afford land elsewhere, moved to the frontiers, where they viewed the Indians not as fellow victims but as rivals for the marginal lands to which both had been driven. They brought their cows and hogs with them; they brought their guns; and they brought a smoldering resentment, which they had been unable to take out on their betters. The Indians, they had been taught (if they needed teaching), were not their betters.[10]

9. See Lurie, "Indian Cultural Adjustment," p. 52, or Nash, *Red, White, and Black*, p. 65.
10. Morgan, *American Slavery, American Freedom*, p. 232.

By 1670 Virginia had grown large enough to create its own frontier and its own class of frontiersmen. These white squatters wanted to end the separation of Indian and white lands which the treaty of 1646 had supposedly established. They demanded that the Virginia government open up for white settlement the lands of the surviving Powhatan Indians which were north of the York River. Yet, the events that set off a civil war in Virginia did not occur along the York River but began along the Potomac River, well north of the territory inhabited by the Powhatan Indians. An attempt by Doeg Indians to take some hogs from a Virginia planter, possibly as repayment of a trade debt, ended in the death of ten of the Indians. Raids and counter-raids followed. The fighting soon escalated to include the formerly friendly Susquehannocks. When the Susquehannocks took their revenge on the Virginia frontiersmen, the frontiersmen struck out at former members of the Powhatan Empire who had not taken up arms but who had moved into lands that the Virginians coveted.

The reluctance of Virginia's governor, William Berkeley, to follow a firm course of action helped to expand the scope of the rebellion. The frontiersmen, whose first objective had been to annihilate the Indians, soon began to plunder not only the villages of their red victims but also the plantations of Berkeley's supporters. The unexpected death by disease of the rebellion's leader, Nathaniel Bacon, followed shortly by the arrival of armed vessels from England, soon ended this chaotic episode. The greatest losers in the rebellion were Virginia's Indians who, whether peaceful or belligerent, were indiscriminately attacked. The Indians had not formed an alliance to attack the frontiersmen, as some rumors claimed, but the frontiersmen had united to attack the Indians. As a result, Bacon's rebellion ended any claim to political separation and independence for the Indians within the borders of the Virginia colony. Many Indian survivors left the colony to be absorbed by other native communities. The survivors who remained behind had by 1700 only a few thousand acres of communally owned land in all of the Virginia colony. Some landless Indians of the colony tried to settle near their ancestral homelands, first as squatters and later as renters and owners, if possible. The men continued to hunt, fish, and gather wild foods on uncultivated lands. Eventually they would take up the women's work of agriculture. For the most part, these small, mixed remnant communities of the former Powhatan Empire remained isolated from other Indian societies, but they maintained an Indian identity down to the present day through their social separation into what one anthropologist calls "geographical enclaves."[11]

On the Virginia frontier neither unity nor disunity produced predictable

11. Ibid., pp. 250–69; Nash, *Red, White, and Black*, pp. 129–31; Lurie, "Indian Cultural Adjustment," pp. 55–60; and Rountree, "Change Came Slowly," pp. 6–7.

political results. For example, the Powhatan Indians had demonstrated great military unity in 1622 and 1644 but had lost. By 1676, the English were numerous and disunited but were still powerful enough to defeat diverse native groups. The eventual domination by the English in Virginia involved, in part, the application of European technology—but not in warfare so much as in transportation. Put another way, sailing ships more than clumsy, hand-loaded muskets were what determined English victory. The Powhatan Indians, their population often reduced by disease, could not match the growth of the English population through transoceanic migration. They also did not share the English view that conquest could mean annihilation as well as subjugation. The Powhatan Indians fought for revenge or to establish sources of tribute. They sought to control both people and their lands. The English sought to control the lands for settlement or cash-crop agriculture; people were expendable. The Indians' bows and arrows were probably as effective at killing as the early English guns, but the Powhatan Indians, even after their efforts in 1622 and 1644, seemed either unwilling or unable to carry out killings on the same scale as the English.[12]

In comparison to other frontiers of North America, the entire scale of conflict in Virginia was simple and nearly self-contained. Interaction between Virginians and Powhatan Indians centered on trade, warfare, and treaty making. Missionaries, for example, were not well established among the Indians and so played no role in improving or worsening relations. In addition, European international rivalries had not intruded on the Virginia frontier of the 1600s to affect the political relationships between Indians and whites. Indeed, beyond the efforts of the Powhatan Empire toward conquest, few intracultural political connections among the Algonkians and other native peoples had been of influence. The apparent simplicity of these political developments in colonial Virginia seem not unlike the situation around Cape Town beginning in 1652.

MACRO-CONTEXT: DEPENDENCE AND IMPERIALISM ON THE FRONTIERS OF NEW FRANCE

In contrast, developments on the frontiers of New France were not so simple. International, intercultural, and intracultural conflicts and alliances greatly influenced political developments. Unlike the English, who came to Jamestown with no clear commercial enterprise in mind, the French returned to the Saint Lawrence Valley after their initial contact in 1534 with a commitment to profit from the fur trade with the Indians. In 1608, Samuel

---

12. Rountree, "Change Came Slowly," p. 1, compares English firearms with Indian bows and arrows.

de Champlain established his base at the narrows of Quebec, 130 miles up-river from the center of the old summer coastal trade at Tadoussac. In its early years fewer than twenty men wintered at this fortified outpost, which boasted cannon, moat, and drawbridge.[13]

Champlain had good cause for concern about warfare. The Quebec region had become a "no-man's land" between native societies engaged in wars brought on, in large part, by economic motivations tied to the fur trade which had slowly developed since 1534. The acquisition of European metal goods (especially weapons) gave any native group a certain economic and military advantage over its neighbors. In addition, the Indians who were in direct contact with the European traders tried to assume the role of middle-men, which meant they took—sometimes by force, sometimes by trade—the furs trapped by other Indians. In effect, the activities of European traders, off the Atlantic coast or up the inland waterway of the Saint Lawrence, had set off a chain reaction of wars among Indians to control the new commerce.[14]

Warfare, on a small scale, was nothing new to the native Iroquoian peoples of the area. For them, warfare had long centered on the blood feud, which demanded counter-raids and formal revenge for any killings. To prevent the blood feud's deleterious impact, neighboring Iroquoian communities, perhaps as early as the mid-1400s, had begun to form larger confederacies. These larger polities existed primarily to prevent warfare among member communities. The Iroquoian confederacies were not powerful, centralized governments. For the membership of a central council, the women of each village chose the sachems, or chiefs, of traditional clans and leading families. These sachems were civil, not war, leaders. They met from time to time to administer the affairs of the confederacy, but their authority was limited, especially in the case of revenge or warfare against nonmembers of the confederacy. In fact, individual warriors remained free to carry out raids if others wished to follow them. Given such freedom of action, the sachems of the confederacy could establish few united policies. The separate villages of the confederacy, with their matrilineally determined clans and leading families, remained the most significant unit for active decision making. In effect, the foreign policy of each member village could differ greatly, and the blood feud could be carried on outside the confederacy. This individual initiative in external aggression increased greatly in frequency and scale once war became a way to control trade as well as a way to gain revenge.[15]

At the time of the first French settlement, the two major Iroquoian con-

13. Eccles, The Canadian Frontier, p. 23.

14. Bruce G. Trigger, The Children of Aataentsic: A History of the Huron People to 1660 (Montreal, 1976), 1:214–24.

15. Ibid., 1:156–63.

federacies were located to the southwest of Quebec. The Huron confederacy consisted of four agricultural polities which may have numbered as many as thirty-five thousand people. They were densely settled in villages of as many as two thousand in a small region northwest of Lake Ontario, between Georgian Bay and Lake Simcoe. The other major confederacy, the Five Nations of the Iroquois (often called simply the Iroquois), consisted of no more than fifteen thousand people on extensive ancestral homelands southeast of Lake Ontario. Both Iroquoian confederacies relied on the agricultural production of corn, beans, pumpkins, and melons raised by the women of the villages. Women also fished, and the men carried on hunting, raiding, and trade. The Hurons and the Iroquois already had a tradition of animosity, no doubt due to the operations of the blood feud between the two confederacies. The Hurons, in addition, had established an effective alliance in the fur trade with their Algonkian neighbors to the north. The Algonkians and Hurons, in turn, functioned as middlemen for other Indians farther north and west, who exchanged their furs for the French goods controlled by these two native peoples.

Champlain soon realized that cooperation between the Huron Confederacy and his traders at Quebec would be necessary to insure commercial success. Since the French presence in North America was always small in number, such dependence on powerful native trading partners became standard practice. Over the next century and a half, as the French expanded their commercial empire westward and down the Mississippi Valley, the role of middlemen was taken up by other Indians, such as the Ottawas, the Miamis, and the Illinois. These native partners not only acquired furs by their own use of trade, raid, or trapping, but they also helped distribute French textiles, metal goods, and weapons.

Yet this mutual dependence readily progressed beyond trade to a *military* relationship which involved the French and their native partners in each other's wars. For example, in the summer of 1609 sixty Hurons and Algonkians asked the French to aid them in an attack against the Mohawks of the Iroquois Confederacy. Champlain and two companions accompanied these raiders and used their harquebuses in a skirmish with some two hundred Mohawks. The Iroquois warriors had never been exposed to European firearms, so they soon fled the field of battle. But firearms were not always so effective. In October of 1615, Champlain and twelve French volunteers joined a Huron raid against the fortified village of another polity of the Iroquois Confederacy, the Onondagas. The French firearms had little impact on the thick log palisades of the Iroquois defenders, and the Hurons, after suffering several losses, withdrew to their homelands.[16]

16. Eccles, *The Canadian Frontier*, pp. 24–31.

Within a few years, the Dutch established their own trading post on the Hudson River at Albany. The Iroquois Confederacy, which had been at a disadvantage against the Hurons in trade and warfare, could now function as middlemen for another European power. Soon they acquired their own muskets. Yet, the effectiveness of such firearms as superior killing weapons was questionable. The accurate but slowly hand-loaded rifle did not become common in the American colonies until the early 1700s. Even when repeating handguns and rifles appeared in the mid-1800s, the Indian bow with steel-tipped arrows still proved to be a formidable killing weapon.[17] Nonetheless, American Indians from the earliest days of trade sought European firearms. Their appeal may have initially been attributable to the terror which the guns' noise and flash induced. Arrows could be shot more quickly and quietly, but muskets, and later rifles, did have a power and range which bows could not match. So these firearms may have given the native user a greater impression of personal strength, which in turn may have psychologically supported an increased scale of warfare. Whatever the case, the expanded warfare between the two Iroquoian confederacies culminated with the fall of the Hurons to a massive Iroquois invasion.

In the autumn of 1648, the Iroquois, mainly Senecas and Mohawks, organized a large expedition of nearly a thousand warriors who wintered without detection in small groups in the forests north of Lake Ontario. In mid-March the warriors struck, captured a Huron village, made it their fortified camp, and began a campaign of terror. Already gripped by famine after a poor harvest and hard winter, and with the enemy in their midst, the Hurons burned their villages and fled. Their confederacy was ended.

Unwittingly, the French had aided the Huron's demise because of the policies of Jesuit missionaries who first appeared among the Huron in 1634. To encourage Hurons to convert to Christianity, the Jesuits had insisted that only Christian Hurons be supplied guns, and even then in small numbers. This policy also helped to assure the safety of the Jesuits, who lived among the Hurons; but it did not insure the safety of the Hurons, whose old adversary, the Iroquois, had no meddling missionaries to limit their supply of arms. Beyond this problem, the issue of conversion had created factional divisions between traditionalists and Christians. In addition, many more Hurons traveled away from their villages to participate in the fur trade than did the Iroquois. So the commercial and religious activities of the French produced negative political/military results among the Hurons, who in comparison to the Iroquois were divided, underarmed, and undermanned.[18]

17. Thomas L. Hall, see "guns," in *The Reader's Encyclopedia of the American West,* Howard R. Lamar, ed. (New York, 1977), p. 476.
18. Trigger, *Children of Aataentsic,* 2:762–67, 849–50.

The Iroquois attack in March of 1649 showed how the small-scale vengeance raids of the blood-feud era had given way to large-scale wars of conquest resulting from the competition for European trade and weapons. After the fall of the Hurons, the Iroquois continued to pursue an aggressive foreign policy against other Indians with the aim of making their confederacy the dominant middleman of the fur trade. By the 1690s, the Iroquois had been in conflict with the Ottawas and the Illinois to the west, the Susquehannas of the Delaware Valley to the south, and a host of intermediate and more distant peoples. Even some French settlements in the Saint Lawrence Valley had come under attack. These belligerent activities took their toll of Iroquois warriors, but the cultural tradition of adopting defeated opponents helped replace some of the losses. Many of these raids did not come at the direction of Iroquois sachems. Small parties could act out of the personal motivation of their members, regardless of the confederacy's concerns. Yet these independent actions still increased the influence the Iroquois wielded through terror.[19]

In regard to the European powers, the Iroquois had entered a three-sided pattern of competition and dependence among themselves, the French (centered at Montreal since the 1640s), and the English (who had replaced the Dutch at Albany with their conquest of New Netherland in 1664). All three powers, because of their desire to control the supply of beaver, created a new commercial/military frontier among the western Indians in the Ohio River valley, the Illinois country, and areas beyond the Great Lakes. For the Iroquois, control meant the acquisition of new hunting lands as well as raid or trade with other Indians who had trapped the beavers. They sought to dominate the western Indians through native military power. The French, on the other hand, sought to gain influence among the western Indians through economic and military alliances. Gifts rather than raids characterized the French effort. Beyond a few settlements, predominately in the Saint Lawrence Valley, the French only "occupied" the western lands with trading posts, missions, or the yearly expeditions of the *coureurs de bois*. They needed the friendship of the indigenous residents; the Iroquois did not.

Indeed, the French saw the belligerency of the Iroquois as an aid to their own efforts. Not only did Iroquois terrorism help create many native allies for the French, but the Iroquois also served as a barrier between the western Indians and the English merchants at Albany. On the other side of this barrier, the English of the New York colony saw their own commercial success as tied to that of the Iroquois. Beyond trade, the English viewed the Iroquois as the crucial element in political relations with other Indians. Beginning

19. Allen W. Trelease, "The Iroquois and the Western Fur Trade: A Problem in Interpretation," *Mississippi Valley Historical Review* 44 (June 1962): 32–51.

with the administration of Edmund Andros in the 1670s, the colonial governors in New York and later in Pennsylvania tried to certify Iroquois dominance over other Indian polities through the establishment of a series of
treaties called the "covenant chain." These treaties continued into the
1740s and attempted to formalize the tributary status of various native polities who, for the most part, had already been subjugated by the Iroquois.
Apparently the Iroquois welcomed this recognition of themselves as a superior power in the colonial treaties, but the so-called tributaries seemed to
have viewed the covenant chain as an interrelated system of alliances with
both the Iroquois and the colonial governments.[20]

This elaborate English effort to turn the Iroquois into unwitting surrogates through the establishment of the covenant chain had only mixed results because the fact remained that the Iroquois could act independently.
Most significantly, in the North American theatre of the imperial wars between France and England that occurred from 1688 to 1763, the Iroquois
chose to remain neutral from 1701 to 1759. They had been disappointed by
the lack of English support in their invasion of the French settlements during King William's War of 1689–97, and were greatly distressed when the
English sent no military aid after the French and their allies retaliated
against Iroquois villages. Only when the conquest of New France seemed
imminent, in the midst of the Seven Years' War, did the Iroquois end their
neutrality. In the interim, independent elements of the distinct Iroquois polities had fought on occasion with one European power or the other, but the
full military force of the confederacy had not come into play for nearly sixty
years.[21]

During this period when the English were deprived of Iroquois support,
the French held a military advantage through the use of their allies. Indeed,
the imperial policies of New France had transformed the frontier of trade
among the western Indians into a frontier of military alliances. This process
began in the 1680s, when small military garrisons were sent out to man the
trading posts of the western regions. In effect, military officers replaced
frontier merchants, and the interconnections of the fur trade took on a military dimension. No doubt selected native partners now had a readier supply
of firearms than before, but most significantly, the military control of the
frontier posts opened a new line of communication within the French Empire. As Canadian historian W. J. Eccles recognized, "Orders could be sent
from Versailles to a military trading post in the heart of the continent, four
thousand miles away, and when these orders did not run counter to the pri-

20. Eccles, *The Canadian Frontier*, pp. 7, 31–32, 103; Francis Jennings, "The Constitutional Evolution of the Covenant Chain," *Proceedings of the American Philosophical Society*
115 (1971): 88–96.
21. Nash, *Red, White, and Black*, pp. 245–48, 265–68.

vate interests of the commandants, or were too imperative to be ignored, they were obeyed. The writ of the King of France now extended much more firmly over half the continent. . . ."[22]

During the years of the Anglo-French wars, the French in North America could rely on their network of military posts and Indian alliances to launch attacks against the English, who by 1750 had 1,250,000 settlers in thirteen colonies along the Atlantic seaboard. This large English population had displaced the predominately Algonkian coastal peoples, from present-day Maine south to Georgia, in ways which the fate of the Powhatan Indians of Virginia exemplified. Beyond the Appalachian mountains to the north and west of these English settlements, the French area of influence stretched from the Saint Lawrence River across the Great Lakes and down the Mississippi River to the port of New Orleans. By 1750, the French had only some 60,000 settlers in this entire region.

Geographically as well as politically, four major Indian confederacies were in the middle between the French and English. These confederacies were the Iroquois near the Great Lakes and the somewhat differently organized polities of the Cherokees, Creeks, and Choctaws in the southeastern region. Both the British and the French had some success in establishing trade with elements of each confederacy but, as with the Iroquois, these confederacies gave only limited military support to either European power and so remained effectively neutral. Up until the final stages of the Seven Years' War, these four large confederacies held the balance of power in the North American theatre of the Anglo-French conflict. The English would have preferred to see these confederacies serve as a shield on the western peripheries of the Atlantic colonies, because the French and their Indian allies often attacked across this neutral zone with hit-and-run raids.[23]

This style of combat showed how French imperial policy had adapted to the particular circumstances of the North American frontier. Some French missionaries might desire assimilation of the natives, but the French Empire had incorporated native societies through a system of economic/military alliances which did not necessitate either cultural absorption or armed conquest. Subsequently, although the French were far less numerous than the British, they had many native allies who fought as an effectively mobile, mixed force. The English, on the other hand, had tried to incorporate Indian lands more than they had tried to enlist Indian aid. In time of war, therefore, they could not turn to large numbers of native allies within their zone of conquest and settlement. The four largest native polities on the periphery of the English settlements could not be persuaded by increased trade or lavish

22. Eccles, *The Canadian Frontier*, p. 116.
23. Nash, *Red, White, and Black*, pp. 265–75.

gifts to side with the British colonies, so these colonies had to rely on support from the metropole to resolve the Anglo-French wars. Imperial power, not political adaptations in North America, proved to be the colonies' greatest ally. In the Seven Years' War, William Pitt's policy of massive economic and military aid turned the tide of battle in North America and led to the conquest of New France.

The end of the French Empire in North America, certified by the Treaty of Paris in 1763, removed an important alternative in intercultural politics. With the minor exception of the Spanish in Florida and in previously French Louisiana, one European power now laid claim to all the lands of the cis-Mississippi. For native peoples this change was monumental. No longer could confederacies such as the Iroquois or Cherokees remain neutral and play the French off against the English. In addition, the mutual dependence which characterized the French imperial system beyond this neutral zone was transformed by the British and later the Americans. Quite simply, the French, because of their small numbers of settlers, had needed Indian allies to carry on the fur trade and to attain military control of their vast North American empire. For the French, the frontier was their empire. For the British (and later on the United States), the frontier was the area into which their empire must expand. In this Anglo-American context, Indians served as military allies or trade partners in an interim relationship on the periphery of an expanding zone of settlement. Ultimately, the British and Americans did not need the Indians because their empire could survive on European immigration. These Euro-Americans could trap their own beaver and fight their own wars. Indeed, they were numerous enough to fight among themselves and create a new nation. In macro-context, the balance of power on the frontier shifted in 1763. Once more, as in 1521, a broad frontier of survival opened, but in this case the political question was Indian, not European, survival.

RESOLUTION: THE FRONTIER OF NATIONAL EXPANSION

Along the western Great Lakes region and through the Ohio River valley, the Indians seemed well aware of the shift in the balance of power in 1763. Lord Jeffrey Amherst, a victorious commander in the Seven Years' War, established an austere policy toward the former native allies of the French. After British forces took over the French forts of the region, Amherst reduced appropriations for trade and ended the practice of issuing gifts to native leaders. Former trading partners of the French, such as the Ottawas, Potawatomis, and Ojibwas, soon launched a nearly spontaneous uprising. The best planned attacks came in May of 1763 against Fort Detroit and were directed by Pontiac, an Ottawa warrior. Other native peoples such as the Shawnees and Delawares joined in the rebellion, which saw numerous British forts either fall to the Indians or, like Fort Detroit, come under extended siege. By July, the British had lost control of their newly acquired territory north and west of the Appalachian Mountains. Amherst had to send in two expeditions of regular British troops to put down this native resistance. These campaigns were eventually successful, although Pontiac and his followers did not accept peace terms until May of 1765.[24]

This fierce native resistance to the British, which many historians call Pontiac's Rebellion, had its origins not only in the collapse of the old French-Indian alliances but also in the general disruption of Indian life on the frontier. Besides the example of Pontiac's siege of Fort Detroit, a messianic figure, the Delaware Prophet, had helped fan the flames of warfare. This religious leader talked of the loss of the old ways of life and how the Indians of the region, as revealed to the prophet by the Creator, could regain their pristine early life if they drove the white men out of their country. The Delaware Prophet had begun his preachings about 1762, and many native groups of the Great Lakes and Ohio region, including Pontiac and his followers, accepted his message. Pontiac's Rebellion, therefore, demonstrated Indian resistance in both political and cultural terms. Yet, this resistance was pan-Indian only in the way that such events as the Ghost Dance of the 1890s on the Great Plains were pan-Indian. An organized, political conspiracy had not occurred; but a generalized spirit of opposition did exist.[25]

As a response to Pontiac's Rebellion and in an effort to prevent further costly Indian wars, officials in London established the Proclamation of 1763. This latter action initiated an attempt to provide an orderly administration of the frontier, controlled from the metropole. The Proclamation of 1763 plus the Plan of 1764 prohibited settlement and speculation and restricted trade within the trans-Appalachian region. Settlers had to return to the East; private speculators could not purchase land from the Indians; and traders now needed licenses to do business with the Indians and were forbidden to deal in rum and rifles. For the management of Indian affairs in the region, two superintendencies were established, divided by the Ohio River into northern and southern. The two superintendents had the responsibility of negotiating treaties which would establish a clear line separating the lands of white settlers and Indian communities.

Although this policy at first had the temporary result of changing the trans-Appalachian region of the cis-Mississippi into an Indian reserve, the

---

24. Thomas D. Clark, see "Pontiac's Rebellion" in *The Reader's Encyclopedia of the American West*, p. 948.

25. Anthony F. C. Wallace, *The Death and Rebirth of the Seneca* (New York, 1969), pp. 115–21.

line of separation worked no better in this macro-context than it had in the micro-context of Virginia in 1646. Land speculators from Pennsylvania and Virginia pushed for the renegotiation of treaty agreements and succeeded in having a vast area between the Tennessee and Ohio rivers reopened for white settlement—and personal profit.[26]

Once it gained its independence in 1783, the United States government also claimed control over the trans-Appalachian and all subsequent frontiers. Yet, as with the British after 1763, the United States also accepted, almost without question, expansion of white settlement. The U.S. Ordinances of 1785 and 1787 erected a framework for the survey and governance of politically unorganized territories which permitted their eventual recognition as member states in the Union, once enough settlers had arrived. Significantly, the federal government of the United States reserved for itself the power to make treaties, as had the British imperial government in 1763. Through this treaty power, first the British and then the United States government attempted to remove Indians peacefully from the zone of white settlement.

In 1763, it appeared that the British might permit a large section of the trans-Appalachian frontier to be reserved for Indians. In this case, the boundary lines were soon renegotiated and the Indian territory reduced. A similar fate awaited the various reserves established by the treaties of the United States. Any conjecture that the loss of native lands would have been abated by the continuation of British imperial rule neglects the compromises soon imposed on the Proclamation of 1763 and the Plan of 1764. These compromises indicated that the metropole could not control white expansion on the frontier. Within a decade, additional events showed that the metropole could not even control its own colonies.

The full resolution of Anglo-American independence from Great Britain required two major wars over a forty-year period from 1775 to 1815. From the American Revolution through the War of 1812, the major Indian polities of the cis-Mississippi also saw the issue of their own independence largely resolved. Continued disunity within each polity, as well as among the different polities, often contributed to the final result. The fate of the Six Nations of the Iroquois (who had added the Tuscaroras in 1722) exemplified this process. The political organization of the Iroquois Confederacy had never included full control over the warfare of the individual "nations." The overall neutrality of the Six Nations from 1701 to 1759 had not prevented some Senecas from joining in French raids and some Mohawks from siding with the British. In the war of the American Revolution, the sachems of the Iroquois Confederacy announced at Albany in August of 1775 that the Six

26. Frederick Merk, *History of the Westward Movement* (New York, 1978), pp. 67–71.

Nations would remain neutral, but by 1777 British agents had enticed the Senecas with gifts and feasts to join in the war. Soon Joseph Brant and many of his fellow Mohawks also fought openly alongside the British. In response, the Continental Congress sent out agents who convinced some Oneidas and Tuscaroras to cooperate with the rebel forces.

By far the greater number of Iroquois fought with the British. Throughout the rest of the war one thousand Iroquois raiders and five hundred Tory rangers devastated the frontier belt of settlements from northern New York to the Ohio Valley. These forces were never effectively defeated, but they did pay a high price for their success. In the fall of 1779, American troops under General John Sullivan destroyed the villages and fields of the pro-British Iroquois. The next year, in retaliation, the British launched attacks against the villages of the pro-American Iroquois.[27]

One unified alliance with either side in the American Revolution might have prevented the two invasions of the Iroquois lands. But instead the Iroquois polities fought on either side, and so sometimes they fought each other. As the American colonies broke from Great Britain to form their own confederacy, the old Iroquoian confederacy of the Six Nations simply broke apart. Within thirteen years after the end of the war, those Iroquois who had not fled to reserves in British Canada remained on small reservations in New York State. The fact that this rapid loss of land occurred through negotiation, not conquest, revealed how weakened the Iroquois were after the American Revolution.

The first and perhaps the largest of these negotiated cessions took place in 1784 at Fort Stanwix in New York, where the Iroquois gave up by treaty large tracts of western lands, especially in the Ohio River valley. In native terms, the Iroquois had not dominated this area nor prevented white intrusion since the days of the trade wars. Their cession of these lands had as little realpolitik as the American claim by right of conquest to all lands east of the Mississippi. With the Iroquois now in collapse and unable to offer protection, the native peoples of the Ohio region soon organized their own resistance to American hegemony. These people created an informal confederacy, composed of Shawnees, Miamis, Ottawas, and others, which raided white squatter settlements. The English, despite the 1783 Treaty of Paris, still held nine forts in the Old Northwest and supplied some arms to the Indians.[28]

The same disruption and displacement of traditional Indian ways which had fueled Pontiac's Rebellion in 1763 may explain these uprisings in the

---

27. Washburn, *The Indian in America*, pp. 148–50; and Wallace, *Death and Rebirth of the Seneca*, pp. 127–48.

28. Washburn, *The Indian in America*, pp. 157–63.

Ohio region of the Northwest Territory. Instead of a formal alliance among established polities, this Indian confederacy may have resembled a loose aggregation of remnant bands and displaced villages with different cultural backgrounds. In this respect, the membership of this informal confederacy may bear some resemblance to the Griquas of southern Africa. Whatever the case, in 1790 and 1791, the new federal government of the United States, which had replaced the short-lived American confederacy, responded with two major military expeditions into the area. Both failed. A third effort in 1794 produced victory at Fallen Timbers and a treaty of peace. But this was not the end of native resistance in the Old Northwest.

After the turn of the century, a larger-scale political and religious organization began to coalesce around the Shawnee brothers Tecumseh and Tenskwatawa. The latter was known as the Shawnee Prophet, and his religious message that white ways be rejected and old ways reestablished, as much as Tecumseh's dream of a grand Indian alliance, explained the success of their efforts. Diverse native groups of trans-Appalachia either visited the Prophet at his settlement on the Tippecanoe River in the Indiana Territory or were visited themselves by the charismatic Tecumseh. As a political strategy, Tecumseh wished to avoid war with the United States until his plan for pan-Indian resistance gained more strength. In general, native peoples of his own region, perhaps because of the disruption of their traditional lifestyles, accepted Tecumseh's concepts, whereas those in other regions, particularly members of still well-established polities, were less receptive. For example, Pushmataha, a major leader of one faction of the Choctaws in Mississippi, openly and successfully opposed Tecumseh's plan because it threatened his own prestige, which was based on conciliation toward the whites.

In 1811, Governor William Henry Harrison of the Indiana Territory forced the issue of war with his advance against Tenskwatawa's settlement, Prophet's Town. Tecumseh was absent on a journey to the south, but Tenskwatawa had remained behind. Harrison managed to provoke a battle and then burned the village. Enraged by the start of a war he had sought to delay, Tecumseh broke with his brother but carried on with the fighting. Their attempt at pan-Indian unity across different regions collapsed in the aftermath of the battle of Tippecanoe.[29] At no other time in the frontier context of the United States would the opportunity for the construction of a pan-Indian confederacy to halt white expansion seem so bright. Yet, if two Indian brothers could not remain united, how could culturally diverse polities and remnant groups? At most, native alliances remained a factor of cultural tradi-

29. P. Richard Metcalf, articles on "Pushmataha," "Tecumseh," and "Tenskwatawa," in *The Reader's Encyclopedia of the American West*, pp. 987–88, 1162–63, 1165–66.

tion and compatibility within one region. Such had been the case among the earlier Iroquoian confederacies, and such was the case with Tecumseh and Tenskwatawa's alliances in the Old Northwest.

The remnant of Tecumseh and his followers became British allies during the War of 1812. The Shawnee chief died early in the hostilities at the Battle of the Thames, an end symbolic of the fate of other American Indians during that war. Indeed, it may be said that the United States fought two wars from 1812 to 1815, one against the British and one against the Indians. The war against the British did not go well, and the United States was lucky not to lose any territory to an invasion down from Canada or up the Mississippi. The war against the Indians went much better, in part because the Indians again demonstrated little unity even within their own polities.

The major campaign of the "Indian War" involved Andrew Jackson and the Tennessee Volunteers in what had begun as a civil war among the Creeks. The belligerent, traditionalist Red Sticks held strong views against white incursion but had exerted their wrath on the acculturated faction of their own village-based, Creek confederacy, who were often called "progressives." In August of 1813, the Red Sticks attacked Fort Mims on the lower Alabama River, where some progressives had sought refuge. In the ensuing massacre, a thousand Red Stick warriors killed over five hundred people, the majority of them white settlers. Jackson now had a reason to march his volunteers into Creek territory. Progressive Creeks joined the Tennessee forces along with like-minded Cherokees and Choctaws. These last two confederacies also had traditionalist factions but had not lapsed into civil war. With his native allies, Jackson nearly annihilated the Red Sticks at the battle of Horseshoe Bend in March of 1814. Yet in the aftermath of this victory, Jackson dictated a treaty of massive land cessions which did not distinguish between his Creek allies and his Creek opponents. The treaty did benefit his white friends, land speculators and cotton planters who had cast a covetous eye on the Creeks' territory.[30]

Jackson's campaign against the Creeks had little direct connection with the United States' war against Great Britain, for the Creeks were not allied with the British. Nonetheless, other Indian groups such as Tecumseh and his Shawnees did join with British forces in what proved to be the last major war in which American Indians could side with a foreign power. Whether allied or not, the Indians of the cis-Mississippi experienced the same consequences. At the Treaty of Ghent, which produced an armistice in the Anglo-American War, the British did not establish any special provisions for the recognition of an "Indian barrier state," despite promises they had made

30. Michael Paul Rogin, *Fathers and Children: Andrew Jackson and the Subjugation of the American Indian* (New York, 1975), pp. 145–59.

to their red allies. As a result, in the words of historian William T. Hagan, "From 1815 on, the red man had to deal strictly on American terms."[31]

Before the War of 1812, Indians inhabited and to some extent controlled much of the state of Georgia and nearly all of what was to become Alabama and Mississippi. Also large sections of western Tennessee and Kentucky, northwestern Ohio, and most of what remained of the Old Northwest could be called Indian land. By 1840, with the exception of a few small enclaves, none of this land could be labeled Indian. In less than three decades, the United States government had removed American Indians from the cis-Mississippi as a political, though not a social, presence. Some groups managed to stay behind on official reservations, such as the Senecas in New York, or as outlaw, unlanded remnants, as was the case with some traditionalist Seminoles in the swamps of Florida, Cherokees in the mountains of North Carolina, and Choctaws in the scrublands of Mississippi. Nonetheless, the overwhelming majority of native peoples had either been removed to the trans-Mississippi or had died in the process of moving.

Astoundingly, this mass exodus was predominately peaceful. Armed resistance occurred among the Seminoles in Florida, with limited success, and among a small faction of the Sauk and Fox Indians of Illinois, with no success. The major Indian challenge to the policy of removal came within the legal system of the United States, a fact which demonstrated that native independence had nearly lapsed. The often mixed-blood "progressive" faction of the Cherokees, many of whom had established farms and schools and had converted to Christianity, helped initiate two cases that came before the federal Supreme Court in 1831 and 1832. These suits produced a strong restatement of federal, not state, control of Indian affairs. The Cherokees and all Indian polities were defined by the court as "domestic dependent nations" who, according to the opinion of the chief justice, "occupy a territory to which we assert a title independent of their will, which must take effect in point of possession when their right of possession ceases. Meanwhile they are in a state of pupilage. Their relation to the United States resembles that of a ward to his guardian."[32]

The Cherokees' suits had sought to block the actions of the state of Georgia, which had passed laws to terminate Cherokee jurisdiction over Cherokee lands within the state boundaries. In effect, the Supreme Court announced that the state of Georgia could not carry out actions which would bring on the removal of the Cherokees; only the federal government could legally act against the Cherokees. The new president of the United

31. William T. Hagan, *American Indians* (Chicago, 1961), p. 65.
32. Quotation of Chief Justice John Marshall from Ronald N. Satz, *American Indian Policy in the Jacksonian Era* (Lincoln, Neb., 1975), p. 45.

States, Andrew Jackson, heartily endorsed the policy of removal, but he did not endorse, or even enforce, the Supreme Court decisions. Jackson was happy to see the Indians removed by any and all levels of white government. Under such pressure, a faction of the Cherokees signed a *federal* treaty at New Echota in 1835, and the question of jurisdiction over removal became moot.

Andrew Jackson was no friend of the Indians. Jackson's views on Indian affairs had evolved during his boyhood in the backcountry Waxhaw settlement of South Carolina and during his formative adult years in the frontier community of Nashville, Tennessee. Although they acted within different historical settings, Andrew Jackson and Nathaniel Bacon could easily have found agreement on topics such as the corruption of established wealth, the rights of common settlers, and the "proper" fate of the Indians. Of course, Nathaniel Bacon failed to bring his frontier-fermented ideas to a position of power in colonial Virginia, whereas Andrew Jackson had become president of the United States.

To confront Jackson, the Indians needed their own white friends, and indeed, missionaries and other philanthropic characters recognized the red man's plight. These "friends" often came from areas well removed from the frontier, such as New England, but they believed the future of the Indian to be assimilation within white society, not independence from it. Some of these philanthropists supported the Cherokee lawsuits in order to stop removal, but others advocated removal because it would place Indians beyond the negative influence of white settlers who were not appropriate models for assimilation.[33]

Once Indians needed philanthropic friends instead of military allies, the era of political equilibrium on the cis-Mississippi frontier had closed. White hegemony could be assumed, and the important question for Indians became the nature of that control. Would white policies be beneficial or detrimental, and at what risk could they be ignored? The way in which members of native societies answered these questions created numerous factions over an ideological range extending from obstinate traditionalism to pliant accommodation. In many cases these internal factions may have merely amplified earlier, prefrontier divisions of clan and kin. In the past, traditional divisions had often helped to determine who would be the religious and political leaders in many native societies. Now clans and families may have become yet another source of continued disunity.[34] Whatever the case,

33. Bernard W. Sheehan, *Seeds of Extinction: Jeffersonian Philanthropy and the American Indian* (Chapel Hill, N.C., 1973), pp. 265–79.

34. The study of factions among American Indians is a new emphasis in scholarship influenced by the research and speculations of Robert F. Berkhofer, Jr. See his article, "The Political

native politics had begun to function within an enclave created by the con-trolling power of the federal government. The removal policy created the first major enclave across the Mississippi in the so-called Indian Territory, and more enclaves followed during the closing of the trans-Mississippi frontier.

This western frontier of the United States closed politically in less than a century, whereas the cis-Mississippi frontier had remained open for nearly three centuries. To some extent a more rapid denouement occurred in the trans-Mississippi because of the diversity of native alliances and enmities which prevented any unified resistance, and because of the astounding flood of white settlers who came west primarily to mine, raise cattle, or farm. Yet the federal government of the United States played perhaps the most signifi-cant role in the closing of the trans-Mississippi frontier, because of its pro-gram of political domination developed to close the cis-Mississippi frontier. As had been the case for removal, the federal government used military ag-gression and treaty cessions to enclave Indians. In political terms, enclave-ment meant that the federal government, not the native polity, set the boundaries of the native area of residence. The purpose of this enclavement centered either on removing Indians from the path of white migration and settlement, or on freeing Indian lands for white exploitation, which usually meant mining, farming, or railroad development. In effect, the government often anticipated white demands for more land.[35]

Yet government domination in the trans-Mississippi did not progress in an unbroken string of successes. Treaties were ignored or misinterpreted by both parties, and the United States Army was often undermanned. Many native peoples, such as the Teton Sioux of the Northern Plains, resisted en-clavement because it would disrupt their wide-ranging lifestyle, which for them included buffalo-hunting and horse-raiding. In addition, the Teton Sioux and some other native societies, such as the Mescalero Apaches, proved extremely difficult to subjugate because their political organization reached no higher than the level of the band, so that no single battle or treaty could produce submission of all members of the society. The Teton Sioux, in effect, presented a *disunified* resistance. Still, in the aftermath of the discovery of gold in the Sioux lands of the Black Hills and with the loss

Context of a New Indian History," *Pacific Historical Review* 40 (August 1971):357–82. Native factions remain a topic more easily discussed than researched.

35. John D. Unruh, Jr., has found that both the federal government and the Indians could be supportive, indulgent friends to migrants crossing the trans-Mississippi region to settle in Oregon and California. This revelation shows how much the government sustained settlement of the West and also demonstrates that the Indians often failed to perceive emigrants crossing their lands as a threat. See Unruh, *The Plains Across: The Overland Emigrants and the Trans-Mississippi West, 1840–1860* (Urbana, Ill., 1979), pp. 156–243, passim.

of General Custer and his command at the Battle of the Little Big Horn, the federal government had to respond in force. A massive military campaign in the winter of 1876–77 was launched against the scattered Teton Sioux bands and compelled either surrender or flight into Canada.[36]

By the time of this government victory on the Northern Plains, enclavement had spawned a policy which insisted that native peoples stay on their assigned reservations and assume white ways. Yet, whatever the policy on the reservation, the act of enclavement meant that the Teton Sioux, like other American Indians, had lost the independent control of their place of residence. Whether or not they were located on ancestral homelands, these residences—these "reservations"—were determined and maintained, not by the political organization and cultural traditions of the native peoples, but by the legal, legislative, and financial indulgences of the United States' government. At any time legislation, or the lack of it, could curtail services to the reservation. In the 1880s, with the loss of the buffalo, such services included necessary food supplies. Congress could even attempt to close down reservations entirely, as occurred in the 1950s for the Wisconsin Menominees. For American Indians, such government actions were a challenge to social and cultural survival, not to political independence. Only legal precedent, based on written treaties, and popular opinion, based on romantic stereotypes, today prevent the Congress or the president from terminating more reservations. Such is the contemporary realpolitik for many native Americans. For them, enclavement has produced a nearly powerless situation.

When English settlers first arrived at Jamestown and French traders first came to Quebec, these Europeans were also in a nearly powerless situation. They survived because of the indulgences of native neighbors, often in the form of trade. After this frontier of survival passed, conflicts and confrontations emerged, but so did patterns of alliances—some of them cross-cultural, some of them traditional. A zone of English settlement was established along the Atlantic coastal region. New France became a frontier empire based on trade and alliances with native peoples. Then, in 1763, the balance of imperial power shifted, and in broad terms, native survival became the issue. American Indians now needed alliances among a wider range of native polities, but such pan-Indian, interregional connections did not evolve. Instead, disunity continued to characterize the native political response. Meanwhile, the federal government of the United States had begun to take a firmer role in the frontier of national expansion. Ultimately, despite various forms of resistance, American Indians found themselves ei-

36. Robert M. Utley, *The Last Days of the Sioux Nation* (New Haven, Conn., 1963), pp. 6–19.

ther enclaved on reservations or ignored as unlanded, marginal peoples. The survival of American Indians now lay with the friendly indulgences of philanthropic individuals and the federal government. This reversal in the positions of power since 1607 leaves open the question of whether the relationship between white Americans and red Indians will continue to evolve into total rejection of Indians by whites, thus marking the complete transposition of the roles that existed in 1521 with the failure of the earliest European settlement on the cis-Mississippi frontier.

6

CHRISTOPHER SAUNDERS

Political Processes in the Southern African Frontier Zones

We should imagine a hundred frontiers, not one, some political, some economic, and some cultural.

—Fernand Braudel, *The Mediterranean and the Mediterranean World in the Age of Philip II*

I

In the past, most historians of the American and southern African frontiers have either ignored the indigenous peoples or treated them as obstacles to the forces of "progress," represented by the advancing white frontiersmen. Now, however, we recognize that frontiers have two sides. As William Christie Macleod pointed out over fifty years ago, "To understand fully why one side advances, we must know something of why the other side retreats."[1] Accordingly, the frontier, here conceptualized as a zone of settlement and colonization in which there were competing sources of power and authority,[2] must be seen from both sides—and so from no "side" at all.

Even when that point is grasped, it is still easy to assume that there was

For helpful criticism I would like to thank John Hopper, Margaret Kinsman, Jeffrey Peires, Robert Ross, John Wright, and members of the Africa Seminar of the University of Cape Town. I am especially indebted to Colin Webb, who provided much of the initial inspiration and many of the ideas incorporated here, and to Leonard Thompson, who helped me to clarify what I was trying to say.

1. W. C. Macleod, *The American Indian Frontier* (New York, 1928), p. vii. In South Africa, Eric Walker spoke of the need to understand "both sides of the frontier" in "A Zulu Account of the Retief Massacre," *The Critic* 3, no. 2 (January 1935):69. W. M. Macmillan had, to a limited extent, attempted this in *Bantu, Boer, and Briton* (London, 1929).

2. W. K. Hancock contrasted this American-type frontier, "primarily an economic thing," with the "political," European-type frontier, the sharp edge of an established sovereign state (*Survey of British Commonwealth Affairs*, 2 vols. in 3 [London, 1937–42], vol. 2, pt. 1, p. 3). Given the many possible definitions of *frontier*, Hancock might have said that it, too, was, like imperialism, "no word for scholars." Were the frontier merely a newly settled area, all South Africa might be termed "frontier," or at least the trekker republics by comparison with the more settled Cape.

a predetermined process in North American and southern African frontier history: the subjection of the indigenous peoples to white control—in the southern African case, the subjection first of the Khoisan peoples who occupied the western part of the region and then of the Bantu-speaking peoples farther east. But on closer scrutiny it becomes apparent that there was no straightforward, unilinear process by which white power became dominant throughout the region. As in North America, there were periods when indigenous peoples maintained their dominance, followed by periods of equilibrium. Ultimately, white power was everywhere consolidated, but before that happened power relations took many different forms. There was no simple, dichotomized white-black frontier with two monolithic, antagonistic blocs facing each other, as Max Gluckman pointed out in a famous essay.[3] Both blacks and, in the nineteenth century, whites, were divided among different political units, and different groups competed for power within each unit. The result was that in frontier situations white factions interacted with black factions in a variety of ways.[4] In addition, the power exercized from metropolitan centers frequently had a crucial bearing on processes in frontier zones.

During the initial period in a frontier zone—the "open" phase—whites often lacked the will or the means to establish hegemony and there was a rough balance of power between whites and blacks. The frontier began to "close" when the whites began to dominate. In white-Khoisan frontier zones, which we consider first, the open phase was relatively short-lived. It was usually longer in frontier zones where whites competed with groups of mixed descent or with Bantu-speaking Africans.[5]

In this work, we are focussing on the frontier processes initiated by European expansion. However, to understand those processes we need to be aware of the human situation into which Europeans were penetrating. First, while recognizing for analytical purposes that southern Africa was inhabited by three categories of people distinguished from one another by different modes of production—hunter-gatherers (San, whom whites have called Bushmen), pastoralists (Khoikhoi, whom whites have called Hottentots), and mixed farmers (the Bantu-speakers)—it is important that we should also realize that there was extensive intermixing among all these peoples, and that there was no precise correlation between physical type,

3. Max Gluckman, "The Bonds of the Color Bar, South Africa," reprinted in Paul Baxter and Basil Sansom, eds., *Race and Social Difference* (Harmondsworth, Middlesex, 1972), esp. p. 285.

4. On the importance of factionalism in North America, see esp. Robert F. Berkhofer, "The Political Context of a New Indian History," in *The American Indian*, ed. Norris Hundley (Santa Barbara, Calif., 1974), pp. 117–24. Thanks to the term "faction fight," *faction* has become a dirty word to some South Africans ignorant of its wider usages.

5. Once closed, then, there was no longer a frontier. The sense in which the frontier "reopens" is discussed below, p. 169 and n. 67.

language, and economic activity.[6] Second, the indigenous polities were de-limited by kinship ties and personal allegiance rather than by geographical boundaries.[7] Third, frontier processes had existed in southern Africa (as in North America and elsewhere) long before the European intrusion began. In the western part of the region, a major factor since early in the Christian era was the frontier process created by pastoralists as they moved onto land pre-viously used exclusively by hunter-gatherers;[8] and in the eastern part of the region a central theme since early in the Christian era was the frontier pro-cess created by mixed farmers as they broke away from their parent commu-nities and moved southward onto land previously occupied exclusively by hunter-gatherers or pastoralists.[9] Finally, we shall also recognize that the ad-vent of whites did not put an end to these dynamic relationships among the indigenous peoples.

We lack detailed evidence about these processes. But we do know that they had generated modes of thought and action which people spontane-ously applied to the new types of frontier situations created by European penetration. When whites entered zones where blacks were already deeply involved in struggles for power, blacks inevitably treated them as potential allies or enemies in that competition. For example, Khoikhoi pastoralists naturally regarded whites as potential allies against their traditional en-emies, the hunter-gatherers who raided their livestock. Similarly, Bantu-speaking mixed farmers often sought white aid in their internal power struggles for which the white intruders were not responsible; in doing so, they were applying strategies they had fashioned in earlier frontier situations.

II

During the century and a half after Vasco da Gama opened up a new route from Europe to Asia in 1497, white seamen occasionally landed at the Cape and traded with the indigenous Khoikhoi pastoralists. As time went on, the

6. For whole groups of Khoikhoi becoming Xhosa, see for example, Robert Ross, "Ethnic Identity, Demographic Crises and Xhosa-Khoikhoi Interaction," *History in Africa*, vol. 7 (1980). Gerrit Harinck argued that there was no frontier between Xhosa and Khoikhoi because they were not "completely autonomous corporated groups existing independently" ("Interaction be-tween Xhosa and Khoi: Emphasis on the period 1620–1750," in *African Societies in Southern Africa*, ed. Leonard Thompson [London, 1969]). But before groups of Khoikhoi were incorpo-rated as Xhosa, there was competition for power between Xhosa and Khoikhoi, which would seem to justify use of the term *frontier*. See J. B. Peires, "A History of the Xhosa c. 1700–1835" (M.A. thesis, Rhodes University, 1976), esp. pp. 56–60.

7. Though among the Xhosa, for example, belts of unpopulated country separated groups. See n. 51 below.

8. Richard Elphick, *Kraal and Castle* (New Haven, Conn., 1977).

9. R. R. Inskeep, *The Peopling of Southern Africa* (Cape Town and London, 1978).

Khoikhoi became increasingly suspicious of white motives, but they nevertheless sought to use the whites in their internecine quarrels. In 1617, for example, Coree persuaded a Dutch party to march inland to help him attack his neighbors. By 1652, Richard Elphick argues, those whom he terms the Peninsular Khoikhoi "had learned to distinguish the different European nations, and were well aware of the advantages of playing one off against the other."[10] Thus, even before the Dutch East India Company founded a permanent refreshment station at the Cape in 1652 a pattern had been set of active involvement of the one society in the politics of the other.

Like the Dutch in New York, in the early years of their settlement the Dutch at the Cape were well aware of the precariousness of their position.[11] Trade required friendly relations with at least some groups, and costly wars were to be avoided. Jan van Riebeeck, the first Dutch commander, therefore sought to exploit divisions among the Khoikhoi: he was told to "employ every imaginable means to detach these Cape fellows from the Saldanjars;"[12] he mediated between Peninsular subgroups; and he sought an alliance with Oedasoa of the Cochoqua, a powerful local ruler.[13] Not all the Khoikhoi of the southwestern Cape saw the whites as the major threat against which they should unite. Though 1652 marks the beginning of the assertion of exclusive territorial claims by the Europeans,[14] at first such claims affected only certain Peninsular Khoikhoi. Others took time to perceive the threat and then had to decide whether outright resistance or some form of collaboration was in their best interests. Had Oedasoa come to the aid of the Peninsulars in the first Dutch-Khoikhoi war, the Europeans might have been driven from the region, but instead he was prepared to use the Dutch against the Peninsulars, with whom his people had been at enmity for at least a generation.[15] In the mid-1660s he again sought Dutch aid against his rivals to the southeast.[16] When the Dutch attacked Oedasoa's successor in 1673 and 1674, they were in effect intervening in an inter-

10. Elphick, *Kraal and Castle*, p. 86.

11. Allen W. Trelease argues that the weakness of the Dutch forced them to follow a policy of appeasement. *Indian Affairs in Colonial New York: The Seventeenth Century* (Ithaca, N.Y., 1960), esp. p. 115.

12. D. Moodie, ed., *The Record, or a Series of Official Papers Relative to the Condition and Treatment of the Native Tribes of South Africa* (reprinted Amsterdam, 1960), p. 99.

13. Elphick, *Kraal and Castle*, pp. 113, 122; H. B. Thom, eds., *Journal of Jan van Riebeeck*, 3 vols. (Cape Town, 1952–58), 3:443–46.

14. Unlike—say—Xhosa society, Dutch society was almost entirely exclusive, not open to the incorporation of aliens, and the Europeans had a concept of private, individual ownership of land which was alien to the indigenous people, who believed that the land belonged to the group. Misunderstanding arose when indigenous people believed themselves to be granting whites the mere use of land, whereas whites regarded it as having been alienated permanently.

15. Elphick, *Kraal and Castle*, pp. 120, 122.

16. Moodie, *The Record*, pp. 274, 289.

Khoikhoi feud, which may have been intensified but was probably not caused by the new trading relationships with the Europeans.[17] We can only infer what the motivations of the Khoikhoi were, but it would seem likely that they regarded their traditional enemies as a greater danger than the European settlers.

It was over two centuries after the arrival of the Dutch settlers in Table Bay before the last of the many Khoikhoi frontiers closed. In describing the complex patterns of collaboration, resistance, and assimilation that characterized European-Khoikhoi relations during that long period, Shula Marks argues that there was initially more equality than has been admitted by historians: in the first war of 1659–60, the Khoikhoi were close to "success"; when the Peninsulars sought peace "they had by no means been conquered"; at the end of the second war in 1677, Gonnema was "still unsubdued."[18] Nevertheless, the undermining of Khoikhoi political and economic independence began at an early stage. One can trace this back even before the 1670s, when the Company for the first time began to treat Khoikhoi as colonial subjects, and it occurred much less because of military conflict than through disease, through a subtle whittling away of their land and cattle, and through their taking employment with the Dutch.[19] It was aided by the extreme fragility of Khoikhoi polities, whose constantly changing composition and leadership Elphick attributes to the pastoral transhumance which the Khoikhoi practiced. Klaas, an influential leader, was unusual in benefitting for twenty years from a close alliance with the Company, but then a corrupt governor seized the herds he had accumulated and imprisoned him on Robben Island. That some Khoikhoi leaders received staffs of office under the Company only made manifest their loss of independent power.[20] To explain exactly how and why that power was lost would, however, require an examination of relations between leaders and followers which is not possible, given the limitations of the available evidence.[21]

17. Elphick, *Kraal and Castle*, pp. 120, 126, 130–31; S. Marks, "Khoisan Resistance to the Dutch in the Seventeenth and Eighteenth Centuries," *Journal of African History* 13, no. 1 (1972):66.

18. Marks, "Khoisan Resistance," pp. 64–67. Elphick sees the relationship as being somewhat more unequal. *Kraal and Castle*, esp. pp. 115–33.

19. Elphick has sought to explain the fact that they did not offer more resistance by referring to their appreciation for "goods and services which economies other than their own could provide" and their familiarity "with a 'labor' system whereby clients from one tribe worked for employers in another," which enabled them to take work with the Dutch relatively easily. *Kraal and Castle*, p. 68.

20. On this, see Monica Wilson's review of Elphick's *Kraal and Castle* in *African Economic History* 5 (Spring 1978):95.

21. The need to do this in the American case was argued by Richard White in "The 'New Indian History': Old Wine in New Models," *Meeting Ground* (Summer 1976), p. 13. However, White did not prove that it could be done.

By the beginning of the eighteenth century the Dutch controlled most of the arable areas in the southwestern Cape, and white frontiersmen were thrusting forward up the coastal plains toward Namaqualand, through the Hex River valley into the Little Karroo, and eastward toward Algoa Bay. Khoikhoi vainly attempted to resist this advance by sporadic raids on the intruders, and as one Khoikhoi group fell back onto the grazing lands of another, inter-Khoikhoi warfare spread. In the face of the trekboer advance, the only way in which either Khoikhoi or peoples of mixed descent could maintain their political independence was by moving into the interior ahead of the trekboers and there creating new communities. The result was a highly confused situation in one zone after another, as intrusive groups and indigenous communities competed for scarce resources such as water, cattle, and firearms and attempted to establish hegemony. The successive frontier zones along and beyond the periphery of the white advance were areas of chronic instability; some observers regarded them as anarchic.[22] In the 1830s, for example, Dr. Andrew Smith reported that the indigenous pastoralists and hunter-collectors in Bushmanland and along the middle Orange "associate in small groups—each carries on its operations independently and no one recognises the right of any other to interfere with it. No regular chiefs are acknowledged except on particular occasions, hence generally speaking each individual follows his own propensities and every party makes war or makes peace just as meets its individual purpose."[23] With land in the north much less desirable for white settlement than land in the east, the slow penetration of this area by colonists went for a long time relatively little noticed in Cape Town. The !Kora, a predominantly Khoikhoi community, who combined hunting with pastoralism and stock-raiding, were quite successful in keeping the white intruders from their fountains. Indeed, some !Kora groups managed to maintain an independent existence along the banks of the middle Orange River until 1878, when it took a strong colonial force to subdue them. That campaign closed the last Khoikhoi frontier.[24]

The history of relations between the white invaders and the hunter-gatherers is even less well documented than those with the herders, and is complicated by the fact that it is likely the "boschiemans-hottentots" of the records were increasingly pastoralists who had lost their livestock rather

22. Martin Legassick, "The Griqua, the Sotho-Tswana and the Missionaries, 1780–1840: The Politics of a Frontier Zone" (Ph.D. diss., University of California, Los Angeles, 1969); idem, "The Northern Frontier to 1820: The Emergence of the Griqua People," in *The Shaping of South African Society*, ed. Richard Elphick and Hermann Giliomee (Cape Town, 1979).

23. Quoted in Robert Ross, "The !Kora Wars on the Orange River, 1830–1880," *Journal of African History* 16, no. 5 (1975): 566. See also P. R. Kirby, ed., *The Diary of Dr. Andrew Smith, 1834–1836*, 2 vols. (Cape Town, 1939–40), 1:128: "The chief has comparatively no power; all are inclined to think and each [is] desirous of adopting his own views. . . ."

24. T. Strauss, *War along the Orange* (Cape Town, 1979).

than hunter-gatherers who had never possessed any. On rare occasions whites shot game for "Bushmen," presented them with sheep, or offered them employment,[25] but white communities never entered into cooperative political relations with them. The usual pattern was for Boer commandos to threaten their very existence with great brutality. In the 1770s, when the whites reached the Sneeuberg mountains of the interior plateau, several bands of hunter-gatherers, for the first and only time, forged a loose alliance to challenge the white advance. Their mode of existence helped them to resist and to survive, and in the late eighteenth century they constituted a more serious threat to the whites than the Xhosa in the east,[26] checking further colonial expansion northeastward for some thirty years. Even after the colonial government had nominally established its authority, it was still sometimes "extremely difficult to say whether one lives in peace or war with the Boesjesmen; they are sometimes quiet for a long while, so that nothing is heard from them, but all of a sudden they appear . . . plundering and destroying everything within their reach."[27] After 1806, the British administration made enough resources available to tip the balance in favor of the colonists and blunt the "Bushman" resistance; but small groups of raiders continued to trouble the colonists into the middle of the century. Ultimately, those "Bushmen" neither exterminated nor forced into service had to retreat to join their fellows who already lived in the rocky fastnesses of the Drakensberg or on the fringes of the Kalahari desert. Some of the latter were the only indigenous people to survive as hunter-collectors beyond the first years of the twentieth century. One "Bushman," who led a mixed community in the northeastern Cape in the second quarter of the nineteenth century, became an active collaborator of the white colonists; but this was highly atypical, and even he ended his days among the caves of the Drakensberg.[28]

III

Whereas in the western Cape first white cultivators and then pastoralists intruded upon widely dispersed indigenous hunter-collectors and pastoralists (whose numbers were never large), from the 1770s the pastoral trekboers, and from the 1830s the Voortrekkers, entered territory inhabited by

25. P. J. van der Merwe, *Die Noordwaartse Beweging van die Boere voor die Groot Trek (1770–1842)* (The Hague, 1937), pp. 156–61; Philip V. Tobias, ed., *The Bushmen* (Cape Town, 1978), p. 86.

26. In the east, the whites clashed mainly with the Gqunukhwebe to begin with, not the main body of the western Xhosa, who were to prove a much more formidable foe.

27. G. M. Theal, ed., *Records of the Cape Colony*, 36 vols. (London, 1897–1905), 9:81.

28. C. C. Saunders, "Madolo: A 'Bushman' Life," *African Studies*, vol. 36, no. 2 (1977).

people whose cattle were a vital element in their lives but who, more importantly, cultivated fields around their villages. These Bantu-speaking Africans—to whom the term *Africans* will here be arbitrarily limited—were not merely more settled than the Khoikhoi and the San. They were less seriously affected by European diseases, they were far more numerous, and they lived in larger, more centralized and coherent polities, in which much greater power could be exercised, thanks to their stronger economic bases and more complex political structures. These Africans, and also those people of mixed descent whose settled core, the Griqua, played a "middle role" between whites and Africans north of the Orange River,[29] were relatively quick to adopt the horse and the gun.[30] But it was not only changes on the black side that made the typical nineteenth-century frontier one on which greater power was exercised than formerly. The number of white frontiersmen also increased, five thousand new immigrants settling directly on the Cape eastern frontier in 1820. Thanks to technological innovations in Europe, white military muscle grew substantially; to the small bands of white settlers was added the organized might of British regiments, and behind the British presence lay, at least in theory, the relatively limitless resources of the empire.

Though the power that whites could wield was in the end to prove decisive, many areas saw quite lengthy periods of rough, if constantly shifting, balances of power between Africans, people of mixed descent, and whites. In such situations relationships were naturally fluid and cross-cutting alliances joining white and black factions common. Whites might have up-to-date firearms, the knowledge of how they might best be used, and a relatively plentiful supply of ammunition, but their parties were often extremely small and, being scattered over large areas, cut off from their fellows. True, the Great Trek flung some fourteen thousand whites in one vast movement far into the interior, but parties went their own ways and reinforcements were not always easy to summon. In the circumstances in which they found themselves, the Voortrekkers, like the trekboers before them, had perforce to form alliances with Africans and to try to set African faction against African faction so that they would not have to face a solid enemy. The very small community of white traders at Port Natal after 1824 entered into client relations with Shaka and then with Dingane; though they accepted refugees from Zululand against the wishes of the Zulu rulers,

29. In his dissertation, cited above, Martin Legassick argues that it was only the Griqua decline in the 1840s that presaged a direct struggle between the whites and the Sotho-Tswana.

30. For example, Peter Delius has shown that by the 1860s the Pedi had acquired large quantities of guns by going out to work for them ("Migrant Labour and the Pedi before 1869," *The Societies of Southern Africa in the 19th and 20th Centuries*, University of London Institute of Commonwealth Studies no. 7 [1977]). See generally, S. Marks and A. Atmore, "Firearms in Southern Africa, a Survey," *Journal of African History*, vol. 12, no. 4 (1971).

they were in no position to offer any greater challenge.[31] The Voortrekkers who entered Natal in 1837, however, sought extensive land for settlement. They hoped to be able to avoid direct confrontation with the Zulu and tried to get land by a treaty from Dingane. Though they were prepared to fight if necessary, and did so with conspicuous success at Blood River in December 1838, when Mpande offered himself as an ally against his half-brother Dingane, they were quick to accept the alliance.

For Mpande an alliance with the Voortrekkers was a means of ensuring that Dingane did not recover his position as Zulu ruler. Many other examples could be cited of ways in which black rulers used whites in their internal power struggles. Two recent biographies of Moshoeshoe of Lesotho have shown how skillfully he exploited white divisions for his own purposes.[32] That a ruler like Mpande had a shrewd grasp of what was in his interest is shown, for example, by his retort, made when the Voortrekkers clashed with the British in 1842, that he would aid whichever party emerged the stronger from the contest.[33]

The cross-cutting alliance between Mpande and the Natal Voortrekkers, which benefitted both parties, was made easier by the fact that on neither side had a large, well-organized state had time to become firmly established. On the Cape eastern frontier, the introduction of administrative control by the British—most notably through the circuit courts, the first of which toured the frontier districts in 1811—coincided with the expulsion of Africans from the Zuurveld and the closing of this, the first of the many frontier zones that opened up along the Cape's advancing eastern border. It took two decades for the whites south of the Vaal to organize themselves into an established polity, and longer for a similar process to occur north of that river. Not only was white power highly fragmented in the early Transvaal as rival leaders ruled with charismatic authority what were almost independent fiefdoms, but in large areas white control was nonexistent, while in others whites and blacks competed for power on virtually equal terms. The Pedi, for example, retained their independence in the eastern Transvaal,

31. Shaka asked them to assist him against his enemies and to arrange an alliance with Britain; Gluckman speaks of them as being "constitutionally absorbed into his political system" ("Bonds of the Color Bar," p. 280). Without competition for political power, this was no frontier zone. The same is true of the settlement of whites along the Mthatha River, which Ngangeliswe of the Thembu allowed to protect his chiefdom from Mpondo raids.

32. When a group of Transvaal trekkers under Pretorius sought his help against the Free State in 1857, however, Moshoeshoe did not exploit the Boer quarrel, probably because he did not know who would emerge victorious. Leonard Thompson, *Survival in Two Worlds* (Oxford, 1975), pp. 236–37.

33. G. M. Theal, *The Republic of Natal, the Origin of the Present Pondo Tribe, Imperial Treaties with Panda, and Establishment of the Colony of Natal* (Cape Town, 1886), p. 39. Theal comments, "on this as on every other occasion of the kind of which South African history furnished a record, the Bantu were ready to join the winning cause."

while in the Zoutpansberg whites lost control in 1867, after which they had to pay tribute to African rulers.[34] On the African side, the larger states the Voortrekkers encountered were products of the recent intra-African Mfecane wars and were still in the process of evolving. Had no Voortrekker invasion occurred, it is by no means certain what their final shape would have been. As it was, the centralizing tendencies did not preclude a continuation of the old practices of segmentation and fission, which in turn facilitated the construction of transfrontier alliances.

Open frontiers beween whites and Africans or peoples of mixed descent were not, of course, all of a kind. Competition for land, and a consequent struggle for power, intensified over time as communities came to jostle each other in a few zones of much sought-after territory, and as this struggle moved to new areas, so new frontier zones opened. In some cases two clear-cut loci of power challenged each other within a narrow area; in others, no single power was capable of exerting its influence over the zone as whole.[35] Metropolitan control over the activities of white frontiersmen on the nineteenth-century Cape eastern frontier was greater than, say, in the mid-century Transvaal frontier zones, where groups raided each other almost with impunity and relations were consequently more anarchic. To illustrate such complexities, let us briefly consider a few examples of frontier zones in the open phases.

In the Cape-Xhosa frontier zone at the end of the eighteenth century there was a rough balance of power. Individual white settlers, with their families and retainers, had moved into the Zuurveld between the Bushmans and Fish rivers, where on three occasions in two decades they clashed with the African groups which had earlier occupied the area. The outcome in each case was stalemate, for neither side was able effectively and permanently to assert its claims to the territory against the other. The whites were not supported by major colonial forces, and the Xhosa groups were weak and divided, political rivals of those farther east, from whom they had earlier broken away, and relative newcomers to the territory themselves. At the be-

34. J. A. I. Agar-Hamilton, *The Road to the North: South Africa, 1852–1886* (London, 1937), p. 35. In the jargon of Jack Forbes, then, the South African frontier was not always one of unilinear expansion: "Frontiers in American History and the Role of the Frontier Historian," *Ethnohistory* 15 (1968):227.

35. Jan Vansina describes how, in the states of Central Africa in the early nineteenth century, "the authority and power of the central government faded away more and more the farther one went from the center toward the boundaries. Thus boundaries between the states were vague, sometimes even overlapping, and there was little conflict of power between the states, since their respective forces on the common border areas were so weak" (*Kingdoms of the Savanna* [Madison, Wis., 1966], pp. 155–56). In South Africa many instances of lack of power and authority could be found—for example, between the Langeberg and the Caledon valley in the early nineteenth century.

ginning of the nineteenth century, after the whites had once again been pushed back, "it appeared that the expansion of the Cape colony might have come to a halt, and even that a retreat westwards was possible."[36] After the council in Cape Town fixed the colonial boundary at the Fish River in 1780, successive governments tried to remove those Africans living in the Zuurveld, believing that rigid territorial segregation would best promote peace on the frontier and reduce expenditure to a minimum; but before 1812 none was able to effect this. Changes of rulers in Cape Town did not, however, leave the frontier zone unaffected: the arrival of the British helped precipitate the third war in 1799; the Batavians stabilized the frontier after that war in a way which the Dutch East Indian Company probably would not have been able to do; and then, ultimately, the British, with greater force at their disposal than any previous regime, were responsible for the crucial expulsion of 1812.

The allegiances of those living in the Zuurveld were divided. Governments in Cape Town claimed authority there, but in fact colonial control in the frontier region, exercised through a landdrost and occasional visits by metropolitan-based officials, was minimal in the late eighteenth century. The trekboers, as pioneers, tended to be individualistic, factious, and reluctant to accept any limitations on their independence imposed from a distant metropolis. Disagreements between them and Cape Town and its agents frequently turned on policy toward Africans or Khoikhoi in the frontier zone, and their search for independence led to actual rebellions in 1795–1801. By 1801, however, it was clear that the white farmers could not win control in the Zuurveld by themselves and they moved toward full cooperation with the central government, demonstrated in the combined operation to clear the Zuurveld in 1811–12.

The fluidity of politics in the frontier zone in this open phase is reflected in the different roles played by Khoikhoi. Many of those who were working for whites in the Graaff-Reinet district fought against the colonists in 1799, in what was, for the whites, the most serious of the early confrontations on the frontier; other Khoikhoi, however, fought for the colonists against the Xhosa in the Cape Hottentot Regiment, which helped to drive the Africans from the Zuurveld in 1811–12.[37]

On the Xhosa side, the small polities in the frontier zone acknowledged the ritual seniority of the paramount, whose seat of government lay east of the frontier zone at this time, but were to all intents and purposes indepen-

36. W. M. Freund, "The Eastern Frontier of the Cape Colony during the Batavian Period (1803–1806)," *Journal of African History* 13, no. 4 (1972): 645.

37. L. W. Swart, "Some Aspects of the History of the Cape Regiment, 1806–1817" (Honours essay, University of Cape Town, 1978).

dent.[38] Like Cape Town on the white side, then, the paramount was unable
to wield effective control in the zone; moreover, he did not have resources of
the kind the white metropole could assert. Local Xhosa chiefs competed for
the allegiance of other factions and were prepared to seek alliance with
whites to strengthen their position. Thus, Shaka of the Gqunukhwebe offered to assist the whites "with all his Kaffirs" against "Bushmen" raiders in
1792, while the following year Ndlambe of the Rharabe Xhosa joined forces
with Barend Lindeque, a leading trekboer, and together they routed the
Gqunukhwebe.[39]

From 1812 the Fish River became the effective as well as the nominal
boundary on which white power directly confronted African power. Seeking
to stabilize this boundary, Governor Somerset actively intervened across it,
recognizing Ngqika as paramount in the hope that he would become a
powerful colonial ally. Though Ngqika claimed equality with Somerset and
answered "that he was much obliged to his Lordship for conferring on him
the honour and title of chief of his Nation, and begged His Excellency would
accept the same compliment from him in return," he admitted the limitations of his power, adding that "where control was required, the other chiefs
should be approached independently."[40] Accepting the title of paramount
cost Ngqika support among his people, who saw him as the tool of whites,
and this loss of support in turn increased his dependence on his white allies.
By 1818, when he was defeated in battle by a combined Xhosa force under
Ndlambe's leadership, the intra-Xhosa feud had become inextricably bound
to the question of relations with the whites. The struggle over who should
rule at home cost the Xhosa much territory; after the resisters had been defeated at the battle of Grahamstown in 1819, the collaborator Ngqika,
whose aid was now of less importance to the whites, found himself stripped
of much of his best land.

In other circumstances white recognition of African rulers reinforced
and bolstered authority on the African side. One could cite trekker support
for Mpande or British backing for Cetshwayo, both in his rise to power and
again in the 1880s when he returned to Zululand, though in the latter case it
also contributed to his death. Support from whites might always alienate
some followers, but it did not necessarily mean dependence; though they

38. Because the Xhosa groups that broke away acquired only de facto not de jure independence, J. B. Peires speaks of segmentation rather than fission occurring. "A History of the
Xhosa," pp. 224–26.

39. S. Marks, "Khoisan Resistance," p. 60, n. 19, quoting Cape Archives, G.R.1/9, Hurter's
report, 5 June 1792; J. S. Marais, *Maynier and the First Boer Republic* (Cape Town, 1944), pp.
40–41.

40. H. A. Reyburn, "Studies in Cape Frontier History," *The Critic* 4, no. 1 (October
1935): 53.

benefitted from white aid, Mpande and Cetshwayo both exercised effective autonomy as rulers. At the same time, Zulu and white politics were closely intertwined. In Zululand in 1856–57, Mpande backed Mbulazi and the Izig-qoza faction over Cetshwayo, the older brother, whom some of the most powerful men in the kingdom supported in the hope that if he came to power they would be able to exercise that power on his behalf. In this strug-gle for power the role of Europeans was of critical importance. Fynn believed that Mpande "retained the chieftainship so long because Ketchwiyo and his adherents are unsure whether it is the intention of the Natal Government or the Boers to interfere." Mpande was fully prepared to see such interference in order to maintain his position. Rosalind Mael suggests that he assigned Mbulazi land bordering on Natal to facilitate an alliance with that colony, and explains that after the battle of Ndondakasuka he told some Afrikaners that he wanted them "to come here and stop with me. I will then see who will rebel [*sic*] against me."[41]

Similar processes were at work in the eastern Transvaal-Swazi frontier zone in the mid-nineteenth century. Philip Bonner has described how Swazi society at this time was continuing "to divide along both horizontal and ver-tical lines of cleavage: horizontal because many of the chiefdoms incorpo-rated by Sobhuza in the centre and north of Swaziland remained culturally and linguistically differentiated from their Ngwane rulers, so that an unsta-ble ethnic stratification ran through Swazi society; vertical, because the characteristic Nguni propensity for fission within ruling lineages had yet to be fully contained by the evolving institutions of the Swazi state."[42] While in the older days dissidents and younger sons might have hived off to form new polities, in the post-Mfecane, Great Trek period there was no room for them to do so, and conflict was therefore internalized within the polity. There was, moreover, a Zulu claim to Swazi allegiance, and on a number of occasions Zulu armies were sent against the Swazi to enforce it. To meet this challenge, the Swazi ruler in the mid-1840s decided to form an alliance with a group of Boer neighbors.

At this time there was no Transvaal state; isolated groups of trekkers in different parts of what would become the Transvaal Republic claimed con-trol over vast areas but exercised it over only relatively small pockets. Chal-lenged by his elder brother Malambule, who had established friendly rela-tions with Mpande of the Zulu, Mswati regarded the Boer community at

41. R. Mael, "The Problem of Political Integration in the Zulu Empire" (Ph.D. diss., Uni-versity of California, Los Angeles, 1974), pp. 201, 214–15, 231.

42. P. L. Bonner, "Factions and Fissions: Transvaal/Swazi Politics in the Mid-Nineteenth Century," *Journal of African History* 19, no. 2 (1978):222. As the very title of Bonner's article indicates, however, he still thinks in terms of the "Transvaal" and "Swaziland," when in a sense such units did not exist, as he himself admits on p. 237.

Ohrigstad as a potential ally against these internal and external enemies. But the Ohrigstad community was itself divided, with A. H. Potgieter's leadership being challenged by a growing Volksraad party. It was this latter faction which, against Potgieter's wishes, signed an agreement with Mswati in July 1846, at a time when Mpande was about to invade and would give his support to Malambule. With Boer aid, however, Mswati was able to force the Zulu army to withdraw from his country in July 1847. In the next few years the factions realigned themselves. Another ambitious brother obtained aid from the Ohrigstad Boers, and this time Mswati sought an accommodation with Mpande, which enabled him to dispose of his new rival in 1855. On both sides, then, transfrontier alliances were the means whereby factions dealt with internal challenges.

While African chiefs rarely formed alliances against the whites,[43] and never succeeded in uniting all the Africans in a particular area, time and again specific African groups were prepared to join whites in alliances or in joint campaigns against other Africans. There was no well-developed sense of racial identity among Africans,[44] sectional advantage was placed before wider interests, and views of the most appropriate strategy differed as much as they do among black South Africans today. Whites, though by no means united themselves, had a clearer perception of the struggle as a racial one, but were ready to use African allies both against other Africans and in order to extend their influence beyond the limits of their formal control.[45] Some blacks benefitted from their collaboration with whites, notably the Mfengu, who obtained large land grants; all gained the protection of a powerful ally. In the eastern Transvaal, those Tsonga called "government-volk" fought for the Boers and gained protection against the Gaza; in turn, the Boers were for a time dependent on Tsonga aid for survival.[46]

The era of rough equality found formal expression in treaties signed between apparently sovereign parties. Bonner argues that the Swazi-Boer

43. On the Cape eastern frontier there was an increase of scale in African resistance over time. In 1818–19, Ndlambe forged an alliance of Xhosa groups; by 1846–47, Thembu were fighting on the Xhosa side. See further, C. C. Saunders, "The Hundred Years' War; Some Reflections on African Resistance on the Cape-Xhosa Frontier," in *Profiles of Self-Determination*, ed. D. Chanaiwa (Northridge, Calif., 1976).

44. A point made in Monica Wilson and Leonard Thompson, eds., *The Oxford History of South Africa*, 2 vols. (Oxford, 1969–71), 2:246, and for Indians by Nancy Lurie in "Indian Cultural Adjustment to European Civilization," reprinted in Stephen Salsbury, ed., *Essays on the History of the American West* (Hinsdale, Ill., 1975). Moshoeshoe did, however, tell Sekonyela, "We are both black and of one nation." P. B. Sanders, "Sekonyela and Moshoeshoe," *Journal of African History* 9 (1969):449.

45. In *The Grand Strategy of the Roman Empire* (Baltimore, 1976), Edward Luttwak uses the concept "hegemonic empire" for this (see pp. 30, 49, 192). One might cite the Mfengu in Fingoland in the period 1865–79 or the "kinglets" in Zululand in 1879–87 as examples.

46. See especially the dissertation being written for London University by Patrick Harries.

treaty of July 1846, rather than ceding valuable Swazi land, was in fact "a master stroke of Swazi diplomacy" and reflected a real balance of power.[47] However, such balances were relatively short-lived. The treaties were always made on white terms and primarily in white interests—even if an Mswati or a Moshoeshoe could see advantage in them[48]—and they were amended or swept aside as those interests changed. In 1843 Moshoeshoe and Adam Kok III seemed to the colonial authorities to be useful allies to keep order on the northern border, but in 1848 when Sir Harry Smith decided that Britain should take on that task, and again in 1854 when a Boer government was installed in the Free State, the British ignored the interests of the BaSotho and the Griqua. After wool brought new wealth to the Philippolis Griqua, white farmers coveted their land and edged them off it, and the British authorities intervened only to suggest that they move to new territory. On the Cape eastern frontier, similarly, there was a measure of equality implicit in the treaties Stockenström signed with African rulers in the Ciskei in the aftermath of the 1834–35 frontier war. The modifications made in the treaties in 1840 were slight, because it was feared that greater changes would provoke war.[49] However, in 1844 a new British governor bowed to white expansionists who were ready for another war and imposed new treaties, which did lead to war two years later. Maitland's treaty of amity with Faku survived from 1844 into the 1880s because the interests of the two parties did not clash, but the Mpondo were forced to accept violations of it in 1850, 1872, and 1878.[50] That even in the age of rough equilibrium the tide began flowing against African states is perhaps most clearly seen in the case of Moshoeshoe's Lesotho. The identity of that state was probably based initially on allegiance rather than on territoriality.[51] By the mid-1860s, however, Moshoeshoe had not only been forced to accept bound-

47. P. L. Bonner, "Mswati," in *Black Leaders in Southern African History*, ed. C. C. Saunders (London, 1979), p. 66.

48. For example, Thompson, *Survival*, pp. 120–21. In South Africa, treaties did not primarily concern land or the removal of Africans from their land. This was partly because there was not the same need as in North America to legitimize the acquisition of such land in the face of European competitors.

49. John S. Galbraith, *Reluctant Empire* (Berkeley, Calif., 1963), p. 156. On the treaties, see also pp. 140–41, 168–70.

50. D. G. Cragg, "The Relations of the Amampondo and the Colonial Authorities, 1830–1886, with Special Reference to the Role of the Wesleyan Missionaries" (D. Phil. diss., Oxford University, 1959).

51. P. B. Sanders, *Moeshoeshoe Chief of the Sotho* (London, 1975), p. 62. Cf. Thompson, *Survival*, p. 176. Asked if certain people belonged to him, Moeshoeshoe answered, "Cannot you see they send me food?" (Kirby, ed., *Diary of Smith*, 1:129). On another occasion the Sotho leader defined his territory by saying that it was "wherever his foot had pressed the ground or one of his people had ever lived." G. M. Theal, *History of the Boers in South Africa* (London, 1887), p. 212 n.

ary delimitations which cost his people much of the very fertile land west of the Caledon River, but the expansive Free State, pushing on toward the Maloti Mountains, threatened the very survival of the state.

IV

The open phase in the politics of the frontier zones was, then, an inherently unstable one. Given the differential access of black and white communities to technological innovation, the balance of military power could not be indefinitely sustained.[52] The victory of the Zulu at Isandhlwana and of the Sotho in the Gun War were both the results of atypical circumstances.[53] Long before the introduction of the Maxim gun in the 1890s, sheer numbers counted for less, and in any case, the arrival of many more whites in the interior had lessened the Africans' numerical advantage. The whites' fear that the guns which Africans bought in return for labor at the diamond fields in the 1870s would upset the military balance proved, in the event, to be groundless.

The closing of a frontier zone was often an abrupt event, as in the Zuurveld in 1812 when 20,000 Africans were expelled across the Fish; and yet farther east the Cape frontier was not finally closed until the end of Mpondo independence in 1894. The formal extension of rule frequently masked the absence of effective control. British Kaffraria was added to the empire by Sir Harry Smith at the end of 1847, a major war was fought there in 1850–53, and the cattle-killing followed in 1856–57, but even then the Ngqika (western) Xhosa retained considerable power, sufficient to enable them to join the Gcaleka (eastern) Xhosa in resistance in 1878. The end of the frontier must be traced on the ground, in the substitution of magisterial for chiefly authority and the imposition of taxation, rather than through the coloring of maps in government offices in metropoles or the rhetoric of claims to sovereignty. The Transvaal's northern boundary was said to be the Limpopo decades before the last of the many frontiers opened up by the Great Trek closed with the suppression of Mphephu's resistance in Vendaland in 1898.

Though in the age of rough equality the balance of power often began to move against the Africans, yet overall the turning point came in the 1870s. By the end of that decade it was clear that independent African rule could not long survive anywhere; the balance of power had shifted fundamentally.

52. The extent to which race determined this differential access is a controversial matter that demands closer attention than it has been given to date.
53. The Zulu were aided by the element of surprise and by incompetence on the British side, the Sotho by the terrain and the relatively large number of guns they possessed (and the absence of imperial troops).

Even though the African societies now possessed large quantities of fire-arms, the power imposed by the white metropoles overturned the balance. The crucial factor—as in the Zuurveld in 1811–12 or the Ciskei in 1834–35, 1846–47 and 1850–53—was often the intervention of British troops. In Lesotho in 1868, the High Commissioner's announcements that he was cutting off the supply of arms and ammunition to the Free State and taking the BaSotho under British protection were backed up by the dispatching of five hundred members of the Cape Frontier Armed and Mounted Police. As on the Cape-Khoisan frontier, the local metropolis might assume an "imperial" role and, by intervening directly in the frontier zone, tip the balance of power there. In the Transkei in the 1870s, imperial and subimperial intervention were interwoven, the High Commissioner working hand in glove with the responsible Cape ministry. In the 1877–78 war, imperial troops played their last major role on that frontier; thereafter, the Cape relied on its own forces, thus gaining greater independence of action.[54]

It is clearly impossible within the scope of this chapter to attempt an overall analysis of the reasons for the many imperial interventions, or to discuss the forces of white expansionism in general—including, say, the political role of missionaries or the sometimes conflicting interests of white settlers and their governments. To claim, however, as Waldemar Campbell does, that "chronic disorder and crumbling tribal societies produced political vacuums which either imperial or settler governments had to fill"[55] is inadequate on several counts. It discounts, for example, both the expansionist drive of a Harry Smith or Bartle Frere[56] and the way in which the Grahamstown gentry, under Godlonton's leadership, sought war for personal aggrandizement through the opportunities it opened up for commercial enterprise and land speculation.[57] Moreover, in suggesting that African societies collapsed of their own accord, Campbell misses the crucial importance of the pressures for labor and land, which were greatly intensified by the needs of the diamond mines and capitalist agriculture from the 1870s, and of the British government's attempts to bring about a confederated South Africa that might both permit Britain to withdraw from formal rule in the subcontinent and provide for further economic expansion.

54. C. C. Saunders, "The annexation of the Transkeian Territories," *Archives Year Book for South African History*, 1976 (hereafter cited as AYB).

55. Waldemar B. Campbell, "The South African Frontier 1865–1885: A Study in Expansion," *AYB* 1 (1959):220. Campbell was inspired by the American parallel to consider the history of the South African frontier (p. x).

56. See also J. Benyon, "The Cape High Commission: Another Neglected Factor in British Imperial Expansion in South Africa," *South African Historical Journal*, vol. 5 (November 1973).

57. Tony Kirk, "Self-Government and Self-Defence in South Africa: The Inter-Relations between British and Cape Politics 1846–1854" (D. Phil. diss., Oxford University, 1972), esp. pp. 58–64, 125–26, and chaps. 5, 8.

In the mid-1870s the Transvaal government was persuaded to act against Sekhukhune of the Pedi, who sought to maintain his independence and the territorial integrity of his chiefdom in the face of encroachment by white farmers. The Voortrekker republic was unable to gain a decisive victory over his forces, and Shepstone used this as a pretext to annex the Transvaal in the interests of confederation. Having assumed the government of that territory, the British felt committed to end the Pedi challenge, and British troops soon reduced Sekhukhune's stronghold. In Zululand, on the other hand, because of the furore over the Anglo-Zulu war, Wolseley partitioned but did not annex, and this remained a semianarchic frontier zone until 1887, when Boer encroachments seemed to threaten Britain's strategic interests. So the closing of the South African frontier zones was shaped in part by what men in a distant metropolis conceived were the interests of a world power. Indeed, Robinson and Gallagher argue that the British government sanctioned Rhodes's move into Zimbabwe in 1890 to prevent Transvaal expansion northward in the interests of British supremacy in the subcontinent, which in turn was important because of the searoute to India.[58]

But though global concerns occasioned the closing of southern African frontier zones, so too did local considerations. Anglo-Afrikaner tensions might play a part—as in 1868 when the British accepted Moshoeshoe's plea for protection rather than see his territory come under Free State rule and his people scattered. Some cases were affected by intercolonial rivalry, as in 1894 when the Cape annexed Pondoland because it believed it could not, for reasons of prestige, allow Natal to expand its territory southward.[59] Intra-African feuds, too, might lead directly to the closing of a frontier. By the mid-1870s the Thembu of the Transkei had a long-standing quarrel with the Gcaleka, their Xhosa neighbors to the southeast, which did not turn on relations with the colonists. Defeated in war by the Gcaleka in 1872, the Thembu ruler in 1875 sought "British protection," presumably on the Lesotho model, to avoid another round of hostilities. The newly self-governing Cape saw in his request an opportunity to extend its influence east of the Kei in the interests of the stability of its eastern border. The colony had to work through the High Commissioner, but the imperial government had no wish to assume new responsibilities in the area. "British protection," then, the Thembu soon discovered, meant Cape magisterial rule.[60] With Thembu-

58. Ronald Robinson and John Gallagher, *Africa and the Victorians* (London, 1961), esp. chap. 7. The most important revisionist article on imperial motivations is A. Atmore and S. Marks, "The Imperial Factor in South Africa in the Nineteenth Century: Towards a Reassessment," in *European Imperialism and the Partition of Africa*, ed. E. F. Penrose (London, 1975).

59. Saunders, "Transkeian Territories," chap. 7. It may be noted here that whereas in the Zuurveld the "closing" of the frontier involved the subordination of colonists to central control, in the Transkei, Cape Town–appointed administrators spearheaded white expansion.

60. Ibid., chaps. 2, 3.

land under Cape rule, the Gcaleka leader, under strong pressure from a war party within his chiefdom, was persuaded to give his support to those who argued that a desperate effort should be made to break out.[61] War with the colony followed a skirmish with Mfengu. Gcaleka resentment against the Mfengu dated from their removal of large herds of cattle from Gcalekaland in 1835, but had been much aggravated in the 1860s by Mfengu settlement on land from which white troops had expelled the Gcaleka in 1858. Against the advanced technology the whites could employ—and Frere believed the newly installed telegraph was as important to the quick colonial victory as the Snider carbines and Seven Pounders[62]—even the combined forces of the Gcaleka and the eastern Xhosa leaders proved helpless. At the close of the war Gcalekaland, too, lay under Cape magisterial rule, and the colonial government repaid the western Xhosa for their participation by removing them en masse east of the Kei into the Transkeian "reserve."

That white-black relations should have taken second place to intra-black conflicts during the open phase is hardly surprising. That this is also true in many cases until the very closing of the frontier zones is perhaps more difficult to understand.[63] In the closing phase, intrablack political cleavages by no means always reflected, as in the Gcaleka-Mfengu case, the white-black cleavage. When BaSotho fortunes were at their lowest ebb, Molapo, Moshoeshoe's second son and one of his most important territorial rulers, signed a separate peace with the Free State. When Boers were already making serious inroads into Zulu territory, the Usuthu faction was prepared to deal with them and give them land in return for their help against Zibhebhu and the Mandhlakazi. The explanation for such apparent lack of perception of the threat posed by whites would seem to lie largely in the fact that each black group sought what seemed to it the best advantage in a situation where it was by no means clear which course of action was most to the advantage of overall black interests. White factions might pose threats, but they were also potential allies, and if one group allied itself itself with a white faction it was only natural for another to seek a powerful ally elsewhere. Conflicts among the black groups—whether the result of fissive forces within Nguni or Sotho society or springing from, say, competition for scarce resources or personal ambition—were often long-standing and deep-rooted. To have subordinated them to a greater unity in the face of the white threat would have required political and institutional changes of major pro-

61. On the war and peace parties in the Gcaleka chiefdom in 1877, see esp. M. Spicer, "The War of Ngcayecibi 1877–8" (M.A. thesis, Rhodes University, 1978), pp. 84–106.

62. Natal Archives, Shepstone Papers, box 15: Frere to Shepstone, 15 October 1877.

63. Evidence of attempts at black unity in the 1870s speaks more of white fear than of reality. Factionalism among blacks continued, of course, into the colonial period. See, for example, R. H. Davis, "School vs. Blanket and Settler," *African Affairs*, vol. 78 (January 1979).

portions, for the old pre-Mfecane fissiparous tendencies survived in the new states borne of that upheaval. And whereas on the Cape eastern frontier the closing was long-drawn-out, for many of the peoples of the interior it came very quickly, allowing little time for adjustments.

Nor should the white role in African cleavages be forgotten. It was often deliberate policy to divide black from black, both in the preconquest phase and during the closing period.[64] It should also be remembered that the whites themselves were by no means a monolithic bloc—though no white group sought to unite blacks against other whites, as the British tried to unite the Indians of the Old Northwest against the Yankees.[65] Given the deep dynastic division within Tswana society, which by the 1880s went back for generations, it was natural that when the Ratlou-Rolong accepted Transvaal Boer aid against their Tshidi rivals under Montshiwa, he should turn to the British for protection; nor was it immediately clear that British rather than Boer "protection" was the lesser of two evils. The white impact was in fact by no means uniformly destructive: even in the Ciskei not all Africans lost their land; and though the Transkei became a "dumping ground" for Africans from the Ciskei, and some Transkeian land fell into white hands, most of it remained in African possession. British intervention in the interior presented what amounted to an alternative model to the massive dispossession so commonplace elsewhere; in Lesotho and in Bechuanaland, part of which was to be incorporated within the Cape in 1895, relatively large compact areas remained in African hands. In the Cape, as in the United States, the era of military conflict ended with the passage of legislation to provide for individual title, but in southern Africa the requirement that alienation needed the governor's approval in fact prevented much alienation.[66]

That black territorial rights were not totally eliminated—though soon more Africans were outside than inside the "reserves" and the High Commission territories—was to be vitally important for the future development of the country. It has been argued that these "reserves" and territories func-

64. At the time of the Xhosa cattle-killing, for example, an administrator wrote that the divisions among the Xhosa were "healing up every day, do what we will to keep . . . [them] open" (quoted by A. F. du Toit, "The Cape Frontier," *AYB* 1 [1954]: 103). Another Ciskeian administrator urged the government to "keep up . . . the old animosity between Kafir and Fingoe," quoted Saunders in "Transkeian Territories," p. 15.

65. See Robert F. Berkhofer, "Barrier to Settlement: British Indian Policy in the Old Northwest, 1783–1794," in *The Frontier in American Development*, ed. David M. Ellis (Ithaca, N.Y., 1969). Whites did, however, use black allies against other whites: see, for example, n. 32 above.

66. Long before the Allotment (Dawes) Act of 1887 and the Glen Grey Act of 1894, attempts had been made in both North America and southern Africa to provide individual title to indigenous peoples; the allotment treaties of the 1830s with the "civilized tribes" presaged later policy more closely than the attempts to grant individual title to Mfengu in the Victoria East district in 1848 and the 1850s (on which, see Du Toit, "Cape Frontier," p. 105).

tioned as places where labor could, despite their widespread poverty by the 1920s, be sustained at no cost to the white employer, who could consequently pay low wages to migrant laborers. In the 1960s these areas of land were to become either independent countries (Botswana, Lesotho, and Swaziland) or prospective "homelands"—territorial bases from which Africans could exert some bargaining power, however limited in size, divided, or poor they might be. In this sense, then, the nineteenth-century frontiers have been reopened, and the reallocation of land is an important issue in South African politics today.[67] In the United States, Indian land claims may help to give the nineteenth-century frontiers a certain contemporary relevance; in southern Africa the reopening of those frontiers may yet tear the country apart.[68]

V

In this chapter I have deliberately ignored the impact of the frontier on the political systems of the peoples involved so as to concentrate attention on the political processes in the frontier zones themselves. This other theme is at least as complex as the one examined here. Martin Legassick has shown, for example, that there is no easy answer to the nature of the impact of the frontier on the development of white racial attitudes.[69] If the frontier promoted democracy at all in southern Africa, as Turner argued it did in North America, then it was *herrenvolk* democracy. The Constitution of the United States served as a model for the Free State constitution of 1854, but the latter explictly excluded blacks from the vote.[70] The incorporation of the fron-

67. In January 1979, the South African prime minister announced that he was prepared to see the 1936 land determination reopened. Jack Forbes speaks of the "re-opening" of a frontier in terms of potentiality for possessing political autonomy ("Frontiers," p. 229). It may be argued that a rebellion momentarily "re-opens" a frontier.

68. In the first half of the twentieth century, South African expansionism opened new external frontier zones to the north, which served as buffers between South Africa and "black Africa." Since the Lisbon coup of 1974, most of these buffer zones have collapsed.

69. M. Legassick, "The Frontier Tradition in South African Historiography," *The Societies of Southern Africa in the 19th and 20th Centuries*, University of London Institute of Commonwealth Studies, no. 2 (1971).

70. J. M. Orpen, *Reminiscences of Life in South Africa* (reprint Cape Town, 1964), pp. 203–04, 292. Leonard Thompson shows how different were the constitutional traditions of the Free State and the Transvaal, in "Constitutionalism in the South African Republics," *Butterworths South African Law Review* (1954); but on the exclusion of blacks, they were at one. For comparative perspectives, see: Kenneth P. Vickery, "Herrenvolk Democracy and Egalitarianism in South Africa and the U.S. South," *Comparative Studies in Society and History*, vol. 16 (1974); Richard B. Ford, "The Frontier in South Africa; A Comparative Study of the Turner Thesis" (Ph.D. diss., University of Denver, 1966); and esp. Hermann Giliomee, "Democracy and the Frontier," *South African Historical Journal*, vol. 6 (November 1974).

tier region east of the Kei within the Cape was a direct cause of measures taken by the Cape Parliament in 1887 and 1892, which had the effect of preventing more Africans from using the vote. Generally, white farmers probably made greater adaptations on the frontier than their African counterparts. The quasi-political, highly flexible, and mobile commando, in particular, was organized to aid white expansion against indigenous peoples. While the segmentary tendencies in African societies made for their expansion, those societies were not restructured for conflict with whites. Like the Khoikhoi, the Xhosa had a history of constant feuding among themselves, but they were not a militaristic people. The Zulu, who became one as a result of the Mfecane, forged no new device to meet the white challenge. Perhaps the Griqua made the greatest adaptations because of their marginality and consequent desire to follow European practices.[71] But to explore such themes adequately would require another chapter at least as long as this one.

Here I have attempted to show that, while one broad theme in southern African history is the subjection of the indigenous peoples to white control, there is a sense in which for much of that history, contrary to the still dominant historiographical tradition in South Africa, there was no simple white-black frontier. Ethnicity by no means always determined the form which political process took on the frontier. Particularly in situations of rough equilibrium, factions on both "sides" of the frontier played many different roles and interacted "across" the frontier in a wide variety of ways. Here one can find parallels in those frontier zones in which Euramericans interacted with Amerindians of the eastern seaboard, who possessed relatively complex social and political systems. Though the political as well as the social and economic contexts within which they operated were very different— the various Xhosa factions were not independent to the extent that the Mohegan-Pequot and Narragansetts were—there were obvious similarities between the ways in which an Uncas and an Ngqika used whites for internal political ends, and also between the ways in which the whites sought to make of the local ruler a "supreme chief" who would keep order and remain a loyal friend.[72]

71. Ross, *Adam Kok's Griquas* (Cambridge, Eng., 1976), esp. pp. 113–18.

72. John Hopper kindly allowed me to read his unpublished comparison between Ngqika and Uncas, entitled "Power and Politics on Interracial Frontiers" (seminar paper, Yale University, 1975). That Uncas was able to preserve his preeminence among the Indians while Ngqika was not, was a product, Hopper suggests, of the respective strength of each man relative both to other indigenous leaders and to the colonists (p. 31). In attempting to make Ngqika a "supreme chief," the colonists misunderstood the dynamics of Xhosa society. Being weaker in his own society, Ngqika was not able to support the colonists to the extent that Uncas did the Puritans.

In the closing of the frontiers, too, there are parallels. The Ngqika Xhosa suffered their "Trail of Tears" forty years after the Cherokee, when they were forcibly removed into the Transkei and pushed back onto other indigenous people. In both southern Africa and North America cleavages within the indigenous societies remain important into, and beyond, the closing of the frontiers. Overall, perhaps, the parallels seem closest, despite the obvious demographic disparity, between the semiextermination of the largely nomadic Plains Indians and that of the San. Both were hunter-gatherers whose political systems were not dissimilar and whose delicately balanced ecosystems were in both cases undermined by white intrusion. Between the closing of the Amerindian frontier and the African frontier in southern Africa, on the other hand, there are striking differences. The Africans of southern Africa retained far greater power than the Amerindians of North America because of their greater numbers relative to the whites, their importance as laborers in the white economy, and the fact that they retained some relatively good land, whereas the Amerindians were pushed onto small reservations on poor land. In the United States the white pioneers had closer links with their colonial base than their equivalents in southern Africa: unlike the pioneers on the Great Plains, the Voortrekkers were seeking independence on the veld from what they considered to be the alien rule of the metropolitan power. Yet in southern Africa metropolitan intervention was massive and decisive in effecting the closing of the frontier.

Such parallels as historians of southern Africa have previously drawn between relations with indigenous peoples on the southern African and on the American frontiers have been made in passing and have not been based on detailed examination of the two cases. Such exact work is necessary before confident generalizations can be advanced. Demography, environment, and the political and economic systems of the groups involved all inevitably shaped political process in each case. They, as well as the nature of that process itself, must therefore be studied in depth, for we remain sadly ignorant of political relationships in many frontier situations. It is to be hoped that more work and reflection on the one case will then help us to understand the other more fully.

4

Social and Economic Processes

7

RAMSAY COOK

The Social and Economic Frontier in North America

I

A North American revolution began with the arrival of the first European fishermen, explorers, and traders in the late fifteenth century. An expanding Europe opened a new frontier on which two distinct societies and cultures made their first contact. Over the next four centuries the European intruder gradually engulfed the indigenous Amerindian. While it was not obvious at the beginning, the long-term advantages in the clash between these two "integral cultures"[1] lay with the Europeans: a growing economy, an increasingly complex technology, an expanding population, and a centralized political system supported by military power. Though the Amerindians "were not at all behind us in natural brightness of mind and pertinence," as Montaigne remarked, the Old World sold the New "our opinions and our arts very dear."[2]

Montaigne's comment places the emphasis in the right place. To understand fully the social and economic processes on the new frontier, it must be clearly seen that the newcomers were more than just fishermen, explorers, and traders: they were agents of Europe. The process, whose beginning their arrival announced, was the "europeanization" of North America. That did not mean simply the creation of replicas of Europe—though names like New France, New England, and Nova Scotia are more than just suggestive. But the North American environment inevitably induced substantial

---

1. Bernard W. Sheehan, "Indian-White Relations in Early America: A Review Essay," *William and Mary Quarterly* 26, no. 2 (April 1969): 285.
2. Ronald H. Frame, ed., *The Complete Works of Montaigne* (Stanford, Calif., 1957), bk. 3, p. 693.

modifications.[3] North America was "europeanized" in the sense that, in the conflict on the new frontier, it was European "opinions and arts" that became dominant and Amerindian "opinions and arts" that became marginal. "In the beginning," John Locke maintained, "all the world was America."[4] By the end of the nineteenth century, most of North America was Europe.

The idea of the "frontier" as an interpretive device originated with Frederick Jackson Turner; he viewed it as a process of Americanizing the European settler, a process that "takes him from the railroad car and puts him in the birch bark canoe." Others, like Harold Innis, the fur-trade historian, viewed the process from an opposing perspective: Europe reached out to draw North America into its orbit.[5] But the distinction was perhaps not so radical. Innis certainly recognized that, to a degree, European survival in North America depended on "borrowing cultural traits" from the Amerindian: indeed, he argued that the beaver, the birch, and the Indian laid the foundations of Canada.[6] And Turner was certainly aware that whatever the frontier did to the European, the outreach of the European also had its impact on the frontier, specifically on native Americans. In fact, two years prior to his most famous pronouncement, he published a little monograph entitled *The Character and Influence of the Indian Trade in Wisconsin*. In that study, whose conclusions were quietly reechoed in the essay on the frontier,[7] Turner set out the broad outlines of the impact of European trading systems on native American societies. His conclusions were similar to those reached by Innis forty years later, and have a strikingly modern ring:

> Upon the savage it [the trading post] has worked a transformation. It found him without iron, hunting merely for food and raiment. It put into his hands iron and guns, and made him a hunter for furs with which to purchase the goods of civilization. Thus it tended to perpetuate the hunter stage; but it must also be noted that for a time it seemed likely to develop a class of merchants who should act as intermediaries solely. . . . The trading post left the unarmed tribes at the mercy of those that had bought firearms, and thus caused a relocation of the Indian tribes and an urgent demand for the trader by remote and unvisited

3. R. Cole Harris, "The Extension of France into Rural Canada," in James R. Gibson, ed., *European Settlement and Development in North America* (Toronto, 1978), pp. 27–45.

4. John Locke, *Two Treatises of Government* (Cambridge, 1960), p. 298.

5. Frederick Jackson Turner, *The Frontier in American History*, ed. R. A. Billington (New York, 1962), p. 3; John C. Juricek, "American Usage of the word 'Frontier' from Colonial Times to Frederick Jackson Turner," *Proceedings of the American Philosophical Association* 110 (1966): 10–34.

6. Harold Adams Innis, *The Fur Trade in Canada* (Toronto, 1961), pp. 384, 392; see also W. J. Eccles, "A Belated Review of Harold Adams Innis, *The Fur Trade in Canada*," *Canadian Historical Review* 60, no. 4, (December 1979): 419–41.

7. Turner, *The Frontier*, pp. 11–14.

Indians. It made the Indian dependent upon the white man's supplies. . . . Instead of elevating him the trade exploited him. . . . By intermarriage with French traders the purity of the stock was destroyed and a mixed race produced. The trader broke down the old Totemic divisions, and appointed chiefs regardless of Indian social organization, to foster his trade. . . . The sale of their lands, made less valuable by the extinction of game, gave them a new medium of exchange, at the same time that, under the rivalry of trade, the sale of whiskey increased.[8]

Both Turner and Innis recognized that the frontier was the scene of a clash between a "relatively complex civilization and a much more simple civilization,"[9] between the agents of Europe and the inhabitants of North America.

II

Innis's contrast between two "civilizations," though at different stages of development, was much nearer to the truth than Turner's conflict between "savagery and civilization."[10] Indeed, it is all too easy from the twentieth-century perspective to exaggerate the disparity between pre-Industrial Europe and pre-Colombian North America. Once the differences in environment have been taken into account, as Nancy Lurie has argued, "there was actually little in the European bag of tricks which the Indians could not syncretize with their own experience . . . despite guns and large ships the Europeans could not wrest a living from a terrain which, by Indian standards, supported an exceptionally large population."[11] Recognition of that fact helps to explain the relative ease and self-confidence which characterized the Amerindian reception of the first Europeans. For the most part, the native inhabitants welcomed their unexpected visitors, offered hospitality, showed a willingness to trade, and provided advice on everything from food and transport to the healing arts. At first the Europeans acted more like tourists and peddlers than like prospective permanent residents. They were

8. Frederick Jackson Turner, *The Character and Influence of the Indian Trade in Wisconsin* (Norman, Okla., 1977), pp. 77–79. Turner and Innis agreed on another fundamental matter, for Turner wrote, "The water system composed of the St. Lawrence and the Great Lakes is the key to the continent" (p. 21). Innis's "Laurential thesis" was founded on that concept.

9. Innis, *Fur Trade in Canada*, p. 15.

10. Turner, *The Frontier*, p. 3.

11. Nancy Oestreich Lurie, "Indian Cultural Adjustment to European Civilization," in James Morton Smith, *Seventeenth-Century America* (Chapel Hill, N.C., 1959), p. 39; see also Erna Gunther, *Indian Life on the Northwest Coast of North America* (Chicago and London, 1972), pp. 249–62; T. J. Brasser, "Early Indian-European Contacts," in Bruce G. Trigger, *Handbook of the North American Indians*, 20 vols. 15 (Washington, D.C., 1978), 15:78–88 (*The Northeast*).

impressed with what they saw in this (to them) new world. "Throughout the eastern woodlands," Carl Sauer concluded in his survey of the earliest contacts, "the observers were impressed by the numbers, size, and good order of the settlements and by the appearance and civility of the people. The Indians were not seen as untutored savages, but as people living in a society of appreciated values."[12]

Yet on closer examination even those earliest contacts bore the seeds of future developments. Jacques Cartier's first meeting with the native people who lived around what he christened the *Baie de Chaleurs* was typical, and its symbolism unmistakable. On July 6, 1534, just after mass, Cartier and his crew, traveling by long boat, were surprised by two fleets of Indian canoes whose occupants signaled their desire to trade. The Europeans, substantially outnumbered, were uneasy, and rather than trade they chose to frighten off their pursuers by loud gunfire. But the Amerindians were undaunted and returned the following day, apparently determined to exchange goods. This time a meeting took place, which Cartier recorded in a well-known passage:

> The savages showed a marvellously great pleasure in possessing and obtaining these iron wares and other commodities, dancing and going through many ceremonies, and throwing salt water over their heads with their hands. They bartered all that they had to such an extent that all went back naked without anything on them; and they made signs to us that they would return on the morrow with more furs.

The inhabitants of this region had obviously met Europeans before. That they wanted to trade was one sign; that they left their women behind was another. Equally interesting was their almost insatiable desire for goods from Europe. Then there was the European sizing up his new acquaintances; there was obviously profitable trade to be had here. But there was still more. "I am more and more of the opinion," Cartier wrote, "that these people would be easy to convert to our holy faith."

With visions of commerce and Christianity in his head, Cartier on July 24, 1534, erected at the mouth of Gaspé harbor a thirty-foot cross emblazoned with the fleur-de-lys. An engraving in gothic print read, "VIVE LE ROY DE FRANCE." Here was a new turn of events, and one the Indian leader, Donnacona, did not expect. He protested vigorously, but to no avail. Under the duress of what amounted to abduction, he apparently accepted Cartier's claim that "the cross had been set up to serve as a land mark and guide post

12. Carl Otto Sauer, *Sixteenth-Century North America* (Berkeley, Calif., 1971), p. 303; see also Cornelius J. Jaenen, "Amerindian Views of French Culture in the Seventeenth Century," *Canadian Historical Review* 55, no. 3 (September 1974):361–91.

on coming into the harbour." But this, surely, was no ordinary traffic-control device. Rather it was a claim to French possessory rights, directed not so much against the native Americans, whose rights seem not to have been consulted, but against other European powers engaged in establishing overseas empires. Cartier's first meeting with the native people of North America, his assessment of their trading and religious potential, and his cavalier assumption that he had the right to erect a traffic sign, typify a whole series of similar events that took place along the Atlantic coast of North America.[13]

The European newcomers had little idea that they had made contact with peoples who had been developing over many centuries as hunting, gathering, fishing, and agricultural societies.[14] Precontact Huronia represented one type of society. It existed on the produce of its natural surroundings: the soil for corn, squash, and beans, "the three sisters"; the lakes for fish; and the animals of the woods and forest for clothing. These were the people of the "Long House." Rivers and streams provided natural roads for their birchbark canoes. Their travels rarely carried them far.[15] The life of the Plains people was different to the extent that their environment required other responses. The buffalo was basic to their domestic economy, providing food and shelter. The bow and arrow and spear were their weapons. When they moved, distances were short, for the carrying had to be done by women and dogs.[16] On the West coast a distinctive culture based on salmon fishing, the collection of shell fish, and the trapping of land and sea animals thrived. Woodworking was highly developed, producing large houses in permanent coastal villages. These peoples' canoes were dugout cedars, suitable for heavy water, their fishing gear highly sophisticated, their sculpture and painting second to none in North America.[17]

In pre-Columbian North America the rhythm of life coincided with the

13. H. P. Biggar, ed. *The Voyages of Jacques Cartier* (Ottawa, 1924), pp. 53, 55–56, 61, 57, 66. Marcel Trudel, *Histoire de la Nouvelle-France*, vol. 1: *Les Vaines Tentatives, 1534–1603* (Montreal, 1963), pp. 81–82; Brian Slattery, "French Claims in North America, 1500–59," *Canadian Historical Review* 59, no. 2 (June 1978): 147, argues for a literal interpretation of Cartier's intent, but that only seems tenable in a strict legal sense. Wilcomb E. Washburn, "The Moral and Legal Justification for Dispossessing the Indians," in Smith, *Seventeenth-Century America*, pp. 15–32.

14. Jesse D. Jennings, *Prehistoric North America* (New York, 1968); J. V. Wright, *Six Chapters of Canada's Prehistory* (Ottawa, 1976).

15. Conrad Heidenreich, *Huronia* (Toronto, 1971), p. 283; Elizabeth Tooker, *An Ethnography of the Huron Indians, 1615–49* (Washington, D.C., 1964), pp. 58–66.

16. John S. Ewers, *The Horse in Blackfoot Indian Culture* (Washington, D.C., 1955), p. 300.

17. Philip Drucker, *Cultures of the North Pacific Coast* (San Francisco, Calif., 1965); Wilson Duff, *Images Stone B.C. Thirty Centuries of Northwest Coast Indian Sculpture* (Toronto, 1975).

cycle of the seasons. The Amerindian's cosmology provided an understanding of the world as he knew it.[18] Ceremonies like the Huron Ononharoia, the Mandan O-Kee-Pa, the Kwakiutl Potlach, or the Ojibwa Midewiwin formed part of a rich religious and social life. Precontact society included some two hundred separate cultures with perhaps as great a variety of languages. Those cultures were not static, but rather growing and changing. But that growth and change had taken place in virtual isolation from the European world.[19] The cultural and biological consequences of that separate existence only became évident after the Europeans arrived, bringing new animals and plants, new technologies, new diseases, new religious beliefs, and new views of social and economic organizations.[20]

III

The expansion of Europe into North America was, in part, the extension of the developing commercial system of early modern capitalism. That economic system, as it spread throughout the new continent, drew North America and its original inhabitants into the European mold. Settlement sometimes accompanied, sometimes followed, commercial contact. Christian missions were the third, sometimes uneasy, partnership in the europeanizing project. Nascent capitalist economic structures brought market economics with profit-oriented trading practices and concepts of private property ownership that were, in most respects, alien to Amerindian customs. The rules of capitalist society, especially those relating to property relations, were contained in complex legal systems which had no real counterparts in North America.[21]

18. Diamond Jenness, "The Indian's Interpretation of Man and Nature," *Transactions of the Royal Society of Canada*, 3d ser. 26, no. 2 (1930): 57–62.

19. Wilcomb E. Washburn, *The Indian in America* (New York, 1975), pp. 10–65. Of the many studies of Indian art, a particularly useful one is Ted J. Brasser, *"Bo'jou, Neejee"* (Ottawa, 1976), which is especially good on the question of contact. Norman Feder's *American Indian Art* (New York, 1971) is also excellent.

20. Alfred W. Crosby, Jr., *The Columbian Exchange* (Westport, Conn., 1972); R. M. Saunders, "The First Introduction of European Plants and Animals to Canada," *Canadian Historical Review* 16, 20, 4 (December 1935): 388–401.

21. Ralph Davis, *The Rise of the Atlantic Economies* (London, 1973). There is a substantial and controversial literature on the topic of the comparative economic organization and motivation of Europeans and Amerindians. It is conveniently summarized and discussed in Arthur J. Ray and Donald Freeman, *'Give Us Good Measure.' An Economic Analysis of Relations between the Indians and the Hudson's Bay Company before 1763* (Toronto, 1978), pp. 10–18. Another viewpoint is presented in Marshall Sahlins, *Stone Age Economics* (Chicago, 1972). On this topic and other aspects of contact, there is much useful information in Carol M. Judd and Arthur J. Ray, eds., *Old Trails and New Directions*, Papers of the Third North American Fur Trade Conference (Toronto, 1980).

The Amerindians' initial contact with European economic organization came through the fur trade. At least in its early phases, that relationship proved satisfactory, even beneficial, to the native Americans. But it also demonstrated the obvious importance of controlling some of the terms of the trade. As the fur trade was succeeded by agricultural settlement and industry, the Amerindian was gradually pressed to the margins of North American society. His way of life was an obstacle to agricultural production organized through private land ownership. His technology and skills, so important in the fur trade, were no longer in demand in the more diversified society. He rarely fitted into the new capitalist economy, even at the lowest level. In North America the proletariat also came from Europe.[22]

In the New England colonies, New France, and in the vast territories of the Hudson's Bay Company, the fur trade provided the framework for a mutually profitable partnership.[23] Indeed, in the early stages the native American had the upper hand because he had so much that the European needed if the trade was to be profitable.[24] Native technology, geographical knowledge, and country foods made penetration of the continent possible.[25] And most important, it was the harvest of furs that financed the founding of European empires in the new world.

The French were quick to recognize the superiority of Indian means of transportation. In 1602, facing the treacherous Lachine Rapids, Champlain wrote:

> The water here is so swift that it could not be more so . . . so that it is impossible to imagine one's being able to go by boats through these falls. But anyone desiring to pass them should provide himself with the canoe of the savages, which a man can easily carry. For to make a portage by boat could not be done in sufficiently brief time to enable one to return to France if he desired to winter there. . . . But in the canoe the savages can go without restraint, and quickly, everywhere, in the small as well as the large rivers. So that by using canoes as the savages do, it would be possible to see all there is, good and bad, in a year or two.[26]

22. This generalization is, of course, subject to many exceptions, for a few Amerindians have entered the capitalist system at almost every level, from high finance to high steel. One interesting study, which demonstrates some of the problems, is Rolf Knight, *Indians at Work. An Informal History of Native Labour in British Columbia* (Vancouver, 1978).

23. Alden T. Vaughan, *New England Frontier: Puritans and Indians 1620–1675* (Boston and Toronto, 1965), pp. 211–34; Innis, *Fur Trade in Canada*, passim.

24. W. J. Eccles, *The Canadian Frontier 1534–1760* (New York, 1969), p. 24: "The French were far more dependent upon the Indians than the Indians on them."

25. Innis, *Fur Trade in Canada*, p. 389; James Axtell, "The Scholastic Philosophy of the Wilderness," *William and Mary Quarterly* 29, no. 3 (July 1972): 335–66. Eric Ross, *Beyond the River and the Bay* (Toronto, 1973), p. 6.

26. Innis, *Fur Trade in Canada*, cited on p. 49; Champlain's point is dramatically sec-

Champlain was too optimistic about the time needed to tour the country, and he still had to learn that in winter another Indian invention would be necessary for the traveler: the snowshoe. Traveling in the interior, by canoe or snowshoe, meant traveling light. For heavy, complicated, and perishable food the Indians substituted *sagamité*: ground corn to which other ingredients could be added if available. At first the French palate revolted against this, especially when, as Father Sagard noted, it was eaten from the same bowls the Indians used when they "found themselves under the necessity of making water" in the midst of a canoe journey.[27] But sagamité quickly became recognized as indispensable for those who wanted to make the long journey into the Huron country. And when corn was not readily available, the Plains Indians provided another readily transportable food: pemmican. It was pemmican that got the Conneticut trader Peter Pond to Lake Athabaska before any other trader in 1777–78,[28] and it was soon a staple of the trade. With canoes and snowshoes, ground corn and pemmican, and, above all, with the aid of Indian guides, the European traders and explorers, the French on the Saint Lawrence, the British on Hudson's Bay, and then the Americans from Saint Louis were able to tap the rich fur resources of the interior of the continent. The fur trade, which magnetically drew the Europeans toward the unexplored interior, was of critical importance in the history of Amerindian-European contact.

In examining the fur trade and the Amerindian place in it, three initial points need to be emphasized. The first is that trade itself, and some of its consequences, preceded the coming of the European. While the precontact trading network of the Hurons, for example, has sometimes been exaggerated in size and importance,[29] there is no question that the trade and the rules of trade between Hurons and their neighbors, especially the Algonkians, had a lengthy history. From that long experience, the Hurons gained the knowledge that helped them in their later trading relations with the French.

---

onded by a modern birchbark-canoe maker. See John McPhee, *The Survival of the Bark Canoe* (New York, 1975), p. 21. For a thorough account of cultural contact in early New France, see Marcel Trudel, *Histoire de la Nouvelle France*, vol. 2: *Le Comptoir 1604–1627* (Montreal, 1966), pp. 353–403.

27. Gabriel Sagard, *The Long Journey to the Country of the Huron*, ed. G. M. Wrong (Toronto, 1939), p. 60. Corn was nearly as important in early New England, where the first settlers learned corn cultivation from the Indians. A. C. Parker, "Iroquois Use of Maize and Other Food Plants," in W. N. Fenton, ed., *Parker on the Iroquois* (Syracuse, N.Y., 1968), pp. 14–15; Bernard Sheehan, *Savagism and Civility: Indians and Englishmen in Colonial Virginia* (Cambridge, 1980), pp. 101–09.

28. Harold Adams Innis, *Peter Pond. Fur Trader and Adventurer* (Toronto, 1930), pp. 84–86; Grace Lee Nute, *Voyageurs* (New York, 1931), p. 54.

29. George T. Hunt, *The Wars of the Iroquois. A Study in Inter-Tribal Trade Relations* (Madison, Wis., 1940), pp. 53–65.

"The introduction of European goods," Bruce Trigger, a leading student of the Hurons, notes, "did not alter the pattern of Huron development so much as it intensified it."[30] In the southern part of the continent another member of the Iroquois linguistic group, the Cherokees, readily developed the techniques and rules of a trading people.[31] Similar precontact trading patterns existed in the Plains areas, where the Mandans, for example, played a leading role as middlemen.[32] In 1738, La Vérendrye observed the Mandans at first hand and was impressed with their business acumen. The Mandans, he recorded, "are sharp traders and clean the Assiniboine out of everything they have in the way of guns, powder, balls, knives, axes and awls."[33]

The role of middleman was well understood by many Indian groups, who jealously guarded that position once the European trade began. Donnacona's reluctance to provide Cartier with information about routes inland in 1535 doubtless stemmed from his desire to preserve the economic and political advantages which his position as go-between gave him.[34] In the Hudson's Bay trading orbit, Assiniboine and Cree middlemen established their dominance in the trade at York Factory. That gave them the power to demand the best terms from the Blackfeet and Gros Ventres, on the one hand, and the French or British on the other.[35] A similar pattern was repeated on the Pacific Coast, where Kwakiutl traders outbid the Hudson's Bay Company and sold to U.S. coastal ships, while Tsimshian and Tlingit chiefs monopolized trade on the Skeena and Stikine rivers.[36]

Although the fur trade unquestionably contributed to intertribal conflict and bloodshed, those conflicts were not initiated by the trade. The serpent, as John Ewers and others have shown, was already in the American Eden. Champlain discovered on his arrival in America at the beginning of the seventeenth century that Hurons and Algonkians were at war with the Mohawks and were anxious to engage the French on their side in the struggle.[37] Precontact Plains Indians fought over hunting grounds, women, and

30. Bruce G. Trigger, *The Children of Aataentsic*, 2 vols. (Montreal, 1976), 1:175. In *Huronia*, p. 219, Conrad Heidenreich argues that the Huron trading network was less developed than Trigger suggests, but he agrees that a precontact network did exist.

31. John Phillip Reid, *A Law of Blood: Primitive Law of the Cherokee Nation* (New York, 1965), p. 124.

32. John C. Ewers, "The Indian Trade of the Upper Missouri before Lewis and Clark," *Bulletin of the Missouri Historical Society* 10, no. 4, 1 (1954):429–46.

33. John C. Ewers, "The Influence of the Fur Trade upon the Indians of the Northern Plains," in Malvina Bolus, *People and Pelts* (Winnipeg, 1972), cited on p. 3.

34. Trigger, *Children of Aataentsic*, 1:187.

35. Arthur J. Ray, *Indians in the Fur Trade* (Toronto, 1974), pp. 51–57.

36. Wilson Duff, *The Indian History of British Columbia*, vol. 1: *The Impact of the White Man*, Anthropology in British Columbia, Memoir no. 5 (Victoria, 1964), p. 58; Gunther, *Indian Life*, pp. 119–38.

37. Eccles, *Canadian Frontier, 1534–1760*, pp. 24–25.

for revenge and prestige.[38] Indeed, one of the trader's main tasks was to attempt to pacify ancient tribal enmities, for in North America, as elsewhere, trade flourished best in conditions of peace and stability. The European peacemakers were not always successful; nor, indeed, were they always peacemakers. They were certainly not above exploiting intertribal rivalries for their own benefit. But war was not a preferred policy, for peace meant better profits.[39]

A second general, if somewhat obvious, point should be mentioned. In the fur trade, as in other aspects of contact, inland tribes were able to preserve their cultural integrity and bargaining power over a longer period than those tribes which came into earliest and most direct contact with the Europeans. The coastal tribes were the first to face the pressures of settlement, disease, and warfare.[40] While, in an unusual case like that of the Micmacs of Acadia, Indians were able to establish "a symbiotic relationship of mutual tolerance and support" with the French, the more common fate of the coastal Algonkians was defeat and subjugation. From the very outset of contact, the trade brought dramatic changes to the life cycle of the coastal tribes. The demands of the trade disrupted the usual winter movements of the Micmacs toward the coast. This meant that they gave up a traditional food source and became dependent on Europeans for subsistence.[41] What saved the Micmacs in Acadia was the confinement of the settlers to the coast, which left the native peoples their interior hunting grounds while "neither group coveted the other's territory."[42] Most other areas on the coast had the opposite experience: white settlers did covet Indian lands. Moreover, the coastal Algonkians sometimes became pawns in a power game between the Europeans and the interior tribes, notably the Iroquois, who used them both as protective buffers and as conduits for trade with the Europeans.[43] The social revolution which followed this first phase of contact was

38. John C. Ewers, "Inter-Tribal Warfare as the Precursor of Indian-White Warfare on the Great Plains," *Western Historical Quarterly* 6, no. 4 (October 1975):397–410; P. Richard Metcalf, "Who Should Rule at Home? Native American Politics and Indian-White Relationships," *Journal of American History* 61, no. 3 (December 1974):651–65.

39. Robin Fisher, *Contact and Conflict, Indian-European in British Columbia, 1774–1890* (Vancouver, 1977), pp. 42–43; Ray, *Indians*, pp. 14–16; but see also Bruce G. Trigger, "The Mohawk-Mohican War (1624–28): The Establishment of a Pattern," *Canadian Historical Review* 52, no. 3 (September 1971):276–86, for a careful examination of the way the trade rivalries of Dutch, French, and British led to the Iroquois wars.

40. Francis Jennings, *The Invasion of America: Indians, Colonialism and the Cant of Conquest* (New York, 1976), pt. 2, passim.

41. Bernard G. Hoffman, *Cabot to Cartier* (Toronto, 1961), p. 214.

42. Andrew Hill Clark, *Acadia: The Geography of Early Nova Scotia* (Madison, Wis., 1968), p. 361. For a full account, see L. F. S. Upton, *Micmacs and Colonists. Indian-White Relations in the Maritimes, 1713–1867* (Vancouver, 1979).

43. T. J. C. Brasser, "The Coastal Algonkians: People of the First Frontier," in Eleanor

rapid, much more so than in the interior.[44] For nearly two centuries, the distant tribes benefitted from continued isolation—an isolation which the fur traders encouraged in the realization that large-scale settlement would destroy their livelihood.[45]

A final general point is that, within the fur-trading system, the role of the native people was certainly not a passive one. Cartier's initial experience was a common one: the Amerindians wanted to trade. They wanted to obtain European goods that were useful to them, and they early demonstrated a penchant for what might be called luxuries or novelties. That the native Americans understood the benefits of competition was apparent from the outset. In 1611 Champlain wrote that the Montagnais "wanted to wait until several ships had arrived in order to get our wares more cheaply. Thus those people are mistaken who think that by coming first they can do better business; for these Indians are now too sharp."[46] Nor had the importance of profit escaped them; guns obtained at York Factory in the late eighteenth century for twelve beaver by the Crees were later sold to the Blackfeet at a 200 percent markup. As long as fur-bearing animals remained plentiful, the fur trade provided a mutually profitable framework for Amerindian-European relations. The Indians, Aruthur J. Ray has made clear, "were sophisticated traders, who had their own clearly defined set of objectives . . . they were astute consumers and not people who were easily hoodwinked."[47]

Many of the complexities of the fur trade can be illustrated by looking at the French-Huron experience. From the outset the part played by the Hurons in that relationship was that of a partner; it was, as W. J. Eccles notes, "a commercial alliance."[48] Since the Hurons had already, in precontact times, developed a significant trading network based upon their large agricultural output, the French found it necessary to adapt themselves to Huron trading practices. That meant at least a partial conformity to the Huron idea that trade had to satisfy more than mere economic motives. It was part of the politics of prestige.[49] Champlain quickly recognized that a successful trading relationship would have to include gift giving, treaties of

Burke Leacock and Nancy Oestreich Lurie, *North American Indians in Historical Perspective* (New York, 1971), p. 73.

44. A. G. Bailey, "Social Revolution in Early Canada," *Canadian Historical Review* 19, no. 3 (September 1938):264–76.

45. Lurie, "Indian Cultural Adjustment," p. 28; Fisher, *Contact and Conflict*, passim.

46. H. P. Biggar, *The Works of Samuel de Champlain* (Toronto, 1925), 2:171.

47. Ray, *Indians*, p. 69; Arthur J. Ray, "Fur Trade History as an Aspect of Native History," in Ian A. L. Getty and Donald B. Smith, *One Century Later* (Vancouver, 1978), p. 10; for an excellent example, see Samuel Hearne, *A Journey to the Northern Ocean, 1769–71–72*, ed. Richard Glover (Toronto, 1958), p. 187.

48. Eccles, *Canadian Frontier, 1534–1760*, p. 6.

49. Heidenreich, *Huronia*, p. 293.

friendship, exchange of European and Huron representatives, and perhaps even intermarriage. Father Sagard, for example, recorded his embarrassment at the repeated suggestion that he take a Huron wife "or at least . . . make a family alliance."[50] While Huron youths went off to Quebec to be educated and Christianized, the coureurs de bois took up residence with the Hurons at least partly as tokens of French trust. As the missionaries soon discovered, however, the coureurs de bois frequently adopted Indian customs and were thus poor examples of what civilization was supposed to offer.[51] Consequently they were replaced by *donnés*, laymen employed and controlled by the Jesuit missionaries. The Huron acceptance of the Jesuit presence was only a matter of convenience, not a demonstration of a willingness to convert. They wanted the benefits of the trade, especially European goods, which they believed could be readily integrated into their way of life. If, as Champlain and his successors insisted, acceptance of the missionaries was the price to be paid for the trading partnership, then they tolerated Brébeuf and his brethren. But only just.[52]

Yet even in the case of the relatively powerful and economically sophisticated Hurons, the fur trade had its disadvantages. It led to a gradually growing dependence on the French. The Iroquois threat increased that dependence. As Conrad Heidenreich and others have pointed out, the most important change was that, prior to contact, the Huron trading system was based on commodities they themselves produced; after contact it relied increasingly on furs and European goods.[53] It is true that Huron dependence never became as total and debilitating as that, for example, of the Montagnais, and at least until the 1630s trade seemed to bolster rather than undermine the Huron culture.[54] But by the late 1630s, the complicated relationship with the French that focused on the fur trade led to the destruction of Huronia and the assimilation of most of the survivors into the Iroquois Confederacy. In simple terms, the Hurons believed that the preservation of the French trading alliance depended on the missionary presence in Huronia. While the trade might not have seriously affected Huron culture, the goal of the Jesuits was to make fundamental changes in it. Their activities in

50. Sagard, *Country of the Huron*, p. 125; Wallis Smith, "The Fur Trade and Frontier: A Study in Inter-Cultural Alliance," *Anthropologica*, n.s. 15 (1973):21–36.

51. R. M. Saunders, "The Emergence of the Coureur de Bois as a Social Type," *Canadian Historical Association Report* (1939), p. 26; Normand Lafleur, *La Vie traditionnelle du coureur de bois aux XIXe et XXe siècles* (Montreal, 1973), pp. 29–70; Louise Déchêne, *Habitants et marchands de Montréal au XVIIe siècle* (Montreal, 1974), pp. 217–26.

52. Bruce Trigger, "The Jesuits and the Fur Trade," *Ethnohistory* 12, no. 1 (Winter 1965):38.

53. Heidenreich, *Huronia*, p. 282. For a parallel in New England, see Vaughan, *New England Frontier*, p. 234.

54. Trigger, *Children of Aataentsic*, 1:361–65, 425–30.

Huronia created serious dissension between Indian Christians and traditionalists, and that dissension weakened the Huron response to the Iroquois threat. And the Iroquois threat was partly the consequence of the competition between French and English fur-trading dominance.[55] In the background was the smallpox epidemic which, in the late 1630s, had wiped out half of the Huron population. While the fur trade alone was not responsible for the smoke that rose from Saint-Marie-aux-Hurons in 1649, it was nevertheless a central part of the French-Huron relationship, and that relationship brought the final disaster.[56]

The destruction of Huronia and the depletion of fur-bearing animals in eastern North America pushed the explorer and the trader deeper into the interior of North America. The new networks that sprang up out of Fort Churchill, Montreal, and Saint Louis followed many of the patterns already observed in the French-Huron trade. Nevertheless, on the western woodlands and plains, where settlement pressure was slight until the middle of the nineteenth century, the partnership of Amerindian and European trader was fruitful. There, moreover, at least until the amalgamation of the Hudson's Bay Company and the Northwest Company in 1821, the tribal hunters often experienced the benefits of a seller's market. Once again the European traders found it necessary to operate in conformity with indigenous trading habits. Once again they found the Indians eager to trade. In 1730 La Vérendrye reported that a Cree spokesman "begged me to receive them all into the numbers of the children of our Father, to have pity on them and their families, that they were in a general condition of destitution, lacking axes, knives, kettles, guns, etc., that they hoped to get all these things from me if I would let them come to my fort."[57] But anxiety for European goods did not mean that substandard goods were acceptable. One Hudson's Bay Company trader, after a bad experience, reported home in 1728 that "never was any man so upbraided with our powder, kettles and hatchets, than we have been this summer by all the natives, especially by those that border near the French."[58] When Jean-Baptiste Truteau was advised to carry out some detailed market research in the early nineteenth century, the Company of Explorers of the Upper Missouri explicitly recognized that the Indian trade could not be taken for granted.[59] The western trading system, then, was

55. Hunt, *Wars of the Iroquois*, pp. 66–104; Trigger, *Children of Aataentsic*, 2:664.

56. Trigger, *Children of Aataentsic*, 2:601.

57. L. J. Burpee, ed., *Journals and Letters of Pierre Gaultier de Varennes de la Vérendrye and His Sons* (Toronto, 1927), p. 146.

58. Ray, "Fur Trade History," cited on p. 11. E. E. Rich, *The Fur Trade and the Northwest to 1857* (Toronto, 1967), p. 103; Edward Umfreville, *The Present State of Hudson's Bay containing a Full Description of That Settlement and Adjacent Country; And Likewise of the Fur Trade and Hints for Its Improvement*, ed. W. S. Wallace, (Toronto, 1954), pp. 31–32.

59. Ewers, "The Influence of the Fur Trade," cited on p. 9.

again a meshing of European market economics and elements of the traditional exchange system, which was political as well as economic in nature. A careful and detailed examination of this trading system concludes that by the end of the eighteenth century market considerations had become dominant.[60]

No specific calculation of the comparative profits and losses of the European and Amerindian partners in the fur trade is even remotely possible. Even the standard of economic measurement would be almost impossible to establish. But that the European merchants and their companies found the business worthwhile goes almost without saying. They stayed in it and, in the case of the Hudson's Bay Company, for example, resisted the encroachments of settlement as long as possible.[61] On the native American side the case is obviously more difficult to assess. When furs were plentiful, the prices high, and the Indians' bargaining power strong, the benefits were evident. On the Pacific Coast the prosperity, the technological improvements, and the intellectual stimulus that came as part of the trade in the early years fostered an impressive cultural flowering.[62] Similar responses were doubtless witnessed elsewhere. But markets fluctuated as fashions changed and fur-bearing animals declined in the face of indiscriminate harvesting. And worse, the trade involved more than economic profits and losses. The same trade routes that brought buyer and seller together also brought epidemic diseases.[63]

IV

Although it was not recognized at the time, nor by historians in a systematic fashion until recently, the most significant consequence of early contact was biological. There is still much controversy over pre-Columbian demography, but there is substantial agreement that traditional, low-population estimates must be adjusted dramatically upward.[64] In the absence of a pre-Columbian census, there is, of course, a necessary tentativeness about all

60. Ray and Freeman, 'Give Us Good Measure,' p. 236.

61. John S. Galbraith, The Little Emperor, Governor Simpson of the Hudson's Bay Company (Toronto, 1976), pp. 188–208.

62. Duff, Indian History, p. 53.

63. Arthur J. Ray, "Diffusion of Diseases in the Western Interior of Canada, 1830–1850," Geographical Review 66, no. 2 (April 1976): 139–57.

64. Henry F. Dobyns, "Estimating Aboriginal American Population: An Appraisal of Techniques with a New Hemispheric Estimate," Current Anthropology 7 (1966): 395–416. For a survey of the literature, see idem, Native American Historical Demography (Chicago, 1976). My figures are taken from William N. Denevan, ed., The Native Population of the Americas (Madison, Wis., 1976), p. 291.

population estimates.[65] Nevertheless, the total population for North and South America at the time of Columbus's arrival would seem to have been in the area of 57 million. About four and one-half million of those Amerindians lived north of Mexico, of whom perhaps a million occupied present-day Canada, Alaska, and Greenland.[66] That figure had fallen to approximately 350,000 by the end of the nineteenth century. By 1890 the Indian population of the United States stood at 250,000; in Canada, Alaska, and Greenland the figure for 1911 was 108,000.[67] That astonishing decline explains why, until recently, even sympathetic observers anticipated the total disappearance of Amerindian culture.[68]

While many factors led to the diminution of the native populations, the "virulent disease frontier" is now generally recognized as the one of primary significance.[69] "The invasion of the New World populations by Old World pathogens," Henry Dobyns, a pioneer in this area of research, has written, "constituted one of the world's greatest biological disasters."[70] While native Americans had suffered from such diseases as hepatitis, encephalitis, polio, and perhaps yellow fever, the Europeans introduced them to the contagions of smallpox, whooping cough, measles, chicken pox, bubonic plague, typhus, malaria, diphtheria, amoebic dysentery, influenza, and a number of helminthic infections. Wherever syphilis originated,[71] it was almost certainly brought to the people north of Mexico by Europeans.[72] The virulence of these diseases among indigenous North Americans is explained by the lack of previous contact. North America was virgin soil, its people lacking in both immunity and, despite a highly developed system of cures for indige-

65. After an extended examination of the discussion of precontact population, Woodrow Borah concluded that only after a great deal of additional research will it be possible to arrive at a hemispheric figure with a margin of error between 30 percent and 50 percent. Denevan, *Native Population*, p. 34.

66. These figures, taken from Denevan, are about 25 percent higher than the now commonly accepted, and very judicious, estimate contained in Harold E. Driver, *Indians of North America*, 2d ed. (Chicago, 1975), pp. 63–64.

67. Driver, *Indians of North America*, p. 257; F. W. Hodge, *Handbook of the Indians of Canada* (Ottawa, 1911), p. 390. By the mid-1960s, the Indian population of the United States had grown to 600,000. In Canada the figure was 200,000 (ibid., pp. 527, 539).

68. See, for example, Lewis Henry Morgan, *The League of the Iroquois*, [1851] (Secaucus, N.J., 1975), p. 145, and Diamond Jenness, *The Indians of Canada*, [1932] (Toronto, 1977), p. 264.

69. Wilbur R. Jacobs, "The Indian and the Frontier in American History—A Need for Revision," *Western Historical Quarterly* 4, no. 1 (January 1973):46. See also Alfred W. Crosby, "Virgin Soil Epidemics as a Factor in the Aboriginal Depopulation of America," *William and Mary Quarterly* 33, no. 2 (April 1976):289–99.

70. Denevan, *Native Population*, cited on p. 5.

71. Crosby, *Columbian Exchange*, pp. 122–64. The most convincing, perhaps even conclusive, discussion of this issue is Francisco Guerra, "The Problem of Syphilis," in Fredi Chiappelli, ed., *First Images of America: The Impact of the New World on the Old* (Berkeley, Calif., 1976), 2:845–51.

72. Virgil J. Vogel, *American Indian Medicine* (Norman, Okla., 1970), p. 211.

nous diseases, medical treatment. The list of known epidemics is lengthy: between 1616 and 1619 a plague swept through New England that reduced the Indian population by 90 percent. A decade later smallpox brought havoc to the Saint Lawrence region, killing tens of thousands of Iroquois. A century later the same disease, perhaps the worst of the Indian killers, reduced the Cherokee population by half, while in 1837 six thousand Blackfeet, two-thirds of the total population, succumbed to the same infection. That same epidemic virtually exterminated the Mandans in the Dakotas. European-imported diseases were probably a major contributing factor in the extinction of the Beothuks of Newfoundland, whose last survivor died of tuberculosis in 1823. An 1862 smallpox epidemic, spreading north from Victoria, reduced the native population from 60,000 to 20,000 in British Columbia.[73]

Knowing nothing of these mysterious diseases, native Americans reacted with anger, fear, and panic. David Thompson, a western explorer, described the devastation of a smallpox epidemic:

> They had no idea of the disease and its dreadful nature . . . more men died in proportion than women and children, for unable to bear the heat of the fever they rushed into the Rivers and Lakes to cool themselves, and the greater part thus perished. The countries were in a manner depopulated, the Natives allowed that far more than half had died, and from the number of tents which remained, it appeared that about three-fifths had perished.[74]

The most obvious consequence of epidemics was drastic population reduction. Though total figures, or even reliable approximations, are virtually impossible to calculate, a reasonable figure would certainly exceed 50 percent. One estimate of the effect of disease on the population of the Northern Plains between 1734 and 1850 indicates that in 1781–82 virtually every tribe—Arapaho, Arikara, Assiniboine, Blackfeet, Cheyenne, Cree, Crow, Flathead, Gros Ventre, Hidatsa, Kutenai, Mandan, Nez Percé, Shoshoni, and Sioux—suffered losses in excess of 25 percent. Nearly half of these tribes were visited by an equally costly epidemic in 1837–38.[75] The Cree, it is interesting to note, escaped this 1837 ravage because of the effective action of

73. Shelburne F. Cook, "The Significance of Disease in the Extinction of the New England Indians," *Human Biology* 14 (1973):487–91; Trigger, *Children of Aataentsic*, 2:499–501; Reid, *A Law of Blood*, 6; Howard R. Lamar, ed., *The American West* (New York, 1977), pp. 702–03; John C. Ewers, *The Blackfeet: Raiders of the Plains* (Norman, Okla., 1958), pp. 65–66; L. S. F. Upton, "The Extermination of the Beothuks," *Canadian Historical Review* 8, no. 2 (June 1977):133–53; Wilson Duff, *The Indian History*, pp. 42–43.

74. J. B. Tyrrell, ed., *David Thompson's Narrative, 1784–1812* (Toronto, 1916), p. 323.

75. John F. Taylor, "Sociocultural Effects of Epidemics on the Northern Plains, 1734–1850," *Western Canadian Journal of Anthropology* 7, no. 4 (1977):78.

William Todd, a Hudson's Bay Company employee, in carrying out a "massive vaccination."[76]

The importance of population loss, no matter how extensive, cannot be measured in numbers alone. Just as significant is the fact that many of the common epidemic diseases cut down men and women in their most productive years, a time when their services to their families and their communities were most critical. Edwin Denig, of the Western Fur Company, recognized this problem when he wrote of the 1837–38 epidemic among the Assiniboine that "generally very old or very young persons were the only ones who recovered. Most of the principal men having died, it took years to recover from the shock. Young men had to grow up, remnants of bands had to be collected, new leaders to be formed, property to be had."[77]

A second consequence of population shrinkage was territorial movement. Tribes most seriously weakened by loss through disease were easily driven from their traditional territories by their enemies. The decimated Mandan, for example, joined with the remnants of the Arikara and Hidatsi in an attempt to preserve fragments of their existence. In fact, their condition was so feeble that they became almost totally dependent upon the assistance of the United States government. By 1862 further epidemics, combined with Sioux depredations, had reduced these three tribes to a single village. The devastating impact of smallpox on the Assiniboine in 1837 opened the prairie parklands to large-scale migrations of Woodland Cree who, having been immunized against the disease, became the numerically dominant group in the area.[78]

Finally, a major consequence of epidemic disease was a breakdown of traditional values and beliefs. It was easy enough for the Indians to hold the Europeans responsible for the frightening new diseases. As early as the 1640s the Hurons were remarking that "since we pray we see by experience that death carries us off everywhere."[79] But the fact remained that their own cures and their own medicine men were totally ineffective when faced with these foreign contagions. Perhaps the Europeans, and especially the missionaries, had already sown the seeds of doubt,[80] but the helplessness of the trusted shaman in the face of smallpox, measles, and cholera produced a more lasting skepticism, with consequences that may have led to serious questioning of traditional cosmology. David Thompson observed this reaction in the Saskatchewan country in 1780:

76. Ray, *Indians in the Fur Trade*, pp. 188–91.

77. Edwin T. Denig, *Five Tribes of the Upper Missouri* (Norman, Okla., 1961), p. 72.

78. Taylor, "Sociocultural Effects of Epidemics," p. 65; Ray, *Indians*, pp. 183–91.

79. Reuben Thwaites, ed., *The Jesuit Relations and Allied Documents*, 73 vols. (Cleveland, Ohio, 1898), 16:39.

80. Vogel, *American Indian Medicine*, p. 35; Trigger, *Children of Aataentsic*, 2:592–30.

About the tenth day we came to the "One Pine." This had been a fine stately tree of two fathoms girth, growing among a patch of Aspens, and being all alone without any other pines for more than a hundred miles, had been regarded with superstitious reverence. When the smallpox came . . . the master of one of the tents applied his prayers to it, to save the lives of him and his family, burned sweet grass and offered upon its roots three horses to be at its service, all he had, the next day the furniture of his horses with his Bow and Quiver of Arrows, and the third morning, having nothing more, a Bowl of Water. The disease was now on himself and he had to lie down. Of his large family, only himself, one of his wives and a Boy survived. As soon as he acquired strength he took his horses and all his other offerings from the "Pine Tree," then putting his little axe in his belt, he ascended the Pine Tree to about two-thirds of its height, and then cut it off, out of revenge for not having saved his family.[81]

Once the value system, already corroded by other aspects of contact, came into question, the final subversion was not far in the future, for the shaman was "a principal barrier to the eradication of Indian culture."[82]

The drastic decimation of the native population through disease may well have produced another quite unforeseen result: a disturbance in nature's balance. That is one possible interpretation of a story that puzzled the observant David Thompson. He wrote:

A strange idea prevails among these Natives, and also of all the Indians to the Rocky Mountains, though unknown to each other, that when they were numerous, before they were destroyed by the Small Pox all the animals of every species were also very numerous and more so in comparison of the number of Natives than at present; and this was confirmed to me by old Scotchmen in the service of the Hudson's Bay Company, and by the Canadians from Canada; the knowledge of the latter extended over all the interior countries, yet no disorder was known among the animals, the fact was certain, and nothing they knew of could account for it.

81. Tyrrell, *David Thompson's Narrative*, p. 324; Alfred Goldsworthy Bailey, *The Conflict of European and Eastern Algonkian Cultures 1504–1700*, 2d ed. (Toronto, 1969), p. 81; Calvin Martin, *Keepers of the Game, Indian-Animal Relations and the Fur Trade* (Berkeley, Calif., 1978), p. 146.

82. Vogel, *American Indian Medicine*, p. 35. In August 1979, a government hospital in Kenora, Ontario, agreed to allow an Ojibwa medicine man to practice in the mental health unit. Though not attempting to cure "white man's diseases," George Councillor said, "there are Indian sicknesses that doctors can't see, like when a bad medicine man puts a curse on somebody. White men call them emotional problems and hallucinations. In our culture you can get sick from many things. If you hurt a small animal or bird you might have problems many years later. It's forbidden by the Great Spirit to be cruel. You have to fit in with the way things work." The

In nature, both hunter—wolf or Indian—and hunted—deer or beaver—are necessary to maintain the equilibrium. The destruction of predators may temporarily cause the hunted to flourish. But rapid food depletion may then bring large population losses. So perhaps disease was the explanation of the observed decline of animals—disease among the Indians.[83]

The destructive effect of epidemic disease upon the native American populations cannot be taken as evidence of weakness or backwardness. Within the demands of their own environment, Amerindian medical knowledge and practice were not only adequate but in some ways superior to European knowledge. Their use of herbs was very sophisticated, their methods of childbirth and birth control effective and humane. Almost every European observer noted the generally sound health and physical condition of the inhabitants at the time of initial contact. The observation of Nicholas Denys in 1672 was fairly typical:

> They were not subject to disease, and knew nothing of fevers. If any accident happened to them . . . they did not need a physician. They had knowledge of herbs, of which they made use and straight away grew well. They were not subject to the gout, gravel, fevers or rheumatism. The general remedy was to make themselves sweat, something which they did every month and even oftener.[84]

The Iroquois understanding of psychology was attested to, often grudgingly, by such a writer as Père Charlevoix, who noted of the shaman that "what proves the power of imagination over men is that these physicians with all their absurdities cure to the full as often as our own." That opinion is emphatically seconded by modern experts. "Iroquois understanding of psychodynamics," Anthony Wallace has written, "was greatly superior to that of the most enlightened Europeans of the time."[85]

---

local clergymen, equally in keeping with their own traditions, opposed recognition of this contemporary Midewiwin. *Globe and Mail* (Toronto), August 29, 1979, p. 9.

83. Tyrrell, *David Thompson's Narrative*, p. 110. Victor G. Hopwood, in *David Thompson: Travels in Western North America, 1784–1812* (Toronto, 1971), p. 32, interprets this passage as evidence that the Indians had developed a myth of a "golden age" before the white man arrived. He neglects to observe that the white man also witnessed this "golden age." Calvin Martin, in *The Keepers of the Game*, pp. 113–56, argues that the relation between the decline in the number of animals and disease can be explained by the destruction of the Indians' belief system, which could not deal with the fact that the Europeans brought disease. The result was that war was declared on the animals, which seemed to have been held responsible. That may be so, but as a speculation it is certainly no more convincing than the argument for an ecological interpretation presented here and based on Aldo Leopold's essay, "Thinking like a Mountain," in *A Sand County Almanac* (New York, 1976), pp. 129–33.

84. Cornelius J. Jaenen, *Friend and Foe* (Toronto, 1976), cited on p. 104. See also J. H. Kennedy, *Jesuit and Savage in New France* (New Haven, Conn., 1950), p. 107.

85. Vogel, *American Indian Medicine*, cited on p. 190; Anthony F. C. Wallace, *The Death and Rebirth of the Seneca* (New York, 1972), p. 63.

The Indian readily shared his medical cures with the European, as Cartier's scurvy-ridden crew learned. But the tragedy was that Indian medical knowledge proved largely ineffective against the virulent diseases planted in the virgin soil of the Americas by the European intruder.[86] Unconscious "germ warfare" was the most important single cause of the depopulation and demoralization of native American societies.

Though disease was an unintended companion of the European trader, one destructive item in the trader's bag of goods was not: alcohol. From the time of the earliest contacts, Europeans discovered both the Indian's almost insatiable desire for liquor and his apparent inability to consume it in moderation. "These skins were bartered for brandy," Nicholas Denys wrote in 1672, "for which they ever since they first began to trade with fishermen are very greedy and they herewith fill themselves up to such an extent that they frequently fall over backwards, for they do not call it drinking unless they overload themselves with this strong drink in a beastly fashion."[87] Given Amerindian proclivities, the temptation to use brandy, whiskey, and other intoxicants in the trade was a temptation which was virtually irresistible. And as the traditional value system of the Amerindians disintegrated as a consequence of various elements of the contact relationship, the Indians lost confidence in themselves and turned more and more to the consolations of intoxication. It may be one of the great ironies of postcontact history that the missionaries, who opposed the brandy and whiskey trade, actually contributed to the native American's reliance upon it through their corrosive impact on native religious beliefs.[88]

But the fur trade cannot be exonerated from blame for the alcohol trade. Faced with price competition between companies and with the demands of the native Americans for better prices, the European traders found that alcohol was the commodity best suited to satisfy demand and protect profits. Its advantages were twofold. Since it was one of the few trade items that the

86. Biggar, *Works of Samuel de Champlain*, pp. 212–13; Vogel, pp. 111–23; John J. Heagarty, *Four Centuries of Medical History in Canada* (Toronto, 1928), 1:269. See also William N. Fenton, "Contacts between Iroquois Herbalism and Colonial Medicine," in *Smithsonian Institution Annual Report 1941* (Washington, D.C., 1942), pp. 503–26, and Raymond D. Fogelson, "Change, Persistence and Accommodation in Cherokee Medico-Magical Beliefs," in William N. Fenton and John Gulich, eds., *Symposium on Cherokee and Iroquois Cultures* (Washington, D.C., 1961), p. 215–25.

87. Jaenen, *Friend and Foe*, cited on p. 110.

88. Trigger, *Children of Aataentsic*, 1:433; André Vachon, "L'Eau-de-Vie dans la société indienne," *Canadian Historical Association Report, 1960*, pp. 28–29; Thomas D. Graves, "Acculturation, Access and Alcoholism in a Tri-Ethnic Community," *American Anthropologist 69*, nos. 3–4 (June–August 1967):307–21. David G. Mandelbaum, "Alcohol and Culture," *Current Anthropology 6* (1965):281–92; Nancy Lurie, "The World's Oldest Ongoing Protest Demonstration: North American Indian Drinking Patterns," *Pacific Historical Review 40*, no. 3 (August 1971):311–32—all deviate from the alienation explanation presented in most work on the Indian and alcohol.

Indians desired in almost unlimited quantities, it could induce the trappers to increase their volume of furs as nothing else could.[89] Moreover, since the cost of alcohol could be controlled by the simple process of watering it down, it effectively protected margins of profit in a seller's market. As an item in gift-giving ceremonies, a practice increasingly used as an inducement to trade, alcohol assumed an enormous importance.[90]

The Northwest Company trader Duncan M'Gillivray cynically anticipated the economic historian's argument when he wrote in 1794 that "when a nation becomes addicted to drinking, it affords a strong presumption that they will soon become excellent traders."[91] Even after the Hudson's Bay Company's monopoly was established and the whiskey trade officially suppressed, M'Gillivray's philosophy continued to animate the illegal trade out of such places as Fort Whoop Up and to contribute to the final disintegration of Amerindian culture on the western plains. As much as 25 percent of the Blackfoot population may have perished from the effects of alcohol in the years between 1869 and 1874 alone.[92] Alcohol, too, was an epidemic disease.

v

The onrush of settlement, shrinking markets, and the reduction—even extinction—of some species of fur-bearing animals all contributed to the fur trade's decline. In a sense, it died of its own success, for success brought the depletion of resources. The gun, the steel trap, and the horse were critical elements in that success and decline. Each played its part in ensuring a greater harvest of animals in the short run. Each played its part in increasing native American dependence on the Europeans, first by expanding the importance of fur gathering in the Indian economy, and then by contributing to that indiscriminate exploitation which led to exhaustion of the resource. In the end all the Indian had left was dependence. That was the essence of the tragedy of the single-crop staple economy.

The danger of the exhaustion of resources was foreseen by some at least as early as the mid-seventeenth century. Father Le Jeune recognized that the Indians were not conservationists when he observed that when the Monta-

89. E. E. Rich, "Trade Habits and Economic Motivations among the Indians of North America," *Canadian Journal of Economics and Political Science* 26, no. 1 (February 1960): 50–53.

90. Arthur J. Ray, "The Hudson's Bay Company Fur Trade in the Eighteenth Century," in Gibson, *European Settlement and Development in North America*, pp. 134–35.

91. A. S. Morton, ed., *The Journal of Duncan M'Gillivray of the Northwest Company at Fort George on the Saskatchewan 1794–5* (Toronto, 1929), p. 47.

92. Paul Sharp, *Whoop Up Country: The Canadian and American West* (Norman, Okla., 1973), pp. 43–50; Ewers, *Blackfeet*, p. 261.

gnais "find a lodge they kill all, great and small, male and female. The danger is that they will exterminate the species in the region, as has happened among the Hurons."[93] If the valuable furs disappeared in the east, the supply on the northwest plains seemed inexhaustible. But that optimistic assessment ignored the potential of the steel trap baited with castoreum when combined with the determination of trappers and traders alike to gather in the maximum harvest. David Thompson assumed that the Indian had invented the use of castoreum, though it, like the steel trap, was apparently a European innovation.[94] But Thompson's account of the fate of the beaver, and those who depended on it, as recounted to him by an elderly Indian in Swan River country, remains a classic:

> About two winters ago Weesaukejauk [the Flatterer] showed to our brethren, the Nepissings and Algonquins the secret of their destruction; that all of them were infatuated with the Castoreum of their own species, and more fond of it than we are of fire water. We are now killing the Beaver without any labour, we are now rich but soon [shall] be poor, for when the Beaver are destroyed we have nothing to depend on to purchase what we want for our families, strangers now ruin our country with their iron traps, and we, and they, will soon be poor.

That prediction of disaster took only four years to be fulfilled, Thompson noted in 1797, and drew an ecologically sound moral: "A worn out field can be manured and again made fertile; but the Beaver, once destroyed cannot be replaced; they were the gold coin of the country, with which the necessities of life were procured."[95] Attempts were made by the Hudson's Bay Company to prohibit the use of steel traps and control the slaughter of beaver, but the effort was unavailing. The trappers did not understand the need for conservation, some traders refused to accept any threat to profits, and no central authority existed to enforce compliance.[96]

The growing scarcity of beaver increased the importance of other animals, notably the buffalo. In 1805, Zebulon Pike had remarked on the critical importance of this huge beast when he wrote: "The Yanctongs and Titongs are the most independent Indians in the world; they follow the buffalo as chance directs, clothing themselves with the skins, and making their lodges, bridles and saddles of the same material, the flesh of the animal fur-

93. Thwaites, *Jesuit Relations and Allied Documents*, 8:57. On the Indian and conservation, see Martin, *Keepers of the Game*, pp. 157–88.

94. Robin F. Wells, "Castoreum and the Steel Trap," *American Anthropologist* 74, no. 2 (June 1972):479–83; Carl P. Russell, *Firearms, Traps and Tools of the Mountain Men* (New York, 1967), chaps. 2 and 3.

95. Tyrrell, *David Thompson's Narrative*, pp. 204–06.

96. Ray, *Indians*, p. 105.

nishing their food.[97] To that list of uses should be added pemmican as a trade item.[98] After 1821 the Indians no longer had the pemmican market to themselves, for many of the *métis*, who had been released from the Company's staff with the reorganization, now turned to the buffalo hunt. When demand for buffalo robes developed, especially in the United States, Indian and métis alike set out to reap the profits.[99]

While the buffalo hunt was by no means dependent upon the rifle and the horse, both of these European additions to native American life contributed to the near extinction of the buffalo.[100] By 1880 the buffalo joined the beaver (though it was only down, not out) and the passenger pigeon as victims of the contact between European technology and markets on the one hand, and the Indian hunting culture on the other.[101] And the disappearance of the buffalo left once proud, even arrogant, tribes like the Plains Crees starving and faced with little alternative but to beg the authorities for sustenance.[102] And the price of the sustenance, from both Canadian and United States governments, was submission to life on a reservation.

That final state of dependence developed only gradually, but it was perhaps inherent in the character of the trade. Furs provided the Indians with the currency to purchase European technology, utensils, and trinkets. Those commodities undoubtedly gave the Indians a higher standard of living, an easier way of life. But it also meant that they discarded native skills. A Montagnais is quoted as saying that "the Beaver does everything perfectly well; it makes kettles, hatchets, swords, knives, bread, in short it makes everything."[103] As the trade became all important, dependency increased because other sources of livelihood were neglected. By the middle of the eighteenth century, Peter Kalm realized that guns had become indispensable to the Indians of New France, for without them "they would starve to death."[104] The Europeans not only supplied guns and ammunition; only

97. Frank G. Roe, *The North American Buffalo: A Critical Study of the Species in the Wild State* (Toronto, 1970), cited on p. 609.

98. Innis, *Fur Trade*, pp. 2, 235.

99. Ray, *Indians*, pp. 205–13.

100. Frank Gilbert Roe, *The Indian and the Horse* (Norman, Okla., 1974), pp. 332–75; Ewers, *The Horse*, p. 318.

101. William N. Fenton and Merle Deardorff, "The Last Passenger Pigeon Hunt of the Cornplanter Senecas," *Journal of the Washington Academy of Sciences* 33, no. 10 (October 15, 1943): 289–315. In *The Passenger Pigeon* (Norman, Okla., 1973), A. W. Schorger writes: "It has been said that the Indian was the most dangerous of the wild enemies of the pigeon. While possibly true in a literal sense, there is no reason to believe that their raids had an appreciable effect until a large commerce was established by the whites" (p. 137).

102. Mandelbaum, *The Plains Cree*, pp. 51–52; Alexander Ross, *The Red River Settlement* (London, 1856), p. 267.

103. Thwaites, *Jesuit Relations and Allied Documents*, 6:297.

104. Peter Kalm, *Travels into North America* (Barre, Mass., 1972), p. 489.

they could repair the often poor-quality weapons. "The old Indians, when speaking of their ancestors, wonder how they could live, as a Beaver was wiser, and the Bear stronger, than them," David Thompson recorded, "and they confess, that if they were deprived of the Gun, they could not live by the Bow and Arrow, and must soon perish."[105]

The horse and the gun went together as the most prized possessions of the Indians of the central plains, where, by the middle of the eighteenth century, "the northeastward moving frontier of the horse met the southwestward moving frontier of the gun."[106] Together they radically altered life on the plains. For one thing, they contributed to the increasing bloodiness of intertribal warfare. The Plains Crees, for example, quickly recognized the importance of the gun in their effort to defeat the Dakotas and take over their hunting territories. Later, when their woodlands hunting grounds were exhausted, the Cree turned their weapons against the Gros Ventres and Blackfeet in a struggle for control of the plains.[107] As for the horse, it not only increased mobility, it also reduced the exhausting tasks of Plains Indian women by providing a new beast of burden. Moreover, it modified social structures, for the ownership of horses became the measure of wealth, allowing the rich to prosper and the horseless poor to grow poorer.[108] But neither increased mobility nor greater firepower could disguise the fact that the traditional foundations of the Plains hunting culture were vanishing. "We have been running wild on the prairie," Lame Bull told the treaty negotiators in 1855, "and now we want the white man's sons and daughters of our Great White Father to come to our country to tame us."[109] The pathetic plea was hardly necessary.

Drastic shifts in the social organization of Indian tribes, in response to the demands of the European trade, were evident among most Indian tribes. The Chippewas, who lived in the vast region around the northern Upper Great Lakes, gradually moved from precontact village organization to more centralized hunting bands in response to fur-trade imperatives. Moreover, here as elsewhere the trade encouraged neglect of other forms of livelihood, notably fishing. That meant that when winter arrived, food had to be purchased from the European traders. And the food the Chippewas bought back was often the same provisions they had earlier sold to the traders for whiskey and trinkets. Thus, whatever equality had originally existed between hunters and traders disappeared.[110]

105. Tyrrell, *David Thompson's Narrative*, p. 113.
106. Ewers, *The Horse*, p. 13.
107. Mandelbaum, *The Plains Cree*, pp. 30–31. Ewers, *Blackfeet*, p. 297.
108. Ewers, *The Horse*, p. 114.
109. Ewers, *Blackfeet*, cited on p. 223.
110. Harold Hickerson, "The Chippewa of the Upper Great Lakes," in Leacock and Lurie, *North American Indians*, pp. 183–89.

For the Cherokees, scattered through the southern Appalachians bordering the Carolinas, Georgia, Tennessee, and Virginia, trade with the British at Charleston also had profound effects on social and economic development. Despite their isolation and their tradition as a trading people, the attraction of European goods, especially the gun, was fatal. In the early eighteenth century the trade, composed of deerskins, dried plants, and slaves, was an exchange between equals. But it was, as John Phillip Reid has remarked, "an unequal equality."[111] While at the outset the British modified their trading patterns and regulations to conform to Cherokee practices, the Cherokee gradually came to need the British more than the reverse. Other factors, familiar elsewhere, also increased the disparity in the relationship. Population reduction through disease forced increasing use of European agricultural tools, which contributed to soil exhaustion. Morever, the growing importance of the herb trade forced neglect of food production. Finally, the time and the energy necessary for the preparation of skins and herbs for market, combined with the decreased population, forced neglect of hunting grounds, where careful management was necessary to ensure the animal supply.[112]

By the 1730s Cherokee dependence upon the British was nearly complete. A conservative group, advocating a return to the old isolation, found little response among the majority, who "did not wish to be without the better kind of hatchet," the European-supplied gun.[113] The assimilation of the Cherokee people was now almost unavoidable, and the trend was accepted and even encouraged. Acceptance of the white man's ways was demonstrated graphically by the gradual adoption of a centralized, coercive authority to replace the almost anarchic, traditional consensual organization.[114] And that new state set about abolishing many traditional practices, such as the clan right of retribution. But the tragic irony of the Cherokees was that they consciously chose acculturation and political organization as a means of protecting the territories they occupied only to discover that even that

111. John Phillip Reid, *A Better Kind of Hatchet: Law, Trade and Diplomacy in the Cherokee Nation during the Early Years of European Contact* (Philadelphia, 1976), p. 189.

112. Thomas Hatley, "The Dividing Path: The Direction of Cherokee Life in the Eighteenth Century," (M.A. thesis, University of North Carolina, 1977), chaps. 1 and 11. There is sometimes a curious twist to the European impact on North American life. It was the writings of a Jesuit missionary in China in the early eighteenth century that brought Ginseng to the attention of a fellow missionary and botanist, Father Joseph-François Lafiteau, in New France. Subsequently, the demands of the China trade, via Europe, became so great that the plant became virtually extinct in Canada. William N. Fenton, ,"Contacts between Iroquois Herbalism and Colonial Medicine," pp. 517–20, and William N. Fenton, "Joseph-François Lafiteau," in *Dictionary of Canadian Biography* (Toronto, 1974), pp. 334–38.

113. Reid, *A Better Kind of Hatchet*, p. 192.

114. Fred Gearing, *Priests and Warriors, Social Structures for Cherokee Politics*, American Anthropological Association Memoir no. 93, 1962, pp. 79–105.

was not enough.[115] Despite the support of the Supreme Court in the famous case of the *Cherokee Nation* v. *the State of Georgia* (1831), the Georgians were successful in removing most of the Cherokee people to the Indian territory west of the Mississippi.[116] That better hatchet proved to be double-edged.

VI

It was certainly not the fur traders' intention to undermine Amerindian culture. His very livelihood depended on its preservation. Unlike the settler who followed in his path, the fur trader needed the Indian.[117] For the most part he tolerated the Indian way of life, sometimes he admired it, and frequently he became intimately involved in it through *mariage à la façon du pays*. From the outset of contact there had been intermarriage and the recognition that such arrangements could be mutually advantageous. In the marriage of Pocahontas and John Rolfe, both Europeans and Amerindians recognized a traditional method of cementing an alliance. At quite another level, intermarriage took place because Europeans, coureurs de bois and "white Indians," were attracted to the native American lifestyle. As Peter Kalm observed, many young men in New France "settle among the *Indians* far from *Canada*, marry *Indian* women, and never come back again."[118] Since the male-female ratio in New England was fairly well balanced, miscegenation was less common there.[119] And it is important to note that inter-

115. William G. McLoughlin, "Thomas Jefferson and the Beginning of Cherokee Nationalism, 1806 to 1809," *William and Mary Quarterly* 32, no. 4 (October 1975):550–51.

116. Reid, *A Law of Blood*, p. 276.

117. Howard R. Lamar, *The Trader and the American Frontier: Myth's Victim* (College Station, Tex., 1977), p. 52.

118. Kalm, *Travels into North America*, p. 492. James Axtell, "The White Indians of Colonial America," *William and Mary Quarterly*, 3d ser. 32 no. 1 (January 1975):55–88. An ingenious and entirely improbable explanation for the liaisons between whites and Indians was offered by a British nobleman at the end of the eighteenth century. He wrote that "[concerning] the infecundity of the North American savages, M. Buffon, a respectable author, and for that reason often quoted, remarks that the males are feeble in the organs of generation, that they have no ardor for the female sex, and that they have few children. . . . A woman never admits her husband till the child she is nursing be three years old, and this led Frenchmen to go often astray from their Canadian wives" (Lord Henry Home Kames, *Sketches of the History of Man* [London, 1807], p. 364). The classic study of intercultural sexual relations in New France and the Canadian West is Marcel Giraud, *Les Métis canadien. Son Rôle dâns l'histoire de l'Ouest* (Paris, 1945). Strongly influenced by F. J. Turner, Giraud's work will long remain a seminal study of the social history of the fur trade.

119. Vaughan, *New England Frontier*, p. 209. But see also Axtell, "White Indians of Colonial America," pp. 58–88. The assumption that Amerindians were always eager for these marriage alliances is not correct. See Jaenen, "Amerindian Views of French Culture," pp. 283–84.

marriage seems to have virtually always taken place between European men and Amerindian or métis women.

Mixed marriages produced many prominent offspring: Cornplanter, the half-brother of the Seneca prophet Handsome Lake; Sequoyah, inventor of the Cherokee syllabary; and Jean-Baptiste Charbonneau, born to the famous Shoshoni, Sacajaweah, and her voyageur husband on the Lewis and Clark expedition. In fact, mixed marriage was a fairly common phenomenon on the nineteenth-century frontier. The 1825 United States census recorded two hundred and twenty-five such marriages among the Cherokee alone; by mid-century mixed marriages were common among the Blackfeet. One Scottish fur trader, his three Cree wives, and twenty-seven children established a distinct new tribe, the Willow Indians, on the Canadian plains at the end of the eighteenth century.[120]

The pattern of these unions usually followed the Indian custom of what might be called common-law marriage. Apart from the mutual satisfactions of cohabitation, these marriages had obvious material advantages for both fur traders and Indians. An Indian wife provided a trader with a skilled traveling companion, interpreter, and a privileged relationship with a particular group of Indians. Daniel Harmon, a Nor'wester from Vermont who never lost his Puritan conscience, left a colorful account of his "country marriage." Two years after arriving in the Northwest, and already acquainted with traders who had Indian wives, he wrote:

> a Chief among the Crees came to the Fort accompanied by a number of his relations who appeared very desirous that I should take one of his Daughters to remain with me, but to put him off I told him that I could not then take a woman however in the fall perhaps I might for I added I had no dislike of her. But he pressed me to keep her at once as he said he was fond of me and he wished to have his Daughter with the white people and he almost persuaded me to accept her, for I was sure that while I had the Daughter I should not only have the Father's hunts but those of his relations also, and of course [this] would be much in the favour of the Company & perhaps in the end some advantage to me likewise—so

---

120. Merle H. Deardorff, "The Religion of Handsome Lake: Its Origin and Development," in William N. Fenton, ed., *Symposium on Local Diversity in Iroquois Culture* (Washington, D.C., 1951), p. 83; Grace S. Woodward, *The Cherokees* (Norman, Okla., 1963), p. 86; William F. Wheeler, "Sacajaweah: A Historical Sketch," *Contributions to the Historical Society of Montana* 7 (1919):271–96; Anne W. Hafen, "Jean-Baptiste Charbonneau," in LeRoy R. Hafen, ed., *The Mountain Men and the Fur Trade in the Far West* (Glendale, Calif., 1965), pp. 205–24. William T. Hagen, "Squaw Men on the Kiowa, Comanche, Apache Reservation: Advance Agents of Civilization or Disturbers of the Peace?," in John G. Clark, *The Frontier Challenge* (Lawrence, Kan., 1971), p. 173; Ewers, *Blackfeet*, p. 71; David G. Mandelbaum, *The Plains Cree*, p. 10.

that interest (and perhaps a little natural inclination also) I found was nigh making me commit another folly, if not a sin,—but thanks be to God alone if I have not been brought into a snare laid no doubt by the Devil himself.

Three years later, after "mature consideration," he succumbed to fourteen-year-old Elizabeth Duval, whose mother was a Cree. She bore him fourteen children. When Harmon returned to Vermont after sixteen years in Indian country, he took Elizabeth and the surviving children with him, and he made the marriage legal. "On the whole," he wrote, "I consider the course which I design to pursue as the only one which religion and humanity would justify."[121]

For the tribe from which the wife came, the marriage provided a guarantee of continued good relations and perhaps trading preferences. For the woman, whose wishes may not have been much taken into account, such a marriage may have provided a slightly easier way of life. Thus the practice of marriage according to the custom of the country reached the highest echelons of the trade in both the United States and British North America.[122] Alexander Culbertson, a leading bourgeois in the American Fur Company, took the daughter of a prominent Blood Indian for his wife. Edwin Denig had two Indian wives and was quite clear about the economic advantages that went along with these liaisons.[123] In Canada the most prominent of the numerous traders who took advantage of the custom of the country was no less a personage than George Simpson, the governor of the Honourable Company.[124]

Naturally the treatment of these women and of their offspring varied. Some, including Medice-Snake-Woman, Culbertson's wife, eventually returned to the tribal life. Others, like Simpson's Betsy, were found other husbands. Others, probably a minority, returned with their husbands to the east for retirement. One woman, Suzanne-Pas-de-Nom, won an important legal case in which the Canadian courts established that her *mariage à la façon du pays* was legally binding.[125] The fate of offspring varied as well. Some

121. W. Kaye Lamb, ed., *Sixteen Years in Indian Country: The Journals of Daniel William Harmon, 1800–1816* (Toronto, 1957), pp. 28–29, 62–63, 98, 195.

122. Harvey L. Carter and Marcia C. Spencer, "Stereotypes of the Mountain Men," *Western Historical Quarterly* 6, no. 1 (January 1975), p. 31, estimate that 36 percent of the mountain men in their sample had Indian wives.

123. John S. Ewers, "Mothers of the Mixed Bloods," in his *Indian Life on the Upper Missouri* (Norman, Okla., 1968), pp. 62–64; Lewis O. Saum, *The Fur Trader and the Indian* (Seattle, 1965), pp. 85–86.

124. Galbraith, *The Little Emperor*, pp. 67–71.

125. Sylvia Van Kirk, "The Custom of the Country: An Examination of Fur Trade Marriages," in Lewis H. Thomas, *Essays in Western History* (Edmonton, 1976), pp. 49–68; Sylvia Van Kirk, "Women and the Fur Trade," *The Beaver*, Winter 1972, pp. 4–21; Jenifer Brown, "A

were sent off to established schools, where they were provided with the manners and knowledge necessary for future careers in Canada and Great Britain.[126] Others were less fortunate, perhaps. Left to grow up in the west, they led a seminomadic, semiagricultural life, in the trade, the buffalo hunt, and a little agriculture. French-language métis and English-speaking "country-born" made up the majority of the inhabitants of Red River in 1869, when one of their number, Louis Riel, called them together to resist Canadian manifest destiny.[127]

It is difficult to make any sure assessment of the significance of miscegenation in the overall relationship between Europeans and Indians. Apart from the personal benefits and costs of intermarriage, the end result was probably disadvantageous to the native Americans. It doubtless contributed to the breakdown of traditional family and kin relationships, introducing European patterns of male-female relationships. Within the structure of the fur trade, intermarriage worked well enough, apparently, but it declined rapidly with the arrival of settlement and European women. In short, it was a convenience which the Europeans discarded once its usefulness was exhausted. In some settlement areas, the relatively happy country marriages seem to have been succeeded by prostitution and a much more unpleasant kind of concubinage.[128] While the offspring of the mixed marriages might have provided a bridge between the two cultures, that rarely happened. Acceptance by one or other of the two cultures apparently offered the most satisfactory life for most of these people. Certainly the fate of most Canadian métis, since the final defeat of Louis Riel in 1885, has been a miserable one for most of these survivors of the fur trade's golden years.[129] In the last analysis, the fur trade failed to prepare the Indian or mixed blood for the world that arrived with large-scale settlement.

Demographic Transition in Fur Trade Country: Family Size and Fertility of Company Officers and Country Wives," *Western Canadian Journal of Anthropology* 6, no. 1 (1976): 61–71. Jenifer S. H. Brown, *Strangers in Blood: Fur Trade Company Families in Indian Country* (Vancouver and London, 1980).

126. Jenifer Brown, "Ultimate Respectability: Fur Trade Children in the Civilized World," *The Beaver*, Winter 1977, pp. 4–10, and Spring 1978, pp. 48–55.

127. John E. Foster, "The Origins of Mixed Bloods in the Canadian West," in Thomas, *Essays in Western History*, pp. 71–80, and John E. Foster, "The Country-Born in Red River, 1820–1850" (Ph.D. diss., University of Alberta, 1973), pp. 66–70. In Red River alone the métis population grew from 500 in 1821 to 12,000 in 1870, an astonishing rate of increase, especially when contrasted with the parallel decline of Indian populations (Ray, *Indians*, p. 205). See also Margaret McLeod and W. L. Morton, *Cuthbert Grant of Grantown* (Toronto, 1963), and George Woodcock, *Gabriel Dumont* (Edmonton, 1975).

128. Fisher, *Contact and Conflict*, pp. 113 and 209.

129. Washburn, *The Indian in America*, p. 94; Edmund Wilson, *Apologies to the Iroquois* (New York, 1960), p. 171; Howard Adams, *Prison of Grass* (Toronto, 1975); and Maria Campbell, *Halfbreed* (Toronto, 1973).

VII

The encroachment of white settlement, wholesale removal of long-established tribes, and finally confinement on reservations, in both Canada and the United States, marked the last stage in the closing of the "frontier." That process reduced once-dominant Amerindian societies to a status of marginality in North America. The relationship to the land had been fundamental to the shape, functioning, and much of the belief system of Amerindians. The making over of North American land-holding patterns in the image of Europe therefore radically undermined the native culture. At Tippecanoe, Tecumseh protested vainly against the apparently inexorable process:

> The Great Spirit gave this great Island to his red children; he placed the whites on the other side of the big water; they were not contented with their own, but came to take ours from us. They have driven us from the sea to the lakes; we can go no further.[130]

Placing the native Americans on circumscribed territories and dividing the rest of North America into individually owned properties was the most conclusive sign of the Europeanization of North America. While Amerindian concepts of property varied from tribe to tribe, they all reflected the needs of societies whose existence depended upon the products of nature. Usufruct, not registered legal land title, was fundamental, and common ownership was frequent.[131] European contact brought profound changes. The fur trade had already led to some important alterations in property relations. Among the Montagnais, who had traditionally practiced common ownership of hunting grounds, the competition of the trade led to the establishment of "family hunting territories," though changes in available food sources may also have encouraged this development.[132] Moreover, the traditional Montagnais family organization, which was bicentred, became predominantly patrilocal in response to the demands of the trade.[133]

130. Benjamin Drake, *The Life of Tecumseh and His Brother the Prophet* (Cincinnati, 1852), p. 124.

131. Driver, *Indians of North America*, pp. 269–83; Reid, *A Law of Blood*, pp. 131–41; George S. Snyderman, "Concepts of Land Ownership among the Iroquois and Their Neighbours," in Fenton, *Symposium on Local Diversity*, pp. 15–34.

132. Jenness, *Indians*, p. 124; Eleanor Leacock, *The Montagnais "Hunting Territory" and the Fur Trade*, American Anthropological Association Memoir no. 78, 1954, pp. 1–23; Rolf Knight, "A Re-Examination of Hunting, Trapping, and Territoriality among the Northern Algonkian Indians," in Anthony Leeds and Andrew P. Vayda, *Man, Culture and Animals* (Washington, D.C., 1965), pp. 27–42.

133. For a survey of this controversial topic, see A. G. Bailey, "Retrospective Thoughts of

Similar changes were experienced by other tribes. In the process of land purchase, whether by fair means or otherwise, patrilineal laws of property were gradually forced upon such groups as the Iroquois, who had traditionally followed matrilineal lines of inheritance.[134] This change transformed the status of both men and women in Iroquois society. Traditionally, the Iroquois and other Amerindian women had worked the soil, a custom which revealed not their subordination but rather their ownership of the land. The pattern of the European way of life, where men assumed the farming role, may have eased women's physical burdens, but it similarly reduced her to a status "more like her white sisters."[135] For the male the change was no less crucial. Now the landowner, the male also found himself relegated to doing "women's work" and being more dependent on his wife and children for help than he had ever been in his hunting and warring roles.[136] Those traditional concepts of property and the division of labor were probably major reasons for the resistance of Indians to confinement on reserves and acceptance of European agricultural practices.[137] The white man's "lazy Indian" was a man whose occupation had disappeared.

European settlement, even on a limited scale, challenged the Amerindian understanding of land ownership. The Indian did not "own" the land in the European sense of holding a legally enforceable title. Nevertheless, there was recognition, both tribal and intertribal, that defined areas—village sites, agricultural plots, fishing places, hunting territories, and berry patches—belonged to specified groups.[138] Alden T. Vaughan's claim that "the disparity between English and Indian concepts of land tenure was actually rather slight"[139] is accurate enough if one ignores, for the moment, the European legal system.

But the arrival of European immigrants, European governments, and European laws brought customary Indian title into jeopardy. Europeans now laid claim to the lands either through proprietary right, various forms of purchase, or by simple occupancy. To continue to hold land legally, native Americans were forced to recognize the validity and authority of the newly installed system. In short, European law came to define Amerindian prop-

an Ethnohistorian," Canadian Historical Association, *Historical Papers*, 1977, pp. 14–29; and the essays by Frank Speck, Eleanor Leacock and Adrian Tanner, in Bruce Cox, ed., *Cultural Ecology* (Toronto, 1973), pp. 58–114.

134. William N. Fenton, "Locality as a Basic Factor in the Development of Iroquois Social Structure," in Fenton, *Symposium on Local Diversity*, p. 43.

135. Reid, *Law of Blood*, p. 68.

136. Martha Champion Rundle, "Iroquois Women, Then and Now," in Fenton, *Symposium on Local Diversity*, p. 174.

137. Ewers, *Blackfeet*, p. 214.

138. Duff, *Indian History*, p. 8.

139. Vaughan, *New England Frontier*, p. 105.

erty rights. Given that dominant fact, the question of whether Amerindians received a fair return for their property becomes an interesting but distinctly subordinate consideration.[140]

Yet even acceptance of the new system did not guarantee inalienable claims to property. Large tracts of land which were not exploited according to European prescriptions could be considered vacant, and then be occupied. A report of a committee of the Canadian legislature examining Indian policy in 1844 approvingly quoted a passage from Emmerich de Vattel's *Le Droit des gens* (1758):

> The earth . . . belongs to mankind in general, and was designed to furnish them with subsistence. If each nation had from the beginning resolved to appropriate to itself a vast country that the people might live only by hunting, fishing and wild fruits, our globe would not be sufficient to maintain a tenth part of its present inhabitants. We do not, therefore, deviate from nature, in confining the Indians within narrower limits.[141]

Natural philosophy thus aided land hunger as Indians throughout the continent felt growing pressure to surrender or sell their lands. As the Six Nations, who had stood by the British in the American Revolution, learned to their sorrow, even solemn agreements could be modified at the will of the dominant partner. The reward for their loyalty in 1783 had been more than one-half million acres of productive land along the Grand River in Canada. By 1841, a series of complicated transfers and controversial sales had reduced that tract by more than 50 percent.[142] Indians in British Columbia learned that the size of a reservation could vary according to government response to settler pressures.[143] In the United States, the removal of Cherokee, Choctaw, Chickasaw, and Creek, under various forms of persuasion, gave full meaning to Chief Justice John Marshall's apt description of the Cherokees (and by inference, Amerindians generally) as a "domestic, dependent, nation."[144]

The American West, in the post–Civil-War decades, was the scene of a series of bloody wars against the Sioux, the Cheyenne, and most of the other Plains tribes. As a result, the Indians were forced to accept reservation life,

140. Jennings, *The Invasion of America*, pp. 128–45.

141. *Journals, Legislative Assembly, Canada, 1844–45*, "Report on the Affairs of the Indians of Canada," Appendix E.E.E.

142. Charles M. Johnston, ed., *The Valley of the Six Nations* (Toronto, 1964), pp. lv–lxix, 120–92; Sally Weaver, "Six Nations of Grand River, Ontario," in Trigger, *Handbook*, pp. 525–36.

143. Fisher, *Contact and Conflict*, pp. 175–201.

144. Frances Paul Prucha, "Andrew Jackson's Indian Policy: A Reassessment," *Journal of American History* 56 (1969): 527–39.

and the last unsettled lands were opened to whites. To the north the pressure of settlement was less intense and the process much more peaceful, but the end result was remarkably similar. After the abortive Métis rebellion in Red River in 1869, Canada acquired the Hudson's Bay Company Territories. To prepare the way for settlement a quasi-military constabulary, the North West Mounted Police, was organized to oversee the signing of treaties and the establishment of reservations for increasingly destitute Indians.[145]

The Amerindians, through land sales, treaties, and wars, were to be moved, confined—and eventually "civilized"—to make way for the inflow of Europeans. An instruction to the lieutenant governor of the Canadian North West Territories stated the policy frankly enough:

> while assuring the Indians of your desire to establish friendly relations with them, you will ascertain and report to His Excellency the course you may think the most advisable to pursue, whether by Treaty or otherwise, for the removal of any obstructions that might be presented to the flow of population into the fertile lands that lie between Manitoba and the Rocky Mountains.[146]

As elsewhere across the continent, the "obstructions" were systematically removed. What the Indians received in exchange for "fertile lands" evoked this description from a Canadian missionary at the end of the nineteenth century: "The new mode of life on a Reserve, dwelling in filthy houses, badly ventilated, has induced disease; the idle manner of living, being fed by the Government, and having little to do; the poor clothing worn in the winter; badly cooked food, the consciousness that as a race they are fading away."[147]

VIII

When Frederick Jackson Turner, speaking ex cathedra, proclaimed the closing of the American "frontier" in 1893, he was right in at least one sense. The frontier that Columbus, Verrazzano, Cabot, Cartier, and Hudson had opened, and on which the drama of European-Amerindian contact had com-

145. Washburn, *The Indian in America*, pp. 197–208; R. C. MacLeod, *The North-West Mounted Police and Law Enforcement, 1873–1905* (Toronto, 1976), pp. 27–31.

146. René Fumoleau, *As Long as the Land Shall Last* (Toronto, 1973), cited on p. 24. Fumoleau's study and Alexander Morris, *The Treaties of Canada with the Indians* (Toronto, 1880) provide an account of the dispossession process. In "Protection, Civilization, Assimilation: An Outline History of Canada's Indian Policy," *Western Canadian Journal of Anthropology* 6, no. 2 (1976): 13–30, John Tobias looks at post–treaty treatment.

147. John MacLean, *Canadian Savage Folk* (Toronto, 1896), p. 302.

menced, was closed by the end of the nineteenth century. If all the world had once been America, then by 1890 most of North America was Europe.[148] Cartier's traffic sign had pointed the way for explorers, missionaries, traders, and settlers who had gradually changed, dispersed, and enclosed the native populations. In the mythical struggle between Aataentsic's children, Tawiscaron and Iouskara, for control over the world on the turtle's back, Tawiscaron the Creator had won the day. In the post-Columbian world, the Amerindian must often have concluded that the victory had gone to his destructive brother.[149]

The Indians who joined Louis Riel for his last stand at Batoche in 1885 were the brothers of those who marked "the symbolic end of Indian freedom" at Wounded Knee five years later.[150] What had begun in fragile sailing ships had been completed by the railways, the Northern Pacific and the Canadian Pacific. They brought soldiers to pacify and settlers to occupy. They bound the new European-sponsored nations together and reminded the old Amerindian nations that the new technology had triumphed. Unexpected consequences had flowed from small beginnings. "Simple people, with simple trades and simple goods," V. S. Naipaul wrote of Africa, though it might have been of America, "but agents of Europe."[151]

148. Of course, even today the "frontier" is not entirely closed. The search for oil in Northern and Arctic territories has raised again all of the old problems of contact. See *Northern Frontier, Northern Homeland. The Report of the Mackenzie Valley Pipeline Inquiry*, vol. 1 (Ottawa, 1977).

149. William N. Fenton, "This Island, The World on the Turtle's Back," *Journal of American Folklore* 75, no. 298 (October–December 1962): 283–300.

150. Dee Brown, *Bury My Heart at Wounded Knee* (New York, 1970), p. 13; Hugh Dempsey, *Crowfoot* (Edmonton, 1972), pp. 154–94.

151. V. S. Naipaul, *A Bend in the River* (New York, 1979), p. 249.

8

ROBERT ROSS

Capitalism, Expansion, and Incorporation on the Southern African Frontier

Ever since Frederick Jackson Turner introduced the concept of the frontier into the analysis of expanding societies it has had a double meaning. Turner hoped to explain American development by "the existence of an area of free land, its continuous recession and the advance of . . . settlement," but he recognized that this area had to be won by "a series of Indian wars."[1] In other words, the land was empty, available to be taken into cultivation, but it was inhabited by members of another culture who had to be driven off the land before the processes could start whereby, as he saw it, America was Americanized.

Whenever there is expansion of an ethnic group—defined not in terms of race but as the bearers of a particular culture, with its associated systems of production—this dialectical relationship between the two facets of the frontier exists; and nowhere more so than in South Africa. It is not necessary to ascribe South Africa's ills to the survival of frontier attitudes into the twentieth century[2] to appreciate, first, that the modern boundaries of South

---

1. F. J. Turner, "The Significance of the Frontier in American History," reprinted in *The Frontier in American History* (New York, 1920), pp. 1, 8–9.

2. It is ironic that the "Frontier Thesis" of the origins of the South African way of life is in many ways similar in its logic to the "germ" theory that Turner was combating, even though, to take a single example, the time gap between 1800, when MacCrone's historical investigations ended, and the 1930s, when he did his social-psychological testing, is far less than that ignored by H. B. Adams, who claimed that "the origin of the English constitution, as Montesquieu long ago declared, is found in the forests of Germany." See I. D. MacCrone, *Race Attitudes in South Africa: Historical, Experimental and Psychological Studies*, 2d ed. (Johannesburg, 1965), and Richard Hofstadter, *The Progressive Historians* (New York, 1969), p. 66. The irony would be doubled if the recent arguments of Alan Macfarlane were accepted since, very cautiously, they tend to resuscitate the "germ" theory, seeing the origins of capitalist individualism in the kinship system of the Germanic peoples. See *The Origins of English Individualism* (Oxford, 1978), esp. pp. 170, 206.

Africa are to a very large extent the limits of trekboer settlement before 1880, and second, that the incorporation of Africans into the labor process dominated by whites was partially a preindustrial phenomenon, even though its scale and the nature of the class conflict it caused were completely altered by industrialization. The relationship between the territorial expansion of the whites and the subjugation of the blacks can be seen by pondering the contrast between that part of the Afrikaner national myth symbolized by the Voortrekker monument overlooking Pretoria, and the fact that, in the pithy words of C. W. de Kiewiet, in South Africa there "was not a romantic frontier, like the American west, or heroic like the North-West frontier of India. Legend has denied the Pondos, for example, a place beside the Pawnees or the Pathans. The stuff of legend is not easily found in a process which turned Ama-Xosa, Zulus or Basutos into farm labourers, kitchen servants or messengers."[3] And even this contrast ignores the important fact that many of those who opened up the interior of South Africa to exploitation by the European-dominated Cape Colony did not find a place in the Afrikaner pantheon.

The Griquas, the Basters of the north-west Cape, and the Afrikaner clan of Namibia—the name is almost ironic—exhibited very much the same characteristics as the rather whiter voortrekkers and trekboers. To a greater or lesser degree, all were stock farmers who originated in the Cape Colony and had an ambiguous relationship to the coastal markets and a drive to subject Africans, generally as laborers. They can generally be described together, although it is also necessary to analyze the forces that drove them apart.[4]

Even taking this into account, the process that produced the myth can only be understood with reference to the national environment in which it occurred. Not that the environment determined the form of the process;

---

3. C. W. de Kiewiet, *A History of South Africa, Social and Economic* (Oxford, 1940), p. 48.

4. Throughout this essay I have used the term *colonial* rather than *white*, except where the process described involves "whites" as a distinct group from so-called coloureds. This term is not strictly accurate, since Namibia, the South African Republic (the Transvaal), and the Orange Free State were not colonies, except intermittently. For a discussion of the problems of anachronistically using "racial" terms, see the preface to *The Oxford History of South Africa*, ed. Monica Wilson and Leonard Thompson (1969), 1:viii–x, especially the statement that "a third assumption—perhaps the most misleading of all—is that physical type, language and economy are *necessarily* connected." On the various "coloured" groups, see Martin Legassick, "The Griqua, the Sotho-Tswana and the Missionaries 1780–1840: The Politics of a Frontier Zone" (Ph.D. diss., University of California, Los Angeles, 1970); Robert Ross, *Adam Kok's Griquas: A Study in the Development of Stratification in South Africa* (Cambridge, 1976); J. S. Marais, *The Cape Coloured People, 1652–1937* (Oxford, 1939), pp. 74–109; H. Vedder, *South West Africa in Early Times*, trans. C. G. Hall (London, 1938); Alan Kienetz, "The Key Role of the Orlam Migrations in the Early Europeanization of South-West Africa (Namibia)," *International Journal of African Historical Studies* 10 (1977):553–72.

rather, it set limits to it, in conjunction with both the technology available at the time and the prevailing ideas about how a society should be organized. In this regard, the salient fact about the interior of South Africa is that, apart from few exceptional areas, it was suitable only for extensive stock-keeping. By the late eighteenth century, sheep were kept in large numbers throughout most of what was to become the Cape Province, both along the coastal belts north and east of Cape Town and farther inland, moving transhumantly between the mountains of the Cape folded belt and the bushy Karroo. Only in the far east of the colony, in the border districts with the Xhosa and Thembu, were there areas where cattle ranching was more advantageous. In the nineteenth century, when colonial settlement began on the highveld of the Orange Free State and Transvaal, cattle ranching was again a more attractive proposition. Even there, though, the presence of white and Griqua herds seems to have led to a steady deterioration of the veld, as the northward advance of the false karroo bushes at the expense of sweet grassveld bears witness. As a consequence, sheep farming became more regular farther north.[5]

Throughout South Africa, nevertheless, the first penetration of any given area came as a result of hunting and trading expeditions. These began early on in the history of the Cape, when Jan van Riebeeck sent out parties to buy cattle from the Khoikhoi,[6] and continued in 1702 with the first meeting between whites from the colony and the Xhosa—a meeting which, almost prophetically, degenerated into a bloody cattle raid.[7] The advance persisted throughout the eighteenth century and well into the nineteenth, with the establishment of trading posts in the Ciskei and Transkei,[8] and with the combined hunting and bartering in the Zoutpansberg of the northern Trans-

5. The classic study is J. P. H. Acocks, *Veld types of South Africa* (Pretoria, 1953).

6. Richard Elphick, *Kraal and Castle: Khoikhoi and the Foundation of White South Africa* (New Haven and London, 1977), pp. 151–70.

7. Ibid., p. 228; Robert Shell, "European Immigration to the Cape Colony: The Forgotten Factor in Frontier Settlement and European Expansion, 1701–1793" (seminar paper, Yale University, 1979).

8. See, for example, the comment of the magistrate of Albany in 1833: "The trade of Albany has greatly increased during the past year, but not only so, it has also materially altered in character. The circulating medium of traffic with the nations of the interior was formerly beads, buttons and other worthless articles of that description, but of late demand has been for blankets, kersey, iron, iron pots, axes and other manufactured articles of a like description. The returns consist principally of hides, horns and Ivory, of which the quantity obtained during the last 12 months may be estimated at the value of £40,000. This trade with the interior has also lost its fluctuating character which it once had and it is now more equally stable with the trade carried on with any commercial people" (P.R.O. London, C.O. 53/70, 347). That this trade was largely with the Ciskei and Transkei can be seen from its great diminution during the frontier war of 1835 (P.R.O., C.O. 53/72, 301). For a later period, see W. Beinart, "European Traders and the Paramountcy in Pondoland, c. 1878–1894," paper presented to African Studies Association (United Kingdom) Conference, Oxford, 1978.

vaal,[9] through eastern Botswana,[10] and even into Ngamiland and Barotse-land.[11] Later still, the Afrikaner settlers of southern Angola[12] and Kenya[13] followed much the same pattern. Nevertheless, major responsibility for the expansion of the Cape Colony and its successors lies squarely with the stock farmers. The characteristic southern African frontier, whether early in the southwestern Cape or 150 years later in the Transvaal and Namibia, was one where stock farmers searching for new land interacted with Africans, who themselves were generally in possession of cattle and/or sheep. With few exceptions the colonists fought the Africans in order to capture grazing ground or stock, not to control trade routes or agricultural land;[14] and in those exceptional cases where the object of the whites was the acquisition of labor, the captives were used as herdsmen.

In time the first hunters and traders transformed themselves into, or were replaced by, people who were predominantly stock farmers. As P. J. van der Merwe has argued, "throughout the course of our history the pioneers of the frontiers lived, to a greater or lesser extent, by hunting, and saved their stock for the market;"[15] and what was true for the Afrikaner trekboers with whom van der Merwe identified was also true for other South African frontiersmen. Van der Merwe took a rather more nuanced position than has been attributed to him[16] on one of the major debates in the history of colonial expansion in southern Africa. This concerns the extent to which the stock farmers of the interior were dependent on the market and were pulled deeper into the country by the commercial opportunities which this mode of existence offered or, to see the problem inversely, the degree to which the

9. Roger Wagner, "Zoutpansberg: Some Notes on the Dynamics of a Hunting Frontier," University of London, *Collected Seminar Papers on Southern Africa* 6 (1975):32–42.

10. See, for instance, R. G. Cumming, *Five Years of a Hunter's Life in the Far Interior of Southern Africa*, 2 vols. (London, 1856); Neil Parsons, "The Economic History of Khama's Country in Botswana, 1844–1930," *The Roots of Rural Poverty in Central and Southern Africa*, ed. Robin Palmer and Neil Parsons (London, 1977), p. 116–19.

11. See David Livingstone, *Family Letters, 1841–1856*, ed. I. Schapera, 2 vols. (London, 1959), 2:147–51; James Chapman, *Travels in the Interior of Southern Africa, 1849–63*, 2 vols., ed. E. C. Tabler (Cape Town, 1971), 1:194–95.

12. W. G. Clarence-Smith, "The Thirstland Trekkers in Angola: Some Reflections on a Frontier Society," University of London, *Collected Seminar Papers on Southern Africa*, vol. 6 (1975).

13. M. P. K. Sorrenson, *Origins of European Settlement in Kenya* (Nairobi, 1968), esp. pp. 229–30.

14. The Africans may, of course, have seen the land as much as a locus for agriculture as for stock-raising. Nevertheless, it is notable that the major field of conflict in the Eastern Cape was the *Zuurveld*, first-rate summer grazing. Herman Giliomee, "The Cape Eastern Frontier, 1770–1812," in *The Shaping of South African Society*, ed. R. Elphick and H. Giliomee (Cape Town, 1979).

15. P. J. van der Merwe, *Die Trekboer in die Geskiedenis van die Kaapkolonie (1657–1842)* (Cape Town, 1938), p. 45 (my translation).

16. For example, W. K. Hancock, "Trek," *Economic History Review*, 2d ser. 10 (1957–58):333–36.

stock farmers were driven onward by their need for subsistence. One of the poles of this debate was taken by S. D. Neumark, when he argued that "even if the frontiersmen were 99 percent self-sufficient, it was the 1 percent that tipped the scale, for it constituted the minimum factor in the frontiersman's economy."[17] Against this, Leonard Guelke has argued that "under frontier conditions . . . in the midst of abundant resources, a small number of settlers were able to enjoy a modest standard of living with scarcely any participation in an exchange economy,"[18] since "an early view of the South African frontier that maintained that the *trekboeren* were essentially subsistence farmers was not far from the truth, although it overlooked their few important links with the outside world."[19] In a sense this is an unreal debate, or rather one in which at least three separate strands have become entangled. It is worthwhile attempting to unravel them.

First, there is no doubt that for the major part of their own subsistence the frontiersmen were dependent on what they produced themselves. It is impossible to be specific as to what proportion of a frontier family's requirements came from the farm itself. If sufficiently detailed sources exist—which I doubt—they have yet to be investigated quantitatively. Nevertheless, it is possible to give a variety of indications respecting the various sectors of the frontier economy. Perhaps it is best to distinguish the basic needs of the households from luxuries. Almost none of the former came through the market. In particular, food was almost entirely home-produced. The major component of the frontier diet was meat, when possible venison but more generally either mutton or beef. But it should be stressed that the monotonous consumption of mutton was by no means invariable. In all the frontier districts some farmers sowed grain, even if it was not always possible to harvest it. The climate of the interior of at least the Cape Province is such that unirrigated grain fails at least as often as it succeeds. Occasionally attempts were made to supplement the otherwise exclusively carnivorous diet by purchasing grain from other districts;[20] but that was a rare occurrence, not surprisingly when the problems of transport are taken into account. Even in Cape Town around 1800, bread was more expensive than meat per pound.[21] Thus, when the butcher C. H. Olivier was asked what the eastern farmers lived on, he replied: "Meat and milk. Many of them have

17. S. D. Neumark, *Economic Influences on the South African Frontier, 1652–1836* (Stanford, Calif., 1957), p. 4.

18. Leonard Guelke, "Commentary," *Annals of the Association of American Geographers* 67 (1977):466.

19. Leonard Guelke, "Frontier Settlement in Early Dutch South Africa," *Annals of the Association of American Geographers* 66 (1976):41.

20. For example, *Belangrijke Historische Dokumenten over Zuid Afrika*, ed. G. M. Theal (London, 1911), 3:359.

21. For example, John Barrow, *An Account of Travels into the Interior of Southern Africa*, 2 vols. (London, 1801–04), 2:169.

not tasted bread for six years. They used to get meal from the corn farmers, but these now rather prefer to sell their grain to the troops on the Frontier for money, than to barter it for cattle. They try to grow corn every year, but unless there is rain in January and February, the crop is burnt up and the seasons have been very bad."[22] Thus, as Lichtenstein described for a sheep-herding district: "Six hundred wethers are requisite for feeding a family the year through, including the slaves and Hottentots, and in many a colonist's family no other food but mutton is ever tasted."[23]

Clothing was generally homemade, and was initially very largely of soft buckskin, although a growth in prosperity would replace this with European cloth.[24] It is also notable that in almost all the frontier villages the first items to be manufactured were hats.[25] Fuel was collected on the farm itself and was more likely to be cow-dung than wood, to the detriment of the land's fertility.[26] As for shelter, the first colonial inhabitants of any area were almost certain to live in the movable, mat-covered *hartebeeshuisjes* they copied from the Khoikhoi;[27] but as settlement became more permanent, sol-ider houses were to be constructed. They were no doubt built by the farmer and his family themselves—sometimes very badly even in those districts where there was abundant good wood.[28] Elsewhere it might require a consid-erable journey to collect the requisite materials. The Griquas of Philippolis, for instance, had to journey to the Kat River to obtain timber for the frames of their houses.[29] Occasionally, also, substantial constructions of corbelled stone were built in the treeless districts of the Karroo.[30]

Second, it is clear that no frontiersman in southern Africa was outside the gambit of the market and of the money economy, even if they were mar-ginal to him. To give perhaps the most striking example, in 1783 two broth-ers, Jacob and Carel Kruger, managed to escape justice and flee to the Or-ange River from the frontier districts of Karroo, where they had been living as traveling teachers. Their crime was forging the newfangled paper money and distributing it among their neighbors, a crime clearly unimaginable without at least a rudimentary money economy.[31] More prosaically, it is im-possible to ignore the point made by Neumark that no frontier farm could

22. *Records of the Cape Colony*, ed. G. M. Theal, 36 vols. (London, 1897–1905), 29:478.
23. H. Lichtenstein, *Travels in Southern Africa in the Years 1803, 1804, 1805*, trans. Anne Plumtre (Cape Town, 1929–30), 1:446.
24. R. G. Cumming, *Five Years*, 1:140.
25. Cape of Good Hope, *Statistical Blue Book for 1840*, p. 300.
26. W. J. Burchell, *Travels in the Interior of South Africa, 1822*, ed. I. Schapera, 2 vols. (London, 1953), 1:83.
27. Van der Merwe, *Trekboer*, pp. 222–23.
28. Ibid., p. 217.
29. Ross, *Adam Kok's Griquas*, p. 42.
30. A. J. Christopher, *Southern Africa* (Folkestone, Eng., and Hamden, Conn., 1976), p. 79.
31. Case of 25 March 1784, *Algemeen Rijksarchief*, The Hague, V.O.C. 4313.

operate without at least a few articles which could not be produced on the farm itself. The most notable of these were wagons, which, given the trans-humant nature of most stock farming, functioned as dwellings in addition to their distributive task, and firearms, gunpowder, and lead, which were perhaps the most important instruments of production, at least in the far-thest districts.[32] These had to be purchased, and it was therefore necessary for each farmer to market his produce regularly. Perusal of the genealogies published by C. C. de Villiers demonstrates that in the eighteenth century almost all whites visited the southwest Cape at least once every two years, to have their children baptized if for no other purpose,[33] and it is reasonable to assume that these visits were combined with commercial activities. Later, as the farmers moved farther into the interior, so did the commercial system, first in the hands of itinerant traders (*smouse*), until, with the foun-dation of small market towns, it became more firmly rooted.[34]

In general, the farmer attempted to cover as high a proportion of his costs as possible, not by selling his stock to the butcher or as draught oxen, but rather by marketing such goods as soap, tallow, butter, wax, dried fruit, hides, skins, or horns. By thus diversifying his wares, he was attempting to preserve the major component of his capital which, in a time when land was cheap and unimproved, was his stock. It was rational to maintain the flocks and herds at the highest possible level with the available grazing, since there was the ever-present threat of losing the complete herd, either to the depre-dations of Khoisan—or, later, Xhosa or Sotho—or to drought and disease. Given the highly mobile and rootless nature of frontier life, what this did to the long-term quality of the veld was not the farmer's concern. However, because of the high costs of bulk transport, he was often obliged to market those of his possessions that could walk—in other words, sheep and cattle. Indeed, farmers were clearly fully aware of the market value of their stock and attuned to the fluctuations in it. In the 1790s, for instance, attempts to maintain an artificially low price level for meat in Cape Town foundered as a result of the Graaff-Reinet farmers refusal to sell at a rate they considered unacceptably low.

There is no doubt that all sections of the farming community were ea-ger to exploit such commercial activities as were available. In this, as in so

32. On the importance of the trade in firearms to such frontiersmen as the Griquas, see *Records*, ed. Theal, 28:384, 437.

33. Robert Ross, "The 'White' Population in South Africa in the Eighteenth Century," *Pop-ulation Studies* 29 (1975):220.

34. A *smouse* was a traveling pedlar. Ample evidence for the process of town foundation in the Cape Colony can be found in the Cape of Good Hope *Statistical Bluebooks of the Colony* (an annual publication). Farther north, there is no such readily available source, and it is neces-sary to rely on such incidental descriptions as that of Potchefstroom in the 1850s by James Chapman in his *Travels*, 1:14–16.

many other respects, the Philippolis Griquas were typical of "frontier" farmers. Although during the 1820s, when they arrived in what was to become the southern Free State, they were far from wealthy, within a few years they had built up their herds to such an extent that the farmers of the northern districts of the Cape were complaining of the unfair competition that they experienced from the Griquas, who had access to better pastures and could thus command higher prices in the markets of Graaff-Reinet and Grahamstown.[35] At the same time, the Griquas were diversifying their activities. In 1836 one man opened a hotel on the road between the Orange River and Philippolis, since the traffic had become large enough to justify it,[36] while others traded, probably in grain and horses, into Lesotho.[37] Certainly most Griquas were concerned to make a profit from the presence of British troops north of the Orange during the 1840s and 1850s,[38] while, particularly after the discovery of the wagon routes to Ngamiland in 1850, many of the Philippolis Griquas, along with individuals from many other backgrounds in South Africa, took advantage of the temporary ivory boom this discovery caused.[39] At the same time, with the large-scale introduction of merino sheep north of the Orange, some Griquas were able to convert their flocks into wool-bearers, so that the 1850s became a boom decade for Philippolis, at least in economic terms.[40]

Numerous similar responses to new economic possibilities could be described for all the frontiersmen of southern Africa. For much of the eighteenth century, the opportunities were limited to elephant hunting[41] and aloe cultivation,[42] but thereafter, with the increasing commercialization of the country, they were enjoyed by far more of the interior men. Examples range from the Mossel Bay farmers who invested heavily in the 1780s, when there was the chance of opening up the bay as a market for grain (and who suffered very considerable losses when the project was aborted);[43] via the

35. P. J. van der Merwe, *Die Noordwaartse Beweging van die Boere voor die Groot Trek, 1770–1842* (The Hague, 1937), p. 310.

36. W. B. Boyce, *Notes on South African Affairs . . .* (Grahamstown, 1838), pp. 155–56.

37. See *Basutoland Records*, ed. G. M. Theal, 3 vols. (Cape Town, 1883), 1:413; E. Casalis, *My Life in Basutoland* (London, 1889), pp. 136–39; Peter Sanders, *Moshoeshoe, Chief of the Sotho* (London, 1975), pp. 47–48; R. C. Germond, *Chronicles of Basutoland* (Morija, So. Africa, 1967), pp. 438–39.

38. Robert Ross, *Adam Kok's Griquas*, p. 53.

39. See Livingstone, *Family Letters*, 2:147–51; Chapman, *Travels*, 1:194–95.

40. Ross, *Adam Kok's Griquas*, pp. 66–81.

41. Shell, "European Immigration."

42. Anders Sparrman, *A Voyage to the Cape of Good Hope . . .*, ed. V. S. Forbes, trans. J. and I. Rudner, 2 vols. (Cape Town, 1976–77), 2:258–60.

43. See C. F. J. Muller, *J. F. Kirsten or die Toestand van die Kaap Kolonie in 1795, 'n kritiese Studie* (Pretoria, 1960), p. 61; *Belangrijke Historische Dokumenten*, 3:36–38; D. G. van Reenen, *Die joernaal van Dirk Gysbert van Reenen*, ed. W. Blommaert and J. A. Wiid (Cape Town, 1937), p. 285.

eastern cattle farmers who profited from the presence of the British army in Algoa Bay (Port Elizabeth);[44] to Jan Viljoen, veld-cornet of the Marico district of the western Transvaal in the 1850s, who was so concerned to preserve his privileged position on the "Missionaries' Road" to Botswana and the north that he ordered the Griqua, Adam January (alias Apé), to constrain any Britishers from moving north of Molopolole—an order that was obeyed.[45]

Still, to establish on the one hand that the frontiersmen were very largely, if never entirely, self-sufficient and on the other that they were responsive to market opportunities—that, each in his own way, both Guelke and Neumark are correct—does not provide any deep insight into the dynamics behind the rapid spread of colonial structure throughout what was to become South Africa. This is because the economistic arguments they propose cannot penetrate the actual motivation as a whole—far less the economy as a whole. An explanation for frontier expansion in South Africa must necessarily attempt to be an explanation for an immense number of individual decisions to move out and found a new farm in territory as yet unexploited by the colonists. It is most persuasive to view these decisions as stemming from the structure of the colonial family and the tendencies within that institution that led to its regular fission.

In a sense, the most obvious explanation for the regular breaking up of colonial families was their immense size and the consequent high rate of population growth. It is known, for instance, that in the course of the eighteenth century the free population of the Cape Colony (excluding Khoisan) grew by about 2.6 percent per annum, and that this was only marginally the result of immigration.[46] Of course, population growth was a necessary cause of colonial expansion, though not a sufficient explanation for it. But certain problems remain.

First, what was the cause of the population growth? To a certain extent, it was the good nutrition of the colonists, who were able to enjoy the fruits of newly cultivated land and were cushioned from the effects of otherwise debilitating demographic crises by the slaves and the Khoisan doing their hard work for them. There can have been few hungry white men or women in South Africa before, perhaps, the 1880s,[47] and in consequence it is reason-

44. See n. 22 above.

45. See Jan Viljoen to Adam Januarie, 11 June 1852, LMS Archives, South Africa Odds 12/2/C, copy in the handwriting of David Livingstone; Chapman, *Travels*, 1:50.

46. Ross, "White Population," pp. 221–22. It should be noted that when I wrote that article, I had not examined the original lists (held in the Algemeen Rijksarchief, The Hague) and was therefore unaware that the figures given in C. Beyers, *Die Kaapse Patriote*, 2d rev. ed. (Pretoria, 1967), pp. 339–48 include large numbers of free blacks, especially in the Cape District.

47. See Carnegie-kommissie, *Die Armblanke-vraagstuk in Suid-Afrika*, vol. 1: *Plattelandsverarming en plaatsverlating*, by J. F. W. Grosskopf (Stellenbosch, 1932), pp. 19–20.

able to suppose that the death rate was both relatively low and, more importantly, not subject to massive fluctuations. But population growth as rapid as that of early white South Africans also requires a high birth rate, which was certainly to be found. Again, in part it was the health of the population which increased its fecundity, but the effects of this in the long term were probably minimal. Rather, the most important cause of the high fertility[48] of the colonists, and thus ultimately of their sharp increase in numbers, was low age at first marriage, particularly of women. In the eighteenth century, over half the women who ever married did so before they were twenty, while in Potchefstroom in the earliest days of the Transvaal, this proportion had risen to 82 percent.[49] In a precontraceptive society, the effects of such a low age of first marriage for women on the birth rate are clear.

Now, although such a low age at first marriage for women is the rule rather than the exception in world perspective, for a northwest European population it is highly abnormal;[50] and, as will be shown below, the family structure of the colonists was in other respects fairly typical of their continent of origin. In colonial society—and not only in South Africa[51]—the constraints against early marriage had clearly been lifted. In Europe, to generalize shamelessly, such constraints were largely economic. A man could not marry until he was independent, and he often chose a relatively old bride (say, in her late twenties) in an attempt to reduce the size of his future family.[52] There is indeed some evidence that in South Africa, at least the first of these constraints was operative. However, in southern Africa the generally low age at marriage and consequent population increase derived from the opportunities for independence provided, ultimately, by the open frontier in land. As the frontier closed, the age at marriage went up.[53] In other words, it is wrong to explain southern African frontier expansion

48. It is important to realize that fertility rates are calculated on the basis of all women between the ages of fifteen to forty-five, whether or not they are married or otherwise indulging in regular sexual activity.

49. G. A. Kooy, *Een Eeuw Boerenleven in Zuidoost-Transvaal, Mededelingen van de Landbouwhogeschool, Wageningen,* 65/7 (1965), pp. 117–18.

50. See J. Hajnal, "European Marriage Patterns in Perspective," *Population in History,* ed. D. V. Glass and D. E. C. Eversley (London, 1965).

51. See, for example, J. Henripin, *La Population canadienne au début du XVIIIe siècle, Travaux et documents de l'I.N.E.D., Cahier No. 22* (Paris, 1954); P. J. Greven, Jr., *Four Generations: Population and Land in Colonial Andover, Massachusetts* (Ithaca and London, 1970).

52. This is argued, for instance, by E. A. Wrigley, "Family Limitation in Pre-Industrial England," *Economic History Review,* 2d ser., vol. 19 (1966).

53. It is notable that in 1875 the proportion of women between twenty and twenty-four who were married (which is obviously an inverse index of the age at first marriage) was considerably higher in the Eastern Province of the Cape Colony than in the Western. Also, in both divisions there was a strong positive correlation between the proportion who were married and the proportion who were members of the Dutch Reformed Church.

solely in terms of population increase, since to a considerable extent that very increase was encouraged by the presence of the frontier.

The reasons for this independence were partly endogenous and partly imported from Europe. It should be remembered that the institutions and many of the settlers of the Cape Colony came from the Netherlands, and within the Netherlands from the Province of Holland. This was perhaps the classic locus of individualism in Europe,[54] by far the most urbanized region of the continent,[55] and one which, if it had ever had a peasantry in the true sense of the term, had lost it well before the mid-seventeenth century, to give way to highly commercialized agriculture.[56] It was only in the middle of the eighteenth century that the Dutch East India Company began to recruit large numbers of sailors from the areas of genuine European peasantries in central Germany, and by then the pattern of colonial society had been set.[57] Moreover, all immigrants to South Africa had been torn away from their own societies (except for those who came from a seafaring community in the first place) and were therefore not likely to attempt to reconstruct a "traditional" way of life which had rejected them, or at least placed them in a disadvantageous position. Only in the southwestern Cape, far from the frontier, were there incentives to establish a way of life built around a family farm passed on from generation to generation. Mobility was always too easy, and was, moreover, never discouraged in any way by the actions of government or any other institution.[58]

It must be admitted, though, that in rural South Africa the role of kinship came to be far greater than it was in Holland. The high frequency of

54. Probably even more so than England. See Macfarlane, *Origins*, and H. P. H. Jansen, *Hollands Voorsprong*, inaugural lecture, Leiden, 1976.

55. W. Jappe Alberts and H. P. H. Jansen, *Welvaart in Wording, Sociaal-Economische Geschiedenis van Nederland van de Vroegste Tijden tot het Eind van de Middeleeuwen* (The Hague, 1977), p. 263.

56. For this subject, see the magnificent work of Jan de Vries, *The Dutch Rural Economy in the Golden Age* (New Haven and London, 1974).

57. J. R. Bruijn, "De personeelsbehoefte van de VOC overzee en aan boord, bezien in Aziatisch en Nederlands perspectief," *Bijdragen en Mededelingen betreffende de Geschiedenis der Nederlanden* 91 (1976):235.

58. In a comparative work, it is worth stressing the similarities in terms of social structure of the Netherlands and England, and indeed of their respective colonies. It has been argued that "the only areas that never had peasantries at all were those colonized by England: Australia, New Zealand, Canada and North America" (see Daniel Thorner, "Peasantry," *International Encyclopedia of Social Science*). Although there may well have been peasantries in South Africa (though this point is debatable), the white farmers could not be so described. It was not that they "seized privacy and intimacy for themselves as soon as they came off the boat," and thus did not establish the public, nonintimate peasant society, as Edward Shorter argues in *The Making of the Modern Family* (London, 1976), p. 202. Rather, the immigrants to South Africa did not come from a peasant society any more than those to the British colonies did. This argument, of course, largely follows Macfarlane, *Origins*.

marriages among kin would seem to bear witness to this. Nevertheless, there is never any suggestion of anything approaching lineage formation among the white (or Bastard) South Africans, but rather a loose, cognatic kindred, whose members were in all probability highly egocentric and in no sense corporate. It is far more likely that the prevalence of marriage among kin is a construct, first, of the low population density, coupled with large-sized families, which would have meant that a high proportion of available marriage partners were in fact kin, and second, of incipient economic stratification on the *platteland*.[59]

The essential structure of colonial South African rural society can be seen in the mode and the effects of the transmission of property between the generations. This institution, after all, is crucial to the reproduction of social order, and has indeed received considerable attention by students of European peasantries and other rural groups.[60] It is useful to distinguish between two separate processes—namely, succession to property at the death of a member of the older generation, and grants made by the older to the younger generation during the former's lifetime, or, to use more technical legal terms, between succession post mortem and transfers inter vivos. As for the former, the Holland system of rigid partibility was introduced into South Africa.[61] While it was possible to make a will, there were considerable limitations on this, and indeed there was no movement toward unigeniture. This meant that on the death of a man his property was divided, half going to the widow and the other half being distributed among his children. As a consequence, when a man died, his farm would be sold and the proceeds divided among the widow and offspring, a custom much denigrated by those who advocated agricultural improvement.[62] The family group would then conclusively divide as any sort of economic unit, adding considerably to the motive for expansion.[63]

This process could, of course, be accelerated if sufficient property to allow independence was transferred during the lifetime of the father. Here there is a considerable difference between the wine and corn farmers on the one hand and the stock keepers on the other. An agricultural holding is difficult to divide, whereas a sheep flock is very easy, and in any case it seems to

59. This impression, as yet untested quantitatively, has been gained from perusal of C. C. de Villiers, *Geslagsregisters van die Ou Kaapse Families*, 2d ed., rev. C. Pama, 3 vols. (Cape Town and Amsterdam, 1966), and Eugen Fischer, *Die Rehobother Bastards und das Bastardierungsproblem beim Menschen* (Jena, Germ., 1913).

60. *Family and Inheritance, Rural Society in Western Europe, 1200–1800*, ed. Jack Goody, Joan Thirsk, and E. P. Thompson (Cambridge, 1976).

61. J. A. van der Chijs, *Nederlandsch Indisch Plakkaatboek* (Batavia, [Jakarta], Indonesia, 1891), 1:401–90.

62. Barrow, *Travels*, 2:426.

63. For example, Lutz Berkner, "Inheritance, Land Tenure and Peasant Family Structure: A German Regional Comparison," in *Family and Inheritance*, ed. Goody et al., pp. 71–96.

have been the custom to give a newborn child a few cattle or sheep that could be the nucleus for a herd. There were also more possibilities for acquiring a herd by entering some form of client relationship with a wealthy man. The results[64] of this practice in stimulating the independence of young stock farmers can be seen in the fact that, although the average age at marriage for men in both stock-keeping and agricultural districts was more or less the same, the degree of variation in marriage age among the pastoralists was far less. They did not have to wait for their fathers to die before they could become independent.[65] One example will have to suffice as flesh for these dry statistical bones. On 29 October 1805, the members of the *Commissie van Veeteelt and Landbouw* arrived at the farm Groote Valleij, on the Oliphants River, which was owned by Johannes Lubbe. It was a prosperous farm that made its profits from citrus sold in Cape Town, although Lubbe also grew rice, for which there was both water and land in sufficiency. As always, the transportation costs to the market were a major problem for the development of the farm, but in this case it also seemed to the *Commissie* that "industry and hands were somewhat lacking." Nevertheless, Johannes's son, Schalk Willem, who was already married but had not yet become a father,[66] "intended to trek into the veld with a handful of sheep to begin his career," although the *Commissie* attempted to persuade him to remain and intensify the farming on the many unused stretches of his father's farm.[67] I cannot say whether or not he did in fact trek away, as his father had almost certainly done before him.[68] But the point is that he was able to do so and expected to do so.

It would of course be ridiculous to suppose that the structure of authoritative relations within the South African family was the only motive for colonial expansion, even if it may well have been the main one. There were certainly those who moved out to the frontier because of the material advantages it offered, whether in terms of market opportunities or because subsistence could be gained with relative ease in contrast to the more competitive commercial world to the south and west, where considerable capital was needed to become established as a farmer.[69] The Swedish botanist Sparr-

64. Sparrman, *A Voyage.*

65. See also the case of Scandinavia as reported by Jack Goody, *Family and Inheritance,* p. 8.

66. It is uncertain when he married. De Villiers, *Geglagsregister,* p. 511, has him marrying in 1799, at the young age of eighteen, but considering that he is not recorded as having any children until 1806, it would seem possible that there was confusion with another Schalk Willem Lubbe who married in 1804 but did not have any children until 1814. By this late date the genealogies were becoming somewhat less complete and trustworthy.

67. *Belangrijke Historische Dokumenten,* 3:402–05.

68. Johannes's father had apparently lived in the area, though precisely where is not certain, while his brother Frans lived at Biedouw, some 20 kilometres away.

69. I owe this point to Leonard Guelke's critique of the draft of my paper during the Seven. Springs conference in April 1979.

man relates how, when he was on the eastern fringe of white settlement in the 1770s, he received advice on how to set himself up as an independent farmer and on the benefits of so doing.[70] He did not follow that advice, but no doubt others did, and indeed, in this period there were various highly commercial farmers with land far in the east of the colony.[71] Again, after 1836 there were obviously some farmers who moved deeper inland for political reasons, the most clearcut case being those who left Natal after the British conquest.[72] There were also, it should be remembered, those who were forced out. In 1835, Carel Kruger told Dr. Andrew Smith that, twenty years previously, he had been forced to leave his farm in the Warm Bokkeveld as a result of a conspiracy among the leading farmers of the area and with the connivance of the landdrost of Tulbagh. His dark skin made him an easy target for men who wished to increase their holdings in that increasingly prosperous district, and he was thus forced north, eventually to the Orange River, where he became a Griqua.[73] Or again, half a century later, the first colonists in what became East Griqualand were unreconstructed Kat River rebels such as Smith Pommer.[74] These may have been exceptional cases, but the Bastards, and indeed many of the Khoi group along the Orange River and north into Namibia, were driven there by the pressure of white colonists in such districts as the Hantam, the Bokkevelds, and the Roggeveld.[75]

These examples demonstrate a wider truth—namely, that the expansion of colonial settlement had the effect of alienating large numbers of the original inhabitants of South Africa from independent access to the means of production. Indeed, the labor force of colonial South Africa was composed in part of those who were imported to fulfill various tasks in the production process and in part of those indigenous peoples for whom an independent existence was made impossible by the process of colonial expansion. This contrast between the immigrant and the autochthonous can be found between slaves and Khoisan in the seventeenth and eighteenth centuries, and again later with the Indians in Natal from the 1860s and the Chinese on the Witwatersrand in the 1900s. Perhaps weaker parallels could be drawn with

70. Sparrman, *Travels*, 2:133.

71. Susie Newton-King, "Background of the Khoikhoi Rebellion of 1799–1803," University of London, *Collected Seminar Papers on Southern Africa*, vol. 10 (1981).

72. The best general survey of these events is still E. A. Walker, *The Great Trek*, 2d ed. (London, 1936).

73. A. Smith, *The Diary of Dr. Andrew Smith*, ed. P. R. Kirby, 2 vols. (Cape Town, 1939–40), 1:152–53. For the white point of view in this case, see P. J. Venter, "Landros en Heemrade; 1682–1827," *Archives Year Book for South African History* 2 (1940):35.

74. It was estimated around 1860 that there were about 400 "coloured" rebels in the area. G. M. Theal, *History of South Africa since 1795*, 5 vols. (London, 1908), 3:445.

75. See Marais, *Cape Coloured People*, pp. 10–12; Lichtenstein, *Travels* 2:303–04; Fischer, *Rehobother Bastards*, p. 47–57; Vedder, *South-West Africa*, pp. 169–71.

the modern contrast between the migrant laborer and the permanently ur-banized; but in this case there exists the important difference that the areas from which labor is recruited—"pressed out" might be a better descrip-tion—themselves lie within the orbit of the South African economy, which in turn has exerted the pressures that have driven the workers out. In this sense the autochthonous have become migrants.

But this is only the current stage in a long process which began shortly after the foundation of the Dutch colony at the Cape of Good Hope. It was also, especially in its preindustrial phases, largely a frontier phenomenon almost by definition, since it was a consequence of the interrelationship of individuals of different cultures. Indeed, it could be argued that the frontier closed in any particular region, at least in southern Africa, when control over the means of production passed definitively to the colonists. This, at least in that part of the world, is what "legitimate authority" is based on.[76] Even where Africans managed to maintain their de jure possession of land, as in the so-called reserves, their increasing dependence on migrant labor for new necessities—and indeed for many of the old ones—shows how far the inhabitants had been incorporated as inferior members of the white-ruled society.[77]

This incorporation of Africans into the colonial economy as laborers was generally the result of the slow destruction of their indigenous system of production. In the early stages the progress was often brutal and individ-ual. In the more prosperous regions near the coast, workers could be im-ported either as slaves (until 1807) or as indentured laborers (between 1860 and 1911).[78] On the frontier, in contrast, de facto slave labor was often used, but it was of local origin. In the Cape Colony of the eighteenth century, those few prisoners who were taken in the bloody wars with the Khoisan were generally distributed among the farmers who had taken part in the commando. Normally these were children, since adults were indiscrimi-nately slaughtered.[79] Indeed, the carnage on these expeditions was so great that clearly the labor so provided was nothing but a minor by-product. How-ever, in itself it was no doubt welcome, even if the farmers could never fully

76. For this concept as applied to the frontier, see Legassick, "Griqua."

77. The literature on this subject is vast. For a recent survey, see Francis Wilson, *Migrant Labour in South Africa* (Johannesburg, 1972); J. Leeuwenberg, *The Transkei: A Study in Eco-nomic Regression* (London, 1976); Duncan Innes and Dan O'Meara, "Class Formation and Ide-ology: The Transkei Region," *Review of African Political Economy*, vol. 7 (1976); and M. C. Legassick and Harold Wolpe, "The Bantustans and Capital Accumulation in South Africa," in ibid.

78. For a view of this process in its international context, see Hugh Tinker, *A New System of Slavery: The Export of Indian Labour Overseas 1830–1920* (London, 1974).

79. For example, in Graaff-Reinet district alone, 2,504 San were killed in the commandos of the decade 1786–95, as against 669 taken prisoner. Marais, *Cape Coloured People*, pp. 17–18.

trust the bondsmen they acquired in this way. However, considering the small numbers involved, this slavery cannot have been the major course of labor in any district of the eighteenth-century Cape. The wars were fought for other reasons—above all, for the right to run sheep on the traditional hunting grounds of the Khoisan.

In the Transvaal after the Great Trek, the situation may have been qualitatively different. First, there is some evidence that the Transvaalers regularly "bought" children from the various groups of San in the northern Drakensberg, on the border with Natal. Mokazani, a "bushman" interviewed by J. M. Orpen in 1855, was asked whether

> it was a custom among his people to sell their children, or give them willingly? He had never heard of such a thing. Three of his children had been taken away by the servants of some boers . . . but against his will; he only allowed them to be taken because he thought they would have killed him, had he tried to prevent it. He must acknowledge that he had been given a few articles, when the children had been taken away, viz. beads, meat etc. He mentioned the names of nine other men, from whom children had been taken.[80]

But not only San were enslaved. Many of the wars the Transvaal fought against African tribes had as their motive the acquisition of slaves, which were then distributed among the burghers. Indeed, it has been argued that much of the prosperity and power of the Swazi state, in particular, derived from its large-scale participation in slave trading both to Maputo and to the Transvaal. In this way the Swazi aristocracy and royal family were able to accumulate the wealth on which their ascendancy was based.[81]

There were, of course, other less blatant methods of extracting surplus from African tribes. Most important was the imposition of tribute, as was achieved most spectacularly in Namibia, until the Herero revolt led by Maherero against domination of the central plateau by the Afrikaner clan.[82] The levying of tribute was not always successful, as is shown by the failure of the Griqua to establish their hegemony over the southern Tswana in the 1820s.[83] But when it did succeed, as in the Transvaal,[84] it became possible for

80. *Correspondence between his Excellency Sir George Grey, K. C. B., and His Majesty's Principal Secretary of State of the Colonies on the Affairs of Cape Colony, Natal and Adjacent Territories* (Cape Town, 1857), p. 198.

81. P. L. Bonner, "The Rise, Consolidation and Disintegration of Dlamini Power in Swaziland between 1820 and 1889; A Study in the Relationship of Foreign Affairs to Internal Political Development" (Ph.D. diss., University of London, 1977).

82. Vedder, *South-West Africa*, pp. 325–63.

83. Legassick, "Griqua," chaps. 8 and 9.

84. On this, see in particular Stanley Trapido, "Landlord and Tenant in a Colonial Economy: The Transvaal 1880–1910," *Journal of Southern African Studies* 5 (1978):27–58.

the whites to transform their initial exploitation into a more or less regular system for the extraction of rent—in cash, kind, or labor—which often resembled the classic methods used by landlords to extract surplus (and indeed often the necessities for life) from peasants. But the subjected Africans did not form peasant communities,[85] at least in the ideal-typical sense.

Parenthetically, the incorporation of Africans into colonial society as laborers was not invariably the result of pressures emanating from the colonial economy. On the contrary, there are examples of individuals being incorporated as a result of events that were at most marginally the result of colonial expansion. The Twsana, who crossed the Orange River in the 1820s fleeing from the *Difaqane,* looked on the white farms as refuges from the wars and starvation that threatened them farther north. They came to work in large numbers in the districts of Graaff-Reinet and Uitenhage.[86] However, the odds are that most of them did not stay as permanent laborers.[87] Once some degree of peace was established farther north, they moved back, many of them settling in Lesotho under Moshoeshoe.[88] Nor did many Mfengu of the eastern Cape remain permanently as laborers for the white farmers after their 1835 decision to quit Gcalekaland. Some managed to set themselves up in the better-paid positions of the colonial economy, for instance, as surfboat workers in Port Elizabeth, while others were able to transform themselves into small farmers fully within the market economy of the Cape colony.[89] However, this was a normal phase in the eventual subjection of the vast majority of Africans to subordinate and exploited status within the economic system of South Africa.

The recognition of the initial phase of African prosperity consequent upon the expansion of the colonial economy has been one of the major

85. My vision on these has been formed by Macfarlane, *Origins,* pp. 7–33; Eric Wolf, *Peasants* (Englewood Cliffs, N.J., 1966); James Scott, *The Moral Economy of the Peasant: Rebellion and Subsistence in Southeast Asia* (New Haven and London, 1976).

86. C. F. J. Muller, *Die Oorsprong van die Groot Trek* (Cape Town, 1974), pp. 85–134. However, Muller's claim that these immigrants fatally disturbed the delicate balance of forces in the Eastern Cape is patently absurd, since not even the most doctrinaire functionalist could claim that the society in the border region during the 1820s was in any way in equilibrium. Rather, the Tswana were merely one extra element in a fluctuating and highly volatile situation.

87. In 1832, the number of foreign natives in the colony was estimated at only 603 (the three being in Worcester District, the others in Albany, Somerset, and apparently, Graaff-Reinet). The majority of these must have been Xhosa (PRO CO 53/9, 236–37). Two years later, when Graaff-Reinet was enumerated separately, there were 41 "resident strangers" in the district (PRO CO 53/71, 208–09).

88. William Lye, "The Distribution of the Sotho Peoples after the Difaqane," *African Societies in Southern Africa: Historical Studies,* ed. Leonard Thompson (London, 1969), pp. 202–64.

89. Richard A. Moyer, "A History of the Mfengu of the Eastern Cape, 1815–1865" (Ph.D. diss., University of London, 1976).

themes in the recent historiography of southern Africa.[90] Nevertheless, the speedy destruction of the small capitalist farmers has tended to be ascribed too exclusively to the growth of capitalist industry in southern Africa. There were, of course, many groups of commercial farmers who were crushed by the processes of class struggle deriving from the establishment of mining capitalist domination of southern Africa. But although the diamond and gold mines of Kimberley and the Witwatersrand have been the prime movers of southern African history ever since the late nineteenth century, they cannot be considered the only cause of the disruption of African commercial farming for the benefit of the whites. Analogous processes of rise and decline of commercial African groups preceded by decades— even by centuries—the discovery of diamonds. Colonial southern Africa had been within the orbit of capitalism long before the first diamond was mined. It had, after all, been founded by the premier capitalist organization of the time, the Dutch East India Company, and had been taken over by the British at the moment when Great Britain was in the process of transforming itself into the first industrial capitalist nation. In the interest of economy of argument, it would therefore seem valuable to propose an explanation for the subjugation of Africans to white rule that derives from the class struggle engendered by capitalism, and not merely by its local industrial variety. In this way, the paradoxical effects of colonial expansion in southern Africa, in other words of the frontier, can be seen and explained.

The argument begins from the recognition that, as a result of white expansion, a variety of economic opportunities were presented to some of the autochthonous Africans, which they were quick to grasp. Essentially, these derived from the great extension of the market for all products, but more especially for agricultural and pastoral ones.[91] The benefits of this expansion, however, were not equally distributed. Socioeconomic stratification

90. The material of the following paragraphs is clearly derivative, even though, probably, none of the authors on which this argument is based would accept it in its entirety—or perhaps at all. Of particular importance have been: G. Arrighi, "The Political Economy of Rhodesia," in G. Arrighi and John S. Saul, *Essays on the Political Economy of Africa* (New York, 1973); Colin Bundy, "The Emergence and Decline of a South African Peasantry," *African Affairs* (1972), and *The Rise and Fall of the South African Peasantry* (London, 1979); several of the essays in *Roots of Rural Poverty*; Terence Ranger, "Reflections on Peasant Research in Central and Southern Africa," *Journal of Southern African Studies*, vol. 5 (1978). I am well aware that space, competence, and, to a certain extent, my purpose have tended to lead me "to emasculate hard-won and detailed evidence of diversity," for which I apologize to those who have unearthed it. See A. G. Hopkins, "Imperial Connections," *The Imperial Impact: Studies in the Economic History of Africa and India*, ed. Clive Dewey and A. G. Hopkins (London, 1978), cited by John McCracken, "Rethinking Rural Poverty," *Journal of African History* 19 (1978):612–13.

91. This is, of course, in no way to suggest that precolonial economies were stagnant or without developed mechanisms of exchange. But the arrival of the colonial economy presented opportunities of such a quantitatively different order that they amounted to a qualitative change.

among the Africans was intensified, either along precolonial lines or skew to them. Moreover, under the influence of market-oriented agriculture and the individualistic ethos engendered by capitalism, such redistributive mechanisms as there had been in precolonial society atrophied. Their place could not be taken by wage labor within the society, since the new farms were rarely, if ever, of sufficient size to permit the employment of labor. African farmers were able to rely exclusively on their families to fulfill the requirements of cultivation and stock-keeping.

At the same time, and as a result of the same extension of market possibilities, the frontier colonial farmer was enjoying economic opportunities similar to those of his African counterpart, and coming under similar pressure toward internal economic stratification. This was perhaps intensified by the pressure from the descendants of those who had made good on the superannuated frontiers to the south and west.

For the majority of Africans, the combination of land loss and increased stratification within their community made the traditional economic activities of farming and pastoralism decreasingly viable. Therefore, they found themselves obliged to enter the colonial labor market, either permanently or as migrant laborers. The result of this compulsion was that their bargaining position vis-à-vis their employers was weak. Since relatively few, if any, could find employment with African farmers, they were forced to work for whites, either on the land or in the towns, or to take up tenancies on white-owned farms in return for labor, cash, or goods.

In the countryside, then, a three-level stratification developed: large white farmers who employed labor or acted as rentiers; small farmers of all backgrounds (often tenant laborers who had built up their holdings); and agricultural laborers, almost invariably working for the whites. Slowly, the competitive position of the smaller farmers as against the larger deteriorated. Those who were tenants were particularly vulnerable, especially because an increase in the profitability of farming induced the rentiers themselves to farm on a larger scale. Moreover, the larger white farmers had a far more constant access to credit to tide them over cyclical slumps and to rationalize their enterprises. This was not simply a matter of racial prejudice on the part of the banks and other money-lending institutions—though this factor undoubtedly did play its part.[92] Rather, the larger the farm, the better the security that could be offered, and so the operation of "Matthew's Law" was highly rational.[93] Further, since the 1770s the large farmers have almost always been a major element on which the various governments in South

92. Tony Kirk, "Progress and Decline in the Kat River Settlement, 1829–1854," *Journal of African History* 14 (1973): 415.

93. "Unto every one that hath shall be given, and he shall have in abundance: but from him that hath not shall be taken away even that which he hath," Matt. 25:29.

Africa have relied. They have therefore generally been able to enforce compliance with their interests, whether regarding land alienation, labor regulation, or such seemingly mundane matters as the routing of railways.[94] Moreover, and crucially, they were able to maintain their strength by exploiting to the full the labor that had been driven to find work with them, in much the same way as the industrialists and mineowners would do. Thus the same processes which drove the Africans into a dependent position on the land or off it also contributed to the worsening competitive position of those who were able to retain some species of independence.

Conversely, there seem to have been few mechanisms for increasing the size of the small, African-run farms to enable them to compete with the large landowners in supplying the market. Probably, in default of considerable injections of capital, the intensive land use required to produce both a surplus and the family subsistence from these farms meant that the soil quality rapidly deteriorated. Moreover, there was no effective mechanism for accommodating the population increase which resulted from the elimination of subsistence crises by improved transport, from the imposition of peace, and from the increased proportion of monogamous marriages—a consequence of the widespread acceptance of Christianity among these "modernizers." In any case, it seems to have been rare for small farmers to transfer their wealth to succeeding generations. Their heyday lasted around forty years at most, even though it was often the children of these farmers who went to school and used that education to enter the professions as teachers, clergymen, doctors—and politicians. But these were a minority of a minority. Agriculture could not support many of the descendants of the prosperous. Most had no alternative but to become migrant laborers.

At first sight, this analysis would seem to have strayed away from the frontier, at least as that concept is generally apprehended. Certainly, the motives for colonial expansion described earlier in this chapter do not seem fully to accord with the stress on capitalist farming and industry which, I have claimed, together slowly reduced the independent African agriculturalists and pastoralists to a status dependent on wage labor or other forms of subordinate participation in the white-dominated economy, and divorced them from independent access to the means of production. However, even if the initial penetration to the southern African interior was not impelled solely by rational decisions about the maximization of profits and the minimization of risks, the consequence of that settlement was that traders and export-oriented capitalist farmers eventually took over from the original settlers when they themselves did not begin to operate purely along the

94. As W. M. Macmillan pointed out, "to locate the native reserves, it is no bad rule . . . to look for the areas circumvented or entirely missed by even branch railway lines," *Complex South Africa* (London, 1930), p. 212.

principles of commercial farming. Moreover, the clearest example of "the emergence and decline of a South African peasantry," on which much of this argument has been based, occurred in precisely that area which had been—and had remained—the scene of the classic "frontier confrontation" between Africans and settlers—namely, the eastern Cape Colony. To investigate the earlier stages of frontier interaction and to ignore the somewhat later manifestations of the growth of small capitalist farming—or indeed to concentrate solely on the latter to the exclusion of the former—would be misleading. They were clearly two phases of a single, logically progressing historical process.

The process of commercialization and decline can indeed be seen very clearly in the Ciskei. In 1880, regarding the 7,000 Africans under his control, an official conceded that "the people in this neighbourhood who have in one year raised 250,820 lbs of wool of a superior quality and excellent get up, besides 7,484 muids of corn, who attend to 77 wagons, which are mostly employed in the transport business, to say nothing of the labour they undertake . . . cannot fairly be charged en masse with indolence."[95] Even by this stage, however, as Bundy notes, increased economic stratification had begun to create a large group of poor, landless Africans, a process helped by the last of the "frontier wars" in 1879–81.[96]

Groups similar to the commercializing farmers of Herschel, Glen Grey, and Victoria East can be found throughout southern Africa in the decades after the penetration of the colonial economy to any given region. The kholwa of Natal[97] are a clear example of the process, as is the landholder in the Transvaal and the Orange Free State who, with the passing of the Native Lands Act of 1913, became, in the classic words of Sol Plaatje, "not actually a slave, but a pariah in the land of his birth."[98] There were also those who, paradoxical as it may seem now, made Lesotho into the granary of South Africa toward the end of the last century,[99] as well as those maize and tobacco farmers from Rhodesia against whom the white settlers found it difficult to compete.[100] In some ways the most successful—or at any rate

95. Cited in Bundy, "Emergence and Decline," p. 377.

96. Ibid., pp. 378–79.

97. Norman Etherington, "African Economic Experiments in Colonial Natal," *African Economic History*, vol. 5 (1978).

98. Sol T. Plaatje, *Native Life in South Africa before and since the European War and the Boer Rebellion* (London, 1916), p. 4. On Plaatje, see Brian Willan, "Sol Plaatje, De Beers and an Old Tram Shed: Class Relations and Social Control in a South African Town," *Journal of Southern African Studies*, vol. 4 (1978). On agriculture in the Orange Free State, see Tim Keegan, "The Restructuring of Agrarian Class Relations in a Colonial Economy: The Orange River Colony, 1902–1910," *Journal of Southern African Studies* 5 (1979):2.

99. *Roots of Rural Poverty*, pp. 20–22.

100. See, for example, Robin Palmer, *Land and Racial Domination in Rhodesia* (London, 1977), passim; but also Ranger, "Reflections," pp. 118–21.

the most long-lasting—were the generally aristocratic cattle barons of Botswana, who were able to convert their privileged position within Ngwato or Kwena society into relatively permanent wealth on the hoof at the expense of great differences of wealth within the society.[101]

The cycle of stratification followed by a slump, poverty for the many and wealth for the few giving way to poverty and subordination to the whites for almost all the indigenous people, did not begin in the nineteenth century. There are clear parallels among the Khoisan of the seventeenth- and eighteenth-century Cape, although the details of that process of rise and decline were obviously different. The monopolistic policies of the Dutch East India Company were designed to the advantage of the company and its shareholders in *patria*, while the combination of laissez faire and state regulation of black labor during the nineteenth and twentieth centuries was clearly to the advantage of the local employers as well as to overseas capitalists. Moreover, the world economy in the earliest phase of industrialization was not the same as the full flowering of a century later. Nevertheless, it is far from fanciful to see forerunners of the small farmers of the Eastern Cape in individuals such as Herry, Klaas, and Koopman—all Khoikhoi who, albeit temporarily, profited from the commercial opportunities presented during the first half-century of colonial settlement.[102] During the eighteenth century, as the frontier along the Hottentots Holland mountains gave way to the frontier of the Tsitsikamma and the Lange Kloof, so Klaas and Koopman were replaced by Khola (Ruiter)[103] and by those Khoikhoi cattle owners at the mouth of the Gamtoos who sold some three hundred cattle a year to the company before they were driven out of the area under increased pressure from capitalist-oriented white farmers.[104] Similar phenomena can also be seen on the frontier in Namaqualand and, later, in Namibia. A Khoikhoi farmer living high in the Cedarberg was met by George Thompson in 1823. "His farm consists of about fifty-four acres, three of which are sown with wheat. Besides this he raises annually about 100 lb. tobacco, and has upwards of 200 fruit trees in bearing, the produce of which he dries and sells at the drostdy. His live-stock amounted to sixteen head of cattle, twenty goats and forty sheep."[105] Evidently, this man was almost the prototype of the small market-oriented farmer found later throughout the eastern parts of southern Africa. The Basters, too, in particular the community which in

101. Parsons, "Economic History," pp. 132–36.
102. Elphick, *Kraal and Castle*, pp. 105, 141–44.
103. Sparrman, *Voyage*, 2:123; *Reizen in zuid Afrika in de Hollandse Tijd*, ed. Godée Molsbergen, 4 vols. (The Hague, 1916–32), 3:287–89.
104. Newton-King, "Background to the Khoikhoi Rebellion," p. 5.
105. George Thompson, *Travels and Adventure in Southern Africa*, ed. V. S. Forbes, 2 vols. (Cape Town, 1967–68), 2:82.

1860 moved from De Tuin to Rehoboth, deep in Namibia, could be considered as belonging to the same category, even if the reason for their trek was as much the destruction of their homes by !Kora raiders as the pressure from the whites who were at that time beginning to appropriate the grazing land on which their cattle roamed.[106]

There is a considerable problem here. In general, in this chapter I have considered the Basters to be colonists, emanating from the colonial society and usually driven by the same pressure for expansion as their somewhat whiter brethren. Why, then, were they considered to be in competition with the whites, as the De Tuin community certainly was, and as were the Griquas, whether of Kokstad, Philippolis, or Griquatown? Clearly, it is impossible to ascribe this to many of the same factors as caused the decline of the various groups of "progressive" African farmers. The arrival of white farmers in the Griqualands and in Namaqualand put the Basters and the Griquas into a disadvantageous competitive position, especially in financial respects, since the whites had been able, in general, to have built up a more substantial working capital as a result of their closer relationship to the market and their exploitation of Khoikhoi and ex-slave labor farther south. Of course, not all whites were able to manage this, and many were forced to become members of the Baster community, just as a generation or two earlier the Baster community itself had included whites who had been unable to maintain a position within pukka white society farther south. Also, various of the Basters and Griquas were able to maintain their position, and these were slowly assimilated to the white society. But to maintain their position it was necessary for them to "pass." With the intensification of capitalist agriculture and, later, industry, came a far sharper dichotomy between the large landowners and employers, and the small farmers and employees. This conflict became increasingly internalized (at least by the former) as between racially distinct *Ständen*.[107]

At first sight it would seem as if the arguments employed to explain the outcasting of the Basters and Griquas would be equally applicable to the poor whites. Indeed, the slow expansion of the more commercialized economy into the interior of southern Africa brought with it increased stratification among the whites, as within all other communities. It may well have been that these distinctions were sharper than those among the Africans. In

---

106. Marais, *Cape Coloured People*, pp. 88–89; Robert Ross, "The !Kora Wars on the Orange River, 1830–80," *Journal of African History* 14 (1975): 571.

107. There is, unfortunately, no English translation for this Germanic concept; but for its applicability to South Africa, see Robert Ross, "Racial Stratification in Pre-Industrial and Industrial South Africa," *Racism and Colonialism*, ed. Robert Ross (The Hague, forthcoming).

addition to the whites who were able to take advantage of the new conditions, and who very largely created them, there were those who found it impossible to maintain their status as independent farmers and employers of
labor. However, even if they did sink to the level of laborer themselves, they
did not remain there, in contradistinction to many of the Basters and the
Griquas. The opening of the mines of the Rand began to offer opportunities
at the moment when, finally, land ceased to be available in the Transvaal
and the frontier of expansion finally closed. But there was a deeper reason,
related to the different economies within which the poor whites and the
Namaqualand Basters operated. Namaqualand was a sheep-farming region,
where labor was not at a premium. In contrast, in the Transvaal profitability
depended very largely on the exploitation of Africans, whether directly in
agricultural activities or through the extraction of rent. Therefore, the landowners were required to employ considerable numbers of auxiliaries in
order to extract the economic surplus. By preference these were landless
whites, who frequently received remuneration in the form of being allowed
to run stock themselves as bywoners. In this way they foreshadowed the
position of their descendants as supervisors in mining and industry.

If we define the frontier as "a territory or zone of interpenetration between two previously distinct societies" (see p. 7 above), then it is clear that
in South Africa the subordination of the African population to colonial rule
and to the economic system of the colony, and ultimately of the world capitalist system, began on the frontier. Realization of the advantages of this
subordination was not the sole—or even, perhaps a major—cause of colonial expansion, for all that it was the most important result of that expansion. The establishment of the class structure of South African society did
not begin on the frontier, but rather with the introduction and exploitation
of slave labor in the southwestern Cape Colony of the seventeenth century.
Nor did it end there. It has, of course, not yet ended; and the influence of
industrialization on the class structure and ideologies of modern South Africa cannot be overestimated. But neither should the importance of the
"frontier" on the development of the South African way of life be ignored or
devalued. It should not be seen as the single determinant cause, any more
than historians of the United States see the frontier as the only factor in the
Americanization of their country. Nevertheless, one fact is painfully obvious to the observer of modern South Africa: the bulk of the modern South
African labor force are the descendants of those who, in the eighteenth and
nineteenth centuries, were on the "other" side of the frontier as seen from
Cape Town, Bloemfontein, or Pretoria. Aspects of the frontier process in
South Africa may have been comparable to that of the United States. The
effects were radically different. In America, reservations were places where

"useless" peoples were shut away: in South Africa, reserves were sources of that most useful of commodities, black labor. Within this difference, to the extent that it was the consequence of the frontier processes in the two regions, lies the great contrast between the frontiers of North America and southern Africa.

5

Christianity on
the Frontier

9

JAMES AXTELL

The Invasion Within: The Contest of Cultures in Colonial North America

The invasion of North America by European men, machines, and microbes was primarily an aggressive attempt to subdue the newfound land and its inhabitants, and to turn them to European profit. Because it was not totally unlike that of Europe, the land itself could be brought to terms by the increasingly effective methods of Western technology and capitalist economy. The American natives, however, posed a more serious problem. While they shared certain characteristics with the rest of mankind known to Europe, their cultures were so strange, so numerous, and so diverse that the invaders found it impossible to predict their behavior. If the Europeans hoped to harness, or at least to neutralize, the numerically superior natives, they could ill afford to tolerate behavior that was as unpredictable as it was potentially dangerous.

Fortunately, not all natives were inscrutable at all times. European traders quickly discovered that the Indians were no strangers to an economy of barter and exchange. Even without the medium of mutually intelligible languages, Europeans exchanged Indian furs, skins, and food for manufactured goods with the aid of elemental sign languages or trade jargons. Military officers who sought native allies against less receptive natives—or who were sought as allies by native factions—recognized with equal ease the normative behavior of military allies.

But traders and soldiers were soon greatly outnumbered, especially in the English colonies, by invaders whose goals were much less compatible with the lifestyles of the Eastern woodland Indians. When European farmers and townsmen arrived in the New World, they brought no interest in any aspect of Indian culture or behavior. To these colonists—who quickly established the distinctive character of the European invasion—the native possessors of the soil stood as living impediments to agricultural "civilization," differing little from stony mountains, unfordable rivers, and implacable swamps. Since it was highly unlikely that the Indians would vanish into thin air or exile themselves to some arid corner of the continent, the best these invaders could hope for was their pacification and resettlement away from the plowed paths of prosperity. In any event, they had to be rendered predictable to make America safe for Europeans.

As if heaven-sent, a small but determined cadre of invaders offered the ultimate answer to the settlers' prayers. Christian missionaries, who had come to America on the earliest waves of invasion, espoused a set of spiritual goals which colored but ultimately lent themselves to the more material ends of their countrymen. From the birth of European interest in the New World, religious men had ensured that the public goals of exploration and colonization included a prominent place for the conversion of the natives to Christianity. But the Christianity envisioned was not a disembodied spiritual construct but a distinct cultural product of western Europe. Conversion was tantamount to a complete transformation of cultural identity. To convert the Indians of America was to replace their native characters with European personae, to transmogrify their behavior by substituting predictable European modes of thinking and feeling for unpredictable native modes. By seeking to control the Indians' thoughts and motives, the missionaries sought to control—or at least anticipate—their actions, which could at any time spell life or death for the proliferating but scattered settlements on the farming frontier. Unwittingly or not, missionaries lent powerful support to the European assault upon America by launching their own subversive invasion within.

From its inception, the invasion of North America was launched on waves of pious intent. Nearly all the colonial charters granted by the French and English monarchs in the sixteenth and seventeenth centuries assign the wish to extend the Christian church and to save savage souls as a principal, if not the principal, motive for colonization.[1] Even patently economic ventures such as the Virginia, Newfoundland, and Susquehannah companies, as one colonist put it, "pretended, and I hope intended" to hold pagan salvation dearer than pounds sterling.[2]

1. See, for example, *Edits, ordonnances royaux, déclarations et arrêts du conseil d'état du roi concernant le Canada*, 3 vols. (Quebec, 1854–56), 1:3, 5–6; 3:11; Merrill Jensen, ed., *American Colonial Documents to 1776*, in David C. Douglas, ed., *English Historical Documents* (New York, 1955), 9:65, 82, 85, 93.

2. Charles Orr, ed., *History of the Pequot War* (Cleveland, Ohio, 1897), pp. 110–11; Mary Francis Farnham, ed., *The Farnham Papers, 1603–1688*, Documentary History of the State of Maine, vol. 7, *Collections of the Maine Historical Society*, 2d ser. (Portland, Me., 1901), pp. 8–9; Peter Force, ed., *Tracts and Other Papers relating Principally to the Origin, Settlement, and Progress of the Colonies in North America*, 4 vols. (Washington, D.C., 1836–47), vol. 3, no. 1, p. 5, Samuel Purchas, *Hakluytus Posthumus or Purchas His Pilgrimes* [London, 1625], 20 vols.

Obviously the mere desire to convert the American natives was insufficient to accomplish the task. For unless they were potentially convertible they could never become Christian converts, a thought no missionary could entertain for long and remain in his calling. From their map-strewn studies in London and Oxford the cousins Hakluyt described the Indians as people "though simple and rude in manners, . . . yet of nature gentle and tractable."[3] Richard Eburne, a fellow promoter, agreed. His *Plain Pathway to Plantations* was lined with "exceeding[ly] tractable" natives, who were not only "industrious and ingenious to learn of us and practice with us most arts and sciences" but "very ready to leave their old and blind idolatries and to learn of us the right service and worship of the true God."[4] Since none of these men had ever made the American voyage to take personal measure of the natives' capacity, they were drawing on the Christian humanist's faith in the reforming power of education as well as the optimism of early explorers. In 1609, as the Virginia Company was outfitting its third fleet for Western waters, the Reverend Robert Gray gave classical expression to that belief when he told potential investors, "It is not the nature of men, but the education of men, which make[s] them barbarous and uncivill." "Chaunge the education of men," he predicted, "and you shall see that their nature"— corrupted at the source by Adam's sin—"will be greatly rectified and corrected."[5] According to Paul Le Jeune, the Jesuit superior of Quebec, it was optimism such as this that caused "a great many people in France [to] imagine that all we have to do is to open our mouths and utter four words, and behold, a Savage is converted."[6]

While the Indians were felt to be ultimately redeemable, there was one crucial hitch: they were still in a state of "savagery" or "barbarism," which every civilized person knew to be an "infinite distance from Christianity."[7] They were much too "degenerate" for religion to flourish or the Word to work its magic upon them. The heart of the matter was that they could not be trusted with the holy church ordinances "whilst they lived so unfixed,

(Glasgow, 1903–05), 19:406–09; Julian P. Boyd and Robert J. Taylor, eds., *The Susquehannah Company Papers*, 11 vols. (Wilkes-Barre, Pa., and Ithaca, N.Y., 1930–71), 1:255.

3. E. G. R. Taylor, ed., *The Original Writings and Correspondence of the Two Richard Hakluyts*, Publications of the Hakluyt Society, 2d ser., nos. 76–77 (London, 1935), 1:164–65; see also 2:223, 339.

4. Richard Eburne, *A Plain Pathway to Plantations* [London, 1624], ed. Louis B. Wright (Ithaca, N.Y., 1962), pp. 55–56.

5. Robert Gray, *A Good Speed to Virginia* (London, 1609), fols. C1v–C2r. See also Reuben Gold Thwaites, ed., *The Jesuit Relations and Allied Documents*, 73 vols. (Cleveland, Ohio, 1896–1901), 5:33; 6:229–31; 19:39 (hereafter cited as *JR*), and *Father Louis Hennepin's Description of Louisiana* [Paris, 1683], ed. Marion E. Cross (Minneapolis, 1938), p. 145.

6. *JR*, 9:91.

7. *New Englands First Fruits* (London, 1643), in Samuel Eliot Morison, *The Founding of Harvard College* (Cambridge, Mass., 1935), p. 421.

confused, and ungoverned a life."[8] The missionary prospectus was thus drawn for the next century and a half. All the European missionary societies, Protestant and Catholic, began and with few exceptions ended, their American efforts with the belief that it was necessary to "civilize Savages before they can be converted to Christianity, & that in order to make them Christians, they must first be made Men."[9] The English Protestants never questioned this assumption until a few were forced to in the 1760s by an increasing record of crushed hopes and unflattering self-comparisons with the Canadian Jesuits, most of whom, after extensive field experience, by the middle decades of the previous century had ceased to practice what they had once preached.[10] With scarcely a dissenting voice in all those years, the missionaries of North America felt it their clear responsibility to give the Indians "Civilitie for their bodies" before "Christianitie for their soules," for while the second made them *"happy,"* the first made them *"men."*[11]

In implying that the Indians were not yet "men" the Europeans meant one of three things. The first meaning was that the natives were the children of the human race, their passions still largely unrestrained by reason. The second meaning also emphasized their passions, but gave them a much less charitable interpretation; rather than innocent children, the Indians in this view were little better than animals, incapable of reason and enslaved by the most brutal passions. The third and by far the most prevalent meaning, however, was simply that the Indians had not mastered the "Arts of civil Life & Humanity."[12]

Whenever plans were drawn for "humanizing" the American natives, the English missionaries chose a peculiar phrase that speaks volumes about their religious attitudes and cultural preconceptions. Time and again, from the sixteenth century to the American Revolution, it was said that the first goal of the English was to *"reduce"* the Indians from savagery to "civility."[13]

---

8. *Collections of the Massachusetts Historical Society,* 3d ser. 4 (1834):90. See also Chrestien Le Clercq, *The First Establishment of the Faith in New France* [Paris, 1691], ed. and trans. John Gilmary Shea, 2 vols. (New York, 1881), 1:111, 141–42.

9. *The Papers of Sir William Johnson,* ed. James Sullivan et al., 14 vols. (Albany, 1921–65), 7:506 (hereafter cited as *Johnson Papers*). See, for example, Le Clercq, *First Establishment of the Faith,* 1:110–11, 214, 222; *Collections of the Massachusetts Historical Society* (hereafter cited as *Colls. Mass. Hist. Soc.*), 3d ser. 4 (1834):14–15; William Hubbard, *The Present State of New-England* (London, 1677), pp. 86–87 (2d pagination); *Ecclesiastical Records, State of New York,* 6 vols. (Albany, 1901–05), 1:398; John R. Bartlett, ed., *Records of the Colony of Rhode Island and Providence Plantations, in New England,* 10 vols. (Providence, 1856–65), 1:297–98.

10. Jean Delanglez, *Frontenac and the Jesuits,* Institute of Jesuit History Publications (Chicago, 1939), pp. 35–65.

11. William Crashaw, *A Sermon Preached in London before the right honorable the Lord La Warre . . . Febr. 21. 1609* (London, 1610), fols. D4r, K1v.

12. *Johnson Papers,* 5:511.

13. Taylor, *Writings of the Hakluyts,* 2:214; Hubbard, *Present State of New-England,* p.

The phrase is puzzling because we would expect a people with a superior self-image to attempt to *raise* their inferiors, rather than *reduce* them, to their level. Why did they speak as if Indian culture needed a kind of *degrading* before measuring *down* to English civility?

The answer lies in the nature of the wholesale changes in Indian culture required by the English—and the French Recollects, Sulpicians, and early Jesuits as well—to render the natives worthy of religious conversion. From the European perspective, the Indians were deficient in three essential qualities: order, industry, and manners. This meant in essence that they were non-Europeans, the polar opposite of what they should be and should want to be. So, with characteristic confidence, the missionaries proceeded in the heady decades after settlement to prescribe a veritable pharmacopoeia of remedies for the Indians' savage condition.

The immediate concern of the Europeans was to remove the Indians from their "disordred riotous rowtes and companies, to a wel governed common wealth," from what they took to be civil anarchy to the rule of European law. For of all "humane Artes," the missionaries knew, "Political government is the chiefest."[14] To men accustomed to kings and queens, administrative bureaucracies, standing armies, police, courts, and all the punitive technology of justice known to "civilized" states, the Indians seemed to suffer from unbenign neglect. If they were acknowledged to have any government at all, it was usually the capricious tyranny of an autocrat, such as Powhatan in Virginia or Uncas in Connecticut. More prevalent was the view that the "common rules of order in the administration of justice"—the rules followed in Parliament or the Estates General—were not observed in Indian society. Indeed, so subtle and covert were the workings of Indian justice that the colonists were "astonished to find that such societies can remain united" at all.[15] Cast in such a light, these "wild people" obviously needed the Europeans to "bring them to Political life, both in Ecclesiastical society and in Civil, for which," the missionaries assured themselves, "they earnestly long and enquire."[16]

Another disturbing symptom of native disorder was their "scattered and

86 (2d pagination); Farnham, *Farnham Papers*, p. 24; Nathaniel B. Shurtleff and David Pulsifer, eds., *Records of the Colony of New Plymouth in New England*, 12 vols. (Boston, 1855–61), 10:285–86, 368; Gray, *Good Speed to Virginia*, fols. C2v, C4r–v; Clayton Colman Hall, ed., *Narratives of Early Maryland, 1633–1684* (New York, 1910), pp. 20, 84, 90; George Washington to Richard Henry Lee, 8 Feb. 1785, American Philosophical Society, Philadelphia.

14. [George Peckham], *A True Reporte of the late discoveries . . . of the Newfound Landes* (London, 1583), fol. F3r; Gray, *Good Speed to Virginia*, fol. D2r.

15. Adriaen Van der Donck, *A Description of the New Netherlands* [Amsterdam, 1655], ed. Thomas F. O'Donnell (Syracuse, N.Y., 1968), p. 100.

16. *New England Historical and Genealogical Register* 36 (1882):296; *Colls. Mass. Hist. Soc.*, 3d ser. 4 (1834):126, 137.

wild course of life."[17] "Towns they have none," wrote an English visitor with England in mind, "being alwayes removing from one place to another for conveniency of food."[18] The predominantly hunting tribes of Canada and Maine were the least fixed because survival depended on following the non-herding big-game animals in small family groups and living off the stingy land. Even their more sedentary southern neighbors spent only five or six months congregated around their cornfields in villages ranging in size from a few families to a thousand inhabitants. And then they too broke up and moved more than once in search of fish, shellfish, berries, nuts, game, maple sap, "warme and thicke woodie bottomes" to escape the winter winds, more wood for their fires, or simply relief from the fearless fleas of summer.[19]

The natives were considered deficient not only in civil order but in industry as well. In one of his first meetings with the Massachusetts, John Eliot told them that they and the English were already "all one save in two things," the first being that the English were Christians and they were not. The second difference was somewhat less obvious but to English minds nearly as important: "we labour and work in building, planting, clothing our selves, &c. and they doe not."[20] The key word in Eliot's comparison was *labour*. To the idealistic missionaries, many of whom had pursued the life of learning because their constitutions were "unsuited to labour," it did not mean simply "to work" (as Eliot's additional use of that word implies), for even the Indians could be said to "work" by expending energy and thought upon various tasks. Rather, it meant to work *laboriously* in the sense of severe, painful, or compulsory *toil*, the kind that a plowman knows as he walks behind a pair of huge oxen in the late spring heat.[21] In that sense, of course, the Indians had never known work, a deficiency exacerbated by what all Europeans diagnosed as a congenital "national vice"—idleness.

When the colonists found idleness endemic to Indian culture, the cultural norm by which they judged applied to only half the native population—the male half. For upon closer examination it appeared to European observers, almost all of whom were male, that while Indian men were indeed the epitome of slothful indulgence, the work done by Indian women came respectably, even pitiably, close to the missionaries' ideal of "labour." Since such behavior ran counter to their civilized expectations, there was

17. Ibid., p. 269.

18. John Josselyn, *An Account of Two Voyages to New-England Made during the years 1638, 1663* [London, 1674] (Boston, 1865), p. 99.

19. Roger Williams, *A Key into the Language of America* (London, 1643), pp. 46–48; *Colls. Mass. Hist. Soc.*, 1st ser. 1 (1792): 132; Van der Donck, *New Netherlands*, pp. 81–82.

20. *Colls. Mass. Hist. Soc.*, 3d ser. 4 (1834): 50.

21. *Oxford English Dictionary*, s.v. "labour" and "toil."

double cause for raised eyebrows. According to the Reverend Francis Higginson, one of the "discommodities" of *New Englands Plantation* was that Indian "Men for the most part live idlely, they doe nothing but hunt and fish," while "Their wives set theire corne and doe all theire other worke."[22] The reason for this unequal division of labor was, as most colonists saw it, the refusal of the chauvinistic Indian men "to be seene in any woman like exercise" for fear it "would compromise their dignity too much."[23]

Bred like all people to an ethnocentric world-view, the European invaders saw what they expected to see in Indian life. Initially jarred by the half-correct observation that native men were not responsible for the agricultural livelihood of their society, the colonists never recovered their visual focus enough to notice that what was normal behavior in Europe did not always obtain in America, that Indian men played a role in their economy every bit as important as European farmers did in theirs, and that Indian women did not view their social position in the light cast by the male observers from another culture.

On the surface the European criticisms of Indian "industry" were serious enough, but a number of less overt grievances reveal even more about the cultural preconceptions of the colonists, and therefore about the remedial prescriptions that could be expected from the missionaries. The first group of objections, assailing the nature of Indian farming, were stated typically in the form of deficiencies. Not only was native farming done largely by women, but it did not employ the deep-cutting plow harnessed to animal power, fences to enclose the fields, or—particularly symbolic— fertilizer in the form of tame-animal manure.

Thomas Hariot, one of the Roanoke colonists in 1585, observed that the natives "never enrich the soil with refuse, dung, or any other thing, nor do they plough or dig it as we do in England." Nevertheless, their corn reached prodigious heights and "the yield is so great that little labor is needed in comparison with what is necessary in England."[24] Happily for the Massachusetts Bay Company, John Winthrop decided that the New England natives "inclose noe Land, neither have any settled habytation, nor any tame cattle to improve the Land by," and so were devoid of any legal claim to their territory.[25] Although the Indians could watch a European plow "teare up

22. Force, *Tracts*, vol. 1, no. 12, p. 13.

23. Lyon Gardiner Tyler, ed., *Narratives of Early Virginia, 1606–1625* (New York, 1907), p. 101; J. Franklin Jameson, ed., *Narratives of New Netherland, 1609–1664* (New York, 1909), p. 107.

24. Thomas Harriot, *A briefe and true report of the new found land of Virginia* (1588), in David B. Quinn and Alison M. Quinn, eds., *Virginia Voyages from Hakluyt* (London, 1973), p. 56.

25. *Winthrop Papers* (Boston: Massachusetts Historical Society, 1929–), No. 1, 2:120.

more ground in a day, than their Clamme shels [hoes] could scrape up in a month," they preferred their own methods throughout the colonial period.[26] To those colonists who swore by the work ethic, today recognized as having been shared by Protestants and Catholics alike, there was nothing more galling than to discover that wild "savages" reaped the proverbial fruits of the earth without working up a European-style sweat.

Another criticism of Indian farming was implied by the fact that no more equipment was required than a crude hoe and a few handmade baskets. This meant that native technology was as portable as their housing, which rendered them still more difficult to bring to "order." Without horses, barns, carts, harrows, plows, halters, collars, and harnesses—in other words, without a substantial material investment in the capitalist way of life—the Indians could not be securely anchored to one plot of ground where they could always be found (and "distressed" if they got out of line).[27] In addition, without an involvement in the encircling web of credit that husbandry entailed, the Indians could at any time pull up stakes and head for the hinterland, out of reach of Scriptural and European law. Moreover, "they care for little, because they want but little," William Penn tried to explain to his English partners. "In this they are sufficiently revenged on us. . . . We sweat and toil to live; their pleasure feeds them, I mean, their Hunting, Fishing and Fowling."[28]

Penn's characterization of Indian hunting as "pleasure" introduces a second category of English objections to the Indian division of labor. It was bad enough that women should manage the Indian fields without the aid of either their menfolk or the labor-inducing technology of the English, but almost worse was that those truant warriors misspent their days sporting in the woods or the water. Like the founder of Pennsylvania, colonists up and down the eastern seaboard felt that Indian hunting and fishing were more pleasant pastimes than real work. While they could sometimes appreciate that the native men took "extreame paines" in those pursuits, they could not forgive them for expending their energies in places other than plowed fields or fragrant cow-barns.[29]

A southern gentleman put his finger on the true cause of English concern when he noted, after an extensive survey of the Indian country between Virginia and North Carolina, that native men "are quite idle, or at most employ'd only in the *Gentlemanly* Diversions of Hunting and Fish-

26. Wood, *New Englands Prospect*, p. 87.
27. Gavin Cochrane, Treatise on the Indians of North America Written in the Year 1764, Ayer MS "NA" 176, chap. 7, Newberry Library, Chicago.
28. Albert C. Myers, ed., *Narratives of Early Pennsylvania, West New Jersey, and Delaware, 1630–1707* (New York, 1912), p. 233.
29. Tyler, *Narratives of Early Virginia*, p. 103.

ing."[30] By this remark William Byrd II, the English-bred scion of one of the wealthiest families in Virginia, indicated that the Indians' greatest offense was the usurpation of aristocratic privilege, the disorderly crossing of class lines. For in England the only people who hunted were members of the upper classes, who did not kill to eat, or poachers, who did, and risked their ears—or necks—in the attempt. Forests were not public property but belonged to the nobility, who regarded them as private game preserves. Guns were expensive and their ownership was generally forbidden by law.

These, then, were the assumptions that the colonists carried to America, where the forests seemed to belong to no man, where guns became a household fixture, where hunting was often a necessity, and where English class lines failed to replicate themselves. In spite of all the social and environmental changes that should have engendered a different outlook toward hunting (and in some instances did, toward their own), those colonists who did not rely on Indian hunters for marketable furs and skins continued to view the economic activities of Indian men with Old World eyes. Regarded as the social inferiors of all Englishmen, the Indians were harshly judged by semifeudal standards that simply made no sense in the New World, much less in an alien culture.

The English had other, seldom articulated misgivings about Indian hunting that lay just beneath the surface of their vocal disdain. These revolved around the fearful fact that in native society hunting and warfare were two aspects of the same activity. Not only was warfare conducted according to hunting patterns, but hunting was a sort of ritualized warfare, carried on under strong religious sanctions. The education for one was training for both.

Disorder and idleness were thought of as structural weaknesses inherent in native society as a whole; but on a personal level, where most Europeans and Indians met, the natives were also considered woefully deficient. As surely as their government and economy needed reform, so their manners cried out for civilizing treatment. Nothing less then total assimilation to European ways would fulfill the uncompromising criteria of "civility," nothing less than renunciation of the last vestige of their former life; for "Christian" and "savage" were incompatible characters in the invaders' cosmology, and only a willing departure from all he had known, all he had been, could prepare an Indian for a life of Christ. In European eyes, no native characteristic was too small to reform, no habit too harmless to reduce.

One of the first objects of reform were the Indians' names. To European

---

30. *William Byrd's Histories of the Dividing Line betwixt Virginia and North Carolina,* ed. William K. Boyd (New York, 1967), p. 116 (my emphasis).

ears, inured to the peculiar accents of home and the sea, the Algonquian and Iroquoian languages of the eastern woodlands struck a discordant note. Words, including names, were often long and seemingly undifferentiated, full of throaty glottals and short of defining labials. Understandably, the colonists wished to abbreviate, translate, or Europeanize the names of those natives with whom they had any commerce, especially those selected for conversion. Perhaps the easiest way to bestow intelligible European names was to intercept the native child at birth before an Indian name could be given. In praying towns and villages with a resident missionary, this was done most readily at the baptism of the child. On such religious occasions biblical names naturally found favor with the ministers, though just as often Indian parents preferred common French or English names.

If the intimacy of a personal name could be violated, it is small wonder that the missionaries did not hesitate to pass harsh judgment on native sexual mores. The most visible cause for concern was the Indians' state of undress, especially in the summer when visits from the colonists were most frequent. Children remained completely naked until puberty, men sported only skimpy breechclouts, and women, as one colonial admirer testified, "commonly go naked as far as the Navel downward, and upward to the middle of the Thigh, by which means they have the advantage of discovering their fine Limbs and compleat Shape."[31] In European eyes a direct relation existed between such tempting nudity and the Indians' libidinous behavior. Young people took to sexual exploration early in their teens and found nothing shameful about their bodies or their amorous potential; they were certainly strangers to the invaders' concept of "fornication." Although adultery was widely prohibited by tribal law, parents appeared more universally guilty because the Christians did not recognize the validity of Indian divorce, which easily ensued upon the transfer of one spouse's affections and belongings to the lodge of another. By the same token, native polygamy seemed to be rampant when in fact very few tribesmen took more than one wife, and they were usually sachems or men of importance whose obligations of hospitality required more than two female hands.

The intrusive lengths to which the Europeans would go to "civilize" the American natives has perhaps no better measure than the English missionaries' attempts to proscribe "the old Ceremony of the Maide walking alone and living apart so many dayes."[32] This referred to the widespread native belief that a menstruating woman possessed malevolent powers, and was capable of poisoning food with her touch, scaring game with her scent, or injuring a man's health with her glance. In nearly all hunting and most

31. Robert Beverley, *The History and Present State of Virginia* [London, 1705], ed. Louis B. Wright (Chapel Hill, N.C., 1947), p. 166.
32. *Colls. Mass. His. Soc.*, 3d ser. 4 (1834):40.

horticultural tribes, a woman in her "course" withdrew to a small hut in the woods (*wetuomémese* in Narragansett) for the duration, where she lived alone, cooked her own meals with special utensils, and lowered her eyes when a tribesman came near. At the end of her period "she washeth herself, and all that she hath touched or used, and is again received to her husband's bed or family."[33] Despite the intriguing similarity of this Indian custom to the ancient Jewish one, the missionaries wanted not only to move the Indians away from a hunting economy where the menstrual taboo was strongest, but to undercut the whole belief system upon which it was founded. But before they could reeducate the natives in personal hygiene, physiology, and metaphysics, they simply ruled that the Indian woman's time-honored way of dealing with her natural processes was taboo and subject to the scrutiny of foreign men. What the modern women's movement has called "vaginal politics" was clearly not unknown to the Anglo-Protestants who led the invasion within.

However exemplary the Indians' daily—or nocturnal—behavior, one slanted look told the colonists that the natives needed to be clothed in more than modesty. In the eyes of the invaders, native dress was a phantasmagoria of animal pelts, bird feathers, and reptile skins, of colors and textures as wild as the people themselves. Beautifully tanned leathers were thrown together with bird-wing headdresses, mantles of animal heads, feet, and tails, snakeskin belts, smoky fur robes, and swansdown ear decorations. Any exposed skin might be covered with totemic tattoos, shell jewelry, bear grease, or lurid paintings. In all seasons, frail-looking, soft-soled moccasins were worn without stockings—if at all—while men donned buttock-revealing leather leggings as pants against the cold and underbrush. Clearly such uncouth garb would have to be replaced by fashions a la mode in Boston and Quebec. For if an Indian could be persuaded to change his whole lifestyle so that he looked as well as lived and acted like a European, the chances were considered good that he would eventually think European thoughts and believe Christian truths. He would, in effect, cease to be an Indian, the conversion process would be complete, and the colonial "Indian problem" would be solved.

The trick, however, was to get the half-naked forest dwellers to look like European colonists. In some respects this proved to be the easiest task of all, but in the end the Europeans enjoyed only partial success. For in the seemingly indifferent matter of personal appearance they encountered the paramount symbol of Indian identity and the rock upon which most white efforts to "reduce" it were broken.

33. Edward Winslow, *Good Newes from New England* (London, 1624), in Alexander Young, ed., *Chronicles of the Pilgrim Fathers of Plymouth from 1602 to 1625*, 2d ed. (Boston, 1844), p. 364.

Several obstacles stood in the way of an abrupt change of habit by the Indians. The greatest, not surprisingly, was that the great majority of woodland Indians had little use for fitted clothes designed for briarless farms and open fields. As many colonists discovered to their loss, woven cloth garments were quickly shredded in the rough life of the woods. Moreover, European clothes, if they were to present a civilized appearance, had to be washed, ironed, bought in quantities to reduce wear, stored, and frequently replaced—none of which things the Indians were willing or able to do. "Therefore they had rather goe naked," a New Englishman noted, "than be lousie, and bring their bodies out of their old tune, making them more tender by a new acquired habit."[34] Fitted trousers were particularly abhorrent, especially in the South where native men squatted to urinate.[35] The most clothing that the majority of Indians could be induced to buy was a stroud breechclout; a shirt, which they proceeded to wear unwashed until it disintegrated; and a large woolen blanket, which served in turn as overcoat, raincoat, blanket, and nightshirt. The heavy European serges, baize, and fustians, cut into fitted garments that restricted movement and ventilation, found little favor in the native markets of North America—until the missionaries gave their proselytes new reason to buy.

That reason was the European belief that a European appearance visibly segregated their converts from their recalcitrant "pagan" brothers and provided a sign in times of frontier unrest by which "friend Indians" could be readily distinguished from enemies. During the first few decades of settlement this reasoning made some sense. But as the native resistance to foreign cloth weakened, more tribesmen adopted various articles of European dress for their decorative value or because the loss of game made traditional garb impossible. When the woods became such a sartorial hodge-podge, native intentions and allegiances were much more difficult to discern. But even then, the infallible mark of a Protestant "praying Indian" was his English appearance: short hair, cobbled shoes, and working-class suit. So important was European clothing as a badge of "civility" that an Indian's degree of acculturation could almost be read in his appearance. The more he wished to emulate the invaders and to become one with them, the more Europeanized his dress became and the more pains he took to put aside his native costume. In the Eastern woodlands you could often tell a convert by his cover.

But in New England, dress alone was not an infallible guide to the In-

34. Wood, *New Englands Prospect*, p. 73.
35. George Alsop, *A Character of the Province of Mary-land* (London, 1666), p. 72; *[James] Adair's History of the American Indians* [London, 1775], ed. Samuel Cole Williams (New York, 1966), pp. 8–9; Bernard Romans, *A Concise Natural History of East and West Florida*, 2 vols. (New York, 1775), 1:42.

dian's political allegiance, much less to his religious convictions, unless it was accompanied by an equally decisive *uncovering*—short hair. For nothing symbolized the Indian's identity—his independence, his sense of superiority, his pride—more effectively than his long hair. A willingness to cut his long black hair signaled his desire to kill the Indian in himself and to assume a new persona modeled on the meek, submissive Christ of the white man's Black Book. Since this was the missionaries' ultimate goal, they wasted no time in persuading their native proselytes to submit to the barber's shears.

The principal sin of wearing long hair was pride. And seventeenth-century Englishmen did not need reminding that pride was the original sin of their spiritual parents, Adam and Eve. If the Indians had inadvertently or casually worn their hair long, they would still have offended the Protestants' fine sensitivity to personal pride and vanity, but not as grievously as they obviously did. For long hair aptly symbolized the Indians' deeper affront to Anglo-Christianity, which was their characteristic pride and independence.

In describing their religious goals, the missionaries most commonly used the metaphor of placing such "heady Creatures" in the "yoke of Christ" and teaching them to "bridle" their savage instincts.[36] In other words, becoming a Christian was comparable to assuming the posture and character of tame cattle—docile, obedient, submissive. Or, in another popular metaphor, their goal was to "reduce" the Indians' proud independence and godless self-reliance to the total dependence of a "weaned child."[37] Since it was total, this dependence was at once political, social, and religious. In short, the Indians would become "civilized." The "savage" would give way to the "civil man" by repressing his native instincts, habits, and desires, and quietly taking the political bit in his teeth and the religious yoke upon his neck.

Thus, the meaning of the puzzling phrase, "to reduce them to civility," becomes clear. As long hair symbolized pride for the English, so too did the long-haired Indian. In the Christian cosmology, the proud Indian—wandering, lawless, and unpredictable—occupied the higher place: he was puffed up with self-importance, inflated with a false sense of superiority, and unrestrained by law, labor, or religion, not unlike the Devil, whom he was thought to worship. It was therefore an affront to God—and, of course, to

---

36. *Colls. Mass. Hist. Soc.*, 3d ser. 4 (1834):40, 50; John Eliot, *A Brief Narrative of the Progress of the Gospel amongst the Indians in New England* (London, 1671), p. 8. See also *JR* 5:177; 12:61.

37. *Winthrop Papers*, 1:158–59; *Publications of the Colonial Society of Massachusetts* 29 (1933): 147–48. See also *Word from New France: The Selected Letters of Marie de L'Incarnation*, ed. and trans. Joyce Marshall (Toronto, 1967), pp. 77, 84.

his Christian soldiers—that the Indians remained in such an unnatural and undesirable state.

What should also be clear is the sincerity of the religious goals of European colonization. If we interpret "conversion" as the invaders did, not as modern theologians do, there can be no doubt that the conversion of the natives was indeed a primary goal—both logically and chronologically primary. For given the almost unanimous belief that "savages" had to be "civilized" before they could be "Christianized," the initial problem which all the European colonies faced—the natives' dangerous unpredictability—was soluble by "reducing them to civility." If in the process the conquerors were served as much as Christ, who could gainsay their fortune? Certainly not the missionaries, who were keenly aware that "until Christians are the absolute masters of the Indians, missionaries will have scant success without a very special grace of God, a miracle which He does not perform for every people."[38]

The broad consensus about the goals of the Christian missions in North America, emerging from a common Western European experience and ideology, imposed a limited range of conversion methods upon the French and English invaders. Since the "civilizing" and religious conversion of the Indians was essentially an educational task, a process of re-education in effect, the colonists turned naturally to the major social and educational institutions of their own cultures for models and methods. The institution that seemed to promise to work the greatest number of changes in native culture was the town, the European symbol of "civility" (from the Latin civis, citizen) and locus of law and order. The town was expected to fix, restrain, and order Indian life, to direct its licentious energies into productive and predictable channels. Reserves in New France and "praying towns" in New England and elsewhere gave the missionaries some hope of segregating their neophytes and converts from the corrupting example of imperfect colonists and the seductive "paganism" of their native neighbors. Moreover, they were calculated to severely cramp the Indians' mobile style by encouraging them to substitute agriculture for hunting, to build heavy European-style houses, to surround themselves with the cumbersome trappings of European technology, and to remake their civil polity in the European image. Not the least of their attractions for the colonists was that congregations of natives would greatly reduce the required manpower and therefore the economic needs of the missions and provide non-European frontier buffers against enemy war parties.

It took only brief experience in America for the missionaries to con-

38. Hennepin's Description of Louisiana, p. 180.

clude that "if some one could stop the wanderings of the Indians, and give authority to one of them to rule the others, we would see them converted and civilized in a short time."[39] The need, of course, was to give them an economy overnight that would make their seasonal moves unnecessary, for only then could they stay among their fellow converts the year round to receive instruction from a resident priest or pastor and to nurture their new faith. Father Le Jeune was not wrong to observe that "it is the same thing in an Indian to wish to become sedentary, and to wish to believe in God."[40] But his successor as superior of the Canadian missions, Barthelemy Vimont, had a point, too, when he regretted that the Jesuits had "greater trouble in keeping our Christians than in acquiring them. . . . The land that we clear, the houses that we build for them, and the other aid, spiritual and material, that we endeavor to give them, keep them stationary for a while, but not permanently."[41] If the new townsmen could be fed until they became agriculturally self-sufficient, the praying town had a good chance of fostering substantial changes in the native lifestyle, the most important of which were the imposition of new forms of government, discipline, and morality.

The fundamental weakness of Indian life, the missionaries felt, was the natives' belief that they ought "by right of birth, to enjoy the liberty of Wild ass colts, rendering no homage to any one whomsoever, except when they like."[42] Since "they are born, live, and die in a liberty without restraint, they do not know what is meant by bridle or bit."[43] Consequently, no aspect of their "reduction to civility" was more essential than persuading or forcing them to place their necks in "the yoke of the law of God," which translated meant submitting to European-style autocracy, law, and compulsion. When the Jesuit *reserve* of Sillery was settled after 1637, its Algonkian and Montagnais inhabitants felt the need for a civilized form of government to regulate their civil and religious affairs. For the first time in their experience, the men elected by majority vote rather than consensus three magistrates, two moral overseers, and a "Captain of prayers" to assist the hereditary sachem. Four of the winners were "Christians," as was their leader. To prove that the traditional rule of suasion was being replaced by coercion, the new officers borrowed the use of Quebec's dungeon until they could build their own prison to punish (mostly female) breakers of their new adamantine code of morality. "Pagans" who dared to resist their authority were imprisoned,

39. *JR* 12:169. I have translated *sauvage* not as "savage," which has a pejorative ring to modern ears, but as "Indian," which more nearly approximates the neutral descriptive quality of the original. See also *JR* 6:83, 147; 3:143.
40. *JR* 14:215.
41. *JR* 25:113.
42. *JR* 6:243.
43. *JR* 12:61.

chained, whipped, and starved until they learned to obey "a peremptory command" and to submit humbly to "any act of severity or justice." Even the death penalty was seriously considered as a "perpetual" deterrent to moral turpitude.[44]

For most neophytes, French or English, the "yoke of Christ" must have felt anything but "mild and easy," as the missionaries hoped it would.[45] It was virtually impossible not to run afoul of the law when the law proscribed every aspect of traditional life, great and small. In the twenty-four years after 1650, John Eliot gathered some 1,100 Massachusett and Nipmuc Indians into fourteen praying towns. Plymouth's missionaries sponsored eight more towns for 500 persons, and the Mayhews on Martha's Vineyard established still others. Most of the New England towns strongly resembled the seven major Jesuit *reserves* in their puritanical leadership and strict prescription of European ways. Faithful converts who were elected or appointed to office by the missionaries promptly drafted long legal codes to govern the towns, which usually consisted at first of unstable mixtures of zealous converts and resistant traditionalists. Concord's rules, passed in 1647, were typical. Fines up to twenty shillings or whippings were meted out for infractions ranging from fighting, "powwowing" (resorting to traditional medicine men), gaming, "fornication," and lice-biting, to sporting long hair (male) or bare breasts (female), body-greasing, polygamy, mourning with "a great noyse by howling," and menstrual seclusion. (Adultery, witchcraft, and worshipping any deity but the Christian God were punishable by death under colony law, to which the Indians were already subject.) Predictably, the townsmen were expected not only to give up their former habits but to replace them with English ways. Three laws enjoined them to "observe the Lords-Day," to "fall upon some better course to improve their time than formerly," and, most significant, to "labour after humility, and not be proud."[46]

By compelling the natives to avoid idleness, the praying-town laws sought to edge them into a European economy, to transform them from "lazy savages" into *bons habitants* and "laborious" husbandmen. Skilled trades for the Indians were seldom considered and, when they were, quickly shunted aside for fear of providing unnecessary competition for colonial workers. Farming and a variety of marginal home industries such as the manufacture of brooms, pails, and baskets, berrying, and hunting and fishing for hire, were as far as the praying Indians climbed up the ladder of eco-

---

44. *JR* 18:101–07; 22:83–85; *Word from New France*, pp. 105–06. See James P. Ronda, "The Sillery Experiment: A Jesuit-Indian Village in New France, 1637–1663," *American Indian Culture and Research Journal* 3, no. 1 (1979):1–18.

45. *JR* 12:61.

46. Alden T. Vaughan, *New England Frontier: Puritans and Indians, 1620–1675* (Boston, 1965), pp. 346–47.

nomic success. But by anchoring their converts to the soil, the missionaries accomplished two important ends—one for themselves and one for the colonists. As Eliot explained, "a fixed condition of life" enabled the natives to be more trusted with the church ordinances because, "if any should through temptations, fall under [church] Censure, he could easily run away (as some have done) and would be tempted so to do, unless he were fixed in an Habitation, and had some means of livelihood to lose, and leave behind him."[47] And, as an English colonial soldier happily observed, the colonists had it "more in our power to Distress them" if they shook off the civilized bridle or yoke "as we can revenge ourselves on their fixed habitations, & growing corn."[48] Once again the missionaries served Christ and conquest without qualm or contradiction.

Being the scholastic products of book learning themselves, the ministers and officials who designed the American missions inevitably turned to formal institutions of education for help in "reducing" the Indians to "civility," hoping thereby to reform their mental as well as physical habits as early as possible. Throughout the colonial period, the missionaries tried to reach Indian children and adults at the same time, to trap native culture, as it were, in a squeeze between generations. Both the Recollects and the Jesuits established French-style *séminaires* for Indian children during the first years of their missions, but within five years each had folded for lack of funds, students, and success.[49] They then turned their energies toward native *reserves* near the major centers of French population along the Saint Lawrence River and to religious missions to remote Indian villages all over New France. The English, by contrast, were initially frustrated in their attempts to convert native adults, so their emphasis shifted perceptibly toward the young. This was a logical emphasis, because from the beginning the English hoped to train native preachers, teachers, and interpreters to assume the task of converting their brethren to "civilized" Christianity. The only feasible way to train this cadre of native agents was to catch Indian children early in their development, before the hereditary stain of "savagism" became indelible, and "bring them up English."

The instruments the missionaries chose for this task were traditional English schools and colleges, adapted very little to the special needs of Indian students fresh from the forest. Until the eighteenth century, most of them were boarding schools located in English territory, far from the contagion of traditional habits, indulgent parents, and distracting friends. The

47. *Colls. Mass. Hist. Soc.*, 3d ser. 4 (1834):227.
48. Cochrane, Treatise on Indians, Ayer MS "NA" 176, chap. 7, Newberry Library, Chicago.
49. Delanglez, *Frontenac and the Jesuits*, pp. 35–40; Lucien Campeau, *Les commencements du Collège de Québec (1626–1670)*, Cahiers d'Histoire des Jésuites, no. 1 (Montreal, 1972), pp. 51–76.

missionaries agreed with the Jesuits that "the consciousness of being three hundred leagues distant from their own country makes these young men more tractable."[50] Under the nervous eyes and guns of the colonists, the students might have taken an extra stab at docility had they known that their teachers viewed them as "hostages" for the safety of the English in their country and along their borders; chiefs' sons were especially welcome as students for this reason.[51] When they arrived at school, they were effectively quarantined from all contaminating female contact for the duration of their studies, as if they were undergoing a special, long-term puberty rite. In the male world of the missionaries, boys were considered the prime candidates for conversion because it was assumed that they would return to their tribes, assume office by (newly acquired) merit, and lead their "pagan" brethren to "civility." (Girls, when they were noticed at all, were educated separately in the two Rs, religion, and "housewifery" to make them suitable partners for French colonists or Christian Indians.)

The master of such a male school was, of course, a patriarchal figure— serious, pedantic, and strict. Although—or because—Indian parents were "too fond" to "tolerate the chastisement of their children" at home, the missionaries in their colonial strongholds proceeded to institute a birchen government calculated to "humble them, and reform their manners." "Here I can correct & punish them as I please. . . ," admitted the Reverend Eleazar Wheelock at his Indian charity school in Lebanon, Connecticut, "but there, it will not be born." "And who does not know," he asked rhetorically, "that Evils so obstinate as those we may reasonably expect to find common in the Children of Savages, will require that which is severe?"[52]

As in most classrooms, the medium of instruction and discipline was probably louder and clearer than the message of the curriculum, which was unfailingly traditional. In an atmosphere of beetle-browed piety, the students were initiated into the arcana of the Westminster Assembly's *Shorter Catechism*, the English alphabet and grammar, arithmetic, and, in still more abstruse languages, the pastoral classics of ancient Greece and Rome. When the frustration or boredom of their inactive lives erupted in highjinks, the birch rod covered their skin with welts they had never seen at home. By the eighteenth century, the contrast between English schooling and Jesuit proselytizing was blatantly obvious, especially to the Indians. In 1772 the

50. *JR* 12:63.

51. *An Essay towards Propagating the Gospel among the Neighbouring Nations of Indians in North America* (New London, Conn., 1756), p. 16; R. A. Brock, ed., *The Official Letters of Alexander Spotswood, Lieutenant-Governor of the Colony of Virginia, 1710–1722, Collections of the Virginia Historical Society*, n.s. 1–2 (1882–85), 1:121–22, 124, 134, 174; *Word from New France*, 223, 233; *JR* 6:155.

52. *JR* 5:197, 221; 35:251; Papers of Eleazar Wheelock, item 762667.2, Dartmouth College Library, Hanover, N.H.

Onondaga council rejected Wheelock's offer to educate their children with a sharp reproof. "Brother," they said, "you must learn of the French ministers if you would understand, & know how to treat Indians. They don't speak roughly; nor do they for every little mistake take up a club & flog them."[53]

By the fall of Canada in 1760, the English missions had seldom ventured beyond the safety of well-populated and well-fortified colonial settlements. Their praying towns were surrounded by the proliferating towns and farms of southern New England, as were the great majority of their Indian schools. Only a handful of missionaries had ever ventured as far into Indian country as Maine, New York, or the Ohio country, and then with conspicuous lack of success. This timidity was due to three considerations: their ideological insistence on "reducing the Indians to civility" before trying to convert them to Christianity, the belief of many land-hungry farmers and speculators that "the way of conquering them is much more easie than of civilizing them by faire meanes," and a major ecclesiastical deficiency.[54] Until the opening years of the eighteenth century, the English Protestant churches—with the exception of the Church of England, which showed little interest in Indians at the time—were hampered in their missionary endeavors by an ecclesiastical polity that restricted the ministry to those specifically called by an individual congregation of the elect. A minister without a congregation, no matter how holy or how learned he was, was simply a man without the ministry. He could not administer the sacraments of baptism or communion—the only two they recognized—or gather a formal church. Furthermore, despite evangelical assertions to the contrary, the minister was effectively prevented from winning new souls to Christ by being tied to the needs and wishes of his small flock. Unless the unregenerate happened to wander into his congregation on the Sabbath—and understood English—the minister was not likely to encounter many potential converts. "By their principles," an Anglican visitor criticized, "no Nation can or could ever be converted."[55]

By contrast, the Jesuits were organized hierarchically in an international order, freed from parish work to attack heresy and paganism wherever it flourished. From the middle of the seventeenth century, when they gave up the idea of frenchifying the Indians, the Jesuits took their missions into the remote corners of New France, west to Lake Superior, north to Hudson's Bay, south to Louisiana. There they attempted to insinuate Chris-

53. James Dow McCallum, ed., *The Letters of Eleazar Wheelock's Indians* (Hanover, N.H., 1932), pp. 287–88.

54. Susan M. Kingsbury, ed., *Records of the Virginia Company of London*, 4 vols. (Washington, D.C., 1906–35), 3:557.

55. Thomas Lechford, *Plain Dealing: Or, Newes from New-England* (London, 1642), in *Colls. Mass. Hist. Soc.*, 3d ser. 3 (1833):80.

tianity into the natives' lives with methods learned less in the scholastic classrooms of France than in the inhabited forests of America.

The priest's first step was to gain admission to the target village. An ideal way was to talk a leading man or sachem into adopting him, which gave him an extensive set of ready-made relatives, food, shelter, and some measure of physical protection. Then, by his exemplary behavior, the priest made every effort to show the villagers that he was no threat to their continued existence. Without any apparent interest in guns, women, beavers, or land, he sought to convince them that he had left his refined and comfortable life in Europe solely to help them reach God and eternal happiness. He especially courted the favor of the children, who had great power over their parents' affections, not least because he could easily learn the language from them while teaching them their first words of French.

While ingratiating himself by learning their language, the Jesuit began to practice his order's worldwide technique of acculturating themselves to the natives' way of life to win their trust for the task ahead. Unlike the Dominicans and Franciscans within their own church and the Puritans and Anglicans without, the Jesuits articulated and practiced a brand of cultural relativism, without, however, succumbing to ethical neutrality. While they, like all missionaries, sought to replace the Indians' cosmology and religion with their own, they were more willing than their Christian counterparts to adopt the external lifestyle of the Indians until their goal could be realized. Rather than immediately condemn and destroy what they found, they carefully studied native beliefs and practices and tried to reshape and reorient them in order to establish a common ground on which to begin conversion.[56] As Father Vimont put it in 1642, "to make a Christian out of a Barbarian is not the work of a day. . . . A great step is gained when one has learned to know those with whom he has to deal; has penetrated their thoughts; has adapted himself to their language, their customs, and their manner of living; and, when necessary, has been a Barbarian with them, in order to win them over to Jesus Christ."[57] In large measure, whatever success the Jesuits enjoyed was gained not by expecting less of their converts, as the English accused, but by accepting more.

As he learned to adjust his ways to those of the Indians, the priest also began to promulgate his Christian message by appealing to all their senses. In native hands he placed attractive silver and brass medals, rings, crucifixes, and rosaries—not unlike their own wampum belts, medicine sticks,

56. See Peter Duignan, "Early Jesuit Missionaries: A Suggestion for Further Study," *American Anthropologist* 60 (1958):726; J. H. Kennedy, *Jesuit and Savage in New France* (New Haven, Conn., 1950), p. 109; René Fülöp-Miller, *The Power and Secret of the Jesuits* (New York, 1930), pt. 5; *JR* 12:117–25; 33:143–47.

57. *JR* 23:207–09.

and condolence canes—as mnemonic devices to recall his oral message. To their noses he introduced the mysterious fragrances of incense. To their lips he lifted holy wafers. To their eyes he offered huge wooden crosses, candle-lit altars rich with silk and silver, long, brocaded chasubles, and pictorial images of the major scenes in the drama of Christianity. And into their ears he poured sonorous hymns and chants, tinkling bells, and an endless stream of Indian words—haltingly, even laughably, pronounced at first, but soon fluent and cadenced in native measures. Here his long training in logic, rhetoric, and disputation stood him in good stead, once he grasped the novel motivations, interests, and fears of his listeners. Believing that "in order to convert these peoples, one must begin by touching their hearts, before he can convince their minds," the priest sought to manage their dispositions by an adroit use of flattery, bribery, ridicule, insult, "mildness and force, threats and prayers, labors and tears."[58]

If he was at all effective, he would soon succeed in fomenting a serious factional split between "Christians" and "Pagans" at all levels of village society, a division he would quietly work to widen in hopes of placing his converts in all the positions of civil leadership. By administering the sacraments, especially baptism, only to the deserving after considerable instruction and lasting personal reform, he protected the hard-won reputation of his flock and the holy ordinances from familiar contempt.

But the priest's most important goal was to supplant the village shaman, his chief competitor for the minds of the people. By his possession of printed truths (which initially impressed the members of that oral culture), a scientific understanding of nature (whereby a magnet or a compass could be used to attract a following away from a divination rite), and an unrelenting questioning of the habitual (which no cultural practice can long survive), the missionary sought to erode the shaman's prestige and to establish his own in its place. If the fortuitous administration of a cordial, the lancet, or baptismal water happened to rescue a native from the grave, his stock as a functional replacement for the medico-religious shaman would rise dramatically. When the priest saw his converts at the head of village government and himself accepted as the resident shaman, he could consider his mission at least a partial success. While he had not "civilized" his hosts, he had Christianized them without destroying their usefulness to the French as hunters, trappers, and military allies. His only remaining task, as Father Vimont warned, was to keep his Christians in the Faith, a task that a village church would greatly lighten.

While the Jesuits enjoyed several advantages over their English rivals, by no means did they enjoy universal or permanent success in converting

58. *JR* 53:203–05.

the Indians even to Christianity. At the end of two centuries of effort, both the French and the English were forced to admit that they had largely failed to convert the native Americans to European religion and culture.[59] The reasons are not difficult to find. In fact, they are so plentiful and so overwhelming that we should rather wonder how the Europeans achieved as much success as they did. The usual explanations, those most commonly given by contemporaries in a spirit of half-hearted expiation, pointed to the regrettable but inevitable results of contact with European cultures: disease (to which the Indians had no immunities), war (fomented by European trade competition and exacerbated by European firearms), alcohol (for whose use the natives had no cultural sanctions), and the immoral example of false Christians (who, instead of raising the Indians' sights, "reduced them to civility"). Cotton Mather spoke for many when he confessed that the Europeans had "very much *Injured* the *Indians* . . . by *Teaching* of them, *Our Vice*. We that should have learn'd them to *Pray*, have learn'd them to *Sin*."[60]

While no one would deny that these external forces did much to undermine the conversion process, we should emphasize the traits within Indian culture that resisted change, and the defects of the missions themselves.

The first and most serious obstacle was native religion.[61] Several of the first explorers and some of their less perceptive colonial followers thought that the Indians had no religion, just as they appeared to have no laws or government (*ni foi, ni loi, ni roi*). However, a closer look enabled settlers and missionaries to grant the natives a modicum of religious beliefs and observances, though these were seen only as "superstitions" because of their non-Christian character. But one man's superstition is another man's religion, and Indian religion, for all its novelty, was both bona fide and culturally pervasive, capable of explaining, predicting, and controlling the world

59. See, for example, John Halkett, *Historical Notes respecting the Indians of North America* (London, 1825), pp. 214, 218–19, 231–32, 256–57, 295; Alexis De Tocqueville, *Democracy in America* [Paris, 1835], trans. Henry Reeve and Francis Bowen, ed. Phillips Bradley, 2 vols. (New York, 1945), 1:336–55; [Jeremy Belknap], "Has the Discovery of America Been Useful or Hurtful to Mankind?" *The Boston Magazine*, May 1784, pp. 281–85, esp. 283.

60. Cotton Mather, *The Way to Prosperity* (Boston, 1690), p. 27.

61. The following paragraphs are based on a large number of primary sources, such as the *Jesuit Relations* and the Eliot tracts. The following secondary works are also pertinent: Anthony F. C. Wallace, *Religion: An Anthropological View* (New York, 1966); Wallace, *The Death and Rebirth of the Seneca* (New York, 1970); Hartley Burr Alexander, *The World's Rim: Great Mysteries of the North American Indians* (Lincoln, Neb., 1953); Ruth M. Underhill, *Red Man's Religion: Beliefs and Practices of the Indians North of Mexico* (Chicago, 1965); Ruth Benedict, *The Concept of the Guardian Spirit in North America*, Memoirs of the American Anthropological Association, no. 29 (Menasha, Wis., 1923); M. R. Harrington, *Religion and Ceremonies of the Lenape*, Indian Notes and Monographs, 2d ser., no. 19 (New York: Museum of the American Indian, 1921); Akë Hultkrantz, *The Religions of the American Indians*, trans. Monica Setterwall (Berkeley, Calif., 1979); Cara E. Richards, *Man in Perspective: An Introduction to Cultural Anthropology* (New York, 1972), chap. 7.

in emotionally and intellectually satisfying ways. Like all peoples known to ethnology, the various native groups of the Northeast each possessed a religion in that they performed "a set of rituals, rationalized by myth, which mobilize[d] supernatural powers for the purpose of achieving or preventing transformations of state in man or nature."[62] Despite their linguistic and cultural differences, they shared enough beliefs and practices to allow generalization, and, to some extent, comparison with Christianity. For the Indians were not as far from the Christian invaders in religious belief as they seemed to be in practice (or ritual), which partially explains the successes of the missions as well as their failures.

Behind all native religion lay a cosmology, a hierarchy of states of being and a science of the principles of their interaction. The most populous tier consisted of supernatural beings known as "spirits" or "souls," which were continuous "selves" capable of changing form. Though they were invisible, they were audible to men, with whom they could interact directly (such as by shaking a tent) and by whom they were manipulatable in the right circumstances. Possessing will and consciousness, they knew the future as well as the past because of their continuity. Human souls, for instance, could separate temporarily from the corporeal body in sleep, travel to other realms of experience, and return to inform or instruct the person in dreams. Consequently, dreams were regarded by many missionaries as the heart of native religion, for the Indians believed that the supernatural guidance of their lives came from these "secret desires of the soul," which had to be fulfilled if they were to enjoy health, happiness, and success.[63] In death the soul left the body permanently to travel to an afterlife, which was probably vaguely conceived before the Christians began to preach of Heaven and Hell, but which seemed to be an ethereal version of the happiest life they had known on earth, replete with good hunting, abundant fruits, and fine weather. For the long journey to this spirit village in the Southwest, the soul, which had assumed a visible, anthropomorphic ghostly shape, needed food and proper equipment. So the deceased was buried with small pots of food and the tools of his or her calling, the souls of which items would separate from the physical artifacts and accompany the traveler's soul. Although the missionaries managed to alter some small aspects of Indian burial, they seldom persuaded even their converts to deprive the dead of their grave goods.[64]

Just as angels differed in power and character from the Christian God,

---

62. Wallace, *Religion*, p. 107.
63. Wallace, *Death and Rebirth of the Seneca*, pp. 59–75.
64. James Axtell, "Last Rights: The Acculturation of Native Funerals in Colonial North America," *The European and the Indian: Essays in the Ethnohistory of Colonial North America* (New York, 1981), chap. 5.

so Indian spirits and souls differed from the more powerful "guardian spir-its," who enjoyed the ultimate power of metamorphosis, and from the "Mas-ter Spirit." According to native belief, every plant and animal species had a "boss" or "owner" spirit whose experience encompassed all the individuals of the species. Many Indian myths were narratives of the "self" adventures of these spirits. More importantly, a young man—less commonly a young woman—who sought a supernatural talisman of success underwent a quest for a vision alone in the woods in hope of receiving instruction from a guard-ian spirit. If he was successful, the being he saw became his personal help-mate for the rest of his life, during the course of which it would give additional counsel, usually when ritually called upon in time of need. So important was the possession of a guardian spirit or "manitou," wrote a Moravian missionary late in the eighteenth century, that an Indian without one "considers himself forsaken, has nothing upon which he may lean, has no hope of any assistance and is small in his own eyes. On the other hand those who have been thus favored possess a high and proud spirit."[65] The missionary's task was to humble his pride by giving him the meek spirit of Jesus Christ as a new guardian.

The ultimate being in the Indian pantheon, just as in the Christian, was an all-powerful, all-knowing "Master Spirit" or "Creator," who was the source of all good but seldom or never seen. More frequently encountered, especially after the advent of the Hell-bearing Europeans, was an evil god, a "matchemanitou," who purveyed devilry and death if not appeased. Much to the chagrin of the missionaries, most of the Indians' religious worship seemed to center on attempts to deflect the maleficences of this deity in-stead of praising the benefactions of the creator.

The Indians mobilized the supernatural in their world by a number of religious observances and rituals. Just as in the Christian churches, some of these rituals, such as personal prayer, could be performed by any individual, but many were efficacious only when administered in a communal context by a specially qualified priest or shaman, known to the Europeans as a "powwow," "juggler," or "sorcerer." The native priest was almost always a male religious specialist who had acquired, through apprenticeship and vi-sions, extraordinary spiritual power. Unlike his Christian counterparts, however, he possessed *personal* supernatural power that allowed him to ma-nipulate the spiritual cosmology on his tribesmen's behalf; he was not a mere intermediary whose only strength lay in explanation and supplication. But because all spiritual power in the native universe was double-edged, ca-

65. *David Zeisberger's History of the Northern American Indians,* ed. Archer Butler Hulbert and William Nathaniel Schwarze (Columbus: Ohio State Archaeological and Historical Society, 1910), pp. 132–33.

pable of both good and evil, the shaman was as feared as he was revered. For while he could induce trances which made him impervious to pain, influence the weather, predict the future, and interpret dreams for the villagers, he could also cause as well as cure witchcraft—the magical intrusion of a small item into the body or the capture of a soul in dream by any person with spiritual "power," which caused illness and eventually death. Bewitchment was the most feared calamity in Indian life because the assailant and the cause were unknown unless discovered by a shaman whose personal power was greater than that of the witch. Because persons exhibiting strange behavior were usually suspected of malicious intentions, the Catholic missionaries who lived by themselves with no women, read the hieroglyphical pages of a black book, dipped water on the foreheads of native people, fondled crosses and beads, and mumbled incomprehensible incantations always stood the chance of being branded as witches and shunned, if not killed.

By the same token, the Indian shaman was the missionaries' number one enemy because he held their potential converts in the devil's thrall through errant superstition, hocus-pocus, and fear. If he happened to be a sachem as well, as occurred from time to time in New England, the missionary faced a formidable task, for such a man controlled the political and social as well as the expressive and emotional resources of the community. If he could be discredited and supplanted, the missionary might have relatively smooth sailing. But while his opposition persisted, large-scale conversion to a Christian alternative stood little chance of success. So adamant was the resistance of these spiritual leaders, that more than one missionary must have entertained the sentiment of an early Virginia minister, who insisted that "till their Priests and Ancients have their throats cut, there is no hope to bring them to conversion."[66]

The second obstacle to the success of the missions was the Indian languages. Although the colonial French and English encountered only four of the major language groups of North America, each tribe—sometimes each village—spoke a distinct dialect that might be largely unintelligible to their neighbors. Unlike the traders and trappers who also pursued their callings in Indian country, the missionaries were denied the company of those female "sleeping dictionaries" who so quickly formed the strangers' tongues to native vocabularies, syntax, and accents.

Another serious obstacle, especially to the French missions, was native marriage. The Catholic priests, of course, regarded monogamous marriage as one of the seven sacraments and divorce as anathema. The Indians, on the other hand, had always exercised, as Father Vimont put it, "a complete bru-

66. John Smith, *Works, 1608–1631*, ed. Edward Arber (Birmingham, Eng., 1884), p. 563.

tal liberty, changing wives when they pleased—taking only one or several, according to their inclination." Understandably, "conjugal continence and the indissolubility of marriage, seemed to them the most serious obstacles in the progress of the Gospel."[67] When the Indians understood the marital implications of baptism, many pulled up short of the "yoke of single marriage" that the French wished to impose.

The Christian way of life offered many other stumbling blocks for the Indians. Lenten fasting at the end of winter scarcity (even though the Sorbonne declared the beaver to be a fish for religious purposes); discrimination between people after death when in life they had been equals; profession that Christianity was the one true faith when missionaries from many denominations hawked their spiritual wares; confinement of people under the "yoke of God" on the Sabbath when the struggle for life required a full week; obsession with death and the afterlife, especially by the palpable threat of eternal torture by fire; assertion that baptism conferred everlasting life when it was often followed by death—all these practices and more seemed unreasonable to a people who had been raised in a religious tradition that was better adapted to the natural and social world in which they lived.[68]

When the missionaries overstepped the native bounds of courtesy and pressed them to change their thinking, the Indians made two characteristic responses, both of which constituted serious obstacles to their conversion. If, during a theological debate with the missionary, a native leader was not convinced of the wisdom of the Christian position, he would close it with a subtle plea for toleration. "All your arguments," warned Pierre Biard from experience with the Micmacs, "and you can bring on a thousand of them if you wish, are annihilated by this single shaft which they always have at hand, *Aoti Chabaya*, (they say), 'That is the Indian way of doing it. You can have your way and we will have ours; every one values his own wares.'"[69] "If we reply that what they say is not true, they answer that they have not disputed what we have told them and that it is rude to interrupt a man when he is speaking and tell him he is lying."[70] Sometimes the rejection could be quite pointed. The Iroquois at Shamokin minced no words in spurning the offer of the Reverend David Brainerd in 1745 to settle among them for two years, build a church, and call them together every Sunday "as the whites do." "We are Indians," they announced, "and don't wish to be transformed into white men. The English are our Brethren, but we never promised to be-

67. *JR*, 10:63, 18:125.
68. For some of the obstacles the French missionaries had to run, see Alfred G. Bailey, *The Conflict of European and Eastern Algonkian Cultures, 1504–1700*, 2d ed. (Toronto, 1969), chap. 11; Kennedy, *Jesuit and Savage in New France*, chaps. 6–9; André Vachon, "L'eau-de-vie dans la société indienne," Canadian Historical Association, *Report* (1960), pp. 22–32.
69. *JR* 3:123.
70. *Hennepin's Description of Louisiana*, p. 178.

come what they are. As little as we desire the preacher to become Indian, so little ought he to desire the Indians to become preachers."[71] The preacher left the next day.

The Indians could have raised many objections to Christianity—and often did when pushed far enough—but usually only sachems, speakers, or shamans chose to lock minds with the Europeans on their own dialectical turf. Most simply deployed the ultimate Indian weapon against aggressive Europeans, a weapon that has frustrated the best-laid plans of white men for centuries. Louis Hennepin, a Recollect priest who worked the Great Lakes and Illinois country, explained why "a savage must not be regarded as convinced as soon as he seems to approve the statements made to him."

> Complete indifference to everything is a form of politeness with these Indians; they would consider a man ill bred if he did not agree to everything or if he contradicted arguments in council. Even though the most absurd and stupid things are said, they will always answer 'Niaova—that is excellent, my brother; you are right.' They believe, however, only what they privately choose to believe.[72]

On the receiving end of such treatment, not every missionary agreed that it sprang from "mere Civility." Claude Allouez chalked it up to "dissimulation," "a certain spirit of acquiescence," and "stubbornness and obstinacy."[73] After researching the history of the Canadian missions, Pierre de Charlevoix said it stemmed "sometimes from mere complacency, sometimes from some interested motive, more frequently from indolence and sloth."[74] Whatever its origins—and Hennepin was closer to the truth than his Jesuit counterparts—more European missionaries than one must have asked in frustration, "What can one do with those who in word give agreement and assent to everything, but in reality give none?"[75]

While the Indians deployed their secret weapon in the heat of cultural combat, they were seldom if ever the aggressors. For the path of least resistance was an extension of the basic Indian toleration of other religions and the correspondent wish to pursue their own. "The *French* in general take us for Beasts," Adario, the fictional Huron sachem, told his friend Lahontan, "the Jesuits brand us for impious, foolish, and ignorant Vaga-

71. William M. Beauchamp, ed. *Moravian Journals Relating to Central New York, 1745–66* (Syracuse, N.Y.: Onondaga Historical Association, 1916), p. 7.

72. Pierre de Charlevoix, *History and General Description of New France* [Paris, 1744], ed. and trans. John Gilmary Shea, 6 vols. (New York, 1870), 2:77; *Hennepin's Description of Louisiana*, pp. 26–27.

73. Albert H. Smyth, ed., *The Writings of Benjamin Franklin*, 10 vols. (New York, 1905–07), 10:100; *JR* 52:203.

74. Charlevoix, *History of New France*, 2:77–78.

75. *JR* 1:275.

bonds. And to be even with you, we have the same thoughts of you; but with this difference, that *we* pity you without offering invectives."[76] Nor did the contrast end there, as Joseph Le Caron saw as early as 1624. "No one must come here in hopes of suffering martyrdom. . . ," he counseled his Recollect brethren, "for we are not in a country where savages put Christians to death on account of their religion. They leave every one in his own belief."[77] It was true, as every missionary knew. But being Christians they persisted in their attempts to change the Indians.

Yet the missionaries' mediocre showing was due not only to Indian resistance—which took many forms, including the show of arms—but to the missions themselves. The poorest record belonged to the few tardy missionaries who attempted to preach the English gospel deep in Indian country, where the long arm of English law did not reach even in the eighteenth century. Unlike their Jesuit competitors, who came early, stayed long, and strove to understand native ways before altering them, they persuaded none and alienated many with their ethnocentric ineptitude.[78] Only their brothers who worked among the remnant groups of New England enjoyed anything like success.

The English missionaries' performance was closely rivaled by that of the Indian schools, which were also few in number and short-lived. If consumption or smallpox did not carry the native students off prematurely, the racism of their English fellows and masters, the sedentary life of study, corporal punishment, homesickness, and an irrelevant curriculum soon drove them off. Perhaps those who graduated suffered the cruelest irony when they discovered that their polite education earned them no place in English society, where merit faced a color bar, and alienated them from their own people. As an Iroquois council observed in rejecting an offer to send more of their sons to William & Mary, "after they returned to their Friends, they were absolutely good for nothing, being neither acquainted with the true methods of killing deer, catching Beaver or surprizing an enemy."[79] The major difficulty for Indian students was that they came to school too late and left too early, and received no social integration, racial tolerance, or love from the English. The passage from Indian to English culture was simply too long and too hard, and the English did little to make it any easier. The

76. Baron de Lahontan, *New Voyages to North-America* [The Hague, 1703], ed. Reuben Gold Thwaites, 2 vols. (Chicago, 1905), 2:570.

77. Le Clercq, *First Establishment of the Faith*, 1:221–22.

78. James Axtell, "The European Failure to Convert the Indians: An Autopsy," *Papers of the Sixth Algonquian Conference, 1974*, ed. William Cowan, National Museum of Man, Mercury Series, Canadian Ethnology Service, Paper no. 23 (Ottawa, 1975), pp. 274–90.

79. Leonard W. Labaree et al., eds., *The Papers of Benjamin Franklin* (New Haven, Conn., 1959–   ), 4:482–83.

contrast with the Indian way of turning white captives into bona fide Indians could not have been starker.[80]

And yet many Indians did become Christians, both genuine and nominal, and did adopt in some degree European ways during the colonial period. In New England alone, ninety-one praying towns were established before the Revolution, and 133 natives had qualified as teachers, catechists, or preachers to Indian congregations.[81] Many Algonkian and Iroquoian people were also persuaded that the Catholic, Anglican, Moravian, or Congregational faiths spoke more to their spiritual and cultural condition than did traditional religions.[82] How do we explain the existence and variety of these conversions while at the same time accounting for those Indian groups who remained stubbornly traditional?

Any explanation must begin with the continuous, long-term changes in native religion which occurred before the arrival of Columbus and his successors. As archaeology, folklore, and historical linguistics prove without question, no aspect of pre-Columbian Indian culture was static. Therefore we should resist the temptation to judge postcontact changes as either happy or tragic deviations from a norm of noble savage innocence. Purposeful change and adjustment were the only norms.

The first discernible changes occurred very early in the precontact period when native groups borrowed particular beliefs, myths, culture heroes, religious artifacts, ceremonies, and even whole cults from other groups— some at considerable distances via long-established trade routes. Through this continuous process of borrowing and transfer, tribes in contiguous culture areas, such as the northeastern woodlands, came to share a large number of religious traits.

The next round of changes took place in response to the bruited arrival of the Europeans in the period of proto- or indirect contact. Before they actually met any Europeans, many tribes encountered often fabulous stories of white "gods" or "spirits," some products of their awesome technology and their selectively lethal diseases. When the invaders finally appeared in Indian villages, thereby inaugurating the period of direct contact, the crisis of intellect precipitated by rampant sickness and death, novel forms of magic,

80. For the striking contrast between the educational methods of the Indians and the English, see Axtell, *The European and the Indian*, chaps. 4, 7.

81. Frederick L. Weis, "The New England Company of 1649 and Its Missionary Enterprises," *Publications of the Colonial Society of Massachusetts* 38 (1947–51): 150.

82. See, for example, John Wolfe Lydekker, *The Faithful Mohawks* (New York, 1938); Elma E. Gray and Leslie Robb Gray, *Wilderness Christians: The Moravian Mission to the Delaware Indians* (Ithaca, N.Y., 1956); Marion J. Mochon, "Stockbridge-Munsee Cultural Adaptations: 'Assimilated Indians,'" *Proceedings of the American Philosophical Society* 112 (1968): 182–219.

and the unknown was only exacerbated by the need to account for the existence of strange bearded men with white skins and barbarous tongues who were obviously not, like themselves, "original people."[83]

The Indians responded to this general crisis in a variety of ways, depending largely on their geographical and political distance from colonial authority, their economic independence, the health of their population and the succession of leadership, their strength relative to neighbors who may have become allied with the invaders, and their intellectual and emotional flexibility and morale, which were the products of their recent past experience.

Tribes who still enjoyed relatively healthy populations, stable social structures, and political and economic independence could choose to deal with the Christian missionary in at least four ways. They could, as many groups did in New England, direct a steady stream of searching questions at him about the consistency of his theology.[84] Or they could question its applicability to their culture by unleashing their polite but frustrating "secret weapon" of outward agreement and inner disagreement. On the other hand, if the proselytizer annoyed them enough, they could simply ignore him until he despaired and went home; or if he persisted, they could chase him away with arms or kill him as a troublemaker and witch. Whatever course of action the Indians chose, the result was the persistence of traditional religion and the unimpaired authority of the native priest.

Sooner or later, all the eastern tribes began to lose their aboriginal sovereignty and strength. As colonial settlements drew closer, disease tore at the native social fabric, leaving gaps in the web of kinship, political succession, technological expertise, and corporate memory. Trade goods from the shops and factories of Europe became desirable luxuries, then necessities. Entangling alliances forced the tribes into the periodic embrace of the colonial governments when they could no longer play them off against each other. And missionaries were emboldened to plunge into native cantons in search of converts. In these dangerous though not yet fatal circumstances, the native community split into factions, as different individuals and interest groups variously perceived the nature of the problems facing them and the best solutions. A dissident minority always had the option of voting with its feet, as was common in pre-Columbian times, by moving to either a more traditional village or to a Christian praying town or *reserve*. More frequently, a faction stayed to fight for the political and social control of the community resources and its future religious and cultural direction.

Those who saw an urgent need to adjust to post-European conditions

83. Many self-given tribal names simply meant "true" or "original people."
84. James P. Ronda, "'We Are Well As We Are': An Indian Critique of Seventeenth-Century Christian Missions," *William and Mary Quarterly*, 3d ser. 34 (1977): 66–82.

without surrendering their ethnic and cultural identity could exercise two options—if both existed. The first was to join a revitalization movement led by a native prophet or charismatic figure who warned the Indians to reaffirm their ancient beliefs and resume their ancient ways before the Europeans captured their spirits as well as their furs. Many of these leaders, such as the eighteenth-century Delaware Prophet and Handsome Lake in the early nineteenth century, incorporated Christian elements in their religions while clearly rejecting Christianity itself. Many others, however, were intolerant of any foreign intrusions, seeking to restore their culture to an imagined precontact purity.[85]

A second option was also to revitalize native culture, but through the selective use of Christianity rather than nativism. Tribes who escaped the worst maladies of European contact had little need of the full "civilized" cure offered by the Christian doctors; to have taken it would have brought on premature cultural suicide. But the complete prescription did contain some useful ingredients, such as political and military alliance, guaranteed land, economic aid, and trade advantages. If to obtain them the Indians had to swallow the bitter pill of religious conversion, the sacrifice was small enough, considering that Christianity might truly satisfy some new intellectual or emotional hunger. If there was none to be satisfied, the convert could simply, in time-honored Indian fashion, add the power of the Christian God to that of his own deities and proceed to syncretize the beliefs and practices of the new religion with the deep structures of his traditional faith. By accepting the Christian priest as the functional equivalent of a native shaman and by giving traditional meanings to Christian rites, dogmas, and deities, the Indians ensured the survival of native culture by taking on the protective coloration of the invaders' culture. Obviously, this brand of Christianity often lay very lightly on the surface of their lives, its acceptance largely expedient to ensure their independence and group identity. But many Indians found in Christianity genuine sources of spiritual strength that helped them cope with their rapidly changing world. As John Smith noticed very early, "all things that were able to do them hurt beyond their prevention, they adore with their kinde of divine worship."[86]

One group of tribes who responded even more positively to the mission offerings were the coastal Algonkians of southern New England. So seriously were they crippled by a plague in 1616–18, and so thoroughly overrun by the colonial juggernaut in the two decades after, that only John Eliot's complete system of moral rearmament, social reconstruction, and religious revitalization was capable of saving them from ethnic annihilation.

---

85. Charles E. Hunter, "The Delaware Nativist Revival of the Mid-Eighteenth Century," *Ethnohistory* 18 (1971):39–49; Wallace, *Death and Rebirth of the Seneca*, pt. 3.

86. Tyler, *Narratives of Early Virginia*, p. 108.

Lacking any viable options, large numbers of them, led in many cases by traditional leaders of the "blood," converted to Christianity and the English way of life that accompanied it. Even though their conversion entailed wholesale cultural changes, it preserved their ethnic identity as particular Indian groups on familiar pieces of land that carried their inner history. At the cost of a certain amount of material and spiritual continuity with the past, their acceptance of Christianity—however sincere—allowed them not only to survive in the present but gave them a long lease on life when many of their colonial landlords threatened to foreclose all future options. Ironically, the acute English sense of cultural superiority—which was colored by racism before the eighteenth century—helped the Indians to maintain the crucial ethnic core at the heart of their newly acquired Christian personae. In colonial eyes, they were still Indians and always would be, no matter how "civilized" or Christianized they became. Despite the assimilative goal of their missions, the English had serious limitations as agents of social reconstruction. They were far better at "rooting out" than transplanting.

On any frontier, acculturation is normally a two-way process, especially in the early stages of contact. But in colonial North America the direction of religious change—unlike changes in other aspects of culture—was decidedly unilinear, largely because Indian religon was pragmatically incorporative and tolerant of other faiths, whereas Christianity was aggressively evangelical and exclusive. Indian religious culture was forever on the defensive, trying to minimize the adjustments necessary to group survival and independence; Christianity sought to cajole or strong-arm the natives into spiritual submission. Any changes in colonial religion were minor and self-generated, and not the result of native pressure to convert to a False Face or Midéwiwin society. At most, the Indian presence sporadically brought out the evangelical inheritance of some of the colonial denominations and moved them marginally away from their own narrow brand of tribalism.

To be on the defensive, however, does not imply total loss of initiative. The Indians were incredibly tenacious of their culture and lifestyle, but their traditionalism was neither blind nor passive. As the history of the missions clearly shows, the native peoples of the Northeast were remarkably resourceful in adjusting to new conditions, especially in using elements of European religious culture for their own purposes. According to the social and political circumstances in which they found themselves after contact, they accepted the missionaries' offerings in just the amounts necessary to maintain their own cultural identity. They may have made individual or short-term miscalculations of self-interest, white strength, and policy direction—no group is capable of a perfect functionalism—but in general they took what they needed for resistance and accepted only as much as would ensure survival. Because of their creative adaptability and the defects of the mission programs, many Indian people were never fully "washed white in the blood of the lamb." Although their outer lives could be partially "reduced to civility," their inner resources were equal to the invasion within. As long as native people continued to think of themselves as "original people," the religious frontiers of North America remained open.

10

RICHARD
ELPHICK

Africans and the
Christian Campaign
in Southern Africa

In this volume we define a frontier as a zone of interaction among peoples practicing different cultures. But what is a "culture"? It is, I think, best understood as the *totality* of thought and behavior which is patterned (as opposed to individual) and learned (as opposed to instinctual or biological) in human society.[1]

Frontiers are not the only zones of cultural interaction. For example, in the sixteenth century, Asians and Europeans learned something of each others' cultures through the seaborne spice trade. The cultural effects of this trade were, however, comparatively slow and superficial—the exchange of new crops, luxuries, and artistic motifs. Thus the behavior of Asians and Europeans was slightly modified but not their basic thought structures, which were not seriously challenged. Casual cultural interaction of this sort differs greatly from the cultural history of a frontier zone, where, by definition, a decisive struggle for political power is taking place. This struggle imposes strain on the cultures of the contenders as they strive to predict and control each others' behavior.

Early drafts of this chapter were discussed at the Seven Springs Conference on Comparative Frontier History (1979) and in the seminar of the Southern African Research Program (SARP). I am grateful to the many people who offered helpful comments on both occasions. In particular, I wish to thank Leonard Thompson, Robert Baum, Jeffrey Butler, Coleman Cooke, Rodney Davenport, Dunbar Moodie, and Robert Shell for their generosity in providing detailed and constructive critiques of the whole chapter, and Philip Pomper for commenting helpfully on the section on revolutionaries. While writing, I was supported by Wesleyan University and by the Yale-Wesleyan Southern African Research Program, a program funded by the Ford Foundation and the National Endowment for the Humanities.

1. My definition owes much to Clifford Geertz, "Religion as a Cultural System," *The Interpretation of Culture: Selected Essays*, ed. Clifford Geertz (New York, 1973), pp. 87–125, and to A. L. Kroeber and Clyde Kluckhohn, "Culture: A Critical Review of Concepts and Definitions," *Papers of the Peabody Museum, Harvard*, vol. 47, no. 1 (1952).

In southern Africa it was the African losers, rather than the European winners, who reworked their cultures more thoroughly as a result of the frontier experience. This pattern, though common in the history of frontiers, is far from universal: some conquerors, like the Ostrogoths in Roman Italy and the Mongols in China, adopted much of the culture of the peoples they vanquished. There are at least two reasons for the pattern in southern Africa. First, the Africans gradually became convinced that the prowess of Europeans was rooted in deeper aspects of Western culture than military and technological skill. To some degree Africans saw their defeat as a defeat of their world-view; in order to rally from defeat, they decided to rethink their culture, partly along European lines. Second, while they were in a self-critical and impressionable mood, they came under the influence of missionaries, who urged them to alter their culture and offered them various inducements to do so. These two features are common to most nineteenth-century frontiers between Europeans and non-Europeans and differentiate them from frontiers of earlier periods.

The presence of missionaries on the frontier guaranteed that much of the clash and interchange between European and African cultures took place on ground which modern Westerners label "religious." But this fact was not due entirely to the missionaries; for Africans, too, were deeply "religious" in their thinking. Like missionaries, the Africans analyzed many areas—cosmology, social theory, history, education, psychology, medicine—in terms of the actions of noncorporeal beings and nonphysical forces. Religion is thus a sensible focus for a study of frontier culture change.[2] Broadly defined, it embraces more of missionary and of African cultures than it excludes.

"Religious change" is, however, too broad a topic for a chapter of this length. The following analysis focuses, more narrowly, on African responses to the Evangelical mainstream of nineteenth-century missions in southern Africa. It omits detailed consideration of the Roman Catholic missions which, except in a few places like Lesotho, did not became a major force until the end of the century. Nor does it treat movements, like Xhosa millenarianism, which were rooted mainly in traditional African religious thought.

I have sought throughout to find ways in which the frontier may have influenced the intensity, shape, and direction of the religious changes I describe. My findings derive from readings in the secondary literature, and are presented as suggestions to be tested in future research. When scholars have done more detailed work in the primary records of missions—particularly

2. I am employing here a "commonsense" Western notion of religion that excludes systems of thought and practice which many specialists in the field would include. For a more scholarly definition of religion, see Geertz, "Religion as a Cultural System."

on the intellectual and "spiritual" aspects of religious change—we shall have a firmer grasp of the role of the frontier in the broader history of African religions, of Christianity, and of the human quest for security in the cosmos.

TWO WORLD VIEWS

I have spoken of "the clash and interchange" between cultures. This is a very loose form of expression. What actually happened was that *people* practicing different cultures clashed and communicated on the frontier. The culture of nineteenth-century Protestant missionaries was not uniform. They came from many ethnic groups (Dutch, American, English, Scottish, German, French, Scandinavian, and so on), many religious traditions, and many levels of formal education. Nor was their culture static. Europe was in the midst of complex, rapid, and contradictory changes. The advances of science and industry, the flowering of Romantic sensibilities, and the emerging ascendency of the bourgeoisie made European culture more complex, more dynamic, and more at war with itself than any, perhaps, which history had yet seen. Of course, Protestant missionary culture was more uniform, cohesive, and resistant to change than European culture as a whole; but in the end missionaries could not insulate themselves, still less their African charges, from the onrush of Western history.

African culture was not uniform either. There were great cleavages between the cultures of the Khoisan (Khoikhoi and hunter-gatherers) and the Bantu-speakers—cultures which had emerged in different times and places and, despite long interaction with each other, had been sustained by different economies. Less important but just as real were the cultural cleavages among the Bantu-speakers—between the Nguni- and Sotho-speakers and between many locally differentiated groups.

In the early nineteenth century African cultures were in less rapid motion than their European counterparts. Fewer Africans than Europeans would consider abandoning their ancestral wisdom and building a new world on abstract and novel principles. But let us not overstate the contrast. African cultures, like European cultures, exist in history and are far from immutable. They change in response to new circumstances. In normal times, perhaps, these changes are slow and barely perceptible to those who practice the culture. However, the early decades of the nineteenth century were not a normal time for Africans in South Africa. In this era many communities were uprooted or destroyed by forces which, so far as is known, were unconnected with advancing colonial frontiers. Africans called these events the Mfecane, or period of forced migrations. The Mfecane was not merely a breakdown of order, but also a creative era in which Africans invented new military tactics and new forms of social and political organization.[3] We know little about philosophical change during the Mfecane, but we must remember that people do not survive the annihilation of law, the dispersion of their families, and the starvation of their children—they do not wander hundreds of miles to find refuge among peoples of strange speech and customs—without asking hard questions about their inherited models of society, their old views of man and God. We see glimpses, through mission records, of the great Sotho monarch, Moshoeshoe, as he developed a philosophy of pessimistic humanism in the wake of the Mfecane.[4] Surely hundreds of thousands of ordinary Africans similarly reflected and argued about the significance of the things they had seen.

Having asserted that African and missionary cultures were multiform and in flux, I must now treat them for a moment as uniform and static abstractions. For in describing culture change our first task must be to discover points of fundamental compatibility and incompatibility between indigenous and intrusive cultures. These points can only be laid bare by an abstract analysis, which inevitably fails to reconstruct African and missionary cultures in all their variety, color, and concrete detail.

Southern Bantu-speakers, like Protestant missionaries, believed in a High God. They did not, however, conceive him as a creator who inaugurated time when, out of nothing, he fashioned the heavens and the earth. According to Moshoeshoe, his people thought "the world must have existed forever, except, however, men and animals, who, according to us, have a beginning." Even this beginning of man was probably not a "creation" as that term is used in the Hebrew scriptures. The Sotho-Tswana, it seems, believed that men were not created but arrived, already men, from the East or from the bowels of the earth.[5]

The High God of South African Bantu-speakers was particularly associated with phenomena of the sky—clouds, rain, thunder and lightning—which gave the missionaries, with their idea of God "above," an obvious point of contact. He was also, however, associated with earth. The general judgment of students of African religion is that Southern Bantu-speakers, like most Africans, regarded the High God as a distant, shadowy being; that they knew little about him; that they held few rituals in his name; and that

3. J. D. Omer-Cooper, *The Zulu Aftermath: A Nineteenth-Century Revolution in Bantu Africa* (Evanston, Ill., 1969).

4. Leonard Thompson, *Survival in Two Worlds: Moshoeshoe of Lesotho, 1786–1870* (Oxford, 1975), p. 72; David Robinson and Douglas Smith, *Sources of the African Past: Case Studies of Five Nineteenth-Century African Societies* (New York, 1979), p. 51.

5. The quotation is from Robinson and Smith, *Sources of the African Past*, p. 51; see also Gabriel M. Setiloane, *The Image of God among the Sotho-Tswana* (Rotterdam, 1976), pp. 33–34.

they rarely, if ever, invoked him in prayer. Against this consensus, the Tswana theologian Gabriel Setiloane has argued that a great deal is known about "Modimo" and that his presence permeates the thought-world of the Sotho-Tswana to this day. By a careful study of Modimo's praise-names, Setiloane concludes that he is one, invisible, omnipresent, the root of all things, the enabler of human action, the upholder of justice—a being beyond the world yet pervading it. All this is entirely consistent with the classical Judaeo-Christian concept of God. However, Setiloane goes on to argue that there is a major difference between Modimo and the God of the Bible: Modimo is impersonal—an "it" rather than a "him"—and a Being of such importance to Tswana that they do not glibly talk to him or about him.[6]

I suspect that Setiloane's scholarly analysis can be reconciled with the judgment of anthropologists that the African High God is remote and unknown. Setiloane seems to be saying that he is less known and apparently less active than the Christian God, not because he is so small but because he is so large, not because he is too remote but because he is too near. From Setiloane's insights one can perhaps conclude that the essential difference between Modimo and the Christian God is that Modimo is not a god of history. He did not create. He did not reveal himself as a person in history, nor in propositions about himself which Westerners call creeds. He called no nation to perform his will. He did not become man. He works in the world mainly through lesser spirits. Hence the absence of creeds and rituals in his name. Hence the Africans' mixed response when missionaries claimed to know the mind and will of Modimo—horror at the strangers' presumption, fascination at the power they could possibly command.

Closely related to the High God (Modimo) was the other major spiritual category of Southern Bantu-speakers, the ancestors (collectively, in Tswana, *badimo*). *Modimo* and *badimo* are different forms of the same noun, a fact which reflects the belief that the ancestors somehow participate in "numinousness," or the nature of God. The ancestors, though invisible, are still alive and are vitally concerned with the affairs of the community. Their presence is felt by everyone. They continue to occupy their former position in the lineage structure and in the social hierarchy. The living communicate with the ancestors in many ways—through animal sacrifices, libations, and prayers—and seek to please them by adhering punctiliously to rituals and other community norms. In their turn, the ancestors communicate with the living through dreams and trances experienced by specially chosen medi-

---

6. For simplicity of exposition, I shall stick to the conventional masculine pronouns. Benjamin C. Ray, *African Religions: Symbol, Ritual and Community* (Englewood Cliffs, N.J., 1976), pp. 50–64; Monica Wilson, *Religion and the Transformation of Society: A Study of Social Change in Africa* (Cambridge, 1971), pp. 32–33; Setiloane, *Image of God*, pp. 79–86.

ums. If pleased, they impart blessings and protection on the community; if angered, they can inflict misfortune.[7]

Like all peoples, Africans sought to understand sickness, suffering, and death. Their explanations, and their remedies, were complex. They are not easily summarized nor easily categorized as "natural" or "supernatural," "personal" or "impersonal." They attributed some illnesses to what we call "natural" causes, some to the High God, some to the ancestors, some to witchcraft. This last phenomenon is an important form of diagnosis and causal explanation throughout Africa. Witchcraft is seen as originating in the malice of a human heart, but it works through powers inherent in inanimate substances. People may prevent it, sniff it out, and cure it through rituals, medicines, divination, and so on.[8] This whole body of belief—complex, subtle, and differing from community to community—was alien to the thought of Protestant missionaries in nineteenth-century South Africa, who were proud of having sloughed off their mediaeval "superstitions."

Africans did not cling to witchcraft and other theories of causation in supreme indifference to the evidence of their senses. They were, in fact, rather empirical, showing a willingness to test the lore of other peoples and adopt whatever proved useful. Their belief in witchcraft was regularly strengthened when magical protection against it proved efficacious and when convicted witches publicly confessed their crimes. The reality of the living dead was confirmed by dreams and by the otherwise inexplicable phenomena of "possession." Beliefs both in witches and spirits have proven very durable, even among urban Africans with generations of contact with Western civilization.[9]

It seems that the ethical systems of the Southern Bantu-speakers and the Protestant missionaries were fundamentally compatible. According to Eugène Casalis, Moshoeshoe was "greatly struck when we enumerated the commandments of the decalogue. 'That,' said he, 'is written in all our hearts. We did not know the God you announce to us, and we have no idea of the Sabbath; but in all the rest of your law we find nothing new. We knew it was very wicked to be ungrateful and disobedient to parents, to rob, to kill, to commit adultery, to covet the property of another, and to bear false

---

7. Setiloane, *Image of God*, pp. 64–76.

8. Ray, *African Religions*, pp. 150–54; Wilson, *Religion*, pp. 35–38; Setiloane, *Image of God*, pp. 44–63.

9. Monica Hunter, *Reaction to Conquest: Effects of Contact with Europeans on the Pondo of South Africa*, 2d ed. (London, New York, and Toronto, 1961), pp. 307–10; B. A. Pauw, *Christianity and Xhosa Tradition: Belief and Ritual Among Xhosa-Speaking Christians* (Cape Town, London, and New York, 1975), pp. 228–60. On the empiricism of African thought, see Robin Horton, "African Traditional Thought and Western Science," *Africa* 37 (1967): 50–71 and 155–87.

witness.'"[10] Adherents of the two ethical systems did not differ so much on the basic principles as on how to balance and apply them. For example, both sides frowned on adultery, considered divorce undesirable, and agreed that women possessed rights which must be upheld. But they combined these principles in different ways and found themselves in violent dispute over various African institutions. A case in point was *lobola*, or bride-price, which missionaries regarded as the buying and selling of women, and which Africans regarded as a social bulwark to strengthen marriage, discourage divorce, and give women recognition for their important roles as laborers and mothers. Most missionaries were likewise hostile to circumcision and initiation ceremonies, mainly because of the "lewd" practices which accompanied them. For Africans, these rites were essential to social organization, and in some states, to political and military organization as well. Underlying these disputes—and others over beer-drinks, clientship, and polygyny— were different conceptions of the function of morality. The Protestant missionaries tended to see morality as an individual's responsibility to a universal code and an omnipresent God, while the Africans saw it more as a responsibility to continue the harmonious operation of their society.[11]

Africans understood not only their morals but other beliefs as well to be proper to their own, comparatively small-scale communities. That other communities had different rituals, lore, and myths did not surprise or trouble them, though alien customs might have caused them some amusement. They felt no urge to proselytize in the interest of universal values. For them groups, not individuals, gave assent to values and systems of thought. A person could not remain in one society while adopting the beliefs and practices of another. From this assumption derived the "tolerance" of Africans toward alien beliefs. The claims of Christianity, a universal creed which clearly delineated truth from error, came as a challenge to the easy-going assumptions of African religious thought. And Christianity was only the first Western philosophy Africans had to confront. Utilitarianism, liberalism, positivism, and Marxism were to prove no less universalistic and, at times, no less intolerant.

In reviewing the salient differences between African and missionary thought, we must examine the common assertion that the former uses "personal" and the latter "impersonal" symbolic systems for explanation, prediction, and control.[12] In fact, if Setiloane is right, the African system com-

---

10. Robinson and Smith, *Sources of the African Past,* p. 51.

11. Wilson, *Religion,* pp. 76–99; Wallace George Mills, "The Role of African Clergy in the Reorientation of Xhosa Society to the Plural Society in the Cape Colony, 1850–1915" (Ph.D. diss., University of California, Los Angeles, 1975), pp. 49–189.

12. For example, Robin Horton, "African Conversion," *Africa* 41, no. 2 (April 1971): 85–108.

bines an impersonal High God, personal lesser spirits, and impersonal forces of nature. Moreover, it is equally wrong to assume that missionaries relied solely on impersonal, that is, scientific, modes of description and control. In fact, nineteenth-century Protestants strongly believed that God was active in history, not only in the rise and fall of empires but in the minutest events of their own lives.[13] For them the universe was, finally, ruled by a *Person*, with whom one could communicate in prayer; the results of prayer (unlike the results of magic) were never automatic, because they depended on God's loving judgment of what was best. However, this same God had created the universe and had set it in regular courses. The universe itself was not divine and was not personal, but its regularity and predictability were a loving sign of a creator-God who *was* a Person. These regularities could be studied by the scientific method and described by impersonal formulae. It was this complex cosmology—with its supernatural and scientific modes of explanation, and its personal and impersonal codes of description—which sustained early European missionaries. Like most early Victorians, they did not regard religion and science as incompatible. For them the eighteenth-century dispute between rationalism and religion had been laid to rest. Darwin, the biblical critics, and the late Victorian crisis of faith lay in the unknown future.

How, then, did missionary and African thought differ? Both sides agreed that the prime mover in the universe was a God who was one. But the Protestant missionaries, unlike the Africans, made a radical distinction between his actions in nature and in history. They claimed that God had made regularities in nature and had given man a mind to master and use them in acquiring dominion over the earth. They also claimed that God was active in history and that his activity was revealed in the biblical narrative which stretched from the creation of man, through the covenant with Israel, the incarnation of Christ, the spread of the church, to the culmination of all things in the Second Coming of Christ. Whereas God worked in nature through laws, he worked in history through his human agents who, like him, were persons with emotions and will, and were immortal. Nineteenth-century Evangelical Protestants thought that man's duty to God must take precedence over loyalties to any group, tradition, or cultural heritage. For them, man was breaking the bonds of the past, freeing history from nature, and pushing on into worlds previously unimagined.

By severing history from nature, the missionaries, in part unwittingly,

13. Missionary diaries of the early nineteenth century note many incidents of Providential guidance or divine intervention in response to prayer. To take only one example, the Reverend John Campbell, at the end of his first journey in and around Cape Colony, noted: "I have observed a chain of favourable providences during the whole journey, which I [view] as answers to the prayer of many Christians in Britain on behalf of us who were travelling in the wilderness." See John Campbell, *Travels in South Africa* (reprint, Cape Town, 1974), p. 161.

unleashed powerful forces in Africa. On the one hand, they closed nature down; they silenced and deadened it by eliminating personalist and magical strategies of explanation and offering instead the simplifications of mathematics which make possible the technology of industrialism. On the other hand, they blew history wide open with visions of a global brotherhood and endless improvement, all to be accomplished by free men working out the purposes of God. They stamped science on nature; and on history, revolution.

THE MISSIONARIES

Prior to the 1770s, the Cape Colony expanded into areas inhabited mainly by Khoisan (Khoikhoi and "Bushmen" hunter-gatherers). In this period the political structure of traditional Khoikhoi chiefdoms crumbled rapidly, much more rapidly than other aspects of Khoikhoi culture. Moreover, there was little missionary activity among the Khoisan, apart from Georg Schmidt's brief mission at the future Genadendal (1737–44). Thus most Khoisan experienced culture change, neither in a traditional setting nor on mission stations, but on farms owned or rented by whites. Change in this setting was very selective; it was largely unplanned and uncoordinated; and it was chiefly stimulated by the exchange of goods, services, and technologies and by the imposition of new productive relations.[14] The farmers, unlike missionaries, did not set out to transform their laborers' "historically transmitted pattern of meanings embodied in symbols" (one anthropologist's definition of culture).[15] Rather, they merely wanted Khoisan to learn appropriate attitudes to time, to work, and to private property; new political loyalties; skills like shooting and wagon-driving; and appetites for products which the farmer offered as wages. Few farmers before the nineteenth century made efforts to Christianize their laborers. Consequently, large areas of Khoikhoi mythology, cosmology, morality, family life, material culture, and arts, did not come under white scrutiny and were probably touched only indirectly or not at all.[16]

Eighteenth-century missionary endeavor at the Cape was hamstrung by a feature of Calvinist ecclesiology—namely, that missionaries were clergy-

14. Richard Elphick, *Kraal and Castle: Khoikhoi and the Founding of White South Africa* (New Haven and London, 1977), pp. 200–14. Richard Elphick and Robert Shell, "Intergroup Relations: Khoikhoi, Settlers, Slaves and Free Blacks," in *The Shaping of South African Society, 1652–1820*, ed. Richard Elphick and Hermann Giliomee (Cape Town and London, 1979), pp. 155–60.

15. Geertz, "Religion as a Cultural System" p. 89.

16. Elphick and Shell, "Intergroup Relations," pp. 118–19, 159.

men, responsible first for a European congregation and only second for converting non-Christians. But beginning in the 1790s, European and American
Protestants, fired by the Evangelical revival, organized mission societies independent of established church structures. Soon southern Africa, along
with much of the world, was invaded by zealous apostles of change, eager to
replace the culture of blacks, to reclaim the culture of whites, and sometimes even to restructure the relations between blacks and whites in a new
postfrontier society.

In the early decades of the nineteenth century, southern Africa was
among the most intensively missionized parts of the world, along with
North America, India, the Caribbean, and the South Pacific islands.[17] Missions found southern Africa attractive because of its benign climate, its
comparatively supportive government, and its white settlers, some of whom
were not hostile to missionaries but supported them with funds and
manpower.

The missionaries did not represent a cross section of European society.
The Evangelical revival, which stimulated the rise of Protestant missions,
had begun as a movement among the poor. By the early nineteenth century,
it is true, it had gained adherents among all classes and recruited eminent
figures, particularly in commerce and politics. But it was not these who
heeded the call to leave family and home and set sail for Africa. Most missionaries came from a stratum which included the higher ranks of the working class and the lower ranks of the middle class. They were mainly artisans
and skilled workers—that group whom contemporaries called "godly me-
chanics" and whom historians, in another context, have called "the aristocracy of labor."[18] Among the first Methodist missionaries to southeastern Africa were two businessmen, two printers, a joiner, a molder, an upholsterer,
a roper, a wool stapler, and a manual laborer. Of missionaries to the Sotho-
Tswana before 1840, Setiloane has noted a saddler, a carpenter, a black-
smith, a gardener, and a mason. Many of the outstanding missionaries who
shaped African history by the force of their personalities and intellects came
from similar backgrounds. Dr. John Philip had been a weaver; Robert Moffat
was a gardener; John Mackenzie was a farmer's son, apprenticed to a printer;
David Livingstone started his working life in a cotton mill.[19] Nor did the

---

17. This statement applies to Protestant missions only. See B. R. Edwards, "A Missionary Gazetteer," *Fessenden & Co.'s Encyclopedia of Religious Knowledge . . .* (Brattleboro, Vt.,
1936), pp. 1187–1250.

18. The general idea of this and the following two paragraphs owes much to Max Warren,
Social History and Christian Mission (London, 1967), pp. 36–57.

19. Norman Alan Etherington, "The Rise of the Kholwa in Southeast Africa: African
Christian Communities in Natal, Pondoland and Zululand, 1835–1880" (Ph.D. diss., Yale University, 1971), p. 89; Setiloane, *Image of God*, pp. 247–53; William Miller Macmillan, *Bantu,*

class makeup of the missionary force change much over time. Robert Rotberg, after a survey of missionaries in Northern Rhodesia between 1880 and 1924, concluded that "as a group they were descended from craftsmen and tradesmen, and occasionally from fishermen, farmers or graziers."[20]

There were, naturally, some exceptions. The founder of the London Missionary Society in South Africa, Dr. J. T. van der Kemp, was a scholar, medical doctor, former cavalry officer, and companion of the Prince of Orange. Several of the early Paris Evangelical missionaries came from old Huguenot middle-class families. German missionaries tended to come from more rural backgrounds than their British counterparts, but even among them artisans dominated: for example, the first four Moravian missionaries were by occupation a butcher, a tailor, a cobbler, and a cutler.[21]

The class background of missionaries accounts in part for the low level of formal education in some missionary societies. Only fifteen of the first thirty-six Methodist missionaries in southeastern Africa had studied theology. Fewer than thirty-five of two hundred missionaries in Northern Rhodesia before 1924 had a university education. But the pattern was not even. American Board missionaries were required to have both undergraduate and theological degrees.[22] The emphasis on education was strongest among the Scots. The London Missionary Society's remarkable foursome of Philip, Moffat, Mackenzie, and Livingstone all were Scots who had learned from their humble backgrounds to value hard study. Even the less formally educated of the missionaries were usually studious and kept careful diaries. Most showed considerable capacity for practical analysis. But while some of their minds were powerful, they ran in fixed grooves. In dealing with African culture they lacked both the flexibility and the imagination which a university education might conceivably, but not necessarily, have stimulated. They loved hard work. They were inner-directed men, proud of their achievements, too willing to assume that the virtues which had served them in Manchester or Glasgow would serve men and women everywhere.

As for their theology, the vast majority of the early missionaries to South Africa may be labeled Calvinist in the broadest sense, including agents of the London, Glasgow, Scottish, Paris, American, Dutch Reformed,

---

Boer and Briton: The Making of the South African Native Problem, 2d ed. rev. (Oxford, 1963), p. 11; J. du Plessis, A History of Christian Missions in South Africa (reprint, Cape Town, 1965), p. 154; A. Sillery, Sechele: The Story of an African Chief (Oxford, 1954), p. 158; "Livingstone, David," Encyclopaedia Brittanica, 1968 ed., 14:154.

20. Robert I. Rotberg, Christian Missionaries and the Creation of Northern Rhodesia 1880–1924 (Princeton, N.J., 1965), p. 161.

21. Du Plessis, Christian Missions, p. 100; Thompson, Moshoeshoe of Lesotho, pp. 72–73; Bernard Krüger, The Pear Tree Blossoms: The History of the Moravian Church in South Africa, 1737–1869 (Genadendal, 1966), pp. 15, 49; Etherington, "Rise of the Kholwa," p. 134.

22. Rotberg, Christian Missionaries, p. 161; Etherington, "Rise of the Kholwa," p. 89.

and Suisse Romande societies, as well as some Rhenish and some early Anglican missionaries like Allen Gardiner. The important Wesleyans were, of course, explicitly anti-Calvinist in their denial of predestination and their proclamation of free grace, but in style, psychology and general theology they were obvious heirs of English Puritanism or Calvinism. By "Calvinist in the broadest sense" I mean that these groups regarded the Bible as their sole authority for belief and practice, emphasized the fallen nature of man, preached salvation solely by grace through faith, practiced an austere and comparatively nonsacramental form of worship, insisted on an iron discipline in moral matters, and were heirs to an activist tradition of "cleansing church and nation" in the name of God. On this last point they differed from Lutheran and Moravian missions, which tended to quietism in social and political matters. On many other substantial points they differed from the later Catholics, both Roman and Anglican.

However, the message of the Calvinist mainstream was complicated by the fact that virtually every Protestant missionary of the nineteenth century was influenced to some degree by the Evangelical Revival, an international resurgence of Protestant piety concentrated in Great Britain, Germany, and the Anglo-American colonies. In England, America, and Holland, Evangelicalism was not so much a new movement as a renaissance of a declining Puritanism. But it displayed new emphases, techniques, and doctrinal tendencies which later became prominent in the religious lives of whites and blacks in southern Africa. Most importantly, Evangelicals stressed the need for personal, crisislike conversions accompanied by varying degrees of emotion. Several tendencies flowed naturally from the conversionist emphasis. First was a renunciation of the Calvinist doctrine of predestination—explicitly by the Wesleyans, implicitly by most revivalists and missionaries: Evangelicals did not wait for sinners to come to their churches, but pursued them into wheat fields, down slum alleys, and to the uttermost ends of the earth. Second, as emotionalism flourished in religious life, clergy increasingly emphasized spiritual experience rather than doctrinal knowledge as a criterion for church membership. This tendency was most pronounced among Methodists, most resisted among Presbyterians. And, third, there developed from the devaluation of doctrinal purity a spirit of interdenominational cooperation in campaigns against slavery, illiteracy, and so on, and, to some degree, in the mission movement itself. These Evangelical emphases were prominent not only in the Calvinist mainstream but also among the influential Moravians whose general theological background was Lutheran.

The Evangelical tradition required that whites as well as Africans be the targets of missionary enterprise. Evangelicals believed that not only the "heathen" but also nominal Christians, in every generation and in every nation, must be converted. While some went to Africa to convert Africans, others stayed at home to convert Europeans. And not only to convert them: E. P. Thompson's observation that Methodists tried to "uproot preindustrial traditions from the manufacturing districts" of England reminds us that similar Evangelical schemes of culture change in Africa proceeded from more than simple ethnocentrism.[23] The earliest Evangelicals in South Africa—Georg Schmidt in the 1730s and M. C. Vos in the 1790s—preached both to Afrikaners and to their slave and Khoisan laborers. While some groups like the London Missionary Society worked solely among Khoisan and Africans, others like the ubiquitous Methodists made it a principle not to distinguish between their white and black operations. In 1878, for example, all but two Methodist missionaries in Natal were engaged in some kind of interracial work.[24]

Missionaries demanded of Africans a reorientation of thought and behavior which can only be called revolutionary. Consider the comprehensiveness of their program. They expected their converts to abandon belief in witchcraft, an essential facet of the Africans' theory of nature and human society; to relinquish nine-tenths of their cosmology (including belief in the ancestors); and to get along without several essential bonds of community such as polygyny, lobola (bride-price), and most rites of passage. They also wanted to alter the economic base of African communities by turning pastoralists into cultivators, and cultivators into scientific farmers, craftsmen, and traders. They expected traditional herbal and ritual medicines to give way to European drugs. Individual converts were to shift their primary allegiance from kinship groups and chief to a new translineal and transethnic body, the church. And finally the art, music, dance, dress, architecture, community layout, furniture, food, and drink of Africans were (in the more moderate schemes) to be "redeemed" and (in the more radical) forever discarded. One missionary even wanted to change the Xhosa language by purging it of "clicks."[25] From the African point of view this can hardly be called a conservative program.

Modern Westerners cannot understand the early nineteenth-century missionaries without exercising some historical imagination, but missionaries are not so remote from us as to be beyond comprehension. Much of what they thought and did becomes more accessible if analyzed under modern rubrics such as "economic development," "social change," "thought reform," "education," and "community organization." Here I want to develop a single parallel, the resemblance between missionaries and modern revolutionary intelligentsias.

23. E. P. Thompson, *The Making of the English Working Class* (New York, 1966), p. 408.
24. Etherington, "Rise of the Kholwa," p. 97.
25. Krüger, *The Pear Tree Blossoms*, p. 169.

The missionaries were not, of course, intellectuals by profession; nonetheless they formed an earnest, ideologically focused, disciplined group with a theory and tactic of revolutionary change. Like revolutionary intellectuals, they enjoyed some autonomy from the society in which they worked, in part because they were paid from overseas. They went forth to peoples of whom they knew little but whom they deemed socially and mentally oppressed; they strove to "convert" them, that is, to replace their "false" consciousness with a "true" one so that the converts could destroy an old order and create a new in accordance with objective, developing processes of history. The missionaries' theory, like that of many revolutionaries, often proved so irrelevant that they were ignored, rejected, or humiliated by their intended converts; some responded to frustration by sacrificing their principles in the pursuit of victory, becoming intriguers or even enemies of those they had once wanted to help. But the ideal among missionaries, as among revolutionaries, was always a perfect unity of theory and practice, and occasionally a Lenin-like genius could so effectively combine his understanding of divine truth with mundane circumstance that he could shape, if not exactly preside over, changes of extraordinary magnitude. When they succeeded, missionaries ceased to be a revolutionary vanguard and became a bureaucratic elite supervising their converts in the building of a new society. In theory, this missionary "state" should now have withered away. It rarely did, however, and the converts eventually had to mount another revolution against unwanted leaders.

The missionaries invaded South Africa with a well-articulated program, the details of which were debated among its various sects and personalities. The missionaries resembled revolutionaries, and particularly Marxists, in that they justified their actions in terms of history and employed historical analysis as a defense against discouragement and despair; for they knew that they were agents of historical forces which were both progressive and certain to triumph. Thus, among missionaries, as among Marxist revolutionaries, theoretical debate centered on the paradox between objective historical process (Providence, the missionaries' equivalent of dialectic) and human will (the role of the missionary, or party). A major problem concerned the timing of the revolution. Many of the earliest missionaries tried to force God's hand by demanding of their converts total adherence to Western standards before they had adequate understanding or institutional support. This tendency was roughly what Lenin, in his revolutionary movement, called "adventurism." The opposite tendency was more common in later phases of the mission enterprise. Missionaries of this inclination relaxed in the certainty that the revolution would come in "the fullness of time." They convinced themselves that that time had not yet come and devoted themselves to ministering to the short-term desires of Africans for education, medical attention, and so on; this Lenin called economism.[26] In Christian missions, as in revolutionary movements, economism was the most persistent temptation. It drew its strength from the missionary's fear of laying his beliefs on the line and triggering an upheaval with unknown, but surely disruptive, consequences. This fear could always be rationalized by an appeal to biblical texts and an analysis of the historical moment. Today economism is as triumphant in European missions as it is triumphant among European Marxists.

Another debate concerned the role of existing structures. For a political revolutionary the target structure is the state. In *State and Revolution*, Lenin discerned two opposite errors in attempting to change the state. One, "opportunism," was for the revolutionary to cooperate with the existing state; the other, "anarchism," was to destroy existing structures with no plan for replacing them. Lenin argued that one should "smash" the oppressive apparatus of the bourgeois state and replace it with a new apparatus of class oppression, which he called the dictatorship of the proletariat.[27] In the mission movement, the analogue to the state was the existing African culture (including the social structure and the state). Most missionaries were "Leninists": they saw no hope of building a Christian society on an African base, but set out to smash the latter and replace it with the paternalist social structure of the mission station and the aesthetics, morals, and behavioral patterns of the Evangelical lower middle class. Among missionaries the "opportunist" deviation was a minority view in the nineteenth century. Only a few outstanding figures like Bishop John William Colenso of Natal could discern "light" in African culture. Colenso did not attack African institutions head-on, but encouraged their gradual transformation into a mature Christian culture.[28] In the twentieth century this view has gradually gained ascendency in many of the older missionary societies. The "anarchist" deviation among missionaries is perhaps best represented by those who try merely to live a Christ-like life in an alien setting, planting the seed and leaving the harvest to God. This style, characteristic of some Quakers, has had little influence in southern Africa.[29]

A third issue common to missionaries and revolutionaries is the relationship between the vanguard (missionary or party) and the masses. The "Bolsheviks" among missionaries wanted high standards of knowledge and demonstrated character before admitting an African to baptism, to Holy

26. V. I. Lenin, *What Is To Be Done? Burning Questions of Our Movement* (New York, 1972), p. 74–75 and passim.

27. V. I. Lenin, *The State and Revolution* (Peking, 1973), pp. 47–60 and passim.

28. Etherington, "Rise of the Kholwa," pp. 106–12.

29. Roy Harvey Pearce, *Savagism and Civilization: A Study of the Indian and the American Mind*, rev. ed. (Baltimore, 1967), pp. 35–41.

Communion, or to ordination. They envisaged a prolonged and dramatic cleavage between a small but highly dedicated church and the rest of African society. In southern Africa this tendency is best represented by the various Presbyterian bodies. The Methodists, by contrast, were the "Mensheviks" of the missionary movement, arguing for the equivalent of a mass party. They readily admitted persons who had experienced divine grace into their societies and into the network of lay preachers.[30] Most Roman Catholics occupied the middle ground on this question. They made access to baptism comparatively easy, and to the priesthood comparatively difficult.

Of course, these parallels between missionaries and revolutionaries are mainly structural and do not pertain to the goals of the two movements. Moreover, like all historical parallels, they are inexact. But they do bring into relief characteristics of the missionaries which set them off from other proponents of cultural change among Africans, such as white farmers or mine owners. The missionaries, like revolutionaries, were a self-conscious elite, enjoying considerable financial, legal, and social autonomy within their target society; they clearly articulated and debated the scope, nature, and order of change they wanted; and they aspired to comprehensive upheavals that would affect all groups, all regions, and all aspects of life in South Africa.

The parallel is also useful in broaching the question, did the missionaries succeed or fail? The consensus of most recent scholarship is that they failed. And indeed, on most mission fields the going was very rough in the early years. Converts were few, and often of dubious quality. Backsliding was common. Traditional culture remained vital and only half-hidden even on mission stations. And this was not entirely a failure of communication. Many Africans understood Christianity perfectly well yet rejected it totally.[31] As a result, some modern authors have pronounced the whole episode a failure, a rather grotesque sideshow to European imperialism.[32]

Many missionaries also recognized that they had failed. They had not ushered in the kingdom of God. They had not extirpated African culture. They had not created a just South Africa. But should this surprise us? We know, as they did not, something of the coherence of traditional African beliefs and their capacity to explain experience. We know, as again they did not, that entire peoples never discard their world views en bloc; in Europe itself Christianity had not displaced the high culture of antiquity or the folk cultures of the countryside, but had mingled with both for centuries. We

30. Etherington, "Rise of the Kholwa," p. 96; Bengt G. M. Sundkler, *Bantu Prophets in South Africa* (London, New York, and Toronto, 1948), pp. 136–37.

31. Etherington, "Rise of the Kholwa," pp. 151–54.

32. For example, Donald Denoon, *Southern Africa since 1800* (New York, 1972), pp. 64–65.

also know that subsequent revolutionaries, more powerful and ruthless than the missionaries, have failed to realize their visions or cut the present free from the past. The Bolsheviks, even in power, were victims of the "givens" of their situation and of powerful forces beyond their control. Yet their failure was not total; we recognize that they made a difference, that they deflected the course of history. Russia today is not what it would have been if Lenin and his party had never existed.

Roughly the same analysis can be applied to the missionaries. Today the majority of Bantu-speaking Africans in South Africa and the overwhelming majority of "Coloureds" (the mixed descendents of whites, Khoikhoi, and slaves) claim to be Christian.[33] While for many this is a superficial commitment, for many others it is much more profound than one typically finds in churches in the West. Something important happened—if not in the first generation, then perhaps in the second or fifth. The interesting question is not to explain the missionaries' failure, which was to be expected, but to ascertain and explain the rather surprising degree of their success.

THE MISSION STATION

Evangelical missionaries, like Evangelicals in Europe, gauged success mainly by counting conversions and assessing the moral quality of the converts. They expected Africans to respond to the gospel "intelligently" (that is, freely, as individuals), and then to join the church and other voluntary organizations within a broader social and political framework. In doing so, converts would painfully have to renounce some of their former pleasures and associations, but they would not rupture the social fabric by forming religious communities in competition with the family, local government, or the state. Paradoxically, however, Evangelical missions in South Africa created just such ruptures. Almost from the beginning, missionaries created Christian communities that were wholly or partly autonomous from larger units. Moreover, they exercised economic and political power more in the manner of mediaeval bishops than nonconformist ministers from Victorian England. The origin and development of these theocratic communities—the mission stations—must be examined.

The first missionaries to South Africa, the German-speaking Moravians, were unusual among missionaries in having a communitarian heritage: they had all lived in closed, tightly disciplined Moravian villages in

33. The 1970 census puts the percentage of Christians among so-called Coloureds at 90 percent, among "Bantus" at 72 percent. The latter figure is far too high, because the census made no provision for registering adherents of traditional religions (except as atheists) or holders of complex, syncretistic views.

Europe. At first they did not intend to found such villages in South Africa, but in a short time they nonetheless did so. Their first station, Genadendal, and most of their subsequent stations, were founded on colonial territory, that is, in areas where the frontier had closed. The Moravians soon realized that the labor of their Khoikhoi converts was coveted both by the colony's white farmers and by the colonial government. It became clear that they must offer the Khoikhoi an alternative society where they would be protected from exploitation, trained in useful crafts, and taught the Moravian virtues of gentleness and industry. Moravian missionaries made no distinction between their religious, economic, and political roles. They controlled access to the villages, distributed land, exercised discipline, and took charge of economic development. Their transplanted German village of Genadendal won glowing opinions even from Tory governors and freethinking travelers, who, much as they detested Evangelicalism, were charmed by the sight of dutiful and energetic Khoikhoi peasants.[34]

The Moravian model deeply influenced the scholarly and eccentric Dr. J. T. van der Kemp, pioneer of the London Missionary Society (LMS) in South Africa. When, in 1801, van der Kemp negotiated with Governor Dundas for land near Algoa Bay, he made it clear that he visualized a mission village just like Genadendal, in which Khoikhoi converts would labor under the discipline of missionaries.[35] Bethelsdorp, the station he founded, was within the colony but at a more peripheral location than Genadendal. From here the LMS fanned out into many areas of South Africa, almost always by creating self-contained stations under missionary control; only rarely, as at the Kat River, by founding a church in a community organized along secular lines.

Many of these LMS stations were beyond the boundaries of the colony, in regions where political power was weak or divided. For example, the LMS established itself among the Bastaards or Griqua, mixed-blood emigrés from the Cape Colony, who from 1800 began to fashion a new polity in Transorangia.[36] It also sent missionaries into the arid regions along the western stretches of the Orange River; here, the general absence of cultivation, as well as the high incidence of livestock raiding, discouraged the formation of sedentary societies or strong, centralized states.[37] Missionaries of other societies also settled in frontier zones—that is, where African and white polities clashed and colonial economies were encroaching on traditional ones. This was the case in the region east of the Fish River, which was occupied

34. Krüger, *The Pear Tree Blossoms*, pp. 95, 292–95.

35. Jane Sales, *Mission Stations and the Coloured Communities of the Eastern Cape, 1800–1852* (Cape Town and Rotterdam, 1975), pp. 16–17.

36. Martin Legassick, "The Northern Frontier to 1820: The Emergence of the Griqua People," in *Shaping*, ed. Elphick and Giliomee, pp. 261–75.

37. Campbell, *Travels in South Africa*, pp. 399–400.

by Wesleyan and Scottish missionaries after about 1820.[38] These missionaries, and most who followed them to South Africa, were heavily influenced by the Moravian-LMS model of the mission station. Though many had strong theoretical objections to this model, most nevertheless adopted it. Not surprisingly, in frontier zones and other areas of weak or ambiguous political control, the mission stations flourished and became even more self-contained and autonomous than they had been in the Cape Colony.

Soon missionaries also began to settle in areas under firm African control. Here again the LMS blazed the trail with its string of missions among the Tswana, beginning in 1821 with Kuruman. Similar missions were founded by Paris Evangelical missionaries among the Sotho of Moshoeshoe (from 1833) and by various missionaries to the Zulu, beginning in 1836. In such settings, where their lands and liberties were in the gift of an African ruler, the missionaries usually perpetuated the mission-station model. And, in time, the mission communities, even in strong chiefdoms, tended to become distinct from the wider society, and missionaries emerged as a political counterforce to the chief.

It is advisable, then, in explaining the failures and successes of missionaries, to focus on the mission stations, particularly those founded in areas of African control. Such stations, if they survived, inevitably experienced three stages of frontier history: first, the open frontier (when a strong African state came into contact with white neighbors); then the closing frontier (conflict between African and white powers); and finally, the closed frontier (unambiguous white rule). Moreover, insofar as they were successful, the missions experienced an African response which can also be broken down into three stages. In the first, the African ruler allowed, or even urged, a missionary to set up a station in his territory. In the second, Africans began to participate in the life of the station, some by settling there, others by coming intermittently to attend school or church. In the third, Africans affiliated themselves with the church either through a publicly attested conversion, or through baptism, or both. Our task is to suggest connections between these stages in Africans' positive response to missions—permission, participation, affiliation—and the stages of frontier history.

Missionaries who set their sights beyond the colonial borders had first to ask African rulers for permission to settle on their land. The first chiefs who received such requests normally responded with suspicion or hostility, but it was not long before African monarchs were inundating mission societies with more requests for missionaries than they could meet. The chiefs hoped that missionaries would bring to their dominions valuable goods such as guns and foodstuffs, introduce new technologies such as the

38. Du Plessis, *Christian Missions*, pp. 173–75, 182–88.

plow, and serve as gunsmiths, physicians, or dentists. But the prime reason for their enthusiasm was related to the threats posed to their kingdoms by the Mfecane and the advancing frontier. Since missionaries traveled over long distances and communicated even farther by letter, they could provide their ruler with invaluable political and military intelligence. They could also act as his advisers, interpreters, and plenipotentiaries in dealing with colonial officials. Moreover, mission stations were useful as border outposts or, in the case of Moshoeshoe's Lesotho, as vehicles for territorial expansion.[39]

Thus the chiefs' motivations were largely political, but they were not necessarily "secular" or "pragmatic," as modern historians often assume. Chiefs often suspected missionaries of having privileged access to the power of the High God. Thus, especially in the early decades of the mission movement, they expected that the missionary's presence alone would protect them from attacks of both Africans and Europeans. They patronized missionaries just as though they were traditional prophets or healers. Not uncommonly, for example, they would ask their missionaries to heal the sick or produce rain through their prayers. The missionaries, with their Protestant embarrassment about the supernatural, were usually reluctant to submit their faith to such empirical verification. But some consented. Joseph Jackson, Jr., a Methodist, "was elated at the effects of the rain which followed his Sunday prayer in 1861. The people, he said, flocked to him saying, 'Our mouths are now stopped; we can answer you nothing; we see that God is, and that he hears prayers.'"[40]

Quite clearly, then, most chiefs acquired and protected missionaries without manifesting much interest in the missionaries' central concerns— the doctrines of sin, salvation, and everlasting life. They cared, not for the content of Christianity, but for its links with Western civilization and various forms of power. They wanted its adepts, the missionaries, to defend them against the threats posed by the Mfecane and the frontier. But the chiefs' interest did not always end there. Moshoeshoe, for example, established a close friendship with the Paris Evangelical missionaries Casalis and Arbousset; he discussed all manner of theological issues with them and expressed concern about his own sin and need for salvation. Sechele, chief of the Kwena, went even further when, in 1848, he was baptized by David Livingstone. A rather different case was Kgama of the Ngwato, whose father Sekgoma had followed the classic strategy of tolerating a mission station while strengthening traditional religion against its teaching. In 1872 Kgama, who had been baptized in 1860, seized power from Sekgoma's successor,

39. Setiloane, *Image of God*, pp. 134–36; Thompson, *Moshoeshoe of Lesotho*, pp. 80–89.
40. Setiloane, *Image of God*, p. 135; Etherington, "Rise of the Kholwa," p. 146.

Macheng. He subsequently became a paragon of a Christian ruler, whose uprightness and teetotalism were widely publicized in Sunday schools the world over. Two minor chiefs in Natal also fostered the progress of Christianity: Mnini of the Thuli and Mqhawe of the Qadi.[41]

During the second stage in the history of a successful mission, that of participation, Africans, slowly at first, but in increasing numbers, settled at the station, or at least came regularly for instruction. In a few cases their participation was encouraged by the example of their monarch. For example, Moshoeshoe sent his children to the mission school, urged his people to convert, and himself attended church. He was impressed by the personalities of his missionaries and by some of their doctrines; he may even have toyed with using Christianity as a national cult for his recently formed kingdom. Moshoeshoe's patronage led large numbers of his subjects to attend mission schools and significant numbers to be baptized in an era which later missionaries nostalgically called the "golden age" of the Sotho mission (1833–48).[42] This era was succeeded by a massive reaction against Christianity among the Sotho and considerable disillusionment on the part of Moshoeshoe.[43]

The "golden age" in Lesotho—a successful mission on an open frontier—was rather an anomaly in southern African history, though it has parallels elsewhere.[44] The missionaries settled in Lesotho before other Europeans could threaten its independence or present it with disquieting models of "Christian" behavior. Thus missionaries were free of some of the burdens they would carry on later frontiers. However, this fact alone could not overcome the indifference which Africans typically showed toward mission stations newly founded in their midst. The unusual response of the Sotho was largely due to characteristics, not of open frontiers in general, but of Lesotho in particular: an extraordinarily open-minded and influential monarch; an unusually flexible and creative group of missionaries; an era of peace and prosperity coincident with the missionaries' arrival; and a state, newly formed of immigrants and refugees, which had as yet no ancient traditions of its own.

41. Thompson, *Moshoeshoe of Lesotho*, pp. 70–104; Anthony J. Dachs, "Christian Missionary Enterprise and Sotho-Tswana Societies in the Nineteenth Century," *Christianity South of the Zambezi*, ed. Anthony J. Dachs (Gwelo, Rhodesia, 1973), 1:57; J. Mutero Chirenje, *Chief Kgama and His Times c. 1835–1923: The Story of a Southern African Ruler* (London, 1978), pp. 1–16; Etherington, "Rise of the Kholwa," pp. 173–75.

42. Thompson, *Moshoeshoe of Lesotho*, pp. 75–76, 79–80; Claude H. Perrot, "Les Sotho et les missionaries européens au xix⁰ siècle," *Annales de l'université d'Abidjan*, 1970, ser. F, vol. 2, fasc. 1, pp. 13–51.

43. Perrot, "Les Sotho," pp. 52–88.

44. For example, Kongo in the early sixteenth century. See Jan Vansina, *Kingdoms of the Savanna* (Madison, Wis., 1966), pp. 45–58.

The Tswana monarchs Sechele and Kgama also encouraged their people to learn from missionaries. Both were baptized Christians and well-trained students of the Bible. They aimed to create a national church under their own control, an ambition which did not sit well with the congregationalism of their LMS missionaries. Sechele preached regularly to his people in a church where his name was emblazoned on the wall opposite the pulpit. Kgama reformed some Ngwato customs along Christian lines.[45] Significantly, however, the activities of these two monarchs did not foster particularly rapid growth of the missions under their protection,[46] in part, perhaps, because colonial power was encroaching on their kingdoms.

Some Africans came to mission stations, intermittently or permanently, with the aim of learning to read and write. Because Protestant missionaries placed such heavy emphasis on reading the Bible, most made literacy a second priority after conversion itself. In their first contact with Africans, moreover, they often presented literacy and salvation as twin benefits of their teaching. In conversation with a Tlhaping queen, John Campbell and his companions

> explained to her the nature of a letter, by means of which a person could convey his thoughts to a friend at a distance. Mr. A. shewed her one he had received from his wife, by which he knew every thing that had happened at Klaar Water for two days after he left it. This information highly entertained her, especially when told that A. Kok, who brought it, knew nothing of what it contained, which we explained by telling her the use of sealing wax. The bible being on the table gave occasion to explain the nature and use of a book, particularly of that book—how it informed us of God, who made all things; and of the beginning of all things, which seemed to astonish her, and many a look was directed towards the bible.[47]

Without doubt, many perceptive Africans were astounded by literacy. "I will never believe," exclaimed Moshoeshoe's elderly father, "that the word can become visible."[48] The fascination with the written word prompted a few adults and more children to attend mission schools shortly after their founding. In Lesotho, with Moshoeshoe's encouragement, the enthusiasm for

45. Sillery, *Sechele*, pp. 130–31; Dachs, "Christian Missionary Enterprise," p. 57; Chirenje, *Chief Kgama*, pp. 38, 69; Anthony J. Dachs, "Functional Aspects of Religious Conversion among the Sotho-Tswana," in *Christianity South of the Zambezi*, ed. M. F. C. Bourdillon (Gwelo, Rhodesia, 1977), 2:152–53.

46. B. A. Pauw, *Religion in a Tswana Chiefdom* (London, New York, and Toronto, 1960), p. 11, n. 1; Dachs, "Functional Aspects," p. 151.

47. Campbell, *Travels in South Africa*, p. 199.

48. Perrot, "Les Sotho," p. 33.

schooling became something of a craze. Doctor John Philip noted in 1844 that "nothing is more precious to [the Sotho] than a book, nothing pleases them as much as reading, nothing inspires them with as much gratitude as a lesson. If you find them gathered beside their houses or in their fields you will almost always note that they are perusing a book or teaching each other to read."[49]

In most areas, including Lesotho, the initial fascination with literacy wore off, and school attendance stagnated or declined. The fact was that on the open frontier, and even on the closing frontier, the value of literacy—to all but a chief who understood its diplomatic uses—was no clearer than the value of Christian doctrine. Etherington's study of missions in Zululand, Natal, and Mpondoland shows that most scholars in mission schools were people, or children of people, who had already chosen, for other reasons, to live on mission stations. Traditionalists distrusted schools because they were agents of evangelization. Only on the closed frontier, it seems, would the advantages of schooling overcome these inhibitions, as parents came to regard literacy as a passport to advancement in colonial bureaucracies.[50] Then one would find the pattern, so common in colonial Africa, where parents would send their children to missions, not to become Christians, but to learn to read and write.[51]

It seems, then, that chiefly patronage and the appeal of literacy do not fully explain Africans' participation in the life of nineteenth-century missions, except in some specific cases. A more embracing explanation has been suggested by Norman Etherington in his thorough analysis of residents of mission stations in Zululand, Mpondoland, and Natal. Etherington found that only those who had no secure position in traditional society came to live at the stations. Many mission residents had come long distances and were strangers in the district. Some were mixed-bloods, others had lived in chiefdoms annihilated in the Mfecane or had worked in colonial society long enough to have lost their family ties. Still others were outcasts and fugitives from nearby Nguni communities: young people who wished to marry in defiance of their family; twins, cripples, and epileptics sent away by their parents; fugitives from accusations of witchcraft; girls escaping from puberty ceremonies; women running away from husbands. This collection of African flotsam and jetsam appeared despicable and threatening to Nguni living in traditional units, who were almost unanimously hostile to the missionaries, their message, and their following. Etherington's analy-

49. Ibid., p. 34.

50. Etherington, "Rise of the Kholwa," pp. 149, 268, 272; Perrot, "Les Sotho," p. 76.

51. *African Reactions to Missionary Education*, ed. Edward H. Berman (New York and London, 1975); Robert M. Baum, "The Emergence of a Diola Christianity," *Continuity and Change among the Diola*, ed. Francis Snyder and Jose van der Klei (forthcoming).

sis drew on evidence both from areas disrupted by the Mfecane and from the relatively strong polities in Zululand and Mpondoland.[52]

Etherington's conclusions are paralleled by Setiloane's observation that, among Tswana, Christianity was long regarded as "something in which the women and lesser members of society could indulge." Moreover, during the traditionalist reaction in Lesotho after 1848, when most persons of rank withdrew from Christian fellowship, the mission continued to gain a few adherents from the lower ranks of society, particularly women. It seems that Sotho women found opportunities for leadership at the mission which were denied them in traditional political life, as well as specific social benefits such as greater juridical control over their children.[53]

These analyses all suggest that, before the frontier closed, missions attracted mainly the disadvantaged and dispossessed, whose numbers were likely to increase as the Mfecane or the frontier encroached on previously stable African societies. Missionaries, after all, offered two crucial material incentives—land and an alternative social order. Land, it is true, was not yet in desperately short supply in most regions, but many Africans could not find a chief who could offer them both land and a secure environment. For such people, missionaries were the equivalent of local chiefs fashioning new communities out of the social fluidity—in some cases the anarchy—of southern Africa. Whether the mission station was on colonial or African land, the missionary enjoyed considerable autonomy from his overlord. He admitted and expelled people from the community, he allotted land, he controlled marriage, he punished wrongdoers. He also mediated between his subjects and the relevant higher authority, whether African monarch or colonial magistrate. And as time passed, mission communities developed distinct identities. Not only were they laid out along streets radiating from a stone school and church, but gradually their inhabitants erected square, rather than round, houses and cast off their hides and furs to don trousers and petticoats. In this context the missionaries' otherwise absurd insistence that Africans wear Western clothes makes some sense. In Africa, as elsewhere, a community is identified by its apparel.

Before turning to the third stage in Africans' response to missions, let us review our findings on the first two stages and suggest some correlations with frontier history. We may assume that in these earlier stages the content of the missionaries' message was relatively unimportant, being unknown to Africans, or only superficially known by word of mouth. The important determinants of African response were (1) the threats to African

---

52. Etherington, "Rise of the Kholwa," pp. 170–71, 206–21.
53. Setiloane, *Image of God*, p. 143; Perrot, "Les Sotho," pp. 157–62.

societies caused by the Mfecane and the advancing frontier, and (2) the associations of mission endeavor with Western civilization, with colonial power, and with the alternative community of the mission station.

The first stage of African response is fairly easy to understand. African rulers apparently encouraged missionaries to found stations in their territories because they hoped thereby to gain protection from their enemies. As chiefs learned more about the missionaries, and as the disruptions of the Mfecane gave way to the closing frontier, the chiefs' understanding of missionary potential may have drawn less on religious understanding and more on pragmatic calculation, but the goal remained the same.

The explanation of why Africans came voluntarily to the station is more complex. As a rule, Africans who lived in a secure polity on the open frontier would be indifferent to the presence of a mission station in their midst; only minorities and malcontents would be attracted by its economic base and comparative autonomy. When their society came under pressure, however, the Africans' response to the mission would alter significantly. On the one hand, famine, war, and migration would increase the numbers of homeless, poor, and distraught persons who might take refuge at a station. Thus the Mfecane in southeastern Africa produced, not only individual adherents to mission life, but a whole new people of refugees, the Mfengu, who gravitated to mission stations.[54] Similarly, the closing frontier in the northern Cape Colony produced the scattered founders of the Griqua people, who found in Christianity a suitable cult, and in the missionaries suitable advisers, for nation building.

However, the closing frontier also ensured that Africans would associate both missionaries and Christianity with their enemies. Consequently, their indifference to missions often turned to hostility, and the stations survived only because of the chiefs' continuing dependence on missionary diplomatists. Moreover, the closing frontier often threw Africans back on their own religion in a search for knowledge and power to counter the European threat. In Lesotho, during the struggles against Britain and the Voortrekkers (1848–68), there was a strong revival of national customs—circumcisions, dancing, polygamy—which had been under fire in the "golden age" of the Sotho mission. Among Xhosa, the wars with the Cape Colony between 1812 and 1853 spurred prophets to develop the Nguni religious tradition into powerful ideologies of resistance.[55] These features of the closing frontier—the growing numbers of the dispossessed, the increasingly negative associations with missions, and the revitalization of traditional religion—all served

54. Sales, *Mission Stations*, pp. 118, 136.
55. Perrot, "Les Sotho," pp. 77–80; J. B. Peires, "Nxele, Ntsikana and the Origins of the Xhosa Religious Reaction," *Journal of African History* 20, no. 1 (1979): 51–61; John Zarwan, "The Xhosa Cattle Killings, 1856–57," *Cahiers d'études africaines*, vol. 16, pp. 519–39.

to intensify the identification of mission work with minorities and the down-cast. Whether, on balance, these features aided or hindered the growth of mission stations can be determined only by thorough investigation of individual cases.

Just after the frontier definitively closed, however, one would expect a period, however brief, when the identification of Christianity with Western civilization and power would attract Africans to the mission station. At this point the Europeans' victory would appear to have vindicated their world view; the career advantages of a Western education would become more obvious; and the missionaries would appear less threatening, perhaps more useful, than the other Europeans with whom Africans now had to deal, such as farmers, traders, mine bosses, and administrators. We must remember that the Khoikhoi, whose rapid immigration to Moravian and LMS missions had so boosted the early mission movement, were a people on whom the frontier had closed. The Xhosa, who coolly resisted mission pressures for decades, began to respond positively in the 1860s, in the wake of their disastrous defeat in the cattle-killing and of increasing European impact on their society.[56] Among the Sotho, where missionaries had been active and prominent since 1833, widespread and lasting Christianization did not begin until colonial institutions began to undermine chiefly control late in the century.[57] It seems likely, though much research would be needed to prove it, that most Bantu-speakers received a thorough exposure to Christianity only after the frontier had closed.

THE MISSIONARIES' MESSAGE

The third phase in the positive African response to missions—conversion and/or baptism—may often have followed quickly upon an African's decision to participate in the life of a mission station. However, this new stage is logically distinct from its predecessor because Africans publicly declared themselves Christians only after some exposure to the message of Christianity in catechism and school and to the practice of Christianity in worship and daily life. It is, of course, likely that many converts still considered the associations of Christianity more important than its content. In particular, many persons who had chosen to live on a mission station may have decided to adopt the cult of their new community, proceeding on the traditional African assumption that cult and community are coterminous. Moreover, many Africans may have seen other social benefits in baptism,

56. Wallace G. Mills, "The Taylor Revival of 1866 and the Roots of African Nationalism in the Cape Colony," *Journal of Religion in Africa* 8, no. 2 (1976): 114–16.
57. Perrot, "Les Sotho," pp. 164–65.

such as enhanced status in colonial society.[58] Such instrumental motivations for conversion or baptism were almost certainly important and do not imply conscious hypocrisy on the part of Africans, who had a much more sociological understanding of the function of religion than did their Evangelical tutors.

However, these motives cannot fully explain the many well-documented and highly emotional conversions of individuals who quite suddenly changed their allegiances, many attitudes, and values. They also leave us with little understanding of Africans whose Christianity became so intense that they became evangelists themselves and, under missionary supervision, were instrumental in converting hundreds of other Africans outside the mission station. Repeatedly in South African history, it was not the missionary who made the major breakthrough, but African Christians who proclaimed the Christian message in ways that responded to the needs of masses of Africans. Very little research has been done on the emotional and intellectual aspects of religious change in southern Africa. Hence what follows is exploratory and conjectural.

The missionaries' message began with the proclamation that human beings, corporately and individually, are "fallen," that is, alienated from their Creator by an act of willful rebellion. Missionaries thought, of course, that they were proclaiming an *objective* guilt, which existed whether people perceived and felt it or not. The assertion that God and man had been alienated from one another was not necessarily new to African listeners. Benjamin Ray, in his survey of African religions says: "This pattern [of fall] is built into almost every African religious system. Myth posits an original situation against which the world develops. An opposition or division arises between order and disorder, divinity and humanity, sky and earth. The "problem" of religion is to overcome this divine/human polarity through ritual action."[59] However, in European history the power of the Calvinist doctrine of Original Sin has not been due entirely to its plausible explanation of all that is incomplete and broken in human experience. It has also found remarkable resonance among its hearers with *subjective* feelings of guilt. The key question is whether missionaries found this sense of guilt among Africans or had first to create it.

F. B. Welbourn, in an analysis of East African Christianity, has examined this problem by employing a psychoanalytical distinction between guilt-feelings and shame-feelings. Guilt feelings arise when one breaks a moral law and thus displeases a loved one (a parent or God); a sense of

58. Martin Chatfield Legassick, "The Griqua, the Sotho-Tswana, and the Missionaries, 1780–1840: The Politics of a Frontier Zone" (Ph.D. diss., University of California, Los Angeles, 1969), p. 185.

59. Ray, *African Religions*, p. 32.

shame occurs when one fails to perform effectively and thus feels inadequate, out of proportion, or in disjunction with one's society. Welbourn suggests that African societies (and European societies before the seventeenth century) had mythical and ritual means of projecting or otherwise purging guilt feelings; hence they were more likely to be preoccupied with feelings of shame. Only those Africans who had undergone detailed instruction by missionaries were able to respond to the message of sin as missionaries expected. Welbourn attributed early *mass* conversions to the desire of Africans to follow their leaders, that is, to avoid feelings of shame.[60] Quite independently, Eugene Genovese has suggested that African slaves in the United States, for all their eagerness to adopt Christianity, found little use for the doctrine of Original Sin and its accompanying feelings of guilt. For them "Christianity lacked that terrible inner tension between the sense of guilt and the sense of mission which once provided the ideological dynamism for Western civilization's march to world power."[61] It should be noted that the slaves, however degraded their condition, lived in a social order which to them must have appeared stable and sure.

In South Africa one of the toughest barriers to the progress of Christianity was the refusal of many Africans to admit that they were sinners. As Moffat reported on a dialogue with Sotho-Tswana: "When we attempted to convince them of their state as sinners, they would boldly affirm, with full belief in their innate rectitude, that there was not a sinner in the tribe, referring us to the nations whom they dreaded, or with whom they were at war; especially the despised Bushmen."[62]

Yet the missionaries did find people who were tortured by feelings of sin and could find release in Christ, just like people they had known at home. The Khoikhoi, in particular, manifested a lively sense of sin. Almost from their first arrival at Genadendal, the Moravians' meetings were overcrowded with weeping Khoikhoi: "Time and again, they came to tell the brethren how sad they were that the Savior had suffered so much for the sins of men." The Methodist Barnabas Shaw reported his encounter with a Little Nama chief near the Khamiesberg. The chief was "sitting on a solitary rock, a short distance from the place where I had preached. I walked toward him, and found him mourning and weeping aloud. On asking him, 'Chief, why are you mourning thus?' he answered, 'Ik ben al te veel zondig, (I am so exceedingly sinful). All the sins which I ever committed appear to be set before my eyes.'"[63] Many Xhosa also underwent emotional conversions after grap-

60. F. B. Welbourn, "Some Problems of African Christianity: Guilt and Shame," *Christianity in Tropical Africa*, ed. C. G. Baëta (London, 1968), pp. 182–99.

61. Eugene D. Genovese, *Roll, Jordan, Roll* (New York, 1976), p. 212.

62. Setiloane, *Image of God*, p. 116.

63. Krüger, *The Pear Tree Blossoms*, p. 57; Barnabas Shaw, *Memorials of South Africa* (New York, 1841), pp. 267–68. See also Sales, *Mission Stations*, p. 37.

pling with the weight of sin. But they did not do this until the 1860s, after decades of stonily rejecting the missionaries' message. Wallace Mills believes that their new responsiveness was due mainly to the impingement of white society on the Xhosa, a process which had culminated in the cataclysmic cattle-killing of 1856–57.[64]

It appears, then, that missionaries found little sense of guilt (as opposed to shame) among peoples who inhabited a stable social order. By contrast, the Khoikhoi by the end of the eighteenth century and the Xhosa after the cattle-killing had been deprived of comforting certainties, clear boundaries, and a sense of the justness of things. It is perhaps relevant to recall that the first autobiography of a soul's struggle with guilt, as well as the most elaborate development of the doctrine of Original Sin, were written by Saint Augustine when the Roman world order seemed to be collapsing.[65] That there is some correlation between social disintegration and the presence of guilt feelings seems plausible, but at this point in my research I can neither document it fully nor spell out the necessary connections.

A second part of the missionaries' message consisted of biblical narrative—namely, the national history of the Jews, the life of Jesus, and the story of the early Church. For missionaries, the culmination of this history was the birth, death, and resurrection of Jesus, events which they presented (in slightly different ways) as resolving the alienation between God and man. There was no guarantee that Africans would be most struck by the events which missionaries thought central. Indeed, some non-Western peoples have been more impressed by Moses than by Jesus, and Genovese has shown how many American slaves merged these two biblical personages in their minds.[66] It was significant, however, that Africans had had no previous exposure to biblical history. Thus those very events which missionaries regarded as the most important and precious parts of their message, Africans regarded as most novel and interesting. This coincidence accounts in part, I suspect, for the willingness of Africans in many parts of the continent to engage in endless dialogues and disputations with missionaries even when they felt no inclination whatever to "convert."

The problem lay, of course, in deciding what the biblical story meant. The Evangelical missionary anticipated that conversion would occur when an individual despaired of himself, was attracted to the person and sacrifice of Jesus, and transferred his allegiance from self (or other loves) to him. If our earlier analysis is correct, and guilt-feelings were not widespread among

64. Mills, "The Taylor Revival," pp. 114–16; William Taylor, *Christian Adventures in South Africa* (London, 1867), pp. 224–41 and passim.
65. *Confessions* and *City of God.*
66. Genovese, *Roll, Jordan, Roll,* pp. 252–55.

Africans in secure societies, an African convert would not necessarily *"flee to Jesus"* (a typical Evangelical formulation) to escape the wrath to come; but he might still give him his allegiance out of love—that is, because the Jesus portrayed by the missionaries manifested virtues that were admired in the convert's culture. Casalis reported that "what struck [Moshoeshoe] the most, as well as those of his subjects who followed our instructions with assiduity, was the person and work of Christ."[67] Such missionary analyses might, of course, draw heavily on wishful thinking. But nonetheless, I suspect that historians should not look solely for pragmatic and intellectual motives for conversion. Affective and emotional factors, which evidently play a role in conversion to more ritualistic and aesthetic faiths like Catholicism, are probably active in Protestant settings as well; in the latter case, however, the appeal is more to the moral imagination than to the senses. Moreover, we should not forget that personal loyalty was far more important in African societies than in our own. Is it unreasonable to suppose that an African might have seen himself as taking Jesus for his patron?

In Evangelical thought, the sinfulness of man and friendship with Jesus were closely linked doctrines. The first was the problem, the second the solution to it. Hence Evangelical conversion was a rapid transition from anguish to joy, a transition so dramatic that it normally led to alterations in personality—at least for a while. Victorian novelists have left us with savage portraits of one type of Evangelical: the cloying, sepulchral distributor of tracts, epitomized by Miss Drusilla Clack in *The Moonstone*. Another response to salvation by grace, already diagnosed and condemned by Saint Paul in the first century, was antinomianism: let us sin that grace may abound. Some South African critics of Evangelical missions argued that conversion fostered laziness and self-indulgence among Africans who, had they escaped conversion, would be working productively on white farms. This charge was leveled particularly at Bethelsdorp when it was being run by its founder, Van der Kemp.[68] Of course, many of these critics were self-interested, being employers of farm labor themselves, and others held the peculiar conviction that the work ethic was the essence of Christianity. But we must admit that missionary preaching, if unaccompanied by bustling Scottish schemes for improvement, sometimes so enhanced the well-being and self-satisfaction of converts that revolutionary consequences could scarcely ensue.

A third possibility, and one that missionaries should have welcomed, was that converts would become confident, inner-directed men like the missionaries themselves, asserting their dignity as children of God. Evan-

67. Robinson and Smith, *Sources of the African Past*, p. 51.
68. For example, Sales, *Mission Stations*, p. 27.

gelical missions did, in fact, often spawn an entrepreneurial class of converts who became the backbone of a nationalist "middle class." This has
been observed in many parts of Africa and is documented for South Africa
by Etherington's study of the Natal Kholwa and Mills's account of the
Xhosa clergy.[69] Moreover, it seems that from the first arrival of missionaries,
Africans sensed that Christ freed them, not only from sin and guilt, but also
from social inferiority, particularly in relation to settlers. This realization
was particularly striking among the long-degraded Khoikhoi. Let us listen
to a disputation between three "Namaqua" (Khoikhoi) Christians and a Boer
on whose farm the Khoikhoi, in company with a missionary, had been
preaching. (Note that the Boer is trying to conceal his illiteracy.)

> *Boor*: What kind of singing and praying is this you have had? I never
> heard any thing like it, and cannot understand.
>
> *Jacob Links*: I, think, master, you only come to mock us, as many of the
> farmers say we ought not to have the gospel;—but here is a chapter
> (John iii) pray who are the persons that must be born again? (Handing
> the Testament)
>
> *Boor*: Myne osgen [*sic*] zyn niet goed (My eyes are not good), so that I
> cannot see very well, but I suppose Jesus Christ.
>
> *Jacob*: No, master, no such thing;—Jesus Christ says we are all sinners,
> and that we must be born again in the Spirit, or we cannot enter the
> kingdom of heaven.
>
> *Jan Links*: But, master, you once told me that our names did not stand
> in the book, and that the gospel did not, therefore, belong to us
> Namacquas. Will you now tell me master, whether the name of
> Dutchman, or Englishman, is to be found in it? (No answer)
>
> *Jacob*: Master, you who are called Christi menoh (Christians), call us
> heathens. That is our name. Now I find the book says, that Jesus
> came as light to lighten the Heidenen (Gentiles). So we read our
> names in the book. (Farmer silent)
>
> *Hendrick Smit*: That master cannot understand many things in the
> book, is not strange; Paul says, "The natural man receiveth not the
> things of the Spirit of God," 1 Cor. ii, 14.
>
> *Boor*: Who is then the natural man?
>
> *Hendrick*: All men in their sinful and unregenerate state, so that we
> can only understand spiritual things by the help of the Spirit of God,
> &c.
>
> *Boor*: Ik ben geen zendeling (I am no missionary), .therefore cannot ex-
> plain Scripture passages.

69. Etherington, "Rise of the Kholwa," pp. 246–77, 294–342; Mills, "The Role of African
Clergy," passim.

Jacob: But, master, do you ever teach your slaves and servants anything of the gospel?

Boor: Neen, volstrekt niets (No, certainly nothing at all), for were they taught, it would make them equally as wise as myself.[70]

While it is true that the Evangelical message concentrated on themes of sin and salvation, the whole system rested on a cosmology which differed significantly from that of most Africans. Robin Horton has suggested that in the relationship between the two cosmologies can be found much of the dynamic behind conversion in Africa. Horton's "intellectualist" explanation starts from the assumption that African religions rest on a two-tiered cosmology: polytheistic in the lower tier and monotheistic in the upper. On the lower level, as we have seen, are many local forces, in South Africa mainly the spirits of dead humans; these interact with nature and human society in ways which Africans can analyze propositionally and which they seek to control through right behavior and ritual. On the upper level, most African peoples recognize a Creator or High God, but they say little about him and approach him rarely through prayer or ritual. Consequently the High God plays a remote role in the day-to-day affairs of the community.

Horton goes on to argue that the lesser spirits and gods provide a sufficient symbolic apparatus of "explanation, prediction, and control" for people inhabiting a "microcosm," namely, a small-scale, fairly isolated society. However, people who enter into the "macrocosm" of interethnic relations and the social change engendered by colonialism have need of a universal theory of human affairs, which the lore of the High God provides: "The particular position taken up by an individual will depend largely on the degree to which, in his own personal life, the boundaries of the microcosm have ceased to define him."[71] The experience of conquest and colonization made necessary an expression and elaboration of the idea of the High God which Africans already had in embryo. The contemporary arrival of two monotheistic religions, Christianity and Islam, acted as "catalysts—i.e., stimulators and accelerators of changes which were 'in the air' anyway."[72]

Horton's thesis offers an elegant explanation of three incontrovertible but puzzling aspects of African religious history: (1) that tens of millions of Africans have made some sort of public commitment to Christianity and (in other parts of Africa) to Islam, and continue to do so at astonishing rates; (2) that, however, Christianity and Islam do not often make headway against each other; and (3) that Africans' adhesion to monolatry in Horton's upper tier does not usually entail abandoning the traditional lower-tier cosmology.

70. Shaw, *Memorials of South Africa*, pp. 100–01.
71. Horton, "African Conversion," p. 103.
72. Ibid., p. 104.

In other words, Africans continue to practice much of their traditional religion even while being sincere Christians or Muslims.

Still, there are certain profoundly ahistorical features of Horton's thesis which he has sharpened even further in responding to his critics.[73] Most notable is his argument that an elaboration of monotheism was "in the air anyway" in all African societies. This reduction of Christianity and Islam to the role of catalyst entails a counterfactual assertion about a myriad of societies; like all counterfactuals, it is incapable of proof. It also assumes, against common sense, that systems of thought will always respond adequately to new challenges, and it ignores the many civilizations with macrocosmic experiences but predominantly polytheistic religions, like Egypt. Finally, it renders incomprehensible the profound rooting which distinctively Christian and Muslim dogmas other than monotheism have taken in Africa. It is clear, of course, that the missionaries sometimes did act as a catalyst to developments within the African tradition. But their ideas were often more than that: they were additives.

Not that most missionaries would take comfort in my conclusion. They wished, not to add to African culture, but to displace it. Hence they waged unremitting warfare on Africans' allegiance to their lower-tier cosmology of ancestral spirits and their explanatory theories of witchcraft and magic. Protestant missionaries were heirs to the Reformation's battle against magic and "superstition" in the Church, including the whole panoply of priestly powers, charms, amulets, healings, spells, relics, dreams, and prophecies which marked late mediaeval Catholicism.[74] As biblicists, the missionaries could not reject all miracles, but they tended to relegate them to the age of the Apostles. Likewise, they could not deny the existence of all lower-tier spiritual beings (angels, demons), but they downplayed these traditional elements of Christian teaching, particularly in comparison to contemporary Roman Catholics. In practice the early missionaries came to Africa with a modern, scientific conception of nature, and they offered the scientific world view and its technological fruits as consequences of Europe's acceptance of the gospel. They did not, as I have shown, regard Christianity and science as being in conflict. Rather, they combined an attachment to a personal God working through history with a belief in the impersonal, predictable workings of nature.

Africans did not respond to all aspects of this package in the same way. No doubt converts easily picked up the habit of praying to the High God, but such prayer added little to the arsenal of weapons of "explanation, prediction and control" which they already possessed in prayers and rituals to

73. Robin Horton, "On the Rationality of Conversion," *Africa* 45, no. 3 (1975):219–35, and no. 4 (1975):373–99.

74. Keith Thomas, *Religion and the Decline of Magic* (New York, 1971), pp. 51–77.

other spiritual beings. It added little, that is, unless one could empirically demonstrate, as Elijah had done against the priests of Baal, that Jehovah was more powerful than his rivals. This is where the Protestant missionaries were betrayed by their dependence on science. For Africans had been conditioned by their own faiths to expect supernatural aid in dealing with physical disease and with harassment from witches or spirits. Furthermore, as soon as they were exposed to the New Testament, they learned that Jesus and his apostles had had remarkable powers to heal the sick, cast out demons, and confound wizards. But the missionaries simply denied that witchcraft and spirits existed, and in doing so they appeared willful or dotty to their converts and cut them off from Christian resources in areas we call "psychological." As the people of Theopolis told the missionary George Barker, "if witchcraft is not found in the Bible, it is nevertheless a reality."[75] Moreover, the missionaries' meager battery of medicines, which they usually administered under less than ideal conditions, did little to free Africans from the need for "supernatural" weapons against illness. Thus, late in the nineteenth century, African prophets arose who were anxious to appropriate the aid of the Christian God in matters of healing and harassment. After experiencing an anointment of spiritual power from above, they broke with the missions and founded their own "Zionist" churches. The rise of Zionism was an important development in the history of Christianity in South Africa, a sure sign that Christianity was taking root in African soil. Zionism is increasingly being understood, not only as a protest against racial discrimination in southern Africa, but also as an African initiative in finding Christian answers to African questions which the missionaries had ignored.[76]

In this case, then, it appears that Africans grasped an aspect of the Christian tradition and made more of it than the missionaries were able to do. A similar process may have occurred with European views of time and history. It is often said that the European conception of time differs radically from that of traditional Africans. European time stretches far into the past, far into the future, and is linear and progressive. Africans have a somewhat shorter view of the past and little conception of the distant future; indeed, the comparative lack of eschatological speculation in African religions would seem to be one major distinction between them and Judaism, Christianity, and Islam.

Now, if these are true characterizations of traditional South African religious beliefs, it seems obvious that eschatology is one aspect of Christianity which Africans have embraced with enormous enthusiasm. Most

75. Sales, *Mission Stations*, p. 98.
76. See, for example, M. L. Daneel, *Zionism and Faith-Healing in Rhodesia: Aspects of African Independent Churches* (The Hague, 1970).

particularly, they have been attracted to millennial teachings—that is, to speculation about God's intervention in human history at the end of time. The very word *Zionist*, which Sundkler attached to one type of African Independent church, reflects this millennial emphasis.[77] Through the concept of millennium, many Africans have come to see their personal and national travail as part of global historical patterns that will culminate in the establishment of the Kingdom of God on earth.

However, as Wallace Mills has recently pointed out,[78] Christian Africans in South Africa have employed two very different types of millennial speculation, and these correspond rather closely to trends long present in the Christian tradition: postmillennialism and premillennialism. Postmillennialism is the view that Christ will not return until after the thousand-year period of peace prophesied in Revelation 20. It interprets this millennium as the culmination of the era of the Church when God's purposes are gradually worked out in history. Postmillennialism is thus optimistic about the prospects of improvement in the present age, and it encourages one to be actively involved in the world. This view prevailed among European Christians in the early nineteenth century, and also among missionaries. The first generation of Xhosa converts (from the 1860s onward) were postmillennialists, and their eschatology sustained their belief that the spread of Christian principles would undermine racism and discrimination in the Cape Colony. However, these early optimists received serious political and economic setbacks in the 1890s, and many of them were willing, Mills says, to embrace new premillennial theologies which reached South Africa about the same time.

Premillennialism had gained considerable ground among American and English Christians during the nineteenth century. The premillennial view is that Christ will appear *before* the millennium. There is no hope that the present world order can be redeemed; it is distintegrating and will continue to disintegrate until Jesus' coming. Premillennialists in all eras have usually expected the climax of history to come in their own time and have found various ways to withdraw from the world in preparation for the end. For Mills, the rise of Zionist Christian groups among Africans is a premillennial response to oppression in South Africa: he notes that few Zionist prophets or church leaders have been involved in African nationalist politics. In fact, those Africans who rejected the premillennialist outlook remained in the mainline, mission-related churches and moved into increasingly secular and "rational" responses to oppression, such as organizing nationalist par-

77. Sundkler, *Bantu Prophets*, p. 48.
78. Wallace G. Mills, "Christianity and African Conversion: A Contribution to the Horton Thesis" (unpublished).

ties, trade unions, and so on. These responses, moreover, continued to have a strong Christian and utopian flavor.

Mills's thesis is most suggestive. However, I am suspicious of his view that the rise of Anglo-American premillennialism led to the rise of African Zionism. Premillennialism is the prevalent eschatological scheme in the New Testament. It seems possible that biblically educated Africans, imbued with a feeling of defeat, powerlessness, and anxious dread, would appropriate and develop this ancient Christian theme without prolonged tutelage from outsiders. True, one finds white missionaries in the early history of African Zionist churches. However, their role is so transitory that I would be inclined to assign them the Hortonian role I rejected for the first missionaries: that of catalyst.[79] If I am right—and I am only guessing—one can, contra Horton, take seriously Christianity's doctrinal content and potential for development; and also, contra Mills, regard such development as a distinctive, independent African achievement, and not a mere reflex of theological developments elsewhere. According to this view, Africans' activation of Christian millennialism in the face of missionary hostility would parallel their appropriation of doctrines of supernatural healing. Both trends would confirm, not only that Christianity was becoming Africanized, but also that the written word continued to be a threat to established ecclesiastical authority. In a sense, as David Barrett's massive study of African independency suggests, the missionary's worst enemy was, after himself, the Bible.[80]

In this section I have tried to illuminate African conversions by focusing on the content, as well as the associations, of Christianity. The main emotional appeal of Evangelical Christianity lay not, it seems, in its form of worship—though group singing was definitely an attraction at the Moravian missions—but in the solace it offered to the guilt-ridden and poor in spirit. Such persons were more numerous after the frontier had closed, and this fact helps to explain the increase among Africans of emotional conversions similar to those which missionaries had known in Europe.

As for doctrine, we noted Horton's plausible view that, by accentuating monotheism, Christianity helped Africans expand their world view to comprehend experiences imposed on them by colonialism. But missions also brought a new view of nature (which I have called "closed," one of impersonal, regular causation) and a new view of history (an "open" one, in which

---

79. The question is discussed in detail in Bengt Sundkler, *Zulu Zion and Some Swazi Zionists* (London, 1976), pp. 13–67. Even though Sundkler is concerned to highlight the role of missionaries, a role previously neglected by historians, he himself calls the whites "only catalysts" (p. 66).

80. David Barrett, *Schism and Renewal in Africa: An Analysis of Six Thousand Contemporary Religious Movements* (Nairobi, 1968).

God and man actively create a new world). These views implied resources for dealing with needs common to all humankind—curing of illness, rectifying misfortune, and understanding one's place in the cosmos—needs that were, however, intensified by the physical and emotional suffering which accompanied the advance of the frontier. Africans, it seems, were interested in what missionaries taught under both rubrics, but they did not always find the teaching totally satisfying. Before long the early Zionist prophets modified the missionary message to fit Africans' expectations, offering more personal explanations of illness and salvation beyond history, not within it. Zionists sought to strip Christianity of the associations it had acquired on the frontier—associations with Western power and with the autonomous mission station. Zionists also cut away much of the association of Christianity with Western culture. With the beginning of Zionism we have perhaps reached the point where the frontier (but not, of course, its long-term effects) ceased to be of major importance. Africans were now finding in the Christian tradition solutions to problems older (and newer) than the closing of the frontier.

In the last two sections I suggested several connections between the frontier experience and African responses to Christian missions. I argued that, in the early stages of the frontier, the services of the mission station were attractive only to minorities and the disaffected but that the final closing of the frontier gave missions their greatest boost. My analysis of Christian practice and doctrine tended to confirm this view: apparently the emotional and intellectual appeal of Evangelical Christianity intensified as the frontier advanced, guaranteeing that some Africans took refuge, not only in mission stations, but in the teachings and person of Christ.

It is not surprising that Christian missions should owe their limited success to a social crisis. Many religions, Christianity included, easily become civil religions fostering social cohesion and stability. But Christianity in its New Testament form had been a radical protest against law, tradition, entrenched theocratic elites, and national exclusivism; it had won its place in world history in the midst of the collapse of a civilization. And the missionaries strove (with mixed success) to proclaim a New Testament Christianity and to foster revolutionary change. It is not surprising that they were first taken seriously by individuals, and by societies, whose sense of crisis was so deep that they were ready to consider radical solutions.

Further investigation will be necessary, not only to confirm the links I have suggested between the frontier and missions, but also to formulate the links more precisely. Two kinds of clarification are particularly needed. First, the effects of the Mfecane must be disentangled from those of the frontier. This is a difficult task, since the two processes overlapped in some regions and were separated in others by only a decade or two. At the moment one can only suggest that the frontier and the Mfecane both placed similar social and psychological burdens on Africans, but that the frontier, by identifying Christianity with the threatening intruder, presented missionaries with both opportunities and dangers.

Second, we need a more complex model of the closing of the frontier. In this chapter I have assumed that the military closing of the frontier (assertion of European sovereignty) was contemporaneous with economic and social encroachments from European colonies and republics. In practice, of course, this was only very roughly the case, the order of encroachment varying from region to region. We need to learn which aspects of the multifaceted frontier advance most affected religious response. One thing is clear, however. It was not only the objective victories of Europeans which mattered, but also the Africans' subjective realization that they had been beaten. It is striking that the Xhosa suffered through seven wars with the Cape Colony without losing confidence in their traditional world view; it took the disastrous failure of prophecy in the cattle-killing to shake their faith. Religion is part of culture; and in the history of cultures, frontiers close not only on the field of battle but also in the minds of men and women.

LEONARD THOMPSON AND HOWARD LAMAR

Epilogue

When the North American and southern African frontiers closed toward the end of the nineteenth century, the societies in the two regions differed fundamentally. North America had become part of the core of the capitalist economy; southern Africa was still on its periphery. In North America the indigenous polities had disintegrated and the surviving Amerindians formed a negligible fraction of the total population and played no effective part in the economic system. In southern Africa the indigenous cultures were resilient; their members outnumbered people of European origin by more than five to one; and, though they were deprived of political power and economic self-sufficiency, they were indispensable to the regional economy. Despite the presence of a considerable black minority descended from African slaves, North America was irrevocably Europeanized. Southern Africa was an inherently unstable association of African and European peoples and cultures, held together, in the final analysis, by main force.

This contrast was remarkable, considering that both frontier processes were generated and sustained by the same motive force: the explosion of capitalist Europe. The differences among the settlers who went to the two regions—the *habitants* of New France, the Puritans of New England, the Virginians, and the proto-Afrikaners of the Cape Colony—were far less fundamental than those that distinguished them all from all the indigenous peoples of North America and southern Africa. Despite their religious, national, and social cleavages, all European settlers thought of themselves as being members of a common civilization, quite distinct from native Americans and southern Africans. Their first impressions were of striking differences in physical appearance, clothing, and speech; and these were reenforced as they experienced indigenous attitudes toward property—especially land—indigenous political systems, indigenous social bonds and marriage customs, and indigenous rituals and cosmologies. James Axtell and Robert Berkhofer, Christopher Saunders and Richard Elphick have emphasized these differences in their chapters in this volume. The native North Americans and southern Africans were, indeed, small-scale and non-literate societies at the time when white settlers entered their domain. Then, as competition for hegemony occurred in successive frontier zones, the settler communities were sustained and nourished by the lifelines, however tenuous, that they maintained to European culture and technology. For many years they depended on Europe for capital, commodities they could not produce locally, clergy and teachers, and scientific knowledge. The most remote trekboer possessed firearms manufactured in Europe. Until the late eighteenth century in North America and the late nineteenth century in southern Africa, Europe was the settlers' ultimate source of military security. It was a British army, plus local levies, that conquered the Zulu in 1879. Amerindians and Africans had no comparable external sources of strength.

How, then, since both frontiers were branches of the same tree, do we explain the vital contrast between the processes and the outcomes in North America and southern Africa?

The explanation lies principally in two clusters of facts which we shall recapitulate. One is the contrast between the pre-Columbian populations of the two regions—more specifically, between the Amerindians of North America and the Bantu-speaking peoples (though not the Khoisan) of southern Africa. The Bantu-speaking peoples had a far greater capacity to accommodate and survive the impact from Europe than did the Amerindians of North America. They were quite densely settled throughout the more productive lands in the eastern part of southern Africa; they were equipped to withstand the diseases brought by Europeans without catastrophic losses; and their economies had the strength of diversity, since virtually every household derived sustenance from pastoral and arable farming as well as from hunting, and used tools with iron as well as bone, stone, and wooden components. The Amerindian populations of North America, on the other hand, were relatively sparse; they were tragically vulnerable to many of the diseases borne by Europeans; and their economies were relatively fragile, since they had no sheep, no cattle, and no iron technology.

The effects of these differences between the indigenous peoples were compounded by the effects of the differing degrees of commitment of Europe to the two regions, which are demonstrated in the essays by Ramsay Cook and Robert Ross. North America—with its relative proximity to Europe, its river systems providing easy access from the Atlantic deep into the interior, and its resources in fur-bearing animals and fertile soils that could be profitably exploited at each stage of the development of commercial and indus-

trial capitalism—attracted continual infusions of European people and capital, massive enough to generate a complex, diversified trading and farming
economy in the colonial era and a burgeoning industrial economy in the
nineteenth century. In contrast, before the 1870s southern Africa—with its
distance from Europe enhanced by the effects of the equatorial doldrums, its
dearth of navigable rivers, its patchy soils and widely inadequate rainfall—
attracted scarcely any capital and only a miniscule white immigration, and
participated on an insignificant scale in the global economy. Even then, the
opening up of the diamond and gold mines was only the beginning of a long
haul toward a sustaining industrial economy, which would not be achieved
until long after the closing of the frontier.

The other principal frontiers created by the expansion of Europe may be
examined comparatively in this perspective. Australia proves to be a relatively simple case. The indigenous societies of Australia were even weaker
than those of North America, and the region provided considerable potential for capitalist farming and industry, but it lay in the far antipodes from
Europe. Consequently, the history of the Australian frontier is similar to the
history of the North American but was later starting, slower developing,
and smaller in scale. In Meso-America, on the other hand, some factors
resemble those in North America, others those in southern Africa, but
the indigenous people suffered from the fatal flaws of political brittleness
and susceptibility to diseases imported by Europeans. The region possessed
mineral resources that attracted the attention of Europe, but climatic conditions limited the mode and the scale of European settlement. The outcome
in Meso-America was therefore an amalgam between European and native American societies, with stronger indigenous survivals than in North
America and greater cultural and biological integration than in southern
Africa.

Throughout this book we have considered that the frontier processes in
North America and southern Africa "closed" toward the end of the nineteenth century. However, in all historical transitions there are continuities
as well as discontinuities, and we should qualify the closing concept in two
respects. First, although people of European origin had established their *political* hegemony in both regions by 1900, the *economic* and *cultural* processes that began in the frontier contexts have continued with increasing
momentum into the twentieth century. This is particularly true of southern
Africa. In 1900 that region was only in the early stages of industrialization
and most of its inhabitants were scarcely touched by Western education or
Christianity. Today, though South Africa is a rigid, castelike society with
great inequalities of wealth and status, its economy is one of the strongest

in the world, most of its people are baptized Christians, and most of the younger generation are literate.

Second, during the twentieth century white people in both regions have been agents of frontier processes beyond their effective nineteenth-century limits. Although Alaska became de jure an American territory in 1867, in 1900 it was still, in other respects, an open frontier zone; it had less than five thousand Americans, and they were confined to a few coastal and river-side enclaves. Now, Alaska has a burgeoning capitalist economy and over 300,000 Americans from the forty-eight lower states.

The scarcity of white population in Alaska up to the Second World War, and the general neglect by the federal government of that vast territory until 1941, meant that its indigenous peoples—the Aleuts living in the island chain stretching from southwestern Alaska toward Asia, and the mainland Indians and Esquimaux—had a better chance of survival than they would have had if Europeans or Americans had settled Alaska in large numbers during the nineteenth century. Even the ruthless efforts of the Russian American Company, in the eighteenth and nineteenth centuries, to plunder Alaskan furs, by using a hostage-debt peonage system to maintain a labor force of natives as well as Russians did not destroy the Esquimaux and Indian cultures, although the Aleut population was decimated by disease and exploitation. Moreover, statehood (home rule) came for Alaska at a time when blacks and Indian Americans were mounting a successful civil rights movement in the continental United States. The result for Alaska has been, not only a persistence of native peoples and cultures, but also a new respect for both, and the inclusion of indigenous peoples in the political process.

Alaska demonstrates once again how frontiers opening and closing at different times in different environments and with different demographic makeups may follow recognizable sequences yet have remarkably dissimilar outcomes. Today Alaska is a treasure house of natural resources, the benefits of which the inhabitants of the state wish to reserve for themselves. The contests between Alaskans and the federal government, and between the Indian-Esquimaux population and the white entrepreneurs within the state, plus the struggle between the developers and the environmentalists, provide an intriguing variation on the theme of the frontier as a zone of the economic and cultural conflict that has so often been described in this volume. The fact that white Alaskans consider themselves twentieth-century frontiersmen and subscribe to the mores of a frontier culture makes comparative studies all the more compelling; for while the political and cultural frontiers may have closed or reached a state of equilibrium, the economic frontier seems to have remained "open."

In southern Africa, too, at the end of the nineteenth century Mozambique, Rhodesia, and South West Africa still had many of the characteristics of open frontier zones. There, too, white settlement and capitalist penetration increased until quite recently. Now, however, the indigenous peoples have regained control of Mozambique and Zimbabwe; and at the time of writing, the future of Namibia is uncertain and the areas on either side of the Kunene River—its boundary with Angola—are the scene of intense military activity.

The Amazon forest in the interior of Brazil is perhaps the last frontier arising directly from the processes dealt with in this book. There, clusters of indigenous Amerindians were still completely isolated until very recently, but now the modern world is engulfing them in the form of prospectors and settlers, anthropologists and government agents, and diseases are decimating them like their predecessors in North and Meso-America.

Despite these continuities, the frontier processes that were created by the migration of settlers from capitalist Europe to the Americas, Australia, New Zealand, and southern Africa have nearly worked themselves out today; but frontiers of other types abound and are among the most explosive regions in the contemporary world. Several great territorial faults in contemporary human geology are frontier zones along peripheries between major culture areas. The government in Moscow, for example, has to cope with profound problems in the western and southern borderlands of the Soviet Union. In the West, the tensions of an old frontier zone of German-Slav interpenetration are now compounded by ideological factors, as Soviet satellites strive for autonomy; and in the south, non-Slavonic peoples of Muslim faith are still incompletely absorbed into the Marxist-Leninist, Russian-dominated state. In Africa, the Muslim-tropical African fault is an unstable frontier zone, wracked by violence in the Sudan in the 1960s and in Chad in the 1970s and early 1980s. Another type of contemporary frontier conflict is a product of colonialism. For example, the Horn of Africa has a tragic legacy of contested internal boundaries created by the European powers. In the nineteenth century, the disintegration of the Spanish empire led to similar conflicts in Latin America.

Probably the nearest contemporary approach to the kind of frontier dealt with in this book, where rival societies compete for control of the land, is to be found in Israel. There, despite the complex earlier history of Jewish-Arab relations, the contemporary situation is in essence the product of modern Jewish immigration into a territory that had been dominated by Arabs for many centuries. It is a frontier situation with many characteristics that will be familiar to readers of this book: settlement by people with a technology superior to that of the "indigenous" inhabitants and with access to the skills, products, and capital of the industrialized West; their creation of a bridgehead behind the shelter of colonialism; their control of a postcolonial state; and their victories in frontier wars, followed by the incorporation and settlement of conquered territory, the expulsion of many of the indigenous people, and the subjugation and segregation of those remaining. The Israeli frontier is still "open," with raids and counterraids taking place across its contested boundaries; and it remains to be seen whether, when it closes, the state of Israel will be secure or whether it will have been ephemeral, like the white settlements in tropical Africa.

Northern Ireland has a long history as a frontier zone. Settlers from Scotland opened it in the seventeenth century. In 1922 it seemed to many that their descendants had closed the frontier by becoming the dominant majority in a semiautonomous British province detached from the Irish Republic; but Irish Catholics both inside and outside Ulster never accepted that as a final solution, and for more than two decades the province has been the scene of barely controlled warfare, one party depending on Britain and the other party having strong emotional and semiofficial links with the Irish Republic.

During the twentieth century, technological developments have revolutionized conditions in frontier situations. The devastating power of modern "conventional" weapons; the latent threat of nuclear warfare; rapid transportation of people and goods by land, sea, and air; instantaneous communication of news and views by radio and television; snooping by satellite photography and electronic recorders—all such innovations have drastically reduced the autonomy of frontier zones. The most remote regions are now potential victims of great power rivalry, and in nearly every case Washington or Moscow (or perhaps both) is deeply involved, either directly or through surrogates.

Nevertheless, all frontiers possess similar central characteristics. Readers of this book should not be surprised at the political complexities of the Ulster frontier, the effects of capitalist development in Israel, or the resilience of Islam in Iran. Nor should any student of British imperialism in nineteenth-century Africa or of the recent American involvement in Vietnam fail to realize that Soviet intervention in Afghanistan today (and perhaps in Iran or Pakistan tomorrow) may be a somewhat confused response to the suction effect created by a turbulent frontier, rather than an expression of a coherent program of aggression.

In conclusion, the editors of this volume join the contributors to it in asserting that by applying the comparative approach to frontier history we are opening a discussion rather than closing one. Indeed, our primary aim has been to provide a model for further study of the way in which native peoples and Europeans have met and interacted in frontier zones since the time of Columbus and Vasco da Gama. We hope that future discussions will not only proceed analytically, but that they will take place on two levels— that is to say, at the building-block stage as well as at the level of sophisticated concepts. As Robert Berkhofer has written, despite the impression that there was a repetitive pattern in successive frontier zones in North America, we desperately need more studies of specific frontier situations as a basis for strengthening our comparative perspectives.

Large gaps may also be found in the chronicle of the white frontier process, whether North American or southern African. To mention only one of many omissions in the treatment of white frontier society in this volume, it is notable that the role of the family as an important unit of authority as well as an economic unit has had inadequate coverage both here and elsewhere in the literature. Regardless of whether one is speaking of Indians, or blacks, or whites, the role of women in a frontier situation needs to be studied from a number of perspectives, be it from that of helpmates, intermarriage, or as a governing force both within and outside the family unit.

In short, we have only begun to identify the many determining factors—public and private, social and economic, metropolitan and local—that shape a frontier relationship between peoples. What we have conveniently but sometimes incorrectly called a temporary, "anarchic" situation in which no one side is in control, has been a frontier way of life (sometimes brilliantly orchestrated, as in the case of Moshoeshoe) which could last for generations. As the essayists have already demonstrated, it was a way of life that determined local forms of government, the economy, and the culture. It is still a way of life that can and does exist whenever one people intrudes upon another.

At the same time, it is also our hope that the sensitivity and complexity of the comparative approach will offer opportunities to understand the frontier process in ways that imperial, diplomatic, ethnic, political, and economic history do not; for if—as the various authors here contend—Indian-white and black-white relations were secondary in importance to Indian-Indian and black-black relations throughout most of the frontier period, then this fact must be understood in proper context—that is, in the frontier zone and period itself.

The irony of Frederick Jackson Turner's lasting eminence as a frontier historian is that he thought he was describing a zone, a process, a period, and an outcome that were unique to the American experience. What he was actually describing—however inadequately and one-sidedly—was one example of the many frontiers generated by the capitalist system and European settlers, which in turn constitute a particular species of a process that takes place whenever one people intrudes into terrain occupied by another. We hope that these essays will contribute toward the understanding of that universal and still ongoing historical process.

GEORGE MILES   # A Comparative Frontiers Bibliography

Although many scholars have expressed an interest in comparative frontier history, few have actually produced any significant work on the subject. Frederick Jackson Turner himself urged historians to pursue comparative research in a 1904 address entitled "Problems in American History" (later published in *The Significance of Section in American History*, New York, 1932), but the regional specialization characteristic of historians seems to have dissuaded most of them from heeding Turner's call. Few scholars are familiar with the history or historiography of more than one frontier; their comparisons are likely to be superficial at best. This essay seeks to reduce this obstacle by making the basic frontier historiography of North America and southern Africa accessible to the nonspecialist. Its purpose is to introduce Africanists to the American literature and vice versa. As such, it is a preliminary guide; readers should consult the bibliographies cited below for further coverage of the extensive literature which has accumulated on both the southern African and the North American frontiers. Many of the titles cited are still in print. Nearly all will be available at an average college library.

Readers interested in the evolution of comparative frontier history should consult the works cited in the notes to chapter 1. Also helpful are Dietrich Gerhard, "The Frontier in Comparative View," *Comparative Studies in Society and History* 1 (1959): 205–29, and J. L. M. Gulley, "The Turnerian Frontier: A Study in the Migration of Ideas," *Tijdschrift voor Economische .en Sociale Geographie* 50 (1959): 65–72 and 81–91. Alastair Hennessy, *The Frontier in Latin American History* (London, 1978), includes a thorough, thoughtful bibliographic essay which discusses many comparative efforts. For a recent statement on the subject by an American historian,

317

see W. Turrentine Jackson, "A Brief Message for the Young and/or Ambitious: Comparative Frontiers as a Field for Investigation," *Western Historical Quarterly* 9 (1978): 4–18.

Several scholars have already undertaken broad comparisons of North American and southern African frontiers. Louis Hartz, *The Founding of New Societies: Studies in the History of the United States, Latin America, South Africa, Canada and Australia* (Boston, 1964), examines the process by which social "fragments" differentiated themselves from their European origins to become distinct societies. Richard B. Ford, "The Frontier in South Africa: A Comparative Study of the Turner Thesis" (Ph.D. diss., University of Denver, 1966), finds many incongruities between Turner's thesis and the southern African experience. Religious developments on the frontier are examined in M. Boucher, "The Frontier and Religion: A Comparative Study of the United States of America and South Africa in the First Half of the Nineteenth Century," *Archives Yearbook for South African History* 31, no. 2 (1968): 1–114.

Two briefer studies which compare particular aspects of frontier development in North America and South Africa are especially valuable. Hermann Giliomee illuminates political processes in the two regions in "Democracy and the Frontier," *South African Historical Journal* 6 (1974): 30–55. Patterns of land use are explored in R. Cole Harris and Leonard Guelke, "Land and Society in Early Canada and South Africa," *Journal of Historical Geography* 3 (1977): 135–53. Finally, scholars interested in comparing North American and southern African development should be aware of George M. Fredrickson's *White Supremacy: A Comparative Study in American and South African History* (New York, 1980), which makes extremely valuable comparisons of major processes of race relations in the two regions.

PART 1: THE NORTH AMERICAN FRONTIER

Heavily influenced by the ideas of Frederick Jackson Turner, Ray Allen Billington's *Westward Expansion: A History of the American Frontier*, 4th ed. (New York, 1978) and Frederick Merk's *History of the Westward Movement* (New York, 1978) offer comprehensive, systematic accounts of white settlement. Like Turner, Billington and Merk neglect the Indian experience; their surveys should be supplemented with Wilcomb Washburn's *The Indian in America* (New York, 1975). Washburn occasionally oversimplifies, but he combines an informed discussion of patterns in Indian history with a lucid presentation of the frontier's advance across the continent. Scholars wishing to explore a particular region or period of white expansion should consult the *Histories of the American Frontier Series*, ed. Ray A. Billington and

Howard R. Lamar (New York, 1963–71; Albuquerque, 1971–). Many volumes in the series have become the standard authorities on their subjects. For background on people, places, and events, see *The Reader's Encyclopedia of the American West,* ed. Howard R. Lamar (New York, 1977).

The most helpful guide to American frontier historiography is *Westward Expansion*'s superb bibliographic essay, which discusses several thousand titles. Also useful are Rodman W. Paul and Richard W. Etulain, *The Frontier and the American West* (Arlington Heights, Ill., 1977), and George Peter Murdock and Timothy J. O'Leary, *Ethnographic Bibliography of North America,* 4th ed., 5 vols. (New Haven, 1975), which lists nearly every significant study of Indian history or culture published before 1973.

Several journals are especially relevant for students of the American frontier. *The Journal of American History* (Bloomington, Ind.) and *Ethnohistory* (Bloomington, Ind.) publish articles on a variety of frontier-related topics. *The William and Mary Quarterly* (Williamsburg, Va.) concentrates on early American history, while the *Pacific Historical Review* (Berkeley, Calif.) and *The Western Historical Quarterly* (Logan, Utah) generally focus on the history of the Trans-Mississippi West. Articles from all five journals, as well as from some 2,000 other periodicals, are abstracted in *America: History and Life,* ed. Eric H. Boehm (Santa Barbara, Calif., 1964–).

American frontier history has been clouded by the many myths that have enveloped American Indians. By illuminating past misconceptions, Roy Harvey Pearce's *Savagism and Civilization: A Study of the Indian and the American Mind,* 2d ed. (Baltimore, 1965) and Robert F. Berkhofer's *The White Man's Indian: Images of the American Indian from Columbus to the Present* (New York, 1978) clarify our understanding of frontier interaction. Irving Hallowell's "The Backwash of the Frontier: The Impact of the Indian on American Culture," Smithsonian Institute, *Annual Report for the Year Ending June 30th, 1958,* (1959), pp. 447–72, examines the often subtle ways in which Indian culture influenced white society.

For the last quarter-century, American archeologists, anthropologists, and historians have worked together to increase our knowledge of Native American peoples. Their cooperative efforts have culminated in *The Handbook of North American Indians,* ed. William Sturtevant, 20 vols. (Washington, D.C., 1978–) which, when completed, will become the authority on most aspects of Indian history and ethnography. Three volumes, *California, The Northeast,* and *The Southwest, Volume One* have been released; future volumes will complete a regional survey of North America and consider related topics such as the history of federal Indian policy. For a scholarly but nontechnical introduction to Indian cultures, see Robert F. Spencer et al., *The Native Americans,* 2d ed. (New York, 1977).

The recognition that European expansion sent biological shock waves in advance of white settlement has led scholars to increase traditional estimates of pre-Columbian Indian populations. Henry F. Dobyns, *Native American Historical Demography* (Bloomington, Ind., 1976), reviews the literature and discusses new estimates. The process of depopulation is analyzed in Sherburne F. Cook, *The Conflict Between the California Indians and White Civilization* (Berkeley, Calif., 1976) and Alfred W. Crosby, Jr., "Virgin Soil Epidemics as a Factor in the Aboriginal Depopulation in America," *William and Mary Quarterly*, 3d ser. 33 (1976): 289–99. The broader implications of the collision between Old and New World ecosystems are considered in Alfred W. Crosby, Jr., *The Columbian Exchange: Biological and Cultural Consequences of 1492* (Westport, Conn., 1972).

American anthropologists have expended much energy describing and analyzing cultural change among Indian societies. Three valuable anthologies trace their efforts. *Perspectives in American Indian Culture*, ed. Edward Spicer (Chicago, 1961) compares the frontier experiences and acculturative patterns of six Indian communities in an effort to establish a relationship between the two. *The North American Indians in Historical Perspective*, ed. Eleanor B. Leacock and Nancy O. Lurie (New York, 1971) discusses patterns of change among Indian people. *The Emergent Native Americans: A Reader in Culture Change*, ed. Deward E. Walker, Jr. (Boston, 1972) presents a series of outstanding ethnohistorical essays on the theme of cultural interaction. The three anthologies illuminate the pressures and opportunities the frontier brought to Indians as well as the concepts which anthropologists have developed to describe Indian responses.

This essay can cite only a few of the many exciting, innovative works published about early American frontier history in recent years. For a thorough, thoughtful consideration of the literature, see James Axtell, "The Ethnohistory of Early America: A Review Essay," *William and Mary Quarterly*, 3d ser. 35 (1978): 110–44.

Early European explorations are traced in David B. Quinn's *North America from Earliest Discovery to First Settlements: The Norse Voyages to 1612* (New York, 1977). Carl O. Sauer, *Sixteenth Century North America: The Land and the People as Seen by the Europeans* (Berkeley, Calif., 1971) reconstructs the social and natural environments that Europeans encountered. White perceptions of the land and its inhabitants are examined in Peter Carroll, *Puritanism and the Wilderness* (New York, 1969), Richard Slotkin, *Regeneration through Violence: The Mythology of the American Frontier 1600–1860* (Middletown, Conn., 1973), and Karen O. Kupperman, *Settling with the Indians: The Meeting of English and Indian Cultures in America, 1580–1640* (Totowa, N.J., 1980).

For a comprehensive consideration of one Indian community's experience on the early frontier, see Bruce Trigger's monumental study, *The Children of the Aataentsic: A History of the Huron People to 1660*, 2 vols. (Montreal, 1976). Trigger assesses the relative impact of trade and religious proselytization on the Huron and analyzes their response to crises of disease and war. Indian diplomatic initiatives are discussed in Nancy O. Lurie, "Indian Cultural Adjustment to White Civilization," *Seventeenth Century North America*, ed. James M. Smith (Chapel Hill, N.C., 1959), pp. 33–60, and Bruce Trigger, "The Mohawk-Mahican War (1624–1628): The Establishment of a Pattern," *Canadian Historical Review* 51 (1971):276–86.

Among the most controversial issues of early frontier history is the character of Puritan Indian policy. Alden Vaughan, *New England Frontier: Puritans and Indians, 1620–1675* (Boston, 1965), portrays Puritans as sincerely interested in the welfare of Indians. He suggests that cultural differences, not Puritan hostility, prevented accommodation between the two groups. Francis Jennings's *The Invasion of North America: Indians, Colonialism and the Cant of Conquest* (Chapel Hill, N.C., 1975), argues that Puritans exaggerated the differences between Indian and English cultures to obscure the true character of their policy. Jennings also criticizes historians for reinforcing rather than exposing Puritan propaganda. For a judicious consideration of the controversy Jennings has generated, see James P. Ronda, "Beyond Thanksgiving: Francis Jennings' *Invasion of North America*," *The Journal of Ethnic Studies* 7 (1979):88–94. Indian-white relations in the colonial South are addressed in Bernard W. Sheehan, *Savagism and Civility: Indians and Englishmen in Colonial Virginia* (New York, 1980).

Edmund S. Morgan, *American Slavery, American Freedom: The Ordeal of Colonial Virginia* (New York, 1975), illustrates the importance of commercial considerations on the colonial frontier. Morgan reveals the depth of Virginia's dependence on tobacco and explores how the socioeconomic character of the Virginia frontier contributed to the emergence of chattel slavery. The growth of commercial agriculture and its expansion westward are considered in James T. Lemon, *The Best Poor Man's Country: A Geographical Study of Early Southeastern Pennsylvania* (Baltimore, 1972), and Robert D. Mitchell, *Commercialism and Frontier: Perspectives on the Early Shenandoah Valley* (Charlottesville, Va., 1977).

Initially a commercial venture, the colonial fur trade became an important vehicle of political as well as economic interaction. Most studies of the trade have adopted a regional focus and emphasized its social and diplomatic aspects. Among the more valuable accounts are W. J. Eccles, *The Canadian Frontier, 1534–1760* (New York, 1969); Allen W. Trelease, *Indian Affairs in Colonial New York: The Seventeenth Century* (Ithaca, N.Y., 1960), and Verner W. Crane, *The Southern Frontier, 1670–1732*, 3d ed., with an introduction by Peter H. Wood (New York, 1979).

Two recent studies advance radically different views of Indian motives for participating in the fur trade. In *Keepers of the Game: Indian-Animal Relationships and the Fur Trade* (Berkeley, Calif., 1978), Calvin Martin depicts the Indians' aggressive pursuit of furs as less a response to economic opportunity than a holy war against animal spirits which they believed had inflicted the epidemics caused by European expansion. In sharp contrast, Arthur J. Ray and Donald Freeman's *"Give Us Good Measure": An Economic Analysis of Relations between the Indians and the Hudson's Bay Company before 1763* (Toronto, 1978) refutes allegations of noneconomic behavior among Indians and examines how Indians and the Company overcame differences in economic customs to develop a lasting business relationship. Some scholars have applauded Martin's thesis for its imagination and ingenuity, but others have severely criticized it as insufficiently substantiated. The careful analysis of Ray and Freeman seems more likely to influence the course of future research.

There is no adequate survey of Indian-white diplomacy in the eighteenth century, but see Francis Jennings, "The Constitutional Evolution of the Covenant Chain," American Philosophical Society, *Proceedings* 115 (1971): 88–96, for a discussion of the changing character of British relations with the Iroquois and their confederates. White efforts to cultivate Indian allies are explored in Wilbur Jacobs, *Wilderness Politics and Indian Gifts: The Northern Colonial Frontier, 1748–1763* (Lincoln, Neb., 1969), which examines the British and French competition for influence in the Ohio Valley, and Richard R. Johnson, "The Search for a Usable Indian: An Aspect of the Defence of Colonial New England," *Journal of American History* 64 (1977): 623–51, which considers New England's efforts to recruit Indian forces for protection against the French and their Indian allies.

Indian-white relations were never again as balanced as they were in the eighteenth century, nor were they ever again as intimate. The character of the relationship is explored in Gary B. Nash's *Red, White and Black: The Peoples of Early America* (Englewood Cliffs, N.J., 1974). Nash argues that cultural diversity and ethnic interaction are central themes of colonial history. The incorporation of captive whites by Indian societies is discussed in James Axtell, "The White Indians of Colonial America," *William and Mary Quarterly*, 3d ser. 32 (1975): 55–88. For a discussion of white efforts to manipulate relations between blacks and Indians, see William S. Willis, "Divide and Rule: Red, White and Black in the Southwest," *Journal of Negro History* 48 (1963): 157–76.

The most thorough consideration of Indian initiatives on the late colonial frontier is Anthony F. C. Wallace, *The Death and Rebirth of the Seneca* (New York, 1970). Wallace reconstructs the successful efforts of the Seneca, under the direction of the religious leader Handsome Lake, to preserve their cultural integrity and identity despite their loss of political autonomy. Also valuable is Frederick O. Gearing, *Priests and Warriors: Social Structures for Cherokee Politics in the Eighteenth Century* (Menasha, Wis., 1962), which examines Cherokee efforts to develop a political system capable of withstanding the pressures generated by the frontier.

After the American Revolution removed imperial restraints on expansion, Americans quickly incorporated the Trans-Appalachian West within the United States. Reginald Horsman's *Expansion and American Indian Policy 1783–1812* (East Lansing, Mich., 1967) argues that the new government viewed expansion as a vindication of America's republican virtue and expected Indians to accept it as inevitable and desirable. Bernard W. Sheehan's *Seeds of Extinction: Jeffersonian Philanthropy and the American Indian* (Chapel Hill, N.C., 1973) discusses the government's efforts to "civilize" the Indians and make them part of the republic. The failure of the effort is considered in two essays by Reginald Horsman: "The Origins of Indian Removal 1815–1824," The Historical Society of Michigan, *Clarence M. Burton Memorial Lecture for 1969* (n.p., 1970), and "American Indian Policy and the Origins of Manifest Destiny," *The Indian in American History*, ed. Francis Paul Prucha (New York, 1971), pp. 20–28. Horsman concludes that the decision to force eastern Indians to emigrate west of the Mississippi signaled the end of sincere efforts to incorporate Indians as equals into white society and set the tone for future American expansion.

There is no comprehensive study of the Indian experience on the early national frontier; but see *Black Hawk: An Autobiography*, ed. Donald Jackson (Urbana, Ill., 1955) for a classic statement of one Indian's experiences. First published in 1833, the volume recounts Black Hawk's life as a leading man among the Sauk and Fox Indians. Intra-Indian political competition is analyzed in P. Richard Metcalf's "Who Should Rule at Home: Native American Politics and Indian-White Relations," *Journal of American History* 61 (1974):651–65.

Socioeconomic developments among white frontiersmen are explored in Malcolm J. Rohrbough's *The Trans-Appalachian Frontier: People, Societies and Institutions 1775–1850* (New York, 1978) and James E. Davis, *Frontier America 1800–1840: A Comparative Demographic Analysis of the Frontier Process* (Glendale, Calif., 1977). Agricultural expansion is addressed in Paul W. Gates, *The Farmer's Age: Agriculture, 1815–1860* (New York, 1960), while the growth of commercial centers is explored in Richard C. Wade's *The Urban Frontier: The Rise of Western Cities, 1790–1830* (Cambridge, Mass., 1959). Stanley Elkins and Eric McKitrick analyze differences between the northern and southern frontiers in "A Meaning for Turner's Frontier," *Political Science Quarterly* 69 (1954): 321–53 and 565–602.

The religious fervor of the early nineteenth-century frontier was perhaps its most prominent feature. Methodist revivalism is examined in Charles A. Johnson's *The Frontier Camp Meeting: Religion's Harvest Time* (Dallas, 1955). T. Scott Miyakawa, *Protestants and Pioneers: Invididualism and Conformity on the American Frontier* (Chicago, 1964), assesses the social impact of religious institutions. Robert F. Berkhofer, Jr., *Salvation and the Savage: An Analysis of Protestant Missions and American Indian Response, 1787–1862* (Lexington, Ky., 1965), explores missionary efforts to acculturate as well as convert Indians.

The final period of American expansion opened in the 1820s, as traders and explorers began to penetrate the Trans-Mississippi West. The definitive account of their efforts is William H. Goetzmann's *Exploration and Empire: The Explorer and the Scientist in the Winning of the American West* (New York, 1966). Henry Nash Smith's *Virgin Land: The American West as Symbol and Myth* (Cambridge, Mass., 1950) examines how American images of the frontier influenced their conceptions of the Far West. The ideological underpinnings of expansion are analyzed in Frederick Merk's *Manifest Destiny and Mission in American History* (New York, 1966).

In the West, Americans encountered Indian societies that were adjusting to a series of cultural stresses. Preston Holder's *The Hoe and the Horse on the Plains: A Study of Cultural Development among North American Indians* (Lincoln, Neb., 1970) examines the strains which equestrian buffalo hunting on the open plains brought to societies which had farmed in the region's wooded river valleys. In "The Winning of the West: The Expansion of the Western Sioux in the Eighteenth and Nineteenth Centuries," *Journal of American History* 65 (1978): 319–43, Richard White argues that historians must recognize that most Plains Indians feared the Sioux more than they did Americans before they can understand the course of Indian-white relations in the region.

Many scholars have examined the character and influence of the western fur trade. Howard R. Lamar, *The Trader on the American Frontier: Myth's Victim* (College Station, Tex., 1977), reconsiders traditional views and emphasizes the trader's role as mediator between cultures. The increasing dependence of Indians on the trade is examined in Arthur J. Ray, *Indians in the Fur Trade: Their Role as Hunters, Trappers and Middlemen in the Lands Southwest of Hudson Bay, 1660–1870* (Toronto, 1974).

No adequate survey of economic developments on the Western frontier exists, but see John W. Reps, *Cities of the American West: A History of Frontier Urban Planning* (Princeton, N.J., 1980) for a consideration of the crucial role of urban centers in stimulating and organizing economic growth. George Harwood Phillips, "Indians in Los Angeles, 1781–1875: Economic Integration, Social Disintegration," *Pacific Historical Review* 49 (1980): 427–51, analyzes the importance of Indian labor in the growth of Los Angeles and the destructive impact of white systems of labor recruitment. The efforts of town residents to promote their communities are analyzed in Robert R. Dykstra's *The Cattle Towns* (New York, 1976). Rodman W. Paul's *Mining Frontiers of the Far West 1848–1880* (New York, 1963) illustrates the importance of technological developments in unlocking the West's resources, while Allan G. Bogue, *Money at Interest: The Farm Mortgage on the Middle Border* (Ithaca, N.Y., 1955), and Robert P. Swierenga's *Pioneers and Profits: Land Speculation on the Iowa Frontier* (Ames, Iowa, 1968), explore the financial apparatus of agricultural expansion. For a consideration of the farmer's experience, see Gilbert C. Fite, *The Farmers' Frontier 1865–1900* (New York, 1966).

Government efforts to stimulate settlement and economic development are examined in Paul W. Gates, *Landlords and Tenants on the American Frontier: Studies in American Land Policy* (Ithaca, N.Y., 1973), and Wallace D. Farnham, "The Weakened Spring of Government: A Study in Nineteenth Century American History," *American Historical Review* 68 (1963): 662–80. Two older studies which remain valuable are James B. Hedges, "The Promotion of Immigration to the Pacific Northwest by the Railroads," *Mississippi Valley Historical Review* 15 (1928): 183–203, and Paul W. Gates, "The Homestead Act in an Incongruous Land System," *American Historical Review* 41 (1936): 652–81.

Demographic trends are explored in Jack E. Eblen, "An Analysis of Nineteenth Century Frontier Populations," *Demography* 2 (1965): 399–413. The influence of familial relationships is addressed in Blaine T. Williams, "The Frontier Family: Demographic Fact and Frontier Myth," *Essays on the American West*, ed. Harold M. Hollingsworth and Sandra L. Myres (Austin, Tex., 1969) and John C. Ewers, "Mothers of the Mixed Bloods: The Marginal Woman in the History of the Upper Missouri," *Probing the American West: Papers from the Santa Fe Conference*, ed. K. Ross Toole et al. (Santa Fe, N. Mex., 1962).

Political conflict among white settlers generally focused on land. Paul W. Gates, *Fifty Million Acres: Conflicts over Kansas Land Policy 1854–1890* (Ithaca, 1954), emphasizes the local factors which contributed to the creation of "Bleeding Kansas." Ethnocultural conflict and competition for control of land are the central themes of Leonard Pitt's *The Decline of the Californios: A Social History of Spanish Speaking Californians, 1846–1890* (Berkeley, Calif., 1966). Howard R. Lamar's *The Far Southwest, 1846–1912:*

A Territorial History (New Haven, Conn., 1966) places ethnic conflict and the struggle for control of economic resources within the framework of the federal government's territorial system.

The response of western Indians to white encroachment is considered in George Harwood Phillips, *Chiefs and Challengers: Indian Resistance and Cooperation in Southern California* (Berkeley, Calif., 1975), and Robert M. Utley, *The Last Days of the Sioux Nation* (New Haven, Conn., 1963). Religious developments are examined in James Mooney, *The Ghost Dance Religion and the Sioux Outbreak of 1890*, ed. Anthony F. C. Wallace (Chicago, 1965), and Deward E. Walker, Jr., *Conflict and Schism in Nez Perce Acculturation: A Study of Religion and Politics* (Pullman, Wash., 1968). The often fatal consequences of white conquest are vividly depicted in Theodora Kroeber's *Ishi in Two Worlds* (Berkeley, Calif., 1961), a biography of the last survivor of the Yahi Indian community. The valor and dignity of Ishi's story offer an ironic counterpoint to the tragic demise of his people.

The military history of the American frontier is thoroughly surveyed in three volumes. See Francis P. Prucha, *The Sword of the Republic: The United States Army on the Frontier, 1783–1846* (New York, 1969), and Robert M. Utley, *Frontiersmen in Blue: The United States Army and the Indian, 1848–1865* (New York, 1967), and *Frontier Regulars: The United States Army and the Indian, 1866–1890* (New York, 1973). For a discussion of Plains Indian military tactics and objectives, see Marian W. Smith, "The War Complex of the Plains Indians," American Philosophical Society, *Proceedings* 78 (1937):425–61. James Axtell and William C. Sturtevant, "The Unkindest Cut, or Who Invented Scalping," *The William and Mary Quarterly*, 3d ser. 37 (1980):451–72, is a thorough and judicious consideration of the origins of scalping.

Although a consideration of the Spanish-Indian frontier of the Southwest is beyond the scope of this essay, no bibliography of the North American frontier can omit two outstanding pieces of frontier history. Herbert Bolton's "The Mission as a Frontier Institution in the Spanish American Colonies," *American Historical Review* 23 (1917–18):42–61, defined a field of research which has occupied several generations of scholars. For an assessment of Bolton's accomplishment and of the work he inspired, see John Francis Bannon, "The Mission as a Frontier Institution: Sixty Years of Interest and Research," *Western Historical Quarterly* 10 (1979):303–22. Edward Spicer's *Cycles of Conquest: The Impact of Spain, Mexico and the United States on the Indians of the Southwest, 1553–1960* (Tuscon, Ariz., 1962) remains one of the most ambitious and thorough studies of frontier history ever completed. Spicer interweaves concrete detail, anthropological theory, and historical analysis in a skillful manner which makes his account important reading for anyone who wishes to understand more clearly the history of the American frontier in particular or the frontier experience in general.

PART 2: THE SOUTHERN AFRICAN FRONTIER

Southern African historiography has developed three faces in recent years: Afrikaner, Liberal, and Radical. The schools share important concerns but differ sharply on many issues, including the significance of the frontier. None of the schools can be considered apolitical, and the current tension over the future of southern Africa has intensified the scholarly debate, making it unusually acrimonious and highlighting the distinctiveness of each approach.

Few Americans read Afrikaans, the only language in which most studies by Afrikaners have been published. Consequently this essay, while citing several important studies by Afrikaner historians, considers primarily the work of Liberal and Radical scholars.

The development of South African historiography and the character of the current controversy have been the subjects of several studies. Two essays by Leonard Thompson, though somewhat dated, remain useful. "South Africa," *The Historiography of the British Empire-Commonwealth*, ed. Robin Winks (Durham, N.C., 1966), surveys the literature, reviews published records, and describes the archival system. In "Afrikaner Nationalist Historiography and the Policy of Apartheid," *Journal of African History* 3 (1962): 125–41, Thompson considers the relationship between white supremacist ideology and the Afrikaner tradition. Martin Legassick's "The Frontier Tradition in South African Historiography," *The Societies of Southern Africa in the 19th and 20th Centuries* (University of London, Institute of Commonwealth Studies) 2 (1971): 1–33, criticizes Liberal scholars for anachronistically projecting postfrontier circumstances onto the frontier. For further consideration of the issues raised by Legassick, see Harrison M. Wright's *The Burden of the Present: Liberal-Radical Controversy over Southern African History* (London, 1977).

There are many surveys of South African history. Among the most valuable is *The Oxford History of South Africa*, ed. Monica Wilson and Leonard Thompson, 2 vols. (Oxford, 1969, 1971). The editors criticize the ethnocentricity of earlier texts and stress the interaction of Europeans and Africans as the central theme of frontier history. *Beyond the Cape Frontier: Studies in the History of the Transkei and Ciskei*, ed. Christopher C. Saunders and Robin Derricourt (London, 1974) employs an interpretive framework similar to that of *The Oxford History* in order to explore the story of an often neglected region. The Afrikaner perspective is expressed in *Five*

Hundred Years, A History of South Africa, ed. C. F. J. Muller, 2d ed. rev. (Cape Town, 1975) and F. A. van Jaarsveld, *The Afrikaner's Interpretation of South African History* (Johannesburg, 1963) and *Van Van Riebeeck tot Verwoerd, 1652–1966* (Johannesburg, 1971).

Five Hundred Years and *The Oxford History* include extensive bibliographies. The most comprehensive guide to the literature is C. F. J. Muller et al., *A Select Bibliography of South African History: A Guide for Historical Research* (Pretoria, 1966), with a *Supplement* (1974). Isaac Schapera first organized the literature on African peoples in his *Select Bibliography of South African Native Life and Problems* (Cape Town, 1941). Three supplementary volumes have been compiled by scholars following Schapera's tradition. Also useful for students of the frontier is Leonard Thompson et al., *Southern African History Before 1900: A Select Bibliography of Articles* (Stanford, Calif., 1971).

Scholars may keep abreast of the literature through several periodicals. *The Journal of African History* (*JAfH*) (Cambridge, England) frequently considers southern African frontier topics. Also helpful are the *Journal of Southern African Studies* (Oxford) and the *South African Historical Journal* (Bloemfontein). Many important ideas in southern African frontier history have been presented at London University's Institute of Commonwealth Studies and later published in the Institute's annual Collected Seminar Papers on *The Societies of Southern Africa in the 19th and 20th Centuries*. *The Archives Yearbook for South African History* (*AYB*) (Johannesburg) addresses the frontier less often but has published several valuable studies.

The origins and development of African cultures and societies are traced in R. R. Inskeep, *Peopling of South Africa* (New York, 1979), and D. W. Phillipson, *The Later Prehistory of Eastern and Southern Africa* (London, 1977). Although there is no comprehensive ethnographic survey of southern Africa, there are many excellent monographs on individual societies. Monica Wilson's *Reaction to Conquest*, 2d ed. (New York, 1961), a study of the Mpondo, is one example. Isaac Schapera's *Government and Politics in Tribal Societies* (London, 1956; New York, 1967) compares several southern African polities but is limited in the scope of its inquiry. *African Societies in Southern Africa*, ed. Leonard M. Thompson (London, 1969) is a collection of important ethnohistorical essays. It was not, however, intended as an introductory text and should be supplemented with chapters 2, 3, and 4 in vol. 1 of *The Oxford History*, in which Monica Wilson summarizes the early history of southern Africa's indigenous peoples.

The history of the Cape frontier has attracted much attention of late. For an excellent introduction to the recent scholarship, see *The Shaping of South African Society, 1652–1820*, ed. Richard Elphick and Hermann

Giliomee (Cape Town, 1979). Based on extensive archival research, the volume offers fresh insights into nearly every aspect of the early frontier.

The African experience on the Cape frontier is described in Richard Elphick's thoroughly researched and deftly argued *Kraal and Castle: Khoikhoi and the Founding of White South Africa* (New Haven, Conn., 1977). Elphick shows how the socioeconomic customs of the Khoikhoi increased their vulnerability to subjugation by the Dutch. His analysis may be complemented by two essays on African opposition to European expansion: Shula Marks, "Khoisan Resistance to the Dutch in the Seventeenth and Eighteenth Centuries," *JAfH* 13 (1972): 55–80, and Robert Ross, "The !Kora Wars on the Orange River, 1830–1880," *JAfH* 16 (1975): 561–76.

There is no definitive account of early European forays into the interior, but see Norman H. Mackenzie, "South African Travel Literature in the Seventeenth Century," *AYB* 18, no. 2 (1955): 1–112, and Vernon S. Forbes, *Pioneer Travellers in South Africa* (Cape Town, 1965).

The authority on the trekboers is the meticulous P. J. van der Merwe. See his *Die Noordwaartse Beweging van die Boere vor die Groot Trek* (The Hague, 1938), *Die Trekboer in die Geskiedenis van die Kaap Kolonie* (Cape Town, 1938), and *Trek, Studies oor die Mobiliteit van die Pioniersbevolking aan die Kaap* (Cape Town, 1945).

Van der Merwe's interpretation of trekking as a noncommercial, subsistence way of life was challenged by Solomon D. Neumark's *Economic Influences on the South African Frontier, 1652–1836* (Stanford, Calif., 1957). Most reviewers, however, have criticized Neumark for exaggerating commercial considerations. For a trenchant appraisal of the controversy, see W. K. Hancock, "Trek," *Economic History Review*, 2d ser. 10 (1957–58): 331–39. Hancock argues that the question is not whether frontiersmen ever traded their produce, but how important trade was to their lifestyle. That historians have not resolved the issue is illustrated by a recent exchange: see Leonard Guelke, "Frontier Settlement in Early Dutch South Africa," Association of American Geographers, *Annals* 66 (1976): 25–42, and William Norton and Leonard Guelke, "Commentary: Frontier Agriculture: Subsistence or Commercial? With a Reply," ibid. 67 (1977): 463–77.

There is no general account of the tumult which enveloped the Eastern Cape frontier in the late eighteenth century, but several studies tell portions of the story. In *Maynier and the First Boer Republic* (Cape Town, 1944; reprinted 1962), Johannes S. Marais discusses the Afrikaners' reactions to the social and economic crises they perceived. The African experience is discussed in John Alan Hopper, "Xhosa-Colonial Relations, 1770–1803" (Ph.D. diss., Yale University, 1980). The Dutch government's efforts to stabilize the region are examined in William Freund, "The Eastern Frontier of the Cape Colony during the Batavian Period (1803–06)," *JAfH* 13 (1972): 631–45. For an analysis of varied responses to the situation by African religious leaders, see J. B. Peires, "Nxele, Ntsikana and the Origins of the Xhosa Religious Reaction," *JAfH* 20 (1979): 51–62.

Other than Elphick's story of the Khoikhoi, little has been written on economic relations between Europeans and Africans on the early Cape frontier. H. M. Robertson's path-breaking study, "150 Years of Economic Contact between Black and White: A Preliminary Survey," *South African Journal of Economics* 2 (1943): 403–25, and 3 (1935): 3–25, briefly considers the late eighteenth century, but like most work on the topic, it emphasizes nineteenth-century developments.

The Cape frontier's influence on the evolution of racial stratification is a controversial issue. Ian D. MacCrone's *Race Attitudes in South Africa: Historical, Experimental and Psychological Studies* (London, 1937; Johannesburg, 1957) stood as the classic statement on the question for many years, but recently his ascription of white racism to seventeenth- and eighteenth-century frontier conflicts has been severely criticized. In particular, see Martin Legassick's "The Frontier Tradition in South African Historiography" (cited above), which suggests that the early frontier was relatively free of rigid racial divisions.

Many historians have sought the origins of racial stratification in European treatment of the Cape's mixed-blood population, the so-called Coloured people. The seminal work on the subject, William M. MacMillan's *The Cape Colour Question: A Historical Survey* (London, 1927; Cape Town, 1968), contrasts the attitudes of British officials, especially missionaries, with those of Afrikaner frontiersmen. Although subsequent studies owe much to MacMillan's pioneering effort, his work is flawed by oversimplifications. For a fuller, richer consideration of the topic, see Johannes S. Marais, *The Cape Coloured People 1652–1937* (London, 1937).

Recent scholarship on the "Coloured" people has focused on their culture and on their place in the Cape's socioeconomic order. In "The Griqua, the Sotho-Tswana, and the Missionaries, 1780–1840: The Politics of a Frontier Zone," (Ph.D. diss., University of California, Los Angeles, 1970), Martin Legassick explores the pressures and opportunities one "Coloured" community confronted. The demographic origins of the "Coloured" people are investigated in Robert Ross, "The 'White' Population in South Africa in the Eighteenth Century," *Population Studies* 29 (1975): 220–30. Ross elaborates his analysis and considers the demise of autonomous "Coloured" communities in *Adam Kok's Griquas: A Study in the Development of Stratification in South Africa* (New York, 1976).

The insularity of the South African frontier ended in the early nineteenth century, as external events began to impinge on its history. The Zulu

Mfecane, which displaced African societies and opened paths for white expansion, is described in John D. Omer-Cooper's *The Zulu Aftermath: A Nineteenth Century Revolution in South Africa* (London, 1966; Evanston, Ill., 1969). The impact of the British conquest on the frontier and the subsequent flight from British rule of Afrikaner Voortrekkers are discussed in Eric A. Walker's *The Great Trek* (London, 1934; reprinted 1965).

For a consideration of British frontier policy in the wake of the Great Trek, see William M. MacMillan's *Bantu, Boer and Briton: The Making of the South African Native Problem*, rev. ed. (Oxford, 1963). MacMillan dwells on the efforts of the Reverend Dr. John Philip of the London Missionary Society to involve Britain in actions which he believed would ameliorate the Voortrekker impact on Africans. John S. Galbraith's *Reluctant Empire: British Policy on the South African Frontier 1834–54* (Berkeley, Calif., 1963) takes a broader view of the issue and suggests that fiscal conservatism influenced British policy makers as much as humanitarian lobbyists did.

Economic developments on the nineteenth-century frontier have been the subject of much recent research. *The Roots of Rural Poverty in Central and Southern Africa*, ed. Robin Palmer and Neil Parsons (Berkeley, Calif., 1977) investigates the impoverishment of black communities. Though not frontier-oriented, the volume includes several valuable studies on related topics. More explicitly concerned with the frontier, Colin Bundy's *The Rise and Fall of South African Peasantry* (Berkeley, Calif., 1979) shows that many African farmers responded imaginatively and successfully to frontier conditions and that only determined opposition by whites destroyed their initiatives. Norman Etherington offers a similar analysis in "African Economic Experiments in Colonial Natal 1848–1880," *African Economic History* 5 (1978):1–15. An unusual and ill-fated effort by British investors to convert frontier lands into capital is considered in Henry Slater, "Land, Labour and Capital in Natal: The Natal Land and Colonisation Company," *JAfH* 16 (1975):257–83.

Two older studies remain valuable as introductions to their subjects. See Shiela T. Van Der Horst, *Native Labour in South Africa* (London, 1942; reprinted 1971) and H. M. Robertson, "150 Years of Economic Contact between Black and White: A Preliminary Survey" (cited above).

Although European proselytization of Africans increased greatly after 1800, there is no satisfactory account of the missions. J. du Plessis, *History of Christian Missions in South Africa* (London, 1911; Cape Town, 1965) offers a narrative overview of missionary efforts but is analytically inadequate. Bertram Hutchinson, "Some Social Consequences of Nineteenth Century Missionary Activity among the South African Bantu," *Africa* 27 (1957):160–77, and A. J. Dachs, "Missionary Imperialism: The Case of Bechuanaland," *JAfH* 13 (1972):647–58, consider missionaries as agents of white expansion. Religious innovation and its impact on the frontier are addressed in Norman Etherington, "The Rise of the Kholwa in Southeast Africa: African Christian Communities in Natal, Pondoland and Zululand, 1835–1880" (Ph.D. diss., Yale University, 1971), and Wallace-George Mills, "The Role of African Clergy in the Reorientation of Xhosa Society to the Plural Society in the Cape Colony, 1850–1915" (Ph.D. diss., University of California, Los Angeles, 1975).

For consideration of African political initiatives, see Leonard M. Thompson's *Survival in Two Worlds: Moshoeshoe of Lesotho 1786–1870* (Oxford, 1975), which recounts the successful efforts of a remarkable leader to hold his people together despite pressures from Africans, Boers, and Britons. Inter-African political competition is analyzed in Philip Bonner's "Factions and Fissions: Transvaal/Swazi Politics in the Mid-Nineteenth Century," *JAfH* 29 (1978):219–38.

Developments within the Afrikaner community are discussed in B. A. LeCordeur's "Robert Godlonton as Architect of Frontier Opinion (1850–1857)," *AYB* 22, no. 2 (1959):vii–170. The final northward thrust of white frontiersmen is considered in Edward C. Tabler, *The Far Interior: Chronicles of Pioneering in the Matabele and Mashona Countries 1847–1879* (Cape town, 1955) and Waldemar B. Campbell, "The South African Frontier, 1865–1885: A Case Study in Expansion," *AYB* 22, no. 1 (1959):1–242.

Britain's response to Afrikaner expansion is examined in C. W. De-Kiewiet's *The Imperial Factor in South Africa* (Cambridge, Eng., 1937; New York, 1968). While DeKiewiet and most others view British policy as protecting Africans from Afrikaner exploitation, Anthony Atmore and Shula Marks advance a strong counterargument. In "The Imperial Factor in South Africa in the Nineteenth Century: Towards a Reassessment," *Journal of Imperial and Commonwealth History* 3 (1974):105–39, they contend that British intervention usually protected white economic interests and ultimately tipped the balance of power on the frontier into white hands. For a recent examination of the issues, see D. M. Schreuder, *The Scramble for Southern Africa, 1877–1895: The Politics of Partition Reappraised* (Cambridge, Eng., 1980).

African responses to the establishment of white supremacy are considered in Terence O. Ranger's *Revolt in Southern Rhodesia, 1896–97: A Study on African Resistance* (Evanston, Ill., 1967) and in Shula Marks's *Reluctant Rebellion: The 1906–08 Disturbances In Natal* (Oxford, 1970). Terence Ranger examines the spiritual component of African resistance movements in "The Role of Ndebele and Shona Religious Authorities in the Rebellions of 1896 and 1897," in *The Zambesian Past*, ed. Eric Stokes and Richard Brown (Manchester, Eng., 1966), pp. 94–134.

Very little has been written on the military aspects of the South African frontier in any period. The history of the Afrikaner commando is described in G. Tylden, "The Development of the Commando System in South Africa 1715 to 1922," *Africana Notes and News* 13 (1959):303–13, and in G. Tylden, *The Armed Forces of South Africa with an Appendix on the Commandos* (Johannesburg, 1954). For a broader perspective, see a series of essays edited by Shula Marks and Anthony Atmore, "Firearms in Southern Africa: A Survey," *JAfH* 12 (1971):517–77.

Another perspective on European-African frontiers in southern Africa is afforded by several studies of the Portuguese experience on the Zambesi River. See M. D. D. Newitt's "The Portuguese on the Zambezi: An Historical Interpretation of the Prazo System," *JAfH* 10 (1969):67–85, and his *Portuguese Settlement on the Zambesi* (New York, 1973). Also see Allen F. Isaacman's *Mozambique: The Africanization of a European Institution: The Zambezi Prazos, 1750–1902* (Madison, Wis., 1972) and his *The Tradition of Resistance in Mozambique: The Zambesi Valley, 1850–1921* (Berkeley, Calif., 1976). Though not explicitly comparative, the studies provide interesting insights into the different course of development which occurred along the Zambesi frontier.

The Contributors

JAMES AXTELL is professor of history at the College of William and Mary, Williamsburg, Virginia. He is currently at work on a three-volume ethnohistory of colonial North America, and a collection of his essays, *The European and the Indian: Essays in the Ethnohistory of Colonial North America*, is forthcoming. His previous books include (with James Ronda) *Indian Missions: A Critical Bibiliography* (1978) and *The Indian Peoples of Eastern America: A Documentary History of the Sexes* (1980).

ROBERT F. BERKHOFER, JR., is professor of history and director of the program in American Culture at the University of Michigan. He is interested in the history of American social organization, American Indian history, the history of the American frontier, and the theory of history. His major publications include *Salvation and the Savage: An Analysis of Protestant Missions and American Indian Response, 1787–1862* (1965), *A Behavioral Approach to Historical Analysis* (1969), and *The White Man's Indian: Images of the American Indian from Columbus to the Present* (1978).

RAMSAY COOK is professor of history, York University, Toronto, and was visiting professor of history, Yale University, 1978–79. A specialist in the history of French Canada and the history of the Canadian west, his publications include *The Politics of John W. Dafoe and the Free Press* (1963), *Canada and the French Canadian Question* (1966), *The Maple Leaf Forever* (1970), and with R. C. Brown, *Canada 1896–1921: A Nation Transformed* (1974). He is a former editor of the *Canadian Historical Review*, a fellow of the Royal Society of Canada, and was awarded that society's Tyrrell Medal for Canadian History in 1975.

RICHARD ELPHICK studied at the University of Toronto, University of California, Los Angeles, and Yale University. He is the author of *Kraal and Castle: Khoikhoi and the Founding of White South Africa* (1977) and co-editor with Hermann Giliomee of *The Shaping of South African Society, 1652–1820* (1979). An associate professor of history at Wesleyan University, Middletown, Connecticut, he is now investigating the role of Christianity in the formation of South African society.

HERMANN GILIOMEE studied at the University of Stellenbosch, South Africa, where he teaches South African history. In 1973 and 1977–78 he was a research fellow at Yale University. He is the author of *Die Kaap tydens die Eerste Britse Bewind* (1974), coeditor with Richard Elphick of *The Shaping of South African Society, 1652–1820* (1979), and coauthor with Heribert Adam of *Ethnic Power Mobilized: Can South Africa Change?* (1979).

HOWARD R. LAMAR is William Robertson Coe Professor of History at Yale University and Dean of Yale College. A specialist in the history of the Trans-Mississippi West, he has taught courses on comparative frontier history, Indian history, and family history. His publications include *Dakota Territory, 1861–1889: A Study of Frontier Politics* (1956), *The Far Southwest, 1846–1912* (1966), *The Trader on the American Frontier* (1977), and *The Reader's Encyclopedia of the American West* (1977), of which he is editor. He is currently working on a history of the overland trails experience and a comparative study of labor systems in the early West. A member of the Western History Association, he served as its president in 1972. Since 1973 he has worked with Ray Allen Billington as coeditor of *The Histories of the American Frontier Series.*

GEORGE MILES is an instructor in history at Yale University, where he is completing a dissertation on Joseph Brant and Iroquois-white relations in the revolutionary and early postrevolutionary period. He received his B.A. and M. Phil. from Yale university.

CLYDE A. MILNER II received his Ph.D. in American studies from Yale University in 1979 and is currently an assistant professor of history at Utah State University in Logan, Utah. His prize-winning dissertation, "With Good Intentions: Quaker Work and Indian Survival; the Nebraska Case, 1869–1882," will be published as a book by the University of Nebraska Press.

ROBERT ROSS took his B.A. and Ph.D. degrees at Cambridge University and now works for the Centre for the Study of European Expansion of the

University of Leiden, The Netherlands. His major research interest is the socioeconomic history of the Cape Colony in the preindustrial period. He is the author of *Adam Kok's Griquas: A Study in the Development of Stratification in South Africa* (1976).

CHRISTOPHER SAUNDERS, who received his B.A. and D. Phil. from Oxford University, is a senior lecturer in history at the University of Cape Town. His main research interests lie in the nineteenth-century history of the Cape eastern frontier and in the history of Cape Town. His publications include *The Kitchingman Papers* (1976), "The Annexation of the Transkeian Territories," in *The Archives Year Book for South African History* (1978), and, as editor, *Beyond the Cape Frontier* (1974).

LEONARD THOMPSON's publications include *The Unification of South Africa* (1960), *Politics in the Republic of South Africa* (1966), *Survival in Two Worlds: Moshoeshoe of Lesotho 1786–1870* (1975), and as coauthor with Philip Curtin et al., *African History* (1978). He is coeditor with Monica Wilson of the two-volume *Oxford History of South Africa* (1969–71) and with Jeffrey Butler, of *Change in Contemporary South Africa* (1975). A Rhodes Scholar, he was formerly professor of history at the University of Cape Town and at the University of California, Los Angeles. He is now professor of history at Yale University and director of the Yale-Wesleyan Southern African Research Program.

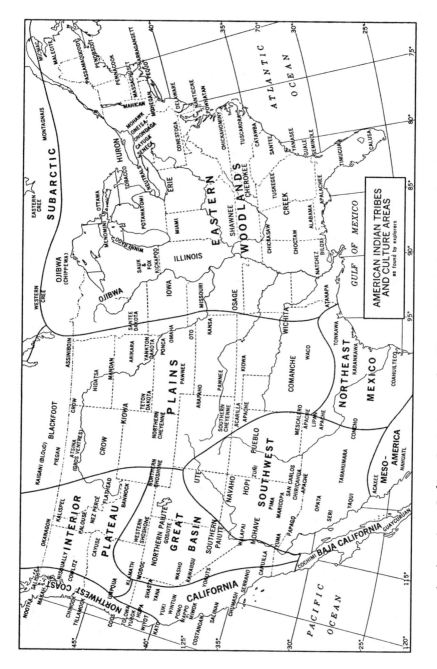

1　American Indian Societies at the Time of First Contact with Whites.
From Annals of America, vol. 6, © copyright 1968 by Encyclopedia Britannica, Inc.

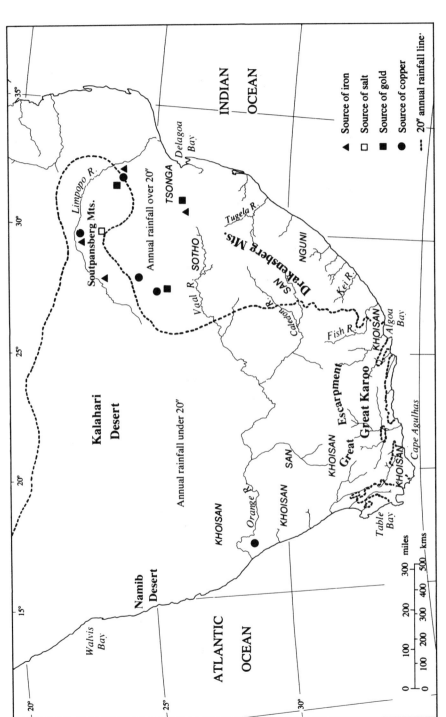

2 Southern African Societies in the Sixteenth Century.

Legend:
- ▲ Source of iron
- ☐ Source of salt
- ■ Source of gold
- ● Source of copper
- - - - 20″ annual rainfall line·

Map labels:
INDIAN OCEAN
ATLANTIC OCEAN
Namib Desert
Kalahari Desert
Walvis Bay
Delagoa Bay
Limpopo R.
Soutpansberg Mts.
Annual rainfall over 20″
Annual rainfall under 20″
TSONGA
SOTHO
Vaal R.
Tugela R.
NGUNI
Drakensberg Mts.
SAN
Ket R.
Caledon R.
Fish R.
Algoa Bay
KHOISAN
Great Escarpment
Great Karoo
Cape Agulhas
Table Bay
Orange R.
35°
30°
25°
20°
15°
20°
25°
30°

Scale:
0 100 200 300 miles
0 100 200 300 400 500 kms

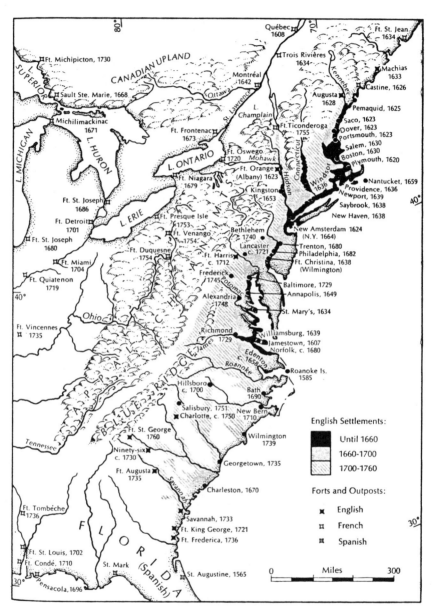

3 English, French, and Spanish Settlements and Outposts in Northeastern America, 1565–1760. From Samuel Eliot Morison, Henry Steele Commager, and William E. Leuchtenberg, *The Growth of the American Republic*, vol. 1 (New York: Oxford University Press, 1969).

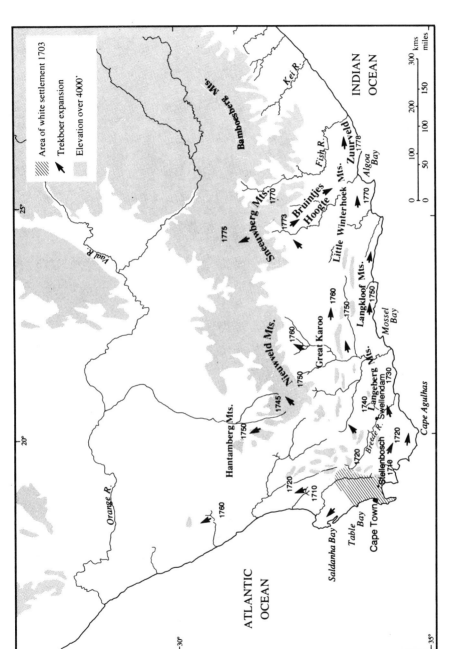

4 White Expansion in Southern Africa, 1652–1780.

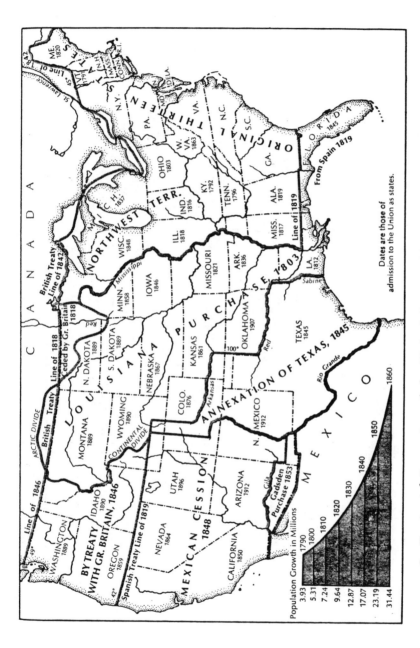

5 Territorial Expansion of the United States, 1776–1853.
From Samuel Eliot Morison, Henry Steele Commager, and William E. Leuchtenberg,
The Growth of the American Republic, vol. 1 (New York: Oxford University Press, 1969).

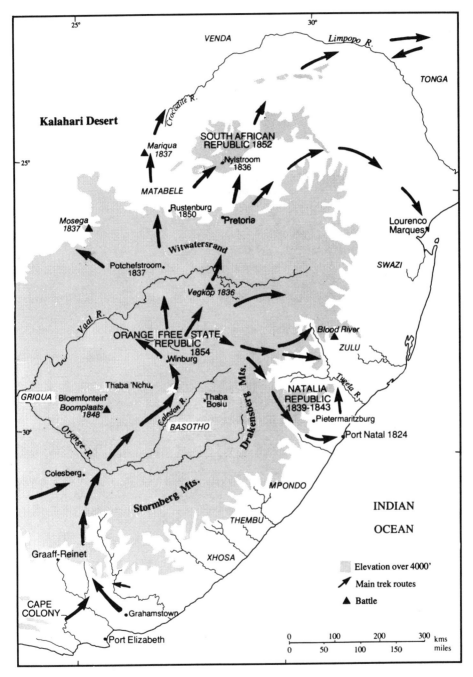

6 The Great Trek: Southeastern Africa, 1836–1854.

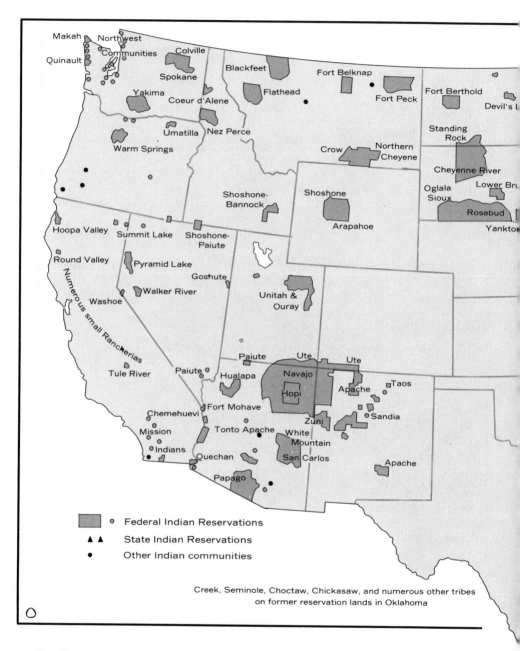

Makah
Quinault
Northwest Communities
Colville
Blackfeet
Fort Belknap
Fort Berthold
Devil's L
Spokane
Yakima
Flathead
Fort Peck
Coeur d'Alene
Standing Rock
Umatilla   Nez Perce
Warm Springs
Crow
Northern Cheyene
Cheyenne River
Oglala Sioux
Lower Bru
Hoopa Valley
Summit Lake
Shoshone-Paiute
Shoshone-Bannock
Shoshone
Rosebud
Yanktor
Round Valley
Pyramid Lake
Goshute
Arapahoe
Numerous small Rancherias
Washoe
Walker River
Unitah & Ouray
Tule River
Paiute
Paiute
Ute
Ute
Hualapa
Navajo
Taos
Chemehuevi
Fort Mohave
Hopi
Apache
Mission
Tonto Apache
Zuni
Sandia
Indians
Quechan
White Mountain
San Carlos
Apache
Papago

▮ ◦ Federal Indian Reservations
▲ ▲ State Indian Reservations
● Other Indian communities

Creek, Seminole, Choctaw, Chickasaw, and numerous other tribes
on former reservation lands in Oklahoma

7   Contemporary Indian Lands and Communities in the United States.
From S. Lyman Tyler, *A History of Indian Policy* (Washington, D.C.:
U.S. Department of the Interior, Bureau of Indian Affairs, 1973).

Major Indian Lands and Communities

d Lake

Grand Portage

Greater Leach Lake

White Earth

Fond du Lac

L'Ance

Ottawa & Chippewa

Sisseton

Oneida

Potawatomi

Winnebago

Miami

aha

kapoo

awatomi

Wyandot

Osage

Micmac

Passamaquoddy

Penobscot

Mohawk

Oneida

Tuscarora

Onondaga

Mohegan

Scaticook

Narraganset

Montauk

Seneca

Mattaponi

Haliwa

Cherokee

Lumbee

Catawba

Choctaw

Choctaw

Creek

Seminole

Seminole

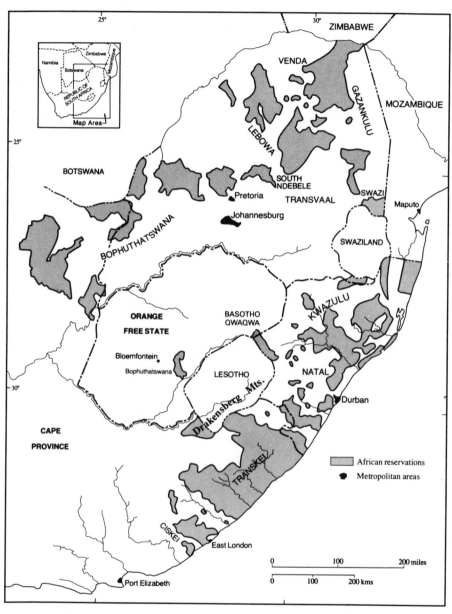

8 The African "Homelands" of the Republic of South Africa.

Index

The following abbreviations are used throughout the Index:

A = African people
I = Indian people
NA = North America
SA = southern Africa

Date D